STUDIES IN THE LANGUAGE AND POETICS OF ANGLO–SAXON ENGLAND

Sherman M. Kuhn

Studies in the Language & Poetics of Anglo— Saxon

By Sherman M. Kuhn

England

KAROMA PUBLISHERS, INC.
Ann Arbor
1984

CONTENTS

Note: Along with the pagination provided at the bottom of each page of this volume, original page numbers have also been retained. This method of dual pagination will enable scholars to cite from both sources.

FOREWORD

In June of this year Sherman M. Kuhn retired after a long and distinguished career as Editor of the *Middle English Dictionary* and Professor of English at the University of Michigan. The usual way of recognizing such an occasion would be to publish a volume of essays by friends, colleagues, and students, but it is our belief that a collection of Professor Kuhn's own essays would be a more appropriate tribute as well as a more important, homogeneous, and lasting piece of scholarship.

Nearly all of Professor Kuhn's scholarly work (outside of the *Middle English Dictionary*) has been on Old English language and literature, and he has acquired a reputation over the years for the methodological rigor of his approach and soundness of his judgments; he is a philologist in the best and most traditional sense of the word, as his scholarship illustrates, with its use of linguistic analysis to solve literary and textual problems. The present collection contains all of his essays on Old English except the two on the Old English digraphs that he wrote in collaboration with Randolph Quirk (both reprinted elsewhere) and the five essays that deal primarily with the *Vespasian Psalter*. Professor Kuhn's major project for retirement is to complete the second volume of his edition of the *Psalter* (we have had the text since 1965), and the latter essays will find their way, in revised form, into that volume.

The thirteen remaining essays collected here divide themselves about equally between Old English language and Old English poetry and poetics (thus the title to the collection). They are all of high quality and from all periods of Professor Kuhn's career (representing forty years of scholarship, 1939–1979) and include essays that appeared in prestigious journals with rigorous selection standards as well as essays that appeared in *Festschriften* (and thus are difficult to come by in libraries), essays that grew out of his teaching ("*Beowulf* and the Life of Beowulf" and "Old English $\bar{A}GLA\bar{E}CA$ – Middle Irish *ÓCLACH*," for example) as well as essays that grew out of his scholarly interests.

We present this collection to Professor Kuhn as a celebration of his distinguished career and as a token of the esteem in which we hold him as friend, colleague, and mentor and wish him "Wæs hal!" for a well deserved, productive retirement.

Robert E. Lewis

Sherman McAllister Kuhn

Sherman McAllister Kuhn was born on September 15, 1907, the son of the Rev. Detmer Thomas Kuhn, a Presbyterian minister from Hooker, Pennsylvania, and Helen (Sherman) Kuhn, a Chicago school teacher. Though his roots have remained in Pennsylvania, part of his childhood and early school years were passed in Alberta, Canada, in the exacting conditions inseparable from homesteading in the western prairies. His high school years, however, 1921-25, he spent at Hopkins High School, Glen Lake, Minnesota, where he enjoyed a well-rounded career of learning and athletics, gaining letters in football and track, besides being on the debating team and valedictorian. He carried these varied interests to Dubuque University, 1925-28, and to Park College, where he graduated with departmental honors in English in 1929. While teaching English and debate at Lincoln Community High School, Lincoln, Illinois, from 1929-32, he attended summer school at the University of Chicago, obtaining his M.A. in American literature in 1933, and his Ph.D. in English linguistics in 1935. His doctoral dissertation, *A Grammar of the Mercian Dialect,* laid the groundwork for much of his future scholarship. It was in this year also that he married Eleanor Jordan of Chicago; they have three daughters, Eleanor Anne, Barbara Jean, and Dorothy Ruth.

His academic teaching career began that same year at Oklahoma A & M College (now Oklahoma State University), with an Assistant Professorship in English, and he became Associate Professor in 1941, and Professor in 1947, having been Visiting Assistant Professor of English at the University of Chicago in the summers of 1938-40. From March 1944 to October 1945 there intervened a stint in the U. S. army, where he served as a cryptographic technician, and achieved the qualification of sharpshooter. In 1948 he came to the University of Michigan as Associate Editor of the *Middle English Dictionary*, and Associate Professor of English. This last was a case of *reculer pour mieux sauter*, and he became Professor in 1955 and Editor of the *Dictionary* in 1961, a post he has held until his recent retirement, June 1983.

In Oklahoma he taught Chaucer, Shakespeare, English and American literature, History of the English Language, and, of course, composition. At Michigan he extended his range widely, giving courses in *Beowulf*, other Old

English narrative poetry, Old English lyric and meditative poetry, surveys of
Old and Middle English literature, Old English and Middle English dialects,
Old Irish, Old Icelandic, Palaeography and Lexicography. He was a deman-
ding teacher, and the best students came to his courses, where they learned
something of his own care, accuracy, and love of medieval literature. Though
never a student in his classes, I have gladly benefitted from working under
him in the *Dictionary*. Never have I met another who would so totally give
his attention to a query, so thoroughly think through all the evidence, and
give so sure and satisfying an answer. It is therefore easy for me to see that
for any graduate student to have him as dissertation director was a great
piece of good fortune. He always revered his own great teacher at Chicago,
Professor J. M. Manly, and his own success as a teacher is demonstrated in
his students who have become scholars in their own right.

Academic honors have followed him. He shared the University of
Michigan Press Award for the *Middle English Dictionary* in 1973, and is to
receive a Distinguished Faculty Award this year. He is a Fellow of the Medieval Academy of America, and was on the Advisory Board of *Speculum*,
1968-70, as well as at different times on the Editorial Boards of *Studies in
Medieval Culture* and *Michigan Germanic Studies*. He will no doubt always
be known chiefly for his long and successful editorship of the *Dictionary*,
where he has proved himself a worthy successor to Hans Kurath in further-
ing the worth and reputation of this project, probably the greatest research
project in the whole field of English studies, and one which he may be
thought to have brought to an even higher plane of amplitude and accuracy.
The greatness of this task is best appreciated by those charged with carrying
on the project after his departure; speaking for myself I feel (to develop a
popular medieval *topos*) like the proverbial pygmy standing on the shoulders
of giants, and rather precariously at that.

The present volume brings before us a number of Professor Kuhn's individual publications, spanning some forty years. These in themselves,
though they may be overshadowed in our minds by the *Dictionary*, entitle
him to be reckoned among the leading scholars of the world. Again and again
he takes up an important topic which previous treatments had left contro-
verted or unsettled; again and again he studies the fundamentals of the
question, brings to bear his complete knowledge and exhaustive research ----
and he usually settles the matter. It is remarkable that in so many areas of
Old English studies, from palaeography to literary criticism, he has made his
mark, and influenced the course of scholarship. These articles serve also to

remind us that Professor Kuhn is expert not only in English and Germanic philology in the older sense, but also in modern linguistic theory. Consequently he fitted into and added his share to the lively intellectual milieu of language studies at the University of Michigan in the post-war years when he first arrived in Ann Arbor. Throughout all, his style has remained in method cautious, in complexity perspicuous, and in controversy courteous.

Professor and Mrs. Kuhn will continue to live in Ann Arbor, and all who know them will wish them a long and happy retirement, to be which, for a man of his interests, it must needs be a productive one.

Lof-dædum sceal in mægþa gehwære man geþeon.

John Reidy

BIBLIOGRAPHY OF THE WRITINGS
OF
SHERMAN M. KUHN

1938   *A Grammar of the Mercian Dialect*. University of Chicago. Pp. i, 1-40.

A Functional Grammar (with N. P. Lawrence and others). New York: Farrar and Rinehart. Pp. viii, 1-206.

1939   "The Dialect of the *Corpus Glossary*," *PMLA*, 54, 1-19.

1940   *A Functional Grammar, Form B* (with others). New York: Farrar and Rinehart. Pp. ix, 1-206.

1941   "The Gloss to the *Vespasian Psalter*: Another Collation," *JEGP*, 40, 344-47.

1943   "*The Vespasian Psalter* and the Old English Charter Hands," *Speculum*, 18, 458-83.

"The Sword of Healfdene," *JEGP*, 42, 82-95.

1945   "*E* and *Æ* in Farman's Mercian Glosses," *PMLA*, 60, 631-69.

1946   Review: H. D. Meritt, *Old English Glosses: A Collection*, in *JEGP*, 45, 345-46.

1947   "Synonyms in the Old English Bede," *JEGP*, 46, 168-76.

1948   "From Canterbury to Lichfield," *Speculum*, 23, 591-629.

Review: D. E. Martin-Clarke, *Culture in Early Anglo-Saxon England*, in *JEGP*, 47, 414-15.

1950   Reviews: Georg Fridén, *Studies on the Tenses of the English Verb from Chaucer to Shakespeare*, in *JEGP*, 49, 104-6.

Claes Schaar, *Critical Studies in the Cynewulf Group*, in *JEGP*, 49, 391-94.

Henning Hallqvist, *Studies in Old English Fractured ea*, in *Language*, 26, 319-23.

1951   "A Damaged Passage in the Exeter Book," *JEGP*, 50, 491-3.

Review: Bertil Sundby, *The Dialect and Provenance of the Middle English Poem, The Owl and the Nightingale*, in *Language*, 27, 420-23.

1952   Review: Bertil Thuresson, *Middle English Occupational Terms*, in *Language*, 28, 135-39.

1952-61 *Middle English Dictionary*, as Associate Editor (with others).
Ann Arbor: University of Michigan Press. Vol. I (A-B), pp.
i, 1-1245. Vol. II (C-D), pp. 1-1371. Vol. III (E-F), pp. ii,
1-952. *Plan and Bibliography*, pp. xii, 1-105.

1953 "Some Recent Interpretations of Old English Digraph Spellings" (with Randolph Quirk), *Language*, 29, 143-56.
Reprinted in Quirk, *Essays on the English Language, Medieval and Modern*. London: Longmans Green, 1968. Pp. 38-
54.

1955 "The Old English Digraphs: A Reply" (with Quirk), *Language*,
31, 390-401.
Reprinted in Quirk, *Essays*, pp. 55-69.
Review: D. T. Starnes, *Renaissance Dictionaries, English-Latin
and Latin-English*, in *Language*, 31, 551-54.

1956 Reviews: H. D. Meritt, *Fact and Lore about Old English Words*,
in *Speculum*, 31, 392-95.
L. F. Brosnahan, *Some Old English Sound Changes: An Analysis in the Light of Modern Phonetics*, in *JEGP*, 55, 491-
93.
J. T. Shipley, *Dictionary of Early English*, in *Language*, 32,
769-74.

1957 "Some Early Mercian Manuscripts," *Review of English Studies*,
n.s. 8, 355-70.

1958 Reviews: R. Quirk and C. L. Wrenn, *An Old English Grammar*,
in *JEGP*, 57, 114-17.
H. Gneuss, *Lehnbildungen und Lehnbedeutungen im Altenglischen*, in *JEGP*, 57, 329-31.

1959 "*The Vespasian Psalter* Gloss: Original or Copy?" *PMLA*, 74,
161-77.

1960 Review: J. J. Campbell, *The Advent Lyrics of the Exeter Book*,
in *Modern Language Quarterly*, 21, 261-62.

1961 "On the Syllabic Phonemes of Old English," *Language*, 37, 522-38.
Reprinted in Charles T. Scott and Jon L. Erickson, eds.,
Readings for the History of the English Language. Boston:
Allyn and Bacon, 1968. Pp. 146-64.
Review: H. D. Meritt, *The Old English Prudentius Glosses at
Boulogne-sur-Mer*, in *Speculum*, 36, 151-53.

1961-83 *Middle English Dictionary*, as Editor (with others). Ann Arbor:

University of Michigan Press. Vol. IV (G-H), pp. 1-1053. Vol. V (I-L), pp. 1-1318. Vol. VI (M-N), pp. 1-1141. Vol. VII (O-P), pp. 1- .

1963   "Treatise of Fishing with an Angle" (Middle English, early printed, and modernized versions) in John McDonald. *The Origins of Angling*. Garden City: Doubleday. Pp. 27-66, 133-79, 251-58.

Reprinted (modernized version only) in McDonald, *Quill Gordon*. New York: Knopf, 1972. Pp. 149-72.

Review: P. Mertens-Fonck, *A Glossary of the Vespasian Psalter and Hymns, Part One: The Verb*, in *Speculum*, 38, 383-88.

1965   *The Vespasian Psalter* (edition). Ann Arbor: University of Michigan Press. Pp. xii, 1-327.

Reprinted by University Microfilms International, Ann Arbor, 1978.

Review: Bertil Sundby, *Studies in the Middle English Dialect Material of Worcestershire Records*, in *Speculum*, 40, 160-66.

1966   "Footnote to a Review," *Medium AEvum*, 35, 182.

Review: Early English Text Society, *The Owl and the Nightingale, Reproduced in Facsimile with an Introduction by N. R. Ker*, in *JEGP*, 65, 158-61.

1967   Review: Alfred Reszkiewicz, *Main Sentence Elements in "The Book of Margery Kempe": A Study in Major Syntax*, in *Linguistics*, 35, 106-10.

1968   "The Preface to a Fifteenth-Century Concordance," *Speculum*, 43, 258-73.

Reviews: M.C. Morrell, *A Manual of Old English Biblical Materials*, in *Modern Philology*, 65, 239-41.

Björn Wallner, *The Middle English Translation of Guy de Chauliac's Anatomy, with Guy's Essay on the History of Medicine*, in *Speculum*, 43, 552-56.

1969   "*Beowulf* and the Life of Beowulf: A Study in Epic Structure," in E. Bagby Atwood and Archibald A. Hill, eds., *Studies in the Language, Literature, and Culture of the Middle Ages and Later*. Austin: University of Texas Press. Pp. 243-64.

1970   "On the Consonantal Phonemes of Old English," in James L.

Rosier, ed., *Philological Essays: Studies in Old and Middle English Language and Literature in Honour of Herbert Dean Meritt*. The Hague: Mouton. Pp. 16-49.

1971 Review: H. D. Meritt, *Some of the Hardest Glosses in Old English*, in *JEGP*, 70, 651-54.

1972 "The Authorship of the Old English Bede Revisited," *Neuphilologische Mitteilungen: Studies Presented to Tauno F. Mustanoja on the Occasion of his Sixtieth Birthday*, 73, 172-80.

"Cursus in Old English: Rhetorical Ornament or Linguistic Phenomenon?" *Speculum*, 47, 188-206.

Reviews: F. N. M. Diekstra, *A Dialogue between Reason and Adversity: A Late Middle English Version of Petrarch's De Remediis*, in *Speculum*, 47, 114-16.

Olof Arngart, *The Middle English Genesis and Exodus*, in *Speculum*, 47, 103-7.

L. W. Daly, *Contributions to a History of Alphabetization in Antiquity and the Middle Ages*, in *Speculum*, 47, 300-3.

M. S. Ogden, *The Cyrurgie of Guy de Chauliac*. Björn Wallner, *The Middle English Translation of Guy de Chauliac's Treatise on Fractures and Dislocations*. Wallner, *A Middle English Version of the Introduction to Guy de Chauliac's "Chirurgia Magna,"* in *Speculum*, 47, 544-48.

1973 "Was Ælfric a Poet?" *Philological Quarterly*, 52, 643-62.

1974 "The Language of Some Fifteenth-Century Chaucerians: A Study of Manuscript Variants in the *Canterbury Tales,"* *Studies in Medieval Culture*, 4, 3 (Kalamazoo), 472-82.

1975 Review: Gillis Kristensson, *A Survey of Middle English Dialects, 1290-1350: The Six Northern Counties and Lincolnshire* (Lund Studies in English, 35), in *Speculum*, 50, 134-39.

1976 "On the Making of the *Middle English Dictionary*," *Poetica*, 4 (Tokyo), 1-23.

Reprinted in *Dictionaries: Journal of the Dictionary Society of North America*, No. 4 (1982), 14-41.

"From Woman to Woperson? A Linguistic Disaster," *Newsday*, January 11. Pp. 7, 11.

1977 "Lecherie," *LSA*, Winter (University of Michigan), pp. 14-15.

"Further Thoughts on *Brand Healfdenes*," *JEGP*, 76, 231-37.

"Wassail," *LSA*, 1, 4 (University of Michigan), 4-5, 17.

1979   "Old English $\overline{A}GL\overline{\cancel{E}}CA$ – Middle Irish $ÓCLACH$," in Irmengard Rauch and Gerald F. Carr, eds., *Linguistic Method: Essays in Honor of Herbert Penzl.* The Hague: Mouton. Pp. 213-30.

"A Report on the *Middle English Dictionary*," *The Chaucer Newsletter*, 1, 2, 19-20.

1980   "The Art of Writing a Definition That Does not Define," in Ladislav Zgusta, ed., *Theory and Method in Lexicography.* Columbia, South Carolina: Hornbeam Press. Pp. 115-21.

"A Second Report on the *Middle English Dictionary*," *The Chaucer Newsletter*, 2, 2, 18.

"Middle English *DON* and *MAKEN*: Some Observations on Semantic Patterning," *American Speech* (Papers in Honor of Thomas Pyles), 52, 5-18.

THE DIALECT OF THE CORPUS *GLOSSARY*

THE Old English words in the Corpus Glossary constitute one of the oldest extant texts in the English language, and one of the three longest in the Mercian dialect. Linguists now agree that the glossary was compiled somewhere in Mercian territory during the eighth century.[1] Palaeographical evidence points to the eighth century as the period of compilation.[2] Concerning two important questions, linguistic opinion seems at present vague and uncertain: First, to what extent is the language of Corpus the result of dialect mixture? Second, what is the relationship between the language of Corpus and that of the most important of the texts now looked upon as Mercian, the Vespasian Psalter?

The first question is significant because, if the glossary contains any considerable number of non-Mercian forms, we must determine the extent and nature of the dialect mixture before we can safely accept much of the evidence which Corpus offers concerning the characteristics of the Mercian dialect. Thomas Wright and Henry Sweet considered the glossary Kentish because of a notation on the first leaf, which indicates that the manuscript belonged, during the thirteenth century at least, to St. Augustin's, Canterbury. There were so many non-Kentish features in the text, however, that Sievers called it Kentish mixed with Mercian. Chadwick, and later Bülbring, reversed the order of Sievers' terms and pronounced it Mercian mixed with Kentish plus an admixture of West Saxon. Luick, writing of the Corpus, Epinal, Erfurt, and Leiden

---

[1] Karl Bülbring, *Altenglisches Elementarbuch* (Heidelberg, 1902), p. 8; H. M. Chadwick, *Studies in Old English*, Transactions of the Cambridge Philological Society, IV (Cambridge, 1899), pp. 249, 252–253; R. Girvan, *Angelsaksisch Handboek* (Haarlem, 1931), p. 7; Karl Luick, *Historische Grammatik der englischen Sprache* (Leipzig, 1921), p. 34; Henry Sweet, *The Oldest English Texts*, E.E.T.S., O.S. LXXXIII (London, 1885), pp. vii, 5; H. C. Wyld, *A Short History of English* (New York, 1927), p. 55.

[2] Wolfgang Keller. *Angelsächsische Palaeographie*, Palaestra, XLIII (Berlin, 1906), I, 18; J. H. Hessels, *An Eighth-Century Latin-Anglo-Saxon Glossary* (Cambridge, 1890), pp. ix-x; Sweet, p. 5.

Reprinted by permission of the Modern Language Association of America from *PMLA*, 54 (1939), 1–19.

Glossaries, remarks that the four are neither West Saxon nor Northumbrian, that they have Kentish characteristics but are not Kentish, and that they are probably of Mercian origin. It is not entirely clear whether he looks upon Corpus as a mixed text at all; if he does, he stresses dialect mixture very little as an explanation of its peculiarities.[3]

The second question is also an important one because there are very definite and striking differences between Corpus and the Psalter, and because the orthographical regularity and the apparent dialectal purity of the Psalter have inevitably made it the standard by which we judge other Mercian texts. Nearly all of the important differences in the consonants and the unaccented vowels as well as many of the differences in the accented vowels may be explained chronologically, as results of phonetic changes which are generally believed to have been incomplete when Corpus was written.[4] In order to account for some of the differences in the accented vowels, investigators have assumed the existence of Mercian sub-dialects. Chadwick did not mention any sub-dialects of Mercian, but he noted differences between Corpus and the Psalter which he was unable to account for by means of any Kentish or West Saxon elements in the former. Bülbring, also without mentioning sub-dialects as such, referred occasionally to the Mercian dialect of the Vespasian Psalter (*merc. Dialekt des VPs.*), as though he felt that there were varieties of Mercian. Luick supposes that there were two important sub-dialects, the one represented by the ninth-century Psalter, the other by Farman's portion of the tenth-century glosses to the Rushworth Gospels. The early glossaries, according to the same authority, are a mixture of the two and contain traces of still a third sub-dialect.[5] On the face of it, this hypothesis seems reasonable; one would expect that a territory with the extent and heterogeneous population of the Mercian kingdom would possess local variations in its speech.[6] But it is doubtful whether some of the peculiarities of Corpus which Luick explains on the basis of sub-dialects are actually the results of local variations. They could, I believe, be explained chronologically.

In this article I hope to shed further light on the two problems out-

---

[3] Sweet, p. 5; Eduard Sievers, *An Old English Grammar*. Translated and edited by A. S. Cook. (Boston, 1899), p. 244; Chadwick, p. 253; Bülbring, p. 8; Luick, p. 34.

[4] For consonants, see Bülbring, p. 190; Chadwick, pp. 232–246; Girvan, pp. 13–14. For unaccented vowels, see Ferdinand Dieter, *Ueber Sprache und Mundart der ältesten englischen Denkmäler* (Göttingen, 1891), I. 45–46; Bülbring, p. 146; Chadwick, p. 246; Girvan, pp. 71, 153–154; Luick, pp. 278, 297–304. For accented vowels, see Bülbring, pp. 42–43, 49–50, 71; Dieter, I, 9–10, 14, 42–43; Luick, pp. 122–123, 171, 216.

[5] Chadwick, pp. 252–3; Bülbring, pp. 35, 63, 96, etc.; Luick, pp. 33–34, 165–166.

[6] The term *Mercian* is loosely used by Luick to include not only Mercia but East Anglia and Essex. Generally, however, the term is applied to Mercia proper.

lined above. Both problems are complicated somewhat by the manner in which the Corpus Glossary was compiled, i.e., from older Latin-English glossaries, interlinear and marginal glosses in Latin texts, and the like.[7] If the compiler had been a mere mechanical copyist, we could have no way of knowing whether his language represented the speech of his own place and time or just a hodgepodge of miscellaneous forms taken from his numerous sources. The investigations of Chadwick make plain, however, that the scribe who compiled Corpus altered many of the spellings which he found in his sources, that he was evidently making a definite effort to modernize his spellings and render them consistent with his pronunciation—in short, that he was more an editor than a copyist.[8] Consequently, although there are frequent archaic spellings, probably copied without alteration, we are justified in treating Corpus as a unified text, and we may reasonably hope to find satisfactory answers to our two questions.

I. To what extent is the language of the Corpus Glossary the result of dialect mixture? Even a cursory examination would reveal that the glossary has *æ* (spelled *ae*, *æ* or *ę*) for the raising and fronting of West Germanic short *a* (e. g. in *dæg*) more often than it has the *e* which seems to be one of the distinguishing marks of the Mercian dialect.[9] Corpus also has *a* frequently for West Germanic *a* before nasal rather than the *o* which one would expect in an Anglian text. Velar-umlaut[10] is irregular in Corpus, especially the velar-umlaut of *a;* unumlauted *e* and *i* appear frequently in open syllables followed by back vowels, while unumlauted *a* is even more frequent than *ea*. The use of *e* and *i* instead of *eo* and *io* might suggest West Saxon influence; the use of *æ* instead of *e*, either West Saxon or Northumbrian influence; the use of *a* instead of *o*, West Saxon or Kentish admixture; the use of *a* instead of *ea*, West Saxon or

---

[7] W. M. Lindsay, *The Corpus, Epinal, Erfurt and Leiden Glossaries*, Publications of the Philological Society, VIII (Oxford, 1912), pp. 1–5; Chadwick, pp. 189, 210. .

[8] For example, many of the items in Corpus are so similar to items in the Epinal and Erfurt Glossaries that they must have been taken from a common source, a lost English-Latin glossary which Chadwick calls "Archetype L" That the compiler of Corpus was altering his materials is evidenced by such things as his elimination of intersonantal *h* in most of the items which he drew from Archetype L. Such correspondences as the following are numerous: Epinal *Villosa—ryhae*, Erfurt *Villosa—ryhae*, Corpus *Villosa—rye*; Ep. *Villis—uulohum*, Erf. *Villis—uulohum*, Cp. *Villis—uuloum*. See Chadwick, pp. 229–232.

[9] The Vespasian Psalter has *e;* and the use of *æ* for West Germanic *e* in such words as *rægn*, *stæfn*, *þægn*, *wæg*, *wæl (bene)* in the Mercian portion of the Rushworth Glosses is hard to explain except on the assumption that WG *a* had fallen together with WG *e*.

[10] The effects of *a-o* and of *u* are so nearly identical in Corpus that it does not seem worth while to distinguish here between *a-o*-umlaut and *u*-umlaut.

Northumbrian or perhaps Kentish influence. But are we justified in attributing these features of Corpus to dialect mixture? The fact that the Vespasian Psalter of the ninth century has *eo, io, e, o*, and *ea* does not lead inevitably to the conclusion that a text written in the same dialect during the preceding century would present exactly the same features. These and some other features of Corpus we shall later attempt to explain chronologically. For the present let us employ more certain criteria in our comparison of the Corpus Glossary with the West Saxon, Kentish, and Northumbrian dialects.

During the period between *i*-umlaut and the ninth century, strict West Saxon must have differed from the dialect of the Psalter: (1) in the breaking of *a* to *ea* before *l* plus consonant, for we can be sure that this change began earlier than *i*-unlaut; (2) in the diphthongization of West Germanic *a, e*, and *ā* to *ea, ie*, and *ēa* after palatal consonants; (3) in the retention of Primitive Old English diphthongs before *c, g, h*, and combinations containing these consonants; (4) in the use of *ie* and *ie-* as the *i*-umlauts of diphthongs; and (5) in the use of *æ* for West Germanic *ā*. An examination of Corpus reveals six Primitive Old English diphthongs before palatal (perhaps guttural?) consonants:[11] *ea* in *mearh* 153, A536; *eo* in *licbeorg* 1771, S45, *-biorg* 1672, P825 (beside *geberg* 1715, R 56 and *baangeberg* 1426, O110); *ēa* in *geac* 965, G87 (beside *gaec* 618, C948, *gęces sure* 58, A131, *ieces surae* 380, C121), *leactrogas* 540, C656 (beside *laec* 154, A545, *-laec* 229, A841, *-laec* 448, C317, *-laec* 1835, S220, *-leec* 113, A419); and *ēo* in *þeohsaex* 1832, S214 (beside *thegh* 556, C747).[12] The proportion of smoothed vowels to unsmoothed Primitive Old English diphthongs is at least twelve to one. There are three *ie*-diphthongs which might suggest West Saxon influence: *alieset* 774, E368, *forsliet* 1135, I413, and the obscure *lendislieg* 316, B167.[13]

---

[11] Figures before the comma refer to the lines in *Oldest English Texts*, pp. 35–107; those after the comma refer to the edition by Hessels. All evidence has been carefully checked by W. M. Lindsay, *The Corpus Glossary* (Cambridge, 1921). The numbering in Lindsay is the same as that in Hessels.

[12] Possibly *bearug* 1284, M38 and *pearuc* 486, C488 belong here. But there is only one clear example of *ea* before *r* plus palatal, and both *bearug* and *pearuc* admit of different explanations. The latter is ordinarily traced to a West Germanic *parruk*, whose *a* would become *ea* by breaking. There is one other possibility. I think it would not be unreasonable to assume that the scribe wrote both words as he pronounced them, and that the svarabhakti *u* was actually pronounced. With this in mind, I have listed the words as examples of velar-umlaut. The word *healecas* (*hēa lēcas*) 218, A773 contains *ēa* by contraction after loss of intervocalic *h*. The Psalter has *hea, hean*, in the oblique cases and in the weak forms, beside *heh* in the strong-nominative-singular-masculine. The form *streagl* A932 is printed by Sweet *stregl* 249. The manuscript has *streal* with *g* over the *a*. Evidently the scribe intended to substitute the *g* for the *a* but forgot to dot out the latter.

[13] The form *gierende* 1986, T41 is not *i*-umlaut, but is probably from *gi-ārendian*, cf.

The significance of these examples is greatly diminished by the presence in the Psalter of a few words containing *ie*, perhaps by *i*-umlaut: *gehie-wade* 32:15; *geðieda* 30:21; *onsiene* 9:4, 26, 32, etc.; *ðieda* 17:44, etc. If there were fewer examples in the Psalter or more in Corpus, the *ie*'s might indicate dialect mixture; as it is, they indicate virtually nothing. There are four good examples of *ǣ* instead of *ē* for West Germanic *ā*: *aethm* 130, A448, *aethme* 2083, U38, *blǣd* 892, F228, *waede* 164, A587. The proportion is about *ē*:*ǣ*::15:1. There are some words containing *ǣ* which are of doubtful origin.[14] Of *ea* before *l* plus consonant there is no trace, and the only examples which might be palatal-diph-thongization occur, like the *ea*'s in *sceadugeardas* 1998, T79, in posi-tions in which we should expect to find *ea* by velar-umlaut or breaking in a Mercian text.

It is hard to compare the dialect of Corpus with eighth century Kentish because nearly all of the Kentish charters were written while Kent was ruled either by Mercia or by Wessex and are very much mixed in their dialect.[15] The other Kentish texts are later than the eighth century. It is possible, however, that early Kentish differed from early Mercian: (1) in the breaking of *a* to *ea* before *l* plus consonant; (2) in the retention of unsmoothed *eo* from velar-umlaut of *e* or *i* before *c* or *g*; (3) in the frequent use of *e* instead of *æ* as the *i*-umlaut of *a* before *l* plus consonant; (4) in the frequent use of *ē* as the *i*-umlaut of *ā* from West Germanic *ai*; (5) in the retention of Primitive Old English diphthongs before *c*, *g*, *h*, and combinations containing these conso-nants.[16] There are no traces of (1) or (2) in Corpus. The six examples of

---

WS *ǣtrendian*, rather than from *gerwan—gierwan*. The form *ðiendi* 1118, I260 is from *þian* (WG *þihan*), cf. similar contracted participles in the Psalter, e.g. *gesiende* from infinitive *gesian* or *gesean*.

[14] Possibly some of the following should have been included: *blaesbaelg* 910, F305, *glaeres* 1958, S688, *naep* 1363, N40, *spręc* (noun) 1852, S299, *spraec* 1769, S43, *suuęr* 633, D26. The first was evidently unfamiliar to the scribe or very corrupt in his sources, cf. *bloestbaelg* 28, Int. 308. In *glaeres* the vowel, according to *NED*, may have been short. In *spręc* the vowel was probably short and probably related to the first or second principal part of *sprecan* rather than the third, cf. Psalter *gespreocu* (nominative-accusative plural). Another *ǣ* which is extremely doubtful appears in *naep* from Latin *nāpus*, for *p* plus back vowel altered the development of *ā*, as in WS *slāpan*. It is true that the Psalter has *slēpan*, but this, like WS *slāpan*, is analogical. Similarly, *suuęr* is analogical like WS *swār*, etc.)— See Bülbring, p. 53; Luick, p. 155.

[15] W. F. Bryan, *Studies in the Dialects of the Kentish Charters of the Old English Period* (Menasha, 1915), pp. 28–29; Chadwick, pp. 182–183.

[16] According to Sievers, pp. 114–115, early vocalization of *g* to *i* at the end of a syllable was a Kentish feature. The following examples appear in Corpus: *romei* 360 (Sweet, p. 667), C89, *iserngrei* 863, F153, *grei* 967, G91, *grei* 981, G117, *omei* 866, F154, *popei* 1516, P166, and perhaps *streide* 1910, S525, although Luick, pp. 219–220, explains the last as a con-tracted form. Chadwick, pp. 173–174, questions Sievers' opinion, presenting evidence of

(5) have already been noted. There are four clear examples—all compounds of the same word however—of *e* as *i*-umlaut of *a* before *l* plus consonant: *edwelle* 908, F300, *eduuelle* 1798, S129, *wellyrgae* 1876, S379, and *eduuelle* 2096, U89 (beside *eduaelle* 137, A490 and *eduuaelle* 2034, T214).[17] There are four examples of *ē* as *i*-umlaut of *ā* from West Germanic *ai: gelestunne* 574, C812, *scultheta* 799, E453, *uuegiδ* 860, F137, *stictenel* 872, F166 (beside *taenil* 868, F162).[18] These examples of (3) and (4) are hardly sufficient to indicate dialect mixture, for the Vespasian Psalter and the hymns which follow it in the manuscript have two examples of *e* for the *i*-umlaut of *a* before *l* plus consonant, *wellan* 113:8 and *wellu* Hy. 2:5, and several examples of *ē* for *i*-umlaut of West Germanic *ai, forδrested, flesc, -ledde, lereδ,* etc.; and the gloss to the Rushworth Matthew, another important Mercian text, has ten of *e* and forty-five of *ē*.[19]

During the eighth century, Northumbrian apparently differed from Mercian in three respects: (1) in the frequent preservation of West Germanic *a* before *r* plus consonant; (2) in the falling together of the breaking diphthongs *ea* and *eo* and of the West Germanic diphthongs *au* and *eu-eo;* (3) in the use of the Northumbrian diphthong *ēi* for long *ē.* Evidence for all three Northumbrian peculiarities is found in Cædmon's Hymn and Bede's Death-Song, both of which date from the eighth century. The fourteen lines of these two poems contain four examples of (1), *uard* twice, *barnum, tharf* (beside one example of *ea middungeard*); one example of (2) *deoth-;* and one of (3), *neidfaerae.*[20] Corpus contains six examples of *a* before *r* plus consonant: *barriggae* 280, B55, *bisparrade* 1451, O221, *gewarht* 567, C780, *sarwo* 88, A281,

---

the change of endosyllabic *g* to *i* from the Northumbrian Liber Vitae and the Saxon Chronicles. The Psalter, also, contains *guiuδu* 24:7 and numerous examples of *i* for the suffix *ig: heſie* (for *heſige* Adj. Nom. Plu. Masc.) 34:13; 54:4; *hweſie* (for *heſige* Adv.) 4:3; *syndrie* 6:7; 7:12, etc.; *weolie* 21:30, etc. In view of the fact that most of Sievers' evidence was taken from Corpus and Epinal, texts which are no longer considered Kentish, and from ninth and tenth century Kentish texts, we may safely assume that Chadwick is correct. Bülbring, p. 204, seems to agree with Sievers, but he repeats Sievers' evidence with little alteration. Girvan, p. 202, has apparently discarded Sievers' view, for he says, "in het vr. kent. *en in naburige dialecten* werd de *g* aan het einde van een woord of letter greep gevocaliseerd" . . . (Italics are mine.)

[17] The double *l* in *scell* "shell" is probably the result of gemination, cf. Gothic *skalja* "tile." Two words, *ellaern* 1775, S55 and *elm* 2149, U237, have *e,* but here the *e* is common Old English and lacks dialectal significance.

[18] *Scultheta* may be corrupt—See Dieter, I, 22. *Werna* 301, B136 should perhaps be added to the list, if it is *wrænna* with metathesis.

[19] Rudolf Zeuner, *Die Sprache des kentischen Psalters* (Leipzig, 1881), I, 15–16, 41; Luick, pp. 172, 173; E. M. Brown, *Die Sprache der Rushworth Glossen* (Göttingen, 1891), I, 29, 69–70.   [20] Sweet, pp. 148–149.

tharme 2140, U210, *þuarm* 1795, S125.[21] The proportion of *a* to *ea* is about one to nine, a proportion which seems rather insignificant in comparison with the *a:ea::*4:1 of the two Northumbrian poems. Corpus contains two examples of *eo* for *ea*, *weorras* 400, C161, *seorwum* 545, C667; one of *ea* for *eo*, *sondgewearp* 1136, I414 (beside *wondeuueorþe* 1975, T19); four of *ēo* for *ēa*, *gefreos* 1402, O28, -*geot* 212, A759 (beside -*geat* 233, A862), *eost-* 460, C375 (beside *east-* 40, A46, 41, A47, 44, A92, 312, B152), and *ōreote* 787, E398 (beside *þreat-* 1265, M1, *threatade* 2169, U291, *þreatende* 1275, M27); one *ēo* for *ēa*, *genaeot* 1117, I245.[22] The proportion for the breaking-*ea* is about *ea:eo::*26:1; for the breaking-*eo*, about *eo:ea::*24:1; for West Germanic *au*, about *ēa:ēo::*10:1. It would seem that there was no significant confusion of the diphthongs under consideration.[23] There are four examples of *ēi* for *ē*: *deid* 728, E90, *eil* 1331, M288, *greig* 850, F115, and *meig* 495, C516.[24] The last two are doubtful. The regular spellings in Corpus are *meg* and *grei*. It is possible that confusion of final *g* and *i* led to the use of *ig* for *g* in both of these examples. The spelling *seign* (for *segn*) 2093, U85, in which the vowel is short, tends to confirm this view. Even if we include the doubtful examples, the proportion of *ēi* is less than one to seventeen.

In summary, the evidence for dialect mixture in Corpus is extremely weak.[25] West Saxon influence may be indicated by four examples of *ǣ* for West Germanic *ā* and six unsmoothed diphthongs. It is possible that some of the latter are merely copied archaisms,[26] for unsmoothed diphthongs would be only slightly more archaic than the retained *h*'s in *faehit* 1582, P407, *raha* 403, C189, *tahae* 141, A494, and *ōhuehl* 641, D56. It is improbable that any West Saxon influence powerful enough to produce the phenomena noted in the first paragraph of this section could have existed without leaving some traces of palatal-diphthongization and of breaking before *l* plus consonant.[27] The case for Kentish is

[21] The forms *barriggae* and *gewarht* are very hard to account for. The former is evidently corrupt and may not even be English. The latter would be as difficult to explain in a Northumbrian text as in a Mercian.

[22] *Sondgewearþ* may contain Germanic *a* before *r* plus consonant, cf. Icelandic *moldvarpa*. The influence of the related verb forms, *weorþan—wearþ*, must also be reckoned with in connection with this word.

[23] The Psalter has examples of *ea* for *eo*, *eo* for *ea*, *ēa* for *ēo*, and *ēo* for *ēa*—Zeuner, I, 22-23, 48-50. Both the Psalter and the glossary show a tendency to confuse the diphthongs resulting from contraction.   [24] The Psalter has *geceigo* 55:10.

[25] The evidence would be stronger, of course, if we included the use of *æ* instead of *e*, *a* instead of *o*, and the other features of Corpus noted in paragraph one of this section. These phenomena are not admissible as evidence because, as we shall see later, all of them have been explained or can be explained satisfactorily as owing to the early date at which Corpus was compiled.   [26] Luick, p. 217, seems to hold this view.

[27] In the Mercian portion of the Rushworth Glosses, there are numerous examples of both of these phenomena. These have sometimes been attributed to West Saxon influence.

slightly weaker. The examples of *e* and *ē*, as we have already seen, mean nothing, except perhaps that a slight tendency to change *æ* (from *i*-umlaut of *a* before *l* plus consonant) and *ǣ* (*i*-umlaut of West Germanic *ai*) to *e* and *ē* existed in the Mercian dialect itself. There is nothing in the glossary, as far as I can see, which we can definitely label Kentish. Northumbrian influence may be indicated by the six examples of *a* before *r* plus consonant and by the four of *ēi*, although two of the former and two of the latter are doubtful. It is unlikely that this Northumbrian influence—if there was one—was potent enough to account for any of the phenomena of paragraph one. Considered in its entirety, the evidence may indicate that the scribe who compiled Corpus was sufficiently acquainted with non-Mercian forms to be occasionally in doubt. He may, as a consequence, have copied a few words from Northumbrian, West Saxon, or Kentish sources without altering them. The evidence can hardly indicate anything further.

II. We are now ready to approach the second of the two major problems with which this study is concerned. What is the relationship between the Corpus Glossary and the Vespasian Psalter? Although the two texts generally agree in the vowels of the accented syllables, they differ markedly in several points.[28] The following disagreements are ordinarily explained chronologically, as results of sound changes which were not yet complete when Corpus was compiled.

		Cp.	*Ps.*
1. WG. *a* followed by nasal	*o,*	*a*	*o*
2. WG. *a* followed by nasal, *i*-umlauted	*e,*	*æ*	*e*
3. WG. *a* followed by *rc* or *rg*	*a,*	*e*	*e*
4. WG. *au* followed by *c, g,* or *h*	*ǣ,*	*ē*	*ē*
5. OE. diphthongs *eo, io, ēo, īo*		Differing treatment.	

1. West Germanic *a* followed by nasal appears as *o* in the Psalter. In Corpus it appears as *o* or *a*, e.g. *aeggimong* 1435, O139, *aegmang* 105, A397. The proportion in the glossary is about *o:a::*5:2. According to Chadwick, the *a*-spelling must have been the regular one in "archetype I," the hypothetical source of the Epinal, Erfurt, and Corpus Glossaries.[29] The accepted explanation is the chronological one. The raising

---

[28] It seemed advisable to omit from consideration the consonants and also the vowels of the unaccented syllables. Such characteristics of Corpus as the frequent use of *b* instead of intervocalic *f* and the frequent use of *æ* instead of *e* in the inflectional endings are commonly accepted as evidence of the early date of the text. No one has suggested, as far as I know, that they indicate any difference between the dialect of Corpus and that of the Psalter.   [29] *Studies,* pp. 189, 203, 250.

and rounding process, it is generally agreed, was still going on during the eighth century and was not complete until about 800.[30]

2. West Germanic *a* before nasal, *i*-umlauted, appears as *e* in the Psalter. Evidently Archetype I had *æ* regularly, *e* seldom.[31] Corpus has *æ* in *doppaenid* 936, F382, *gemęngan* 547, C674, *laendino* 1740, R178, and *maenoe* 599, C387, perhaps also in *wodhae* 583, C840.[32] The proportion is about *e:æ::2:1*; that is, the *e* is about twice as frequent as the *æ* in this position. Scholars have agreed in explaining this difference chronologically.[33] The *a* was not completely rounded at the time of *i*-umlaut. Hence it did not become *oe* as did umlauted West Germanic *o*; but was shifted to an *æ*-sound with very slight rounding, later lost its rounding and then, under the influence of the nasal, was raised to *e*.

3. West Germanic *a* followed by *rc, rg, rh*, or *h* was smoothed in the Anglian dialects. In both Corpus and the Psalter the smoothed vowel appears as *æ* before *h* and combinations containing *h*, although there are sporadic *e*'s, and in Corpus the unsmoothed *ea* in *mearh*. Before *rc* and *rg* the Psalter has *e*, while Corpus has *æ* and *e* in a proportion of approximately *æ:e::3:1*. Again the chronological explanation is the accepted one.[34] The Primitive Old English *æa* (from breaking of WG *a*) was smoothed to *æ*. During the eighth century the smoothed vowel was further palatalized to *e*; e.g. Prim. OE **hæarg* became Corpus *haerg* 1255, L325 (beside *merg* 1308, M195), which corresponds to Psalter *hergas* 134:15 (note also Psalter *merglice* 65:15). In order to account for the retention of *æ* before *h* in the Psalter and other Anglian documents of the ninth century, we must suppose that an *h* hindered the development of the vowel. The Anglian *h* became sufficiently palatal to cause smoothing without becoming palatal enough to permit a further shift of *æ* to *e* to become general.

4. West Germanic *au* followed by *c, g*, or *h* appears as a smoothed vowel in both texts, except for the two words, *geac* and *leactrogas*, mentioned in Section II. In the Psalter the smoothed vowel appears as *ē*, except in the conjunction *ðæh ðe*. In Corpus *ǣ* is more frequent than *ē*. This difference is explained chronologically, and the explanation is simi-

[30] Bülbring, pp. 49–50; Luick, pp. 122–123; Girvan, p. 60.

[31] Chadwick, pp. 204–206, 250.

[32] Sweet and Lindsay print *doppaenid;* Hessels has *doppa. enid* in the text but *dopp-aenid* in the index. For *maenoe*, see Sweet, p. 667. *Wodhae* is corrupt. It glosses *coturno*, which Sweet connects with *coturniz*, Lindsay with *cothurnus*. Sweet considers the word a corruption of *wuduhenn*, or *wudukæn*, cf. Epinal *edischaen* 714. Lindsay, however, thinks *wodhae* is the instrumental singular of *wōð*. It is true that *cothurnus* may have a figurative meaning of "eloquence," or something of that sort, but Lindsay's conjecture seems far-fetched. Is *wōdhenn* a possibility?   [33] Bülbring, p. 71; Luick, pp. 170–171; Girvan, p. 73.

[34] Bülbring, p. 81; Luick, p. 216; Girvan, pp. 34–35, apparently agrees.

lar to that for the short vowel.[35] A prehistoric *bēacn appears in Corpus as -bæcun 1971, S721 (beside -becn 2043, T264), and as -becen 70:7 in the Psalter. An h hindered long ǣ less than it hindered short æ. Probably the first element of the long diphthong was more palatal at the time of smoothing than the first element of the short diphthong.

Chadwick at one time supposed that there was a direct connection between the change of ǣ (from smoothing of ǣa) to ē and the change of ǣ (from West Germanic ā) to ē. He believed, in fact, that they were the same change.[36] He supposed that this shift had taken place later than i-umlaut and smoothing. He explained the use of æ in eighth-century texts, of e in later ones, for the smoothing of æa before rc and rg by supposing that an early lengthening of vowels had taken place before r plus consonant—a lengthening which had preceded the shift of ǣ to ē. The æ was retained before h because no lengthening took place before that consonant. The validity of the entire explanation is destroyed by its failure to account for the retention in the Anglian dialects of the ǣ which resulted from i-umlaut of Primitive Old English ā (from West Germanic ai). It is hardly possible that a spontaneous shift of ǣ to ē. could have occurred after the time of i-umlaut without shifting the umlaut-ǣ to ē. Chadwick's hypothesis has apparently been abandoned.[37]

5. The Old English diphthongs eo, io, ēo, īo are treated somewhat differently in the two texts. The evidence of the Psalter indicates that the diphthongs eo and io (from breaking and velar-umlaut of e and i) had fallen together in the dialect of that text, and likewise the diphthongs ēo and īo (from West Germanic eu-eo and iu). The spelling io for the short diphthong is rare. The spelling io for the long diphthong is still common, but it is frequently used in words which, etymologically, should have eo; and eo-is frequent in words which should have io. In Corpus the distinction between the short eo and io is weak, but not so weak as it is in the Psalter. Before r plus consonant io occurs only once, in -biorg 1672, P825, where etymologically it does not belong. The velar-umlaut of West Germanic i appears as io or eo in a proportion of about io:eo::3:1. The distinction between ēo and īo is better preserved than in the Psalter, but briost- 1672, P825 contains īo for ēo, and double forms like hleor 923, F345—hlior 86, A267 and getreuuade 900, F271— getriowad 857, F134 indicate that the distinction was weakening. We note that Corpus retains long eu and iu frequently, especially before w.[38] These differences between the Psalter and Corpus are explained chronologically. The shift of eu and iu to ēo and īo as well as the falling

[35] *Ibid.*   [36] *Studies*, pp. 96–98, 117.   [37] Luick, p. 130; Girvan, p. 49.

[38] For further examples of īo for īo and īo for ēo in Corpus, see Sievers' article in *P.B.B.*, xviii (1894), 415–416.

together of *io* with *eo* and *ío* with *ēo* occurred during the late eighth and early ninth centuries.[39]

The differences which we have been considering are clearly the results of sound-changes which were incomplete when Corpus was written. The following disagreements between the Psalter and the glossary are more difficult to explain:

	Cp.	Ps.
6. WG. *e* and *i* in open syllable followed by back vowel.	*eo, io, e, i*	*eo, io*
7. WG. *a* in open syllable before back vowel.	........*a, ea*........	*ea*
8. WG. *a* in closed syllable or in open syllable followed by front vowel.	.................*æ, e*..........	*e*
9. WG. *a, e* before *c* or *g* plus back vowel.	..........*a, æ, ea*.......	*æ*
	e ....*e, eo*	

6. West Germanic *e* and *i* in open syllable followed by back vowel underwent velar-umlaut and appear as diphthongs in both texts, but, although exceptions are rare in the Psalter, they are common enough in Corpus to have real significance. If we eliminate all occurrences of *e* and *i* before *c* and *g*, we find that the proportion of diphthongs to unumlauted vowels is about two to one in the glossary.[40] Both Luick and Bülbring have dated velar-umlaut in the seventh and early eighth centuries, i.e., before the time of Corpus.[41] If this dating is correct, the difference in velar-umlaut must be looked upon as a result of local variation within the Mercian dialect, for the frequency of the unumlauted vowels makes it impossible to explain them as archaisms. It is more probable, however, that the sound change has been dated too early. Girvan holds that velar-umlaut was not complete until the ninth century. He points to such forms as *ðueoran* and *ætfealan* in the Vespasian Psalter and *swura* in West Saxon as evidence that smoothing must have preceded velar-umlaut. He further notes the unumlauted vowels in the early Northumbrian texts and in the Epinal and Erfurt Glossaries. Finally, he points to the fact that in the Vespasian Psalter and MS. C of the Cura Pastoralis the *eo* and *io* from velar-umlaut have not fallen together so completely as have the *eo* and *io* which resulted from breaking. The preservation of this distinction seems to indicate that velar-umlaut was a recent change when these texts were produced.[42] Girvan is undoubtedly correct. Cædmon's Hymn and Bede's Death-Song, commonly assigned to the eighth century, contain no examples of velar-umlaut, although the former contain *metudæs, hefæn-,* and *heben*. The Epinal Glossary, which

---

[39] Bülbring, pp. 43, 59; Luick, pp. 135, 236.

[40] A fairly complete list of the diphthongs from velar-umlaut of *e* and *i* will be found in Sievers' article, *P.B.B.,* xviii, 415 ff.

[41] Luick, pp. 34, 266; Bülbring, p. 92.   [42] *Angelsaksisch Handboek,* pp. 92–93.

has never been dated earlier than the eighth century although it may contain some archaic forms from the late seventh, shows only one clear example of velar-umlaut, *geolu* 1064 (beside *gelu* 242, 432, 458 and *ægergelu* 429). Dialect will hardly account for this lack, for *e* and *i* are preserved even before labials and liquids, where the umlaut is supposed to have been common to all of the Old English dialects: *sifun-* 762, *ebor-* 1052, *helustras* 867, etc.[43]

Further evidence may be found. Comparative lateness of velar-umlaut in the dialect of Corpus may be inferred from the infrequency of *eo* and *io* before original back vowels which have been syncopated or changed to *e*. There are two clear examples: *weosend* "bison" 337, B213, *cionecti* 1739, R175. There are two words in which there may have been at one time a svarabhakti *u*: *heolstras* (cf. Epinal *helustras*) 1723, R70, *heolstr* 1838, S228. Or are the diphthongs in these latter two due to some sort of breaking before *l* plus consonant such as we find in Anglian *seolf*? A number of forms are evidently analogical: *ætweosendne* (*aetweosendre* according to Hessels and Lindsay) 1054, I101; *beorende* (cf. Psalter *beorao, beorende,* etc.) 751, E214 and 1677, P841; *eolene* 1057, I111 (beside *eolone* 1453, O 225); *piose* 1208, L147 (beside *piosan* 1586, P414); *screope* 1906, S513 and *aerenscreop* 1935, S574 (beside the verb form *scriopu* 1828, S194). Chadwick thinks that the *eo* in *beorende*, etc. indicates that velar-umlaut took place before the *a* in these words became *e*.[44] It is possible that velar-umlaut began early and continued until the ninth century, as did the shift of *a* to *o* before nasals. But it is much more probable that the *eo* in such words is analogical.

7. West Germanic *a* in open syllable followed by back vowel appears in the Psalter, with a few exceptions, as *ea*. In Corpus the proportion is about *a:ea*::2:1. Velar-umlaut of *a* appears in the following words:[45] *bearug* 1284, M38, *cleadur* 599, C879, *-fearu* 881, F201, *geabules* 813, E518, *geabuli* 96, A321, *geabuli* 648, D69, *geaduling* 914, F318, *geaduling* 1496, P104, *geuueada* 2086, U50, *sceaba* 1755, R231, *sceadu* 1954, S662, *sceadu-* 1998, T79, *-sceaðan* 1579, P391. It is lacking in these words: *apa* P386 (omitted by Sweet), *apuldur* 1273, M24, *-apuldur* 1302, M142, *eorðmata* 2113, U147, *-faru* 186, A696, *gabul-* 469, C416, *gabul-* 1711,

R31, *gelaðade* 90, A287, *-habuc* 118, A432, *-habuc* 826, F10, *-habuc* 1016,
H83. *-habuc* 1890, S438, *-hara* 447, C314, *hara* 1206, L135, *-hara* 1347,
M339, *mapuldur* 51, A120, *maðalade* 586, C854, *nabogaar* 2002, T87,
nabogar 1754, R216, *nabula* 2151, U243, *sadol* 1839, S229, *sadul-* 388,
C130, *sadul-* 1563, P315, *scadu* 1801, S133, *spadan* 2079, U13, *tasul*
2000, T84, *wapul* 835, F37.

According to Luick, this use of both *a* and *ea* results from mixture of
sub-dialects. Mercian split at an early date, he supposes, into the sub-
dialect represented by the Psalter, the sub-dialect represented by the
Mercian portion of the Rushworth Glosses (Rushworth'), and a third
sub-dialect.[46] Luick's reasoning is good as far as it goes, but it does not
go far enough. The Psalter has *ea* generally; Rushworth' has *a* generally;
and, if these two texts represent two sub-dialects, any text written in a
mixture of the two might be expected to have both *a* and *ea*. On the
other hand, Rushworth' has numerous examples of *ea* for *a* before *l*
plus consonant, but Corpus has none; Rushworth' has a fair number of
examples of palatal-diphthongization, in *ceastre*, etc., while Corpus
contains no clear example. The lack of palatal-diphthongization and of
breaking-*ea* before *l* plus consonant may not entirely invalidate Luick's
reasoning, but it certainly leaves his hypothesis open to serious doubts.

I believe it can be shown not only that velar-umlaut of *a* took place,
as Girvan maintains, during the historical period, but also that it was
later than the velar-umlaut of *e* and *i*. In the first place, it is reasonable
to suppose that a sound change which is practically limited to Mercian
and Kentish must have taken place later than a change which is shared
by Northumbrian and West Saxon. One would naturally assume, unless
there were reliable evidence to the contrary, that velar-umlaut of *e* and
i began before Mercian had branched off from the other Old English
dialects and that the velar-umlaut of *a* began after Mercian had become
rather thoroughly differentiated from West Saxon and Northumbrian.
In the second place, the greater proportion of *a* in Corpus would indicate that velar-umlaut of that vowel occurred late. The proportions are
approximately $a:ea::2:1$ and $e,i:eo, io::1:2$. Finally, there are two
clear examples of *eo* and *io* before back vowels which have been reduced
to *e* and several doubtful examples, but there is not a single example of
ea in similar position. The evidence seems to indicate that, when the
glossary was compiled, velar-umlaut of *a* was of so recent origin that
analogical forms, such as Psalter *fearende*, etc., had not had time to
develop.

In order to account for the tardiness of the velar-umlaut of *a*, we
must suppose that *a* was still a back vowel when the tendency which

[46] *Hist. Gram.*, pp. 165, 211.

produced velar-umlaut began. At least, no other explanation appears reasonable. This one would account for the fact that the umlaut affected *e* and *i* earlier than *a*, and it fits our present conception of the phonetics of the umlaut. The generally accepted explanation of the velar-umlaut of West Germanic *a* in the Mercian dialect is that *a* became a front vowel in an open syllable followed by a back vowel, while the back vowel modified the intervening consonant, whereupon a velar glide developed between the fronted vowel and the consonant. The raising and fronting of the Mercian *a* in open syllable before back vowel has been dated in the fifth century.[47] This dating is probably too early. If the change took place during the eighth and early ninth centuries, the effect would be to delay velar-umlaut of *a* in the manner which has been noted. We can in this way account for the difference between Corpus and the Psalter as well as for the difference between the treatment of *e-i* and *a* in Corpus itself.

There is one objection to this explanation. If, during the eighth century, *a* was raised and fronted and then umlauted, why do we find not in Corpus more examples of *æ* in open syllable before back vowel?[48] A fairly satisfactory answer can be found. Velar-umlaut and the raising and fronting process were going on simultaneously. It is not necessary to suppose that *a* was shifted completely to *æ* before umlaut could take place, or that the development was *a* to *æ* to *ea* (i.e. *æa*). The umlaut might occur as soon as the vowel was sufficiently raised and fronted to be definitely different from the following consonant. The development could have been *a* to [*a*ᵃ] to [*æa*]. As long as the vowel was closer in quality to *a* than to *æ*, it might be written *a*. As soon as it reached [*a*ᵃ], it might change immediately to [*æa*] and be written *ea*.[49]

8. West Germanic *a* in closed syllable and in open syllable followed by original front vowel appears as *e* in the Psalter. The only important exceptions are: *a* before *l* plus consonant, e.g. *ald*, and *æ* generally in the unstressed *æt*, *ðæt*, *ðætte*. Corpus shows both of these groups of exceptions; it also shows both *æ* and *e* for West Germanic *a* in those positions in which the Psalter has only *e*. The *æ* is commoner than the *e* in the glossary, the proportion being in the neighborhood of *æ*:*e*::5:1. The following examples of *e* occur:[50] *ceber* 214, A764, *cefer* 326, B187, *-creft*

---

[47] *Ibid.*, p. 266.

[48] There are a number of *æ*'s before *c* or *g* plus back vowel. And *-læppan* 873, F169 may contain an *æ* which has been raised and fronted but not velar-umlauted, cf. Psalter *læppan* 132:2.

[49] The smoothed vowels which appear before *c* and *g* form a group of exceptions. These two consonants were not velarized by following back vowels. Hence the [*a*ᵃ] did not undergo umlaut but developed into *æ*, as in *dægas*, etc.

[50] Some of these examples are doubtful. Sweet prints *gebellicum* as though it were Latin.

217, A772, *gebellicum* 881, F201, *gebrec* 1580, P398, *gebrec* 1717, R58, *gegederung* 549, C686, *gebrec* 190, A709, *gibrec* 2152, U246, *heber* 399, C156, *lebel* 193, A716, *lebil* 1269, M17, *lebl* 2045, T267, *leber* 1823, S186, *lebr* 1804, S141, *-negl* 484, C480, *reftras* 150, A533, *scept-* 156, A548, *sceptog* 145, A517, *snegl* 1220, L180, *snegl* 1283, M37, *sneglas* 531, C630, *tebl* 110, A414, *teblere* 111, A416, *tebleth* 497, C522, *teblstan* 349, C12. The examples of *æ* are too numerous to be listed here. There is only one clear example of *æ* for West Germanic *e*, *saes* 2050, T289, although there are some doubtful examples like *taelg* 934, F379, *caeli* 1748, R204. There are also examples of *æ* for the *i*-umlaut in words which one would expect to contain *e*: *saecg* 977, G113, *waecg* 626, C970, etc. The evidence indicates that the *æ* (from the common Old English raising and fronting of West Germanic *a*, as in West Saxon *dæg*, cf. Psalter *deg*) was just beginning to fall together with West Germanic *e* when Corpus was written, or else that Corpus is a mixture of an *æ*-sub-dialect with an *e*-sub-dialect.

Luick is of the latter opinion and supposes that the use of both *æ* and *e* results from mixture of Mercian sub-dialects.[51] Those objections to the sub-dialect hypothesis which were mentioned in connection with the use of *a* and *ea* apply here as well. In addition there is the fact that Rushworth' has *æ*, not only for the *æ* from West Germanic *a*, but also for West Germanic *e* in about one-third of the words in which that sound occurs.[52] Evidently West Germanic *a* and *e* had fallen together in the dialect of Rushworth'. If, as Bülbring suggests, they fell together under *æ*, the WG *e* having become an open sound,[53] we should expect to find numerous examples of *æ* for WG *e* in Corpus (if Corpus really represents a mixture of sub-dialects). If, on the other hand, the two sounds fell together under *e*, no mixture of a sub-dialect resembling Rushworth' with a sub-dialect resembling the Psalter could produce what we find in Corpus.

Chadwick, p. 195, considers it Old English. Hessels calls it Latin in his edition of the Corpus Glossary, but he has evidently changed his mind on that point—See *A Late Eighth-Century Latin-Anglo-Saxon Glossary* (Cambridge, 1906), p. 228. Lindsay, in his edition of Corpus, calls *gebellicum* Latin, with a question mark. Authority is heavy on both sides, but common sense seems to be on the side of calling the word Old English. *Fiscalis reda—gebellicum* (from **ȝafel-lic?*) *wægnfearu* is a more reasonable reading of the item than *fiscalis—reda gebellicum—wægnfearu*. Sweet considers the vowel of *gebrec* long, but see *N.E.D.*, article "Brake v²" Old Icelandic *snigill*, Old High German *snegil* might lead us to suppose that Corpus *snegl* contains WG *e*. Perhaps it does, but West Saxon *snægel*, early Middle English *snail, snayl*, and modern *snail* point to a Prim. OE. **snagl*. The word *tebleth* belongs here only if it is a relatively late formation based upon *tebl* or *tæfl* (from Late Latin **tab'la*—Latin *tabula*). 　　[51] *Hist. Gram.*, pp. 165–166.

[52] Brown, I, 31–32. 　　[53] *Altenglisches Elementarbuch*, p. 36.

The shift of *æ* to *e* (e.g. *dæg* to *deg*) in Mercian and Kentish has been dated in the fifth century, as has the shift of *a* to *æ* (e.g. *dagas* to *dægas*).[54] The two changes are very similar, and it is logical to suppose that they were closely related and occurred during approximately the same period. Girvan believes that the shift of *æ* to *e* preceded that of *a* to *æ;* otherwise, he believes, the two sounds would have fallen together.[55] Girvan's view needs modification. The change of *æ* to *e* certainly could not have followed that of *a* to *æ*, but the two may have proceeded simultaneously. If the latter were the case, the *a* would become [*aᵉ*] while the *æ* was shifting to [*æᵉ*]; the [*aᵉ*] would become *ea* [*æa*] by velar-umlaut while the [*æᵉ*] became *e*. At no stage would the two sound the same, and hence they would at no time be in danger of falling together.

The date which has been assigned, i.e., the fifth century, is too early. The raising and fronting of Mercian *æ* in closed syllable and in open syllable followed by front vowel should probably be placed in the eighth and early ninth centuries. Its connection with the raising and fronting of Mercian *a* in open syllable followed by back vowel is one reason. The fact that neither change is shared to any great extent by Northumbrian or West Saxon is another. Moreover, the *e* is rare in the Mercian and Kentish texts of the eighth century. In the eighth-century Mercian charters in Sweet's *Oldest English Texts*,[56] we find various combinations of *æðel*- in personal names, beside one example with *e*, *edilbalt*. In the seventh- and eighth-century Kentish charters, we find *aedilmaeri aedilfridi, aethilberhtus, aeðelhuni,* etc., *paeð*, and *caestruuara*. The *æ*'s in the Mercian charters might conceivably be explained by the sub-dialect hypothesis, but what of the Kentish examples? Were there also sub-dialects of Kentish? No one, as far as I know, has suggested that there were, except Chadwick, who made the suggestion only to discard it immediately.[57] The logical inference to be drawn from the rarity of *e* and the frequency of *æ* in eighth-century texts is that the shift of *æ* to *e* was late.

There are two objections to this late dating of the change. Luick argues that the shift must have preceded *i*-umlaut because, if it had taken place later, it would have affected the *æ* (from *i*-umlaut of *a* before *l* plus consonant) in such words as *fællan* and *ældra*.[58] Luick's reasoning is two-edged. If, as he says, the shift of *æ* took place at the same time as that of *a*, and if both shifts took place before *i*-umlaut, the unumlauted *a* in such words as *all* and *ald* would have been affected, as well as that in **falljan* and **aldira*. The result in historic times would be, not only

---

[54] Luick, p. 266.   [55] *Angelsaksisch Handboek*, p. 83.

[56] Pp. 427–433. The importance of the scarcity of the *e* in these charters is somewhat decreased, of course, by the scarcity of words in which the *e* *could* appear.

[57] *Studies*, p. 183.   [58] *Hist. Gram.*, p. 176.

fellan and *eldra*, but *all* and *æld*. Obviously the Mercian shift of *a* to *æ* and of *æ* to *e* (*zweite Aufhellung*) affected neither the *a* in *ald* nor the *æ* in *ældra*—either before or after *i*-umlaut. The explanation must lie in the quality of the combination *l* plus consonant itself; the quality of the combination was apparently such that it prevented the change. We need not suppose that this quality was altogether lost at the time of *i*-umlaut. The commonly accepted explanation of *i*-umlaut is that the *i* or *j* "front-modified" the preceding consonant or group of consonants, which in turn modified the preceding vowel.[59] The combination *l* plus consonant was evidently front-modified sufficiently to cause the umlaut of *a* to *æ* (e.g. *aldira* to *ældra*), but we are not justified in supposing that the modification went much further in the Mercian dialect. The combination could have retained enough of its original quality to prevent a spontaneous shift of the umlaut-*æ* to *e* from becoming general.

Luick bases a second argument against late dating upon the double-umlaut forms *festen* and *efest(i)g* in the Psalter,[60] and other words in which an original *i* or *j* caused umlaut of a preceding *u*, which became *y* and then caused umlaut of the vowel in the stem syllable. Referring to the *zweite Aufhellung*, he says:[61]

Dagegen ist deutlich, daß sie im Mercischen vor einem gleich zu besprechenden Wandel, dem *i*-Umlaut, liegt (§198b und Anm. 3); sie muß also vorhistorisch sein.

In §198, referring to *festen*, etc., he says:[62]

Des *e* in diesen Formen, welches sich genau wie sonstiges *e* entwickelt, aber scharf von *æ* als Umlaut von *a* scheidet, zeigt, daß zur Zeit des Umlautes nicht mehr die Lautfolge *a-u-i* galt (in der sich ebenso *æ* ergeben hätte wie bei *a* vor *l*, §188), sondern schon *æ-u-i*, also die zweite Aufhellung vor dem *i*-Umlaut eintrat.

This objection is not valid, for the evidence which Luick uses proves nothing concerning the date of the *zweite Aufhellung*. If the change of *a* to *æ* and of *æ* to *e* occurred before *i*-umlaut, the *a* in a prehistoric *fastunja* (cf. Old Saxon *fastunnia*) would have become *æ* and then umlauted to *e*. The result would be *festenne* or *festen*. And, if the shift occurred after *i*-umlaut, the *a* would umlaut to *æ*, then be raised and fronted to *e*. The result would be precisely the same, *festenne* or *festen*.

9. Smoothing characterizes both texts. Corpus contains no examples of *eo* before *c* or *g* plus back vowel. The Psalter contains only one example of *ea* in similar position, *hreacan* 113:7,[63] and relatively few

---

[59] Wylde, p. 65.

[60] The Psalter has *festenne* 34:13, etc., *efestgan* Hymn 12:13, *efestigne* Hy. 11:7.

[61] *Hist. Gram.*, p. 166.   [62] *Ibid.*, p. 184.

[63] However, *weagas* (for *woegas*), which appears three times in the Psalter, indicates that *ea* before *g* plus back vowel was not unknown to the glossator.

examples of *a*: *dracan* 90:13; 73:14; *hracan* 134:17; *dagum* 89:15, etc. Corpus contains six examples of *ea*: *heaga-* 962, G63, *heago-* 114, A421, *onseacan* 665, D148, *reagu-* 283, B58, *-ðeaca* 1999, T81, *weagat* 1188, L81; nine of *a*: *asclacade* 1014, H58, *blaco* 1688, P887, *draca* 2027, T182, *gagulsuille* 946, G3, *lundlaga* 1712, R33, *maga* 1934, S573, *-plagan* 1245, L289, *ragu* 1324, M258, *ragu* 1332, M289; eight of *æ*: *asclaecadun* 693, D329, *haeca* 1559, P311, *haegu-* 1897, S473, *hlaegulendi* 317, B171, *naecad* 807, E499, *plaega* 1477, P12, *rægu* 1853, S300, *slaegu* 1230, L247.[54] The Psalter contains a number of examples of *eo*: *gebreocu, spreocu, spreocað, spreocan, spreocende, gebreocendes, steogun; gespreocu, weogum,* etc. In short, *a* is irregularly treated in Corpus, and *e* is irregular in the Psalter. These irregularities are hard to account for.

Perhaps this difference reflects local variation within the Mercian dialect, or perhaps the *eo*'s in the Psalter should be looked upon as evidence of Kentish influence. Neither explanation is generally accepted, however, and Luick suggests that the diphthongs in the Psalter are analogical.[55] •The suggestion seems reasonable. The verb forms could have been influenced by *cweoðu, eotu, meotu, cweoðað, beorað, eotað, bitreodað, eotan, cweoðende, eotende, fortreodendes, -cweodon* and similar forms, both in the Psalter itself and in the spoken language. The nouns could have been influenced by *geofu, geofum, sceopum, weoras,* etc. Similarly, in Corpus the *ea*'s could have been influenced by *sceadu, geuueada, -sceaðan,* etc., the *a*'s by *maðalade, scadu, tasul,* etc. As we should expect, the preponderance of *a* over *ea* before other consonants leads to a preponderance of analogical *a* over analogical *ea*.

This explanation is so neat and convenient that one would like to accept it as it stands, but it needs a certain amount of qualification. The lack of *eo* in Corpus is probably due to the fact that velar-umlaut was in its early stages and analogical forms had not had time to develop. Because velar-umlaut of *a* lagged behind velar-umlaut of *e* and *i*, we should not expect to find analogical *ea*'s either. The orthographical confusion represented by *rægu, reagu, ragu* can be explained in terms of analogy, only if we suppose that the fronting of *a*, the velar-umlaut, and the smoothing tendency were all present. Such a combination of sound changes might lead to the confusion which we have observed.

From the data in this article, certain conclusions may be drawn.

First, the language of the Corpus Glossary is relatively free from dialect mixture, and Luick is correct in minimizing the non-Mercian elements. Out of more than 2200 Old English words only twenty can be taken as evidence of dialect mixture, and four of these are doubtful. We should also bear in mind that Corpus contains very few of the particles like *in, of, se, þæm,* etc., which are the same in all dialects;

---

[54] Here also probably *fraecuð* 695, D331.   [55] *Hist. Gram.*, p. 208.

the proportion of words which could reflect dialect mixture, is large. The major characteristics of the glossary can, therefore, be treated as characteristics of the Mercian dialect.

Second, the language of Corpus does not represent a mixture of a Psalter sub-dialect with a Rushworth' sub-dialect. Luick's sub-dialect hypothesis does not explain the absence in the glossary of some of the most outstanding features of Rushworth'. Moreover, the chief differences between Corpus and the Psalter, including the ones upon which Luick's hypothesis is based, can be explained chronologically, as results of the difference in time between the writing of the two texts. The chronological explanation should not be difficult to accept—the idea that Corpus and the Psalter represent two stages in the development of Mercian rather than two local varieties of the dialect. After all, the difference in time between Alfred and Ælfric is no greater than the difference between the two Mercian texts; yet no one argues that the important differences between Alfred and Ælfric indicate two local sub-dialects.

On the other hand, to conclude that there were no local variations in Mercian, or even that there are no local differences between the Corpus Glossary and the Vespasian Psalter, would be unwarranted. There are minor disagreements in the treatment of the vowels of unaccented syllables which are difficult to account for. There are also a few details (e.g. Corpus *-aeppel* 1512, P137, Psalter *eappul-* 78:1; and Corpus *mettocas* 1709, R19, *meottoc* 2047, T286), for which no one, as far as I know, has been able to find a satisfactory explanation. These disagreements are not at present attributed to local variation, and they may be due to nothing more than the peculiarities of individual scribes; yet it is only by careful scrutiny of such details that real geographical differences —if there are any—will be detected.

Third, certain sound changes probably occurred later than has been supposed. It was necessary to assume late dates for them in order to account for the differences between Corpus and the Psalter when the sub-dialect hypothesis broke down. When the assumptions had been made, they fitted the data, not only of the two texts under special consideration but of the other early Old English texts, better than the accepted datings. In fact, to place velar-umlaut earlier than the eighth and ninth centuries is to ignore the evidence of most of the pre-Alfredian manuscripts. The second raising and fronting of West Germanic *a*, which changed *dæg* to *deg* and *dagas* to *dægas*, must also have occurred, not during the fifth century, but during the eighth and early ninth. Smoothing must have continued at least until 800.

SHERMAN M. KUHN

Oklahoma A. & M. College

THE SWORD OF HEALFDENE

Line 1020 of *Beowulf*, as it appears in the manuscript,[1] reads *forgeaf þa beowulfe brand healfdenes*, that is, "[Someone, clearly Hroðgar] gave then, to Beowulf, the sword of Healfdene." This sword, mentioned again in line 1023, was not only a magnificent gift in itself but a priceless heirloom of the sort whose possession by a foreigner might, under different circumstances, lead to the breaking of sacred oaths and a desperate war of revenge.[2] If the poet had wished to enhance the importance of Beowulf's service to the Danes, nothing could have been more effective than Hroðgar's bestowal of his father's sword upon the conqueror of Grendel.

There is no doubt about the manuscript reading: it is perfectly clear, and no scholar from Thorkelin's day to the present has had any difficulty in making out the word *brand*. Yet the line is now emended to read *Forgeaf þa Beowulfe bearn Healfdenes*, that is, "The son of Healfdene [Hroðgar, of course] gave then to Beowulf. . . . " This change of *brand* to *bearn* eliminates Healfdene's sword, with its wealth of suggestion, substituting a conventional locution and producing a cold, colorless statement of the most commonplace sort. Besides failing to improve the sense or the meter of the line, the emendation tends to obscure an important stylistic feature of the *Beowulf*—its bold use of ellipsis.

When Thorkelin edited *Beowulf* in 1815, he seems to have had no real difficulty with the manuscript reading, *brand*. His transcription and translation of the line were as follows:[3]

Forgeaf þa Beowulfe	*Dedit tunc (Rex) Beowulfo*
Brand Healfdanes	*Lanceam Halfdani*

In his "Index Nominum Propriorum," under the caption *Hrodgar*, Thorkelin cited this passage with the remark, "Illi Healfdani Regis arma donat."[4] He was able, without the aid of modern scholarly equipment, to see that the subject of *forgeaf* is unexpressed and to supply the only possible subject, namely, King

---

[1] See J. Zupitza, "Beowulf. Autotypes of the Unique Cotton MS. Vitellius A xv in the British Museum," *EETS*, LXXVII (London, 1882), 48.

[2] Cf. the Heaðobeard episode, lines 2032–2069.

[3] Grim. Johnson Thorkelin (ed.), *De Danorum Rebus Gestis Secul. III & IV* (Havniæ, 1815), p. 78.   [4] *Ibid.*, p. 263.

Reprinted by permission from *Journal of English and Germanic Philology*, 42 (1943), 82-95.

Hroðgar. Nor did he have any difficulty in identifying *brand* as some sort of weapon, *lanceam* or *arma*.

Emendation was first suggested by Grundtvig in his Danish translation of *Beowulf*, in which the passage containing line 1020 appears thus:[5]

> Det var Halvdans Helte-Søn,
> Guldrund efter Vane,
> Bjowulf han i Kæmpe-Løn
> Gav en gylden Fane,
> Gav ham og, til Herre-Færd,
> Brynje af de Bedste,
> Hjelme-Hat og Belte-Sværd,
> Klinge med Guld-Fæste!

Grundtvig's note indicates his reason for altering the text—"læser jeg: *Bearn Healfdenes*, da Subjectet ellers mangler."[6] The verb *forgeaf*, he assumed, must have an expressed subject, which *bearn Healfdenes* (Halvdans Helte-Søn) could supply but which *brand Healfdenes* obviously could not. In his edition of *Beowulf*, however, Grundtvig gave the manuscript reading in the text and placed his emendation in a footnote.[7]

Since Grundtvig's time, his conjecture has been widely accepted by editors of *Beowulf*. A few have relegated it to a footnote, or have adopted it in translation while retaining the manuscript reading in the text.[8] Most have inserted it in the text, apparently without questioning its validity.[9]

In spite of its wide acceptance, this change of *brand* to *bearn*, with its assumption that a scribe mistakenly substituted

[5] Nik. Fred. Sev. Grundtvig, *Bjowulfs Drape* (Kjøbenhavn, 1820), p. 95.

[6] *Ibid.*, p. 282.   [7] *Beowulfes Beorh* (Kiöbenhavn, 1861), p. 34.

[8] John Kemble, *The Anglo-Saxon Poems of Beowulf*, etc. (London, 1835), p. 73; Kemble, *A Translation of the Anglo-Saxon Poem of Beowulf*, etc. (London, 1837), p. 42; C. W. M. Grein, *Beovulf nebst den Fragmenten Finnsburg und Valdere* (Cassel & Göttingen, 1867), p. 90; Hubert Pierquin, *Le Poème Anglo-Saxon de Beowulf* (Paris, 1912), p. 449.

[9] Benjamin Thorpe, *The Anglo-Saxon Poems of Beowulf*, etc. (London, 1875); C. W. M. Grein, *Bibliothek der angelsächsischen Poesie* (Goettingen, 1857), vol. I; Moritz Heyne, *Beowulf* (Paderborn, 1863); M. Trautmann, *Das Beowulflied*, "Bonner Beiträge zur Anglistik," XVI (Bonn, 1904); W. J. Sedgefield, *Beowulf* (Manchester, 1913); A. J. Wyatt and R. W. Chambers, *Beowulf with the Finnsburg Fragment* (Cambridge, 1920); F. Holthausen, *Beowulf nebst dem Finnsburg-Bruchstück* (Heidelberg, 1921), vol. I; Moritz Heyne and L. L. Schücking, *Beowulf* (Paderborn, 1931); Federico Olivero, *Beowulf* (Torino, 1934); Fr. Klaeber, *Beowulf and the Fight at Finnsburg* (Boston, 1936); etc.

brand for the *bearn* which he found in his exemplar, is not one of those emendations which seem to correct obvious scribal errors. The word *brand* in the sense of "sword" or in any other sense which would fit line 1020 is rare in Old English,[10] whereas *bearn* is a common word which frequently enters into such conventional expressions as *bearn Healfdenes*.[11] Why should any scribe who saw the familiar formula mistake it for the unfamiliar *brand Healfdenes?*

The only objection to the manuscript reading arises from a desire on the part of editors and translators to provide *forgeaf* with an expressed subject. But *forgeaf* needs no expressed subject. In fact, omission of the subject in line 1020 is thoroughly in keeping with the style of the *Beowulf*-poet. Many similar ellipses in the poem, which would be considered solecisms in modern academic prose, apparently seemed innocuous to the writers of former times. The best known discussion of this feature is probably Alois Pogatscher's article,[12] in which he shows that the subject of almost any kind of clause in Old English could be omitted if it were expressed, or even suggested, by a substantive or group of substantives in the preceding or the following clause. For example, the subject of *meahte . . . wiðgripan* in lines 2520–2521 of *Beowulf* is omitted because the *ic* of 2519 can be understood and no ambiguity results from the omission of *ic* in 2520.[13]

	Nolde ic sweord beran,
wæpen to wyrme,	gif ic wiste hu
wið ðam aglæcean	elles meahte
gylpe wiðgripan,	. . . .

Pogatscher's many examples from Old English prose and poetry have been augmented by Ernst Kock,[14] Frederick Klaeber,[15] and others, until the list is decidedly impressive. The specimens range

[10] The only other occurrence in *Beowulf* is in line 1454. A few other Old English examples are given in Bosworth-Toller and the *New English Dictionary*. The meaning *brand* "sword" is defended, superfluously perhaps, by K. W. Bouterwek, "Zur Kritik des Beowulfliedes," *Zeitschrift für Deutsches Altertum*, XI (1859), 84–85.

[11] In *Beowulf*, we find *Ecglafes bearn* 499, *bearn Ecgþeowes* 529, 631, 1383, 1473, *bearn Healfdenes* 469, *Geata bearn* 2184, *gumena bearn* 878, etc.

[12] "Unausgedrücktes Subjekt im Altenglischen," *Anglia*, XXIII (1901), 261–301. [13] *Ibid.*, p. 263.

[14] "Interpretations and Emendations of Early English Texts. III," *Anglia*, XXVII (1904), 218–37; and other articles in same series.

[15] See notes to his edition of *Beowulf*.

from simple ellipses such as the one quoted above to passages like the following, in which the subject of *sceal . . . tredan* is merely suggested by *eorl* and *mægð*:[16]

> þa sceall brond fretan,
> æled þeccean,— nalles eorl wegan
> maððum to gemyndum, ne mægð scyne
> habban on healse hringweorðunge,
> ac sceal geomormod, golde bereafod,
> oft nalles æne elland tredan, ...

Rather numerous examples of the same sort may also be found in Middle and Early Modern English.[17]

Some of the most striking ellipses in *Beowulf* remain untouched by the investigations of Pogatscher and his successors. In the examples which I am about to present, the subject is omitted even though no substantive capable of suggesting it appears in the immediate vicinity.

After a formal speech the narrative may be resumed with a subjectless verb, as in line 2892. Lines 2880–2889 are as follows:

> " . . . .
> Symle wæs þy sæmra, þonne ic [Wiglaf] sweorde drep
> ferhðgeniðlan, fyr unswiðor
> weoll of gewitte. Fergendra [= Wergendra?] to lyt
> þrong ymbe þeoden, þa hyne sio þrag becwom.
> Hu sceal sincþego ond swyrdgifu,
> eall eðelwyn eowrum cynne,
> lufen alicgean! Londrihtes mot
> þære mægburge monna æghwylc
> idel hweorfan, syððan æðelingas
> feorran gefricgean fleam eowerne,
> domleasan dæd. Deað bið sella
> eorla gehwylcum þonne edwitlif!"
> *Heht* ða þæt heaðoweorc to hagan biodan
> up ofer ecgclif, þær þæt eorlweorod
> morgenlongne dæg modgiomor sæt,
> bordhæbbende, bega on wenum,
> endedogores ond eftcymes
> leofes monnes. Lyt swigode
> niwra spella se ðe næs gerad,
> ac he soðlice sægde ofer ealle:
> . . . .

[16] *Beowulf*, lines 3014–3019. The subject suggested is something like "he or she," "one," "everyone," or "each."

[17] See Leon Kellner, *Historical Outlines of English Syntax* (London, 1892), pp. 170–73.

Where is the subject of *heht?* It is clearly Wiglaf who does the commanding. According to Pogatscher, we should find that hero, or his equivalent, in one of the clauses immediately preceding or following the clause in which the verb is underscored. If we look for an expressed subject in the lines preceding 2892, we shall be baffled, indeed, for the nearest mention of Wiglaf by name is in line 2862—thirty lines earlier than *heht*—and the nearest pronoun referring to him is *ic* in line 2880. Pogatscher's principle, unmodified, will hardly fit this passage, for at least seven clauses intervene between *ic* and the subjectless verb: (0) *þonne ic . . . ferhðgeniðlan,* (1) *fyr . . . gewitte,* (2) *Fergendra . . . þeoden,* (3) *þa hyne . . . becwom,* (4) *Hu sceal . . . alicgean,* (5) *Londrihtes . . . hweorfan,* (6) *syððan . . . dæd,* (7) *Deað bið sella eorla gehwylcum* (8?) *þonne edwitlif.* If we look for the subject in the clauses following the verb, we must pass over four clauses in the connecting narrative: (1) *þær . . . monnes,* (2) *Lyt . . . spella,* (3) *se . . . gerad,* (4) *ac . . . ealle.* We must also skip three, perhaps four, in the messenger's speech which follows in lines 2900–3027:

(5) Nu is wilgeofa Wedra leoda, dryhten Geata deaðbedde fæst, (6?) wunað wælreste wyrmes dædum.

(6) Him on efn ligeð ealdorgewinna, siexbennum seoc.

(7) Sweorde ne meahte on ðam aglæcean ænige þinga wunde gewyrcean.

Finally Wiglaf is mentioned, in a connection entirely unrelated to *heht,* in line 2906. Although Pogatscher's explanation does not fit, we know that Wiglaf is speaking in lines 2864–2891. When we reach 2892 and see the verb *heht,* we naturally think of the son of Weohstan as the giver of the command. The subject to be understood was so evident that the *Beowulf*-poet was free to omit it, knowing or unconsciously feeling that no listener or reader could misunderstand.

A similar use of the same verb appears in *Maldon,* line 62— *Het þa bord beran . . . ,* in which the subject of *het* is understood to be Byrhtnoð, although the nearest mention of him is in line 42. His speech of defiance to the invaders intervenes in lines 45–61. There are other examples of this sort in *Beowulf.* The subject of *eode* in line 1232—*Eode þa to setle*—may be suggested by *ic* in the preceding line, but the fact that Wealhþeo has been speaking in lines 1216–1231 would be enough in itself to supply a subject for a singular verb in 1232. An Anglo-Saxon audience would understand, as readily as ourselves, that it was Wealhþeo who went to her seat. The understood subject in the last three examples has been the person delivering the formal speech, but this is not always the case. In line 301—*Gewiton him þa feran* . . ., the verb is plural, and its understood subject is Beowulf and his men rather than the Danish sea-guard who has just spoken.

Digressions of some length may be treated as parentheses—interruptions. Following a passage of this type, even if it be long and involved, the poet may pick up the broken thread of the narrative with a subjectless verb. A good example is *gewat* in line 115. The subject to be supplied—*Grendel*—is plain enough; but if we seek an expressed subject in the lines which follow, we shall find nothing before line 127, unless we can be satisfied with *wiht unhælo* (line 120) in the fifth clause after the one containing *gewat*:

(0) Gewat ða neosian . . . hean huses,
(1) syþðan niht becom,
(2) hu hit Hring-Dene æfter beorþege gebun hæfdon.
(3) Fand þa ðær inne æþelinga gedriht swefan æfter symble;
(4) sorge ne cuðon, wonsceaft wera.
(5) Wiht unhælo, grim ond grædig, gearo sona wæs, ...

If we look for the subject among the clauses preceding *gewat*, we must search even further. Grendel is mentioned by name in line 102; there are kennings, *mære mearcstapa* and *wonsæli wer*, in lines 103 and 105; and in line 106 is the pronoun *him*, which must be considered, since Pogatscher holds that the word suggesting the understood subject need not be in the nominative case.[18] *Gewat* is in the eighth clause after the one containing *him*, the eleventh after the one containing *Grendel*:

(0) Wæs se grimma gæst Grendel haten, mære mearcstapa,
(1) se þe moras heold, fen ond fæsten.
(2) Fifelcynnes eard wonsæli wer weardode hwile,
(3) siþðan him Scyppend forscrifen hæfde in Caines cynne.[19]
(4) þone cwealm gewræc ece Drihten,
(5) þæs þe he Abel slog.
(6) Ne gefeah he þære fæhðe,
(7) ac he hine feor forwræc, (8?) Metod, for þy mane, mancynne fram.

[18] "Unausgedrücktes Subjekt," p. 280.
[19] Some editors place the period after *hæfde* and begin a new sentence with *In Caines cynne*.

(8) þanon untydras ealle onwocon, eotenas ond ylfe ond orcneas, swylce gigantas,

(9) þa wið Gode wunnon lange þrage.

(10) He him ðæs lean forgeald.

(11) Gewat ða neosian, ...

Between *him* and *gewat*, moreover, we find eleven singular substantives representing persons or beings capable of performing the action indicated by *gewat: Scyppend, Caines, Drihten, he, Abel, he, he, hine, Metod, Gode, he.* When repetitions, kennings, synonyms, and pronouns are eliminated, there are still three possible subjects. Yet no one has any doubt whatever as to who it was that "went seeking out the high house." I have never heard of any person who, encountering this passage for the first time, supposed God, or Cain, or Abel to be the subject of *gewat.*[20]

Another example appears in lines 916–920:

> Hwilum flitende   fealwe stræte
> mearum mæton.   Ða wæs morgenleoht
> scofen ond scynded.   Eode scealc monig
> swiðhicgende   to sele þam hean
> searowundor seon.

The subject of *mæton* is easily understood—the warriors returning from the mere. To find an expressed subject of the kind studied by Pogatscher, we must look back at least to *him* in line 866, or better to *heaþorofe* in line 864, or better still to *ealdgesiðas, geong manig,* and *beornas on blancum* in lines 853–856:

> þanon eft gewiton   ealdgesiðas
> swylce geong manig   of gomenwaþe,
> fram mere modge   mearum ridan,
> beornas on blancum.

If we look for an expressed subject after *mæton*, we shall never find it. The expression *scealc monig* in line 918 is a likely looking candidate, for a singular collective noun may suggest the understood subject of a plural verb.[21] But *scealc monig* has no discerni-

---

[20] Thorkelin seems to have had no difficulty in supplying the correct subject—see *De Danorum Rebus Gestis*, p. 11:

> Geweat þa neosian   *Discessit (grendel) speculatum*
> Syþþan niht becom   *Postqvam nox occupaverat*
> Hean huses   *Celsas ædes,*
> . . . .

[21] Pogatscher, p. 284.

ble connection with *mæton*. The clause containing *mæton* is a
return to, or an echo of, lines 864–867 :[22]

> Hwilum heaþorofe   hleapan leton,
> on geflit faran   fealwe mearas,
> ðær him foldwegas   fægere þuhton,
> cystum cuðe.

There is a short transition sentence after *mæton: Ða wæs morgen-
leoht scofen ond scynded.* Then, *Eode scealc monig swiðhicgende
to sele þam hean searowundor seon* tells of the men who came to
Heorot in the morning to see Grendel's arm; *scealc monig* does
not refer to the companions of Beowulf, who had already seen
the arm.

Each of the last two examples follows a digression in which
the poet introduces legendary materials. In the first, he interrupts the flow of the narrative to explain the ancestry of Grendel;
in the second, which might also be looked upon as a speech of
Hroðgar's thegn presented by indirect discourse, the poet introduces legends of Sigemund and Heremod.

In at least one case, it would seem that a subjectless verb
follows neither a speech nor a digression. It occurs in lines 1402–
1407:

>   Lastas wæron
> æfter waldswaþum   wide gesyne;
> gang ofer grundas   gegnum for
> ofer myrcan mor.   Magoþegna bær
> þone selestan   sawolleasne
> þara þe mid Hroðgare   ham eahtode.

Beowulf has recently made a speech, it is true, but that has
ended with line 1396; and, from line 1397 on, the poem is narrative. There is no digression. Yet, as the passage stands in the
manuscript, without emendation, either *for* in line 1404 or *bær* in
the following line is without an expressed subject. As I have
punctuated the passage, *bær* is the subjectless verb, and one
would translate approximately as follows:

Tracks were widely visible along the woodland-paths; the path upon the plains
went straight over the murky moor. [She, i.e. Grendel's dam] bore the best of
the kindred thegns—lifeless—of those who with Hroðgar watched over the home.

It would be possible, however, to place a period after *grundas* and

<hr>

[22] Cf. Johannes Hoops, *Kommentar zum Beowulf* (Heidelberg, 1932), p. 118.

commas after *mor* and *gesyne*, treat *gang* as parallel with *lastas*,[23]
and read "[She, i.e., Grendel's dam] went straight over the
murky moor, bore the best . . . " At any rate, there is a subjectless verb here, the understood subject of which is Grendel's
dam, although the closest definite mention of the old sea-hag is
back in line 1391, several sentences away. Sievers' emendation
[*þær heo*] *gegnum for*,[24] which has been adopted by Chambers,
Holthausen, and Sedgefield,[25] fills out a metrically irregular half-
line and, at the same time, provides a convenient pronoun subject. But this *heo* is grammatically unnecessary, for the understood subject is not in doubt—Grendel's dam is the only creature
who could possibly perform, in this context, the action represented by *bær*.

It should not be surprising that passages of this type are hard
to find outside *Beowulf*. The other extant specimens of heroic
poetry are all very brief, and the religious poetry of the Old
English period differs in poetic style from the *Beowulf*, being less
compact, more tolerant of particles, pronouns, extra syllables,
and the like. Nevertheless, I find two passages, one in *Deor* and
one in *Guðlac*, which may represent the stylistic feature under
consideration; perhaps more thorough study will reveal others.
The *Deor* passage appears in lines 28–34:

> Siteð sorgcearig   sælum bidæled,
> on sefan sweorceð;   sylfum þinceð,
> þæt sy endeleas   earfoða dæl.[26]
> Mæg þonne geþencan,   þæt geond þas woruld
> witig Dryhten   wendeþ geneahhe,
> eorle monegum   are gesceawað,
> wislicne blæd,   sumum weana dæl.

If line 28 were treated as an echo of line 24—*Sæt secg monig
sorgum gebunden*, this example would seem very similar to those
which we have been examining, for *siteð* is separated from the
clause containing *secg monig* by at least three intervening clauses.
Mæg in line 31 is even further removed from any word which
could serve to suggest its subject. The context indicates, however, that the subject of *siteð* is unexpressed because the verb is
indefinite, having for its understood subject "one," "someone,"

[23] As most editors do.   [24] *P.B.B.*, IX (1884), 140.
[25] Klaeber and Schücking reject it.
[26] Some editors treat *siteð* . . . *dæl* as a conditional clause, and use a comma
instead of a period after *dæl*—see Kemp Malone, *Deor* (London, 1933).

"a man," or something of that sort. With this interpretation, the passage differs from the preceding examples, yet it provides definite evidence that poets other than the *Beowulf*-poet would omit the subject of a verb when it was not required for clarity.

There is one objection to the passage: it is possible to treat *sorgcearig* as a substantive adjective—"the sorrowing one," in which case *siteð* would have an expressed subject. Line 28 would then be rendered in Modern English, "The sorrowful one sits deprived of joys . . . " Although this last interpretation is not generally accepted, the possibility is enough to cast a certain amount of suspicion upon the evidence.

The example from *Guðlac* is also doubtful. It appears in line 447. Benjamin Thorpe printed lines 434–448, with their translation, as follows:[27]

guðlac sette.	Guthlac set
435. hyht in heofonas.	*his* hope in heaven,
hælu getreowde.	in salvation trusted;
hæfde feonda feng.	*he* had from *the* fiends' grasp
feore gedyged.	with life escap'd:
wæs seo æreste.	was the first
earmra gæsta.	of *the* wretched spirits'
costung ofercumen.	temptation overcome:
cempa wunade.	*the* champion remained
bliþe on beorge.	blithe on *the* mount,
wæs his blæd mid gode.	his reward was with God;
440. ðuhte him on mode.	seem'd to him in mind,
þæt se mon-cynnes.	that of mankind he
eadig wære.	were bless'd
seþe his anum her.	who here for his own
feore gefreoðade.	soul taketh care;
þæt him feondes hond.	that him *the* fiend's hand,
æt þam ytmestan.	at the last
ende ne scode.	end afflict not,
þonne him se dryhtnes.	when him the Lord's
dom wisade.	doom shall point
445. to þam nyhstan.	to the most near
nyd-gedale.	inevitable separation.
Hwæþre him þa gena.	Yet to him still,
gyrna gemyndge.	earnestly mindful,
edwit sprecan.	*they* spake reproach,
ermþu geheton.	affliction threaten'd
tornum teon-cwidum.	with angry insults:

[27] *Codex Exoniensis* (London, 1842), pp. 128–29. I have made a few minor changes in spelling, substituting *g* for Thorpe's ʒ and undotted *y* for Thorpe's dotted *y*. The line numbers are those adopted by more recent editors.

The narrative is interrupted in line 440 by a short digression containing general reflections upon the value of caring for one's soul and the properest way to approach death. In line 446, the narrative is resumed, apparently without an expressed subject. According to Thorpe's interpretation, *sprecan* in line 447 is a subjectless verb with "they" or "the fiends" understood. As far as grammatical form is concerned, there is no real difficulty: the verb may be looked upon as a late Anglian form of the preterite plural. The *ē* for West Saxon *ǣ* could be an Anglian feature,[28] while the *-an* ending might reflect the late Old English confusion of vowels in the inflectional syllables.[29] Some editors, however, regard *edwit-sprecan* as a compound noun, subject of *geheton* in line 447.[30] The question is whether it is better to treat *sprecan* as a subjectless preterite plural with *edwit* as its object, or to treat *edwitsprecan* as nominative plural of an *n*-stem noun, that is, "shameful-speakers." Which interpretation is more in keeping with Old English poetic style? At present, I can think of no test whereby we might determine with certainty which alternative is preferable.

We have now examined subjectless verbs in three types of context not included in Pogatscher's study: (1) after a formal speech—*gewiton* 301, *eode* 1232, *heht* 2892, *het* (*Maldon*) 62; (2) following a digression—*gewat* 115, *mæton* 917, *sprecan* (*Guðlac*) 447; (3) in an uninterrupted stream of poetry—*bær* 1405, *siteð* (*Deor*) 28, and *mæg* (*Deor*) 31. As far as I can see, the only feature common to all of these examples, and to Pogatscher's as well, is lack of ambiguity. The context in each case tells us exactly what subject is to be understood. We may formulate the general principle underlying this stylistic feature in some such fashion as the following: *An expressed subject is optional in Old English poetry whenever the context and the verb itself are such that omission of the subject will result in no ambiguity.*[31]

---

[28] For similar preterite plurals in *Beowulf*, see *þegon* 563, *þegun* 2633, *gesegon* 3128, *gesegan* 3038, *gefegon* 1627, etc.

[29] Cf., in *Beowulf*, such preterite plurals as *teodan* 43, *sædan* 1945, *gesegan* 3038, *ofgefan* 2846.

[30] For example, G. P. Krapp and Elliott Dobbie, *The Exeter Book* (New York, 1936), p. 62.

[31] This statement is intended as an extension rather than a refutation of Pogatscher's views; naturally, if a noun in an immediately preceding or following clause suggests the subject to be understood, the subjectless verb will not be ambiguous.

To return to *forgeaf*, line 1020, and Grundtvig's emendation, we should have little difficulty in seeing why *forgeaf* needs no expressed subject. The poet tells us in lines 1008–1010 how Hroðgar came to the mead-hall to partake of the feast:

þa wæs sæl ond mæl,
þæt to healle gang   Healfdenes sunu;
wolde self cyning   symbel þicgan.—

Lines 1011–1019, introduced by the formula *Ne gefrægen ic*, describe the behavior of the company, praise the loyalty and friendliness of Hroðgar, Hroðulf, and their retainers. This interruption to the narrative is similar to the legendary and didactic digressions, for the poet is evidently reminding his audience of the hostilities which will one day break out between Hroðulf and the sons of Hroðgar:[32]

Ne gefrægen ic þa mægþe   maran weorode
ymb hyra sincgyfan   sel gebæran.
Bugon þa to bence   blædagande,
fylle gefægon;   fægere geþægon
medoful manig   magas þara—
swiðhicgende   on sele þam hean,
Hroðgar ond Hroþulf.   Heorot innan wæs
freondum afylled;   nalles facenstafas
þeod-Scyldingas   þenden fremedon.—

Then, with *forgeaf* in line 1020, the poet resumes the narrative, telling of the gifts with which someone rewarded Beowulf for his victorious fight:

Forgeaf þa Beowulfe   brand Healfdenes,
segen gyldenne   sigores to leane,
hroden hiltecumbor (hildecumbor?),   helm ond byrnan.
Mære maðþumsweord   manige gesawon
beforan beorn beran.

Is there any doubt as to who gave the gifts? It could hardly be Hroðulf, for the young prince was still a subordinate in rank, not a "treasure-giver." Similarly, among the Geats, Beowulf is never spoken of as rewarding men for heroic deeds during the lifetime of Hygelac, his superior. Someone other than Hroðgar might present gifts, of course, as Wealhþeo does in lines 1188–1201, 2172–2176; but, unless another giver is definitely specified, the logical person to perform the action indicated by *forgeaf* is the king himself. There should be no ambiguity. And, as a matter of

[32] See also the veiled allusions in lines 1162–1165, 1180–1187.

fact, I can find no sign of doubt or hesitation in Thorkelin's translation—*Dedit tunc (Rex) Beowulfo Lanceam Halfdani*—or in his remark in the "Index Nominum Propriorum." Many editors, moreover, have accepted Grundtvig's emendation, but I know of none who has questioned whether Grundtvig was correct in assuming that it was the son of Healfdene, rather than Hroðulf or someone else, who gave the gifts.

Since the understood subject seems to be unmistakable, the only objection to the manuscript reading is not valid; we are no more justified in emending line 1020 than we should be in supplying expressed subjects for the other verbs discussed in this article. We should restore the strong and poetical "sword of Healfdene" and eliminate the weak, colorless substitute which has taken its place for nearly a hundred years.

Two objections may be raised against the unemended reading. It may be objected that Hroðgar would not give so precious a treasure as his father Healfdene's sword out of the family, to a stranger. Would he not preserve it for one of his own sons? The answer is twofold. First, Heorogar, although fond of his son, bequeathed his armor to his brother Hroðgar, who later sent it to Hygelac, a foreigner.[33] Second, Beowulf, so far from being a stranger after the cleansing of Heorot, was the adopted son of Hroðgar.[34]

The second objection is no more serious than the one already mentioned. J. Hoops has noted that the order in which Beowulf presents his four gifts to Hygelac[35] is the same as that in which Hroðgar has previously given them to him; that is, banner, helm, coat-of-mail, sword.[36] By restoring the manuscript reading, we render the two enumerations inconsistent. The inconsistency is not objectionable, however; it is the consistency noted by Hoops which ought to surprise us. Elsewhere in the return-journey section of the poem, the poet avoided anything approaching exact repetition. He omitted numerous details, added the Heaðobeard episode and other matters, and shifted emphasis, even when the facts reported were unchanged.[37] Is it possible that he suddenly

---

[33] Lines 2155–2162.   [34] Lines 946–950, 1175–1176.
[35] Lines 2152–2154.   [36] *Kommentar*, p. 236.
[37] Notice, for example, how he singled out the sword for special mention on the first occasion (lines 1023–1024), but on the second occasion singled out the coat-of-mail (lines 2155–2156).

ran short of devices in lines 2152–2154, when confronted by a simple enumeration of four gifts? The manuscript reading of lines 1020–1022 indicates that he did not, and that here, as elsewhere, he was able to avoid mechanical repetition.

SHERMAN M. KUHN

Oklahoma A. and M. College

E AND Æ IN FARMAN'S MERCIAN GLOSSES

FARMAN'S Mercian glosses to certain parts[1] of the *Rushworth Gospels* have occupied the attention of scholars for more than a century. It would be difficult to find an aspect of the priest or his work which has not, at some time, been investigated. Yet there remain numerous controversial questions, some of them of a very fundamental nature. One of the most difficult concerns Farman's apparently irrational uses of the symbols *e* and *æ*. It will be found that many of the larger conflicts over the position of Rushworth[1] in the general scheme of English phonology are essentially disagreements as to just what values these two letters had in Farman's orthography.

As I examine the work of previous investigators,[2] I cannot help feeling that entirely too much effort has been expended in attempts to force the evidence drawn from the uses of *e* and *æ* into general conceptions of Farman or of the Old English dialects which they cannot be made to fit, with the result that important sections of the evidence have been distorted beyond recognition or, in some instances, completely ignored. The logical procedure would seem to be exactly the reverse. In fact, I believe that many of the uncertainties and contradictions which still envelop Farman's work can be cleared up by the obvious expedient of returning to the evidence itself and re-examining our general theories in the light of what we find.

In this study I shall present all of the evidence relating to Farman's uses of *e* and *æ* in accented syllables, together with a fair sampling of the uses in unaccented syllables, and endeavor to explain each usage in the light of the best modern scholarship. The evidence has been organized under the following heads:[3] (1) Isolative development of West Germanic short *a*; (2) Isolative development of West Germanic short *e*; (3) *I*-

---

[1] Glosses to Matthew, Mark 1–2: 15, and John 18: 1–3, in MS. *Auct. D. ii. 19* of the Bodleian Library, Oxford. Farman's Mercian glosses are often referred to as Rushworth[1].

[2] For systematic recapitulation of the scholarship on Rushworth[1], see E. M. Brown's dissertation, *Die Sprache der Rushworth Glossen zum Evangelium Matthäus*, I (Göttingen, 1891), 3–10, 79–83; and R. J. Menner's "Farman Vindicatus," *Anglia*, LVIII (1934), 1–4.

[3] The general plan and methods of analysis owe much to Karl Bülbring's "E and Æ in the Vespasian Psalter," in *An English Miscellany. Presented to Dr. Furnivall in honor of his 75th birthday* (Oxford, 1901), pp. 34–45. My organization must differ from his, however, since Farman's spelling lacks the comparative regularity and consistency of the *Vespasian Psalter*. In assembling the evidence, I have made use of Brown's dissertation and Ernst Schulte's *Glossar zu Farmans Anteil an der Rushworth-Glosse* (Bonn, 1904); but, wherever either of these differs from W. W. Skeat, *The Holy Gospels in Anglo-Saxon, Northumbrian, and Old Mercian Versions* (Cambridge, 1871–1887), I have followed Skeat.

Reprinted by permission of the Modern Language Association of America from *PMLA*, 60 (1945), 631–69.

umlaut of West Germanic *a*; (4) *I*-umlaut of West Germanic and Latin *o*; (5) Velar-umlaut of West Germanic *a*; (6) Velar-umlaut of West Germanic *e*; (7) Smoothing of Old English *ea*; (8) Smoothing of Old English *eo*; (9) Isolative development of West Germanic *ā*; (10) Isolative development of West Germanic *ē*; (11) *I*-umlaut of West Germanic *ai*; (12) *I*-umlaut of Old English *ō*; (13) *I*-umlaut and smoothing of Old English *ēa*; (14) Smoothing of Old English *ēo*; (15) Contracted forms containing *ē* and *ǣ*; (16) Diphthongs followed by *w*; and (17) Unaccented *e* and *æ*. My own conclusions will naturally appear, but those who cannot accept them, wholly or in part, will at least have all the necessary evidence upon which to base conclusions of their own.

1. Isolative development of West Germanic *a*

WG. short *a*, when its development was uninfluenced by neighboring sounds, was raised and fronted in the Old English dialects from [ɑ], as in German *Mann*, to something approaching the [æ] in Present English *man*. The sound is spelled *æ* (or *ae* or *ę*) in West Saxon and Northumbrian texts, and its early Middle English development is usually written *a*. In the Mercian of the *Vespasian Psalter*, the corresponding sound is almost invariably written *e*, the only important exceptions being *æt*, *ðæt*, *ðætte*, and a few examples of *cwæð* and *ðæs*.[4] The thirteenth-century legends of St. Katherine, St. Marherete, and St. Juliana, which were written in the western part of what had once been the old kingdom of Mercia, contain the same sort of *e*-spellings as the Psalter. It is generally believed, therefore, that West Germanic *a* underwent a further shift, in at least part of the Mercian area, to a sound between [æ] and [e]—perhaps [æ^e].[5]

Farman's glosses, although recognized as Mercian by all modern authorities, seem very different from the Psalter at this point. There are relatively few forms in which WG. *a* is spelled *e*. All of them appear in the following list:[6]

bed (preterite singular of *biddan*) 18, 29; Mk. 1, 40; *bedd* 18, 26; *gebed* 15, 25; 26, 44. *cweþ* (glossing *dixit*) 9, 22; 11, 25; 12, 25; 15, 16; 15, 27; *cweð* 12, 3. *deglicum* 20, 2. *efter* 21, 30. *fretwan* 25, 7. *hefæþ* (present third singular of *habban*) 5, 32. *hweþer*

---

[4] The form *et* appears only once, *ðet* or *det* 10 times, *ðette* or *dette* 4 times. There are three examples of *cwæð*, beside 45 of *cweð*, and two of *ðæs* (genitive singular of *se—ðæt*), beside 30 of *ðes* or *des*.

[5] Bülbring supposed that the further raising and fronting from [æ] to [æ^e] in the dialect of the *Vespasian Psalter* followed immediately after the shift of [a] to [æ], without any "interval of stability"—*An English Miscellany*, p. 35. For my own views on this point, see *PMLA*, LIV (1939), 11–19.

[6] Forms from Mark and John are labeled; all others are from Matthew.

9, 5; 21, 31; *hweþre* 18, 7; 23, 17; 26, 24; 26, 39; *hweðre* 11, 24. *onget* (pt. sg.) Mk.
2, 8. *sett* (pt. sg. of *sittan*) 15, 29; 27, 19; *gesett* 13, 2; 28, 2. *soþfest* 10, 41; 10, 41;
22, 16; 23, 35; *soþfestes* 10, 41; *soþfestę* 23, 28; *soþfeste* 5, 45; 13, 17; 13, 43; 25, 46;
soþfestra 13, 49; 23, 29; *soþfestum* 9, 13; *soþfestnisse* 6, 1; 22, 16. *sprec* (preterite
singular) 12, 22; 13, 3; 13, 33; 13, 34; 13, 34; 14, 27. *toberst* (pt. sg.) 27, 51.
tungulk retftgum 2, 16. *þene* (accusative sg. masculine) 25, 30; 27, 15; *ðenc* 20, 22.
unþwegenum (past participle of *þwean*) 15, 20. *westem* 3, 8; 12, 33; 12, 33; 12, 33;
13, 23; 13, 26; *westęm* 7, 19; *westmas* 7, 17; 7, 18; *westemleas* 13, 22.—*messepreost*
8, 4.

A number of these forms are doubtful in varying degrees, although I
believe the only seriously questionable ones are the forms of *hweþer* and
hweþre, which may contain either WG. *a* or WG. *e*.[7] The *e* in *fretwan*
might be looked upon as the result of *i*-umlaut[8] were it not for the fact
that all other forms of this verb used by Farman are definitely Weak II.
In *tungulkreftgum* and the various forms of *soþfest*, we may have examples
of weakening in the second elements of compounds; the usual forms in
West Saxon and Northumbrian, however, are *tungolcræft-* and *soþfæst*.[9]
Although *þene* seems rather doubtful, existing side by side with *þone*
and *þane* in Rushworth[1], it probably belongs in this list.[10] The word
messepreost, although it contains Latin *i* rather than an original Germanic
a, certainly belongs here.[11]

Even if we accept all doubtful examples at their face value, these *e*-
spellings are few in comparison with Farman's usual *æ*-spellings. He used
æ in *æt* (including the stressed prefix *æt-*), *þæt*, and *þætte*. Excluding these,
which may be matched in the Psalter, we arrive at a proportion of about
æ:*e*::25:2; that is, *æ* is approximately twelve and one half times as frequent as *e*. Farman has *þæs* exclusively for the genitive singular of *se* and
þæt. There are eighty-two examples of *cwæþ* (spelled *cwaþ, cwaeð, cweþ*)
which gloss *dixit* and seem to be definitely preterite singular.[12] Other
æ-spellings are the following:[13]

æfter, æftera, æftere, ahæfen (past ppl. of *ahebban*), *bæclinc, bæd* (pt. sg. of *biddan*),
gebæd, gebęd, bær (pt. sg. of *beran* or *beoran*), *bęr, gebær, bisæc* (glossing *þera*),
blæcne (*nigrum*), *bræc* (pt. sg. of *brecan* or *breocan*), *bręc, cæstre* (beside *ceastre*),

---

[7] Cf. *huæðre, hweðer, hweðre, huoeðer* in the *Lindisfarne Gospels*, Gothic *ƕaþar*, Old
Saxon *hweðar*, Old High German *hwedar*.

[8] I.e. **fratwjan* rather than **fratwōjan*.

[9] The *-ern* of compounds like *berern* and *carcern* contains a definitely weakened vowel,
which appears as *e* in West Saxon. These forms are treated in section 17.

[10] Cf. *þæne* in Farman's glosses and in late West Saxon.

[11] Cf. WS. *mæsse*, Nthb. *mæsse, meassa*. See also Karl Luick, *Historische Grammatik der
englischen Sprache* (Leipzig, 1921), p. 194.

[12] Cf. the six *cwæþ-* and *cweð-*forms listed above.

[13] Repetitions, and a few inflectional or spelling variants have been omitted in this list.

cæstra, cæstras, cæstrum, dæg, dæges, dæge, domdæge, restedæge, fæce (dative sg.), *fæder* (nom., dat., and acc. sg.), *fæderes, fædera, fædra, fæger, fær* (imperative), *oferfæren* (past ppl.), *fære* (dat. sg.), *færennisse, fæss* (*fimbriam*), *frægn* (pt. sg.), *gefrægn, frętwæþ, gefrętwad, gæfles, gæflæs, gæfle, gebrægd* (pt. sg.), *gescræfe, græshoppa, hæfde, hęfde, hæfdon, hæfdun, æfdon* (with omission of *h*), *næfde, næfdon, nęfdun, holstæfes, hrægl, hrægle, hræglę, hrægles, hræglum, rægl* (without *h*), *hræfnað* (probably for *ræfnað*, glossing *sustinebit*), *hræðe, ræþe* (without *h*), *hwænne* (*quando*), *hwæt* (*quid*), *hwæs, gehwæt, hwæþer, hwæþre, læg* (pt. sg. of *licgan*), *lætest* (for *lætemest*), *mæg* (pr.sg. of *magan*), *mæge* (pr. optative), *mægden, mægen, mægene, nægled, genæglad, ofslægen, ısæcę* (pr. opt. of *ondsacan*), *ongægn, togægnes, sægde, sægd, foresægde, gesægde, sægdun, asægdnisse, sæt* (pt. sg. of *sittan*), *sætt, gesæt, sopfæst sopfæste, unsopfæste, gesopfæsted, sopfæstnisse, wisfæstre, spræc* (pt. sg.), *spręc, gespræc, tæppel-, tungulkræftgum, þæce* (dat. sg.), *þæne* (acc. sg. masc.), *wæs* (pt. sg.), *wæss, węs, wæstem, wæstim, wæstmas, wæstma, wæstmum, wæter, wætre, wættres.*

To these should probably be added forty-seven present forms of *habban* (such as *hæbbe, hæfest, hæfeþ*) and the two forms *sægest* and *sægeþ*. The expected vowel in these Weak III presents is *a*, as in *hafast, hafað, nabbende,* and *asagas* of the Psalter. *Segeð* in the Psalter is evidently due to analogy with the preterite *segde;* similarly, West Saxon *hæbbe* and *sægest* as well as these forms in Rushworth[1] are apparently due to analogy with *hæfde, sægde,* and the other preterite forms. If we include *þæs, cwæþ,* and the present forms of *habban* and *secgan,* but exclude the examples of *æt, þæt,* and *þætte,* Farman has more than eight hundred *æ*-spellings for the raising and fronting of WG. *a*.[14]

A few of the examples are doubtful, for example *fæss.* The word *fas* appears with an acute accent once in the *Lindisfarne Gospels,* and A. S. Cook therefore considered the vowel long.[15] Richard Jordan argued for a short *a*.[16] The appearance of *feasum* (*fimbriis*) in the *Vespasian Psalter* seems to indicate a short vowel, for the long *ā* would not have undergone velar-umlaut. Moreover, the acute in Lindisfarne, while it usually indicates either an original long vowel or a late Old English lengthening, appears occasionally over definitely short vowels: *ésne* Lk. 14, 22; *lósað* Mt. 16, 25; *nedró* (acc. pl.) Mk. 16, 18; *unnæhtigo* Lk. 18, 27; *ónsion* Lk. 20, 21; *uósa* (*esse*) Jn. 20, 27. The *æ* in *ongægn* and *togægnes* may be due to *i*-umlaut,[17] in which case it belongs in section three of this study. Other doubtful cases may be explained by reference to Farman's *e*-spellings.

The inconsistency of Farman's spelling is not easily accounted for. The proportion of *e*-spellings is too large for pure West Saxon, pure

---

[14] I count exactly 806.

[15] *A Glossary of the Old Northumbrian Gospels* (Halle, 1894).

[16] *Eigentümlichkeiten des anglischen Wortschatzes* (Heidelberg, 1906), pp. 16–17.

[17] *New English Dictionary.*

Northumbrian, or a Northumbrian scribe copying a West Saxon text. On the other hand, it is far too small for a Mercian writing in the unmixed dialect of the *Vespasian Psalter*.

The proportion of *e* to *æ* is comparable to that of the eighth-century *Corpus Glossary*,[18] which represents an earlier stage of Mercian before the shift of [æ] to [æᵉ] was complete;[19] but, of course, the tenth-century Rushworth[1] is too late to permit a chronological explanation such as may be applied to Corpus. Nor is it possible to suppose that the [æᵉ] of the Psalter dialect was shifting back toward [æ] in the tenth century. If the dialect of the thirteenth-century legends descended from that of the Psalter, the [æᵉ] pronunciation must have persisted well into Middle English times.[20]

To explain the *e*-spellings as purely analogical is dangerous. E. M. Brown, for example, attributes *efter* to the influence of *eft*.[21] Unfortunately for this explanation, Farman's favorite spelling of the latter word is not *eft*, but *æft*.[22] Conventional reasoning about analogical influences would betray us into similar errors with regard to many of Farman's *e*-spellings.

R. J. Menner states that the use of *e* for WG. *a.* in Rushworth[1] is "almost wholly limited to the preterite singular of stray verbs of Class V," and suggests that the *e* in these forms is "probably *ē*, the vowel of the plural being transferred to the singular."[23] Although the latter part of the explanation is worth considering because of the similar preterite singulars in the *Lindisfarne Gospels* and other Northumbrian texts, it in no way accounts for those *e*-spellings in the list above (forty-three out of a total of sixty-five) which are not preterite singulars of Strong V verbs.

---

[18] Loosely, of course. The proportion in the latter is *e*:*æ*::1:5.

[19] The writer, *op. cit.*

[20] Compare the following words from the Katherine-Group with the words listed in this section: *efter, aheven, bed, ber, brec, dei, feder, fedres, feier, hefde, hefden, hwet, hweðer, lei, mei, meiden, mein, meinful, neiles, islein, steðelfest, togeines, seide, set, spec, creft, þene, wes, westum, wettres.* A much longer list might have been compiled from the published editions of the three legends: Eugen Einenkel (ed.), *The Life of Saint Katherine, EETS*, OS, LXXX (London, 1884); Frances Mack (ed.), *Seinte Marherete þe Meiden ant Martyr, EETS*, OS, CXCIII (London, 1934); O. Cockayne and Edmund Brock (eds.), *The Life of St. Juliana, EETS*, OS, LI (London, 1872). The following forms appear in Sir Frederic Madden's edition of *Lagamons Brut* (London, 1847): *iber, iqueð, deie, feier, hefde, whet, wheþer, lei, meiden, togeines, seide, soðfeste, spec, crefte, þene* (acc. sg. masc.), *wes.* The following may be found in the entries after 1100 in the *Peterborough Chronicle*, Benjamin Thorpe (ed.), *The Anglo-Saxon Chronicle* (London, 1861), I, 369–385: *bed* (pt. sg.), *beiet* (pt. sg.), *deʒ, dei, efter, herefter, þerefter, ðerefter, frett* (pt. sg.), *hedde, hefde, hefden, messe, messedei, Candelmesse, sei, seide, seidon, soðfeste, þet, þes* (gen. sg.), *ðes, wes* (pt. sg.), *westme, westmas.* Occasional examples of the same sort occur in the *Ormulum* and other early Midland texts.

[21] *Die Sprache*, I, 14.   [22] *Æft* occurs 17 times, *eft* 11.

[23] "Farman Vindicatus," p. 16.

Farman's treatment of WG. *a*, supported by the presence of other features not found in the Psalter, has led to the view that he was writing a mixture of dialects. Eduard Sievers held that the glosses were Mercian mixed with West Saxon.[24] Bülbring's views were similar, but he saw evidences of Northumbrian as well as West Saxon influence.[25] R. Girvan goes even further, finding Kentish or Southeastern features in addition to the other non-Mercian elements.[26] There is no obvious objection to these dialect-mixture theories, except that the Kentish elements are doubtful and that certain of Farman's uses of the *æ* are not to be found as normal features of any non-Mercian dialect.

Ernst Schulte took the extreme position of supposing that Farman was a Mercian copying a West Saxon archetype—an earlier gloss to the Gospels.[27] According to this hypothesis, the *e*-spellings would represent Farman's own Mercian pronunciation, while the *æ*-spellings would be West Saxonisms copied from his exemplar. Schulte's argument has been attacked, successfully I believe, by Menner.[28]

Karl Luick minimizes dialect mixture as an explanation and argues for the existence of several sub-dialects of Mercian, one represented by the Psalter, another by Rushworth[1].[29] If we adopt Luick's opinion, we may suppose that, in Farman's sub-dialect, WG. *a* was raised and fronted beyond [æ] perhaps, but not completely to [æ*e*], and that the other features in which these glosses differ from the Psalter were also peculiarities of Farman's sub-dialect. The similarity of many of these usages to those of West Saxon and Northumbrian could then be explained only as coincidence.

The evidence presented in this section is hardly sufficient, by itself, to strengthen or refute any of these views. We must look to Farman's other uses of *e* and *æ*.

2. Isolative development of West Germanic *e*

Farman's spelling is unusual in its use of *æ*, not only for the raising and fronting of *a*, but also for the isolative development of WG. short *e*.

---

[24] *Angelsächsische Grammatik* (2nd ed., Halle, 1886), p. 2; *An Old English Grammar.* Translated and edited by A. S. Cook (Boston, 1903), p. 3.

[25] *Altenglisches Elementarbuch* (Heidelberg, 1902), p. 10.

[26] *Angelsaksisch Handboek.* (Haarlem, 1931), p. 8. Girvan's views are evidently based in part on H. M. Chadwick, *Studies in Old English*, Transactions of the Cambridge Philological Society, IV (Cambridge, 1899), 250 ff.

[27] *Untersuchung der Beziehung der altenglischen Matthäusglosse im Rushworth-Manuskript zu dem lateinischen Text der Handschrift* (Bonn, 1903), pp. 22–30.

[28] *Op. cit.*

[29] *Hist. Gram.*, pp. 165–166. Luick does, however, admit the possibility of West Saxon influence—pp. 33–34, 129.

For this sound, West Saxon, Northumbrian, and the *Vespasian Psalter* have almost exclusively *e*. The only exceptions in the last are two examples of *ðæc* for the accusative singular of *þu*—69, 5 and Hymn 12, 6.[30] The Mercian portions of the *Rushworth Gospels* present a very different picture. The following forms with *æ* for WG. *e* appear:

æfne (*tantum*) 5, 47; *æfnðeuw* 18, 33; *efnðeuwe* 18, 31; *æfnþara* 18, 28. *agæfeþ* (present third singular) 16, 27. *cwæþe* (pr. 1 sg.) 5, 39; 5, 44; *cwæþ* (glossing *dico*) 18, 22. *cwæþaþ* (plural indicative) 21, 25; *cwæþað* 11, 18; 11, 19; 23, 16; 23, 30. *cwæþan* (pr. opt.) 5, 11; *cwæþe* 5, 22; *tocwæþe* 21, 3. *cwæþ* (imperative) 20, 21; *gecwæþ* 4, 3; *cwæþað* 26, 18. *cwæþende* 2, 5; 8, 3; 8, 27; 8, 29; 9, 14; 9, 30; 10, 12; 12, 38; 13, 24; 13, 36; 15, 23; 15, 25; 16, 22; 18, 28; 20, 30; 21, 2; 21, 9; 21, 15; 21, 20; 21, 23; 21, 25; 22, 4; 22, 16; 22, 24; 22, 42; 22, 43; 23, 2; 23, 2; 24, 5; 25, 9; 25, 11; 25, 37; 25, 44; 26, 8; 26, 27; 26, 39; 26, 44; 26, 48; 26, 65; 26, 68; 26, 69; 26, 70; 27, 9; 27, 11; 27, 19; 27, 24; 27, 25; 27, 41; 27, 46; 27, 54; 27, 63; 28, 9; 28, 13; 28, 18; Mk. 1, 24; *cwæðende* 18, 26; 21, 4; 21, 10; Mk. 1, 25; *cwæþende* 10, 7; 14, 27; 14, 30; 18, 1; *cwæþendum* 22, 31. *cwæden* (past ppl.) 5, 21; 5, 27; 5, 33; 5, 38; 5, 43; 27, 9; 27, 22; *acwæden* 4, 14; 22, 31; *acwædene* 26, 30; *gecwæden* 5, 31; 8, 17. *forlægennisse* 15, 19; *forlægenisse* 21, 32; *forlægnisse* 19, 9. *forstælan* (pr. opt.) 27, 64. *frægnast* (pr. 2 sg. of *fregnan* or *frignan*) 19, 17. *gewærþe* (pr. opt. of *geweorþan*) 4, 3. *rægn* 7, 25; 7, 27. *sætil* 23, 6. *stæfn* 17, 5; Mk. 1, 11; *stæfne* 24, 31; 27, 50; Mk. 1, 26; *stæfnæ* 27, 46. *swægre* (*socrus*) 8, 14; Mk. 1, 30. *swælteþ* (pr. 3 sg. of *sweltan*) 15, 4. *swæster* 13, 56. *tægþigaþ* (pr. plural of *tegþian* or *teogoþigan*) 23, 23. *tobregdeþ* (pr. 3 sg.) 12, 29. *þæc* (acc. sg. of *þu*) 19, 19; 26, 73; *ðæc* 21, 21. *þægn* 23, 11; *ðægn* 20, 26; *dægne* 5, 25; *þægnas* 5, 1; Jn. 18, 1; *þægnum* 18, 34; 22, 13; 22, 16; 26, 58; Jn. 18, 1; *ðægnum* 14, 2; Jn. 18, 2. *ðægnade* 8, 15; 20, 28; *ðægnadun* 4, 11; *ðægnad* 20, 28; *þægnende* 27, 55; *geþægnade* Mk. 1, 31. *wæg* (*via*) 3, 3; 10, 5; 22, 16; *wæge* 5, 25; 8, 28; 10, 10; 13, 4; 13, 19; 15, 32; 20, 30; 21, 19; *awæg* 19, 22; 22, 5; 22, 15; 22, 22; 26, 14; 27, 60; 27, 66; 28, 11. *wæl* (*bene-*) 5, 44. *wælig* (*dives*) 27, 57. *wær* (*uirum*) 1, 16; *wæs* (imperative) 2, 13; 5, 25.— *gef* (?Usually *gif* in Rushworth[1], but compare Northumbrian and Old Frisian *gef*) 28, 14.

In addition to these, there are more than a hundred examples[31] of *cwæþ* and *cwęþ* which gloss Latin presents, futures, future perfects, and participles: *ait*, *dicit*, *dicet*, *dixerit*, *dicens*, and the like. Schulte was uncertain whether to classify most of these forms as present or as preterite. It is true that *ait* and *dicit* are frequently treated as historical presents in the Northumbrian and West Saxon Gospels, and are rendered by unmistak-

---

[30] Rudolf Zeuner, *Die Sprache des kentischen Psalters* (Halle, 1881), p. 20, cites *ðæs* 7, 18 and 74, 11 as examples of *æ* for WG. *e*. This is a mistake, for both of the pronouns cited are normal genitive singulars of *se*. In 7, 18, *ðæs hestan* glosses *altissimi*, and in 74, 11, *ðæs rehtwisan* glosses *iusti;* cf. *se hehsta* (*altissimus*) 17, 149 *ðæm hestan* (*altissimo*) 49, 14, etc.

[31] There are 105 by my count, 102 according to Schulte's *Glossar*.

able preterites. Yet, as far as form is concerned, Farman's *cwæþ* is not necessarily preterite. An earlier stage of the present third singular, the form found in the *Vespasian Psalter* and occasionally in Rushworth[1], was *cwið*, derived by syncopation and simplification from **kwiþiþ*, itself derived by Primitive Germanic umlaut from **kweþiþ*. In late Mercian, *e* was substituted for *i* through the influence of other present forms. This substitution we can see in Farman's seventeen uses of *cweþ* for the present third singular,[32] all of which, by the way, are classified as present by Schulte. In the final stage, *cwæþ*, we find Farman substituting *æ* for the analogical *e*, just as he was wont to substitute *æ* for *e* in *ðægnadun, stæfn*, and other words having original Germanic *e*. In a similar manner the *æ* found its way into *agæfeþ, swælteþ, tobreġdeþ*, and *fræġnast*.

Although it is possible to trace analogical influences upon many of the individual words in which Farman uses *æ* for WG. *e*, the mass of examples is so great as to make such efforts at explanation seem rather futile. The proportion of *æ*-spellings is very high—approximately *æ:e::5:9*. Among the *æ*'s, I include the examples of *cwæþ* in the present third singular. Among the *e*'s are included Latin *e* in the various forms of *tempel*, Latin *i* in *denera* and *senepes*, the examples of *e* for WG. *i* in footnote thirty-two, and the examples of *e* for Old English *eo* listed in section six.

Various explanations of this use of *æ* for *e* have been offered. Luick could easily have explained it as merely another feature of some anomalous Mercian sub-dialect, but instead he dismisses it as a sort of gigantic scribal error:[33] "In Ru.[1] ist *æ* für jedwedes *e* häufig, doch liegt hier offenbar eine Ungenauigkeit des Schreibers vor."

Bülbring suggested that the *æ*'s pointed to "eine weite Aussprache des *e* als [ę] oder [æ\u1d49]."[34] Apparently he regarded this open pronunciation as a feature of the Mercian dialect, yet he did not attempt to account for the absence of the *æ*-spellings in the *Vespasian Psalter* and other important Mercian texts.

Brown was chiefly interested in proving that Farman's Mercian was a true dialect and not merely a mixture of Northumbrian and West Saxon.

---

[32] The ordinary uses of *e* for WG. *e* need not be dwelt upon since they do not differ from the usage of either the Psalter or strict West Saxon. But the following second and third singular forms of Strong III, IV, and V verbs are worth noting: *agefes* 5, 24; *agefeþ* 17, 11. *bereþ* 1, 21; 1, 23; 3, 10; 7, 17; 7, 17; 7, 19; 12, 35; 12, 35; 13, 23; *bereð* 13, 52. *breceþ* 27, 40; *tobreceþ* 12, 20. *cwebest* 12, 23; *cwebestu* 7, 4; *cweþ* 7, 21; 8, 4; 8, 7; 8, 8; 8, 19; 8, 22; 8, 26; 8, 32; 12, 39; 13, 28; 13, 29; 13, 52; 14, 2; 14, 18; 15, 24; 15, 28; Mk. 2, 14; *cweð* 14, 8; *cwebaþ* (pr. 3 sg.) 12, 32; 12, 32. *eteþ* 9, 11. *geldeþ* 6, 4; 6, 6; 6, 18; 16, 27. *helpeð* 16, 26. *ongeteð* 13, 23. *spreces* 13, 10; *sprecaþ* (pr. 3 sg.) 10, 20; Mk. 2, 7. There are three examples of *e* substituted for WG. *i* in other words: *smere* (imper. sg.) 6, 17; *smerennis* 2, 11; *smerenisse* 26, 12; cf. *smirenisse, smirede*, etc., in the Psalter.

[33] *Hist. Gram.*, p. 264.   [34] *Ae. Elementarbuch*, p. 36.

Accordingly he seized upon the use of *æ* for *e* as a feature not shared to any significant extent by either of the neighboring dialects:[35]

Die Abweichungen vom Nordh. sind zum Teil Annäherung an das Ws., aber nicht alle; in einigen Punkten steht das Merc. ganz für sich da, namentlich

1) AE. festes e wird Merc. zwar meistens auch bewahrt, daneben aber wird es mehr oder minder häufig zu æ . . .

Menner suggests that *e* and *æ* had fallen together in Farman's dialect. "One can hardly escape the conclusion," he writes, "that *e* in this word [*cwæpende*] was very near *æ* in Farman's dialect, and that he naturally wrote it both ways."[36] He points to *stæfn* and *þægn* as examples of the same phenomenon. Apparently he accepts Bülbring's view that *e* was lowered and retracted in the direction of *æ*, but his stand on this point is not entirely clear.

Girvan holds the opposite opinion, that *æ* and *e* in Farman's dialect had fallen together under *e* rather than under *æ*. He associates this feature with southeastern England.[37]

In het kent. en in het merc. dialect van VPs. is æ tot *e* geworden en samengevallen met oerg. *e* . . . Denzelfden overgang vinden wij in de oude glossaria (het duidelijkst in Erf.), waar de æ ook reeds omgekeerd voor de oerg. *e* voorkomt. Deze verwarring . . . schijnt een kenmerk der zuidoostelijke dialecten te zijn, en treedt niet op in het ws., north. en de vr. merc. oorkonden; in R.[1] echter is het onderscheid tusschen æ en *e* volkomen opgeheven, wat men misschien wel aan dezelfde oorzaak kan toeschrijven.

All authorities, except possibly Luick, agree that the isolative developments of WG. *a* and *e* had fallen together to some extent in Farman's dialect. The question is, Did both sounds fall together under *e*, or did both fall together under *æ*? If we consider Farman's usage without reference to related developments, we can use his substitution of *æ* for *e* to prove either that his *æ* had an *e*-sound or that his *e* had a *æ*-sound. But, if we take a broader viewpoint, we shall see at once the difficulties involved in the latter hypothesis.

In the first place, Farman's use of *æ* for *e* was not restricted to the isolative development of WG. *e*. He also substituted *æ* for the *e*'s resulting from *i*-umlaut of WG *a*, *i*-umlaut of *o*, and smoothing of Old English *eo*—as we shall see in the third, fourth, and fifth sections of this article. Consequently, anyone attempting to prove that one of these types of *e* had shifted to a *æ*-sound must show that all the others had shifted as well.

Second, Mercian texts written before the West Saxon conquest of

---

[35] *Die Sprache*, I, 81. [36] "Farman Vindicatus," p. 16. [37] *Handboek*, p. 81.

Mercia show no sign of a shift of *e* to *æ*.[38] They contain sporadic examples of *æ* for *e*, such as ꝺæc in the *Vespasian Psalter*, but no more than one might find in a good West Saxon or Northumbrian text. On the contrary, the evidence afforded by these early and relatively pure Mercian texts would indicate that Mercian *æ* from WG. *a* shifted in the direction of *e* and fell together with the *e* from WG. *e*. Anyone who argues that *e* became *æ* in Farman's section of Mercia must either suppose the speech of that area to have been unrelated to the dialect as a whole and of no real significance in the field of Old English phonology, or else find some means of explaining away the evidence of the other Mercian writings.

Third, a shift of *e* to *æ* in any part of the Mercian territory is unconfirmed by Middle English evidence. There are sporadic examples of *a* for *e* in early Middle English texts, but they are rarer than *æ* for *e* in early Mercian. No one, as far as I know, has ever suggested that WG. *e* descended into Middle English as *a*. On the other hand, we have abundant evidence that the Mercian development of WG. *a* actually entered Middle English as an extremely raised and fronted sound capable of being written *e*. The *e*-spellings of the Katherine-Group, Lagamon's *Brut*, the *Peterborough Chronicle*, and other early Midland texts should be conclusive on that point.[39] Kentish works of Middle English times indicate that the Kentish *e* for WG. *a* also survived the Old English period. Any attempt to prove that a tendency to shift *e* to an *æ*-sound existed in Mercian must account for its disappearance in early Middle English.

Finally, accented WG. *e* has been one of the stablest vowels in the English language. Except where it has been influenced by neighboring sounds, it has approximately the same sound today as it had in West Germanic. The development of WG. *a* has been very different. Regardless of the nature of the neighboring sounds, it has varied and shifted back and forth, at different periods and in different parts of the English-speaking world, among the values [ɑ], [a], [æ], [æᵉ], and even [ɛ]. It is more likely, therefore, that the *æ* (from WG. *a*) shifted in Farman's dialect than that the WG. *e* shifted.

Girvan is correct in holding that *æ* and *e* had fallen together under *e* in Farman's dialect. But his limitation of this feature to Kent and southeastern England is an error. The Middle English evidence indicates that the tendency to raise and front *æ* toward *e* was strong in the West. Although the provenience of the *Vespasian Psalter* is still a controversial question, modern scholars usually assign it to central or western England. There is, moreover, one Old English text exhibiting the shift of *æ* to *e* of

---

[38] I refer especially to the *Epinal* and *Corpus Glossaries*, the *Vespasian Psalter*, and the early Mercian charters.

[39] See footnote 20.

whose provenience we are reasonably certain, the Worcester version of the *Anglo-Saxon Chronicle*.[40]

The *Worcester Chronicle*, written during the eleventh century when Worcester was completely dominated by Wessex, is not a Mercian text; rather it is West Saxon with some Mercian admixture. WG. *a*, raised and fronted, is usually written *æ*, sometimes *a*, as in other West Saxon works, but there are a few *e*-spellings which suggest Mercian influence: *beð* (WS. *bæð*), *deig* (WS. *dæg*), *federen* (WS. *fæder*), *geset* (WS. *gesæt*), *getel* (WS. *getæl*), *hredlice* (WS. *hrædlice*), *messandæg* (WS. *mæssan-*), *ðet* (WS. *ðæt*), *wes* (WS. *wæs*), and others. We note also that, while WG. *e* usually appears as *e* in this chronicle, a number of forms have *æ* and, thus, agree neither with West Saxon nor with any extant Mercian text except Farman's glosses: *asæten* (past ppl. of *asittan*), *awæg*, *cwæden* (pt. ppl.), *forespræcena* (pt. ppl.), *sætle*, *ðægnas*, *wæras*, *wærod*, *wæstseaxna*, and the like.

Evidently the Worcester scribe was a Mercian trying to imitate the official dialect of the eleventh century, the standard English of the time, as it were.[41] In doing so, he occasionally lapsed into the extremely raised and fronted *e* for WG. *a* of his native dialect, but in general he succeeded in substituting the West Saxon *æ*. Then, like most people who cultivate a strange set of speech habits, he went too far: he occasionally substituted *æ* for *e* in words which should have had *e* in Mercian, West Saxon, or any other Old English dialect.

The same explanation holds for Farman. He was a Mercian whose native speech must have been essentially the same as that of the scribe

[40] British Museum MS. *Cotton Tiberius B. IV*, sometimes called "MS. D." of the *Anglo-Saxon Chronicle*.

[41] During the tenth century, after the Danelaw had been reconquered by the kings of Wessex, West Saxon became the standard for all England. It was the dialect of the royal officials, who were appointed or sent out from Wessex by West Saxon kings. It was the speech of many of the church dignitaries, most of whom were either Wessex men or the pupils of Wessex men. As a result, most of the tenth- and eleventh-century texts written in Anglian or Kentish territory are mixed with West Saxon, even when they are not written entirely in that dialect. Karl Wildhagen went so far as to refer to "der westsächsischen χουνή im 10., 11. Jahrhundert"—"Studien zum Psalterium Romanum in England," *Festschrift für Lorenz Morsbach* (Halle, 1913), p. 437. H. C. Wyld writes: "The fact is that all O. E. documents of the later period, with very few exceptions, are written in a common form which in all essential features is W. Saxon . . . so much so that it is now commonly assumed that after Ælfred's time the prestige of Wessex in Government, Arms, and Letters, was such that the dialect of that area became a literary χουνή in universal use in written documents."—*A History of Modern Colloquial English* (Oxford, 1936), p. 49. W. F. Bryan's examination of the Kentish charters reveals that the early ones are mixed with the then-dominant Mercian dialect, the later ones with West Saxon—*Studies in the Dialects of the Kentish Charters of the Old English Period* (Menasha, 1915).

who glossed the *Vespasian Psalter*, but whereas the latter was writing with a minimum of outside influence and thus wrote his own dialect rather consistently, Farman was trying to imitate the language of his temporal and ecclesiastical superiors. As a consequence of this imitation, he introduced numerous Saxonisms into his glosses,[42] among them *æ* instead of *e* for WG. *a*. He, like the Worcester scribe, carried the imitation too far and wrote *æ* frequently for WG. *e*.[43] What his actual pronunciation was, we cannot be certain at present. Perhaps his use of *æ* for *e* was purely orthographical. Or perhaps he actually tried to pronounce WG. *e* with a *æ*-sound.

3. *I*-UMLAUT OF WEST GERMANIC *a*.

For the ordinary *i*-umlaut of WG. *a*, the regular spelling in the *Vespasian Psalter* is *e*.[44] The *e* is normal in the other Old English dialects too, although occasional examples of *æft, sæcgan*, and the like appear in West Saxon, and such spellings as *hwælc* and *to sæcganne* may be found in Northumbrian texts. The Mercian portions of the *Rushworth Gospels* contain an exceptionally large number of *æ*-spellings:

æft 4, 7; 4, 8; 15, 29; 16, 21; 17, 23; 19, 24; 19, 28; 21, 18; 21, 36; 22, 4; 26, 32; 26, 43; 26, 44; 26, 72; 27, 40; 27, 50; 27, 63; *ægsa* 14, 26; 28, 4. *æsnas* 22, 4; 22, 6; *æsnum* 22, 8. *ahæfæþ* (present third singular of *ahebban*) 23, 12. *astęrfed* 15, 13. *bæreflor* 3, 12. *gærwende* 27, 28. *gegærelum* (without *w*) 27, 28. *gesætte* 28, 16. *hæfige* 23, 4; *hæfigra* 23, 23; *ahæfgad* 26, 43. *hwælc* 7, 9; 12, 32; 14, 36; 16, 26; 17, 12; 18, 18; 19, 17; 24, 45. *lægdun* 15, 30; *alægde* 27, 60. *næscum* (without *h*) 11, 8;

[42] Some other features, common in WS. but not in the Psalter, which appear in Farman's glosses are the following: 1. *a* for WG. *a* before nasal—*gangan* 8, 21, *gelamp* 13, 53, etc.; 2. *ea* for WG. *a* before *h*—*geseah* 2, 16, etc.; 3. *ea* for WG. *a* before *l* plus consonant—*ealde* 9, 17, *healfe* 20, 21, etc., 4. *ea* for WG. or Lat. *a* after a palatal—*geatt* 7, 13, *ceastre* 21, 10, etc.; 5. *a* for WG. *a* before palatal plus back vowel—*dagum* 2, 1, *nacud* 25, 36, etc.; 6. *a* for WG. *a* before non-palatal consonant plus back vowel—*faran* 8, 28, *getalu* 24, 30, etc.; 7. *eo* for WG. *e* before palatal—*feoh* 10, 9, *weorc* 5, 16, etc.; 8. *e* or *i* for WG. *e* or *i* before dental or nasal plus back vowel—*metaþ* 7, 2, *nimaþ* 19, 11, etc.; 9. *e* or *y* in *seolf*—*selfe* 1, 21, *sylf* Jn. 18, 1, etc.; 10. *y* for *i*-umlaut of breaking-*eo*—*awyrpeþ* 12, 27, *gewyrð* 13, 32, etc.; 11. WS. unstable *y*—*sylle* 19, 21; 12. *æ* for WG. *ā*—*cwædon* 2, 5, *wæron* 12, 4, etc.; 13. *eā* for WG. *ā* after palatal—*asceadeþ* 13, 49, *sceadenne* 10, 35, etc.; 14. *ēa* for WG. *au* before palatal—*eagan* 18, 9, *þeah* 24, 23, etc.; 15. *ēo* for WG. *eo* before palatal—*fleoh* 2, 13, *-seoke* 12, 22, etc.; 16. *ȳ* for *i*-umlaut of *ēa*—*gehyrde* 22, 7, etc. For further examples in each category, see Brown's dissertation.

[43] By the way, if Schulte's hypothesis needed a coup de grâce, I think Farman's *æ* for WG. *e* would provide it. From what kind of West Saxon exemplar could Farman have copied these *æ*'s? I at one time considered the possibility that Farman was, not a Mercian copying WS., but a West Saxon copying an old Mercian gloss; of course the evidence in this section would refute that view as thoroughly as it refutes Schulte's.

[44] For discussion of the rare exceptions, see Bülbring's article in *An English Miscellany*, p. 37.

11, 8. *sæcgaþ* 21, 16; 21, 24; 23, 3; *sægcaþ* 27, 13; *sæcgað* 27, 64. *sæcge* (pr. opt.) 8, 4; 19, 18; 24, 23; 24, 26; 26, 63; Mk. 1, 44. *sæcge* (imper. sg.) 18, 17; *sæge* 24, 3; *sæg* 22, 17. *sæcgaþ* (imper. plural) 11, 4; 17, 9; 21, 3; 21, 5; 21, 24; 28, 7; 28, 10; 28, 13; *sęcgaþ* 11, 3; *sæcgað* 2, 8; 22, 4. *strægde* 25, 26; *strægdun* 21, 8; 21, 8. *swælce* 18, 5. *swæraþ* 23, 18. *twælf* 10, 1; 14, 20; 26, 20; 26, 53; *twælfe* 10, 5; 26, 14. *-wær-fende* (without *h*) 21, 18. *wærgaþ* 5, 11; *wærge* (pr. opt.) 15, 4; *wærgad* 13, 19; *awærgede* 25, 41.

To these must be added fifty-nine examples of *sæcge, sægce, sęcge,* and *sæcga* used as present first singulars. It would be easy to point out analogical influences which may have affected individual forms. *Æft* may have been influenced by *æfter*, which Farman often wrote *æft* with a curl over the *t*. The *æ*-spellings in present forms of *secgan* may be the result of analogy with the preterites. But as with WG. *e*, the examples listed here are too numerous to be accounted for by individual analogies alone. What we actually have is analogy at work on a grand scale, affect-ing, not single words, but large masses of words having a certain sound in common. As for dialect mixture, Farman may have copied the West Saxon or the Northumbrian usage in *hwælc, sæcgaþ,* and some others; but hardly in *swælce, -wærfende,* and the various forms of *wærgan,* for these would have *y, i,* or *ie* in West Saxon and only occasionally *æ* in Northumbrian. It would seem that Farman was so accustomed to sub-stituting *æ* for *e* that he used *æ* in place of umlaut-*e* just as he used *æ* for West Germanic *e*. The proportion is about *æ:e::*1:2. The *e*-spellings are too regular and commonplace to be listed here.

Six groups of words containing *i*-umlaut of *a* have been reserved for special treatment.

The combination *st* frequently hindered *i*-umlaaut in West Saxon, and Northumbrian, preserving the *æ* in words which would otherwise contain *e*. Farman has the following *æ*-spellings:

fæstæ (preterite singular) 4, 2; *fæste* (pr. optative) 6, 17; *fæstaþ* 9, 14; 9, 14; *fæsten* (opt. plural) 6, 16; 9, 15; *fæstende* 6, 16; 6, 18; 15, 32. *ræste* 11, 29; *ræste-dæge* 12, 1; 12, 5.

With *e*, we find *befest* 1, 18, *gerestedæges* 12, 8, *gereston* Mk. 2, 15, *restaþ* 8, 20, *restæþ* 26, 45, and nine examples of *reste*—12, 2; 12, 10; 12, 11; 12, 12; 12, 43; 24, 20; 28, 1; 28, 1; Mk. 1, 21. The Psalter has *e* in all such words.

There are four examples of double-umlaut, all of which have the *æ* which characterizes West Saxon and Northumbrian rather than the *e* of the *Vespasian Psalter: æfeste* (*að-unsti) 27, 18, *ætgædre* (**-gaduri*) Mk. 2, 15, *ætgędre* 14, 9, *fæsten* (*fastunja) 17, 21.

Words whose roots end in *c* or *cc* seem to belong in a separate group. This arrangement may not appear logical in every instance, but so many of these forms are doubtful that segregation of the entire group seemed advisable. The *e*-spellings are *arecce* (*dissere*) 13, 36; 15, 15; *ðecele* 25, 1; and *gemeccum* 11, 16.[45] The *æ*-spellings are the following:

awæccan 3, 9; 26, 40; *wæcce* 22, 24; *wæcceþ* 10, 8; 26, 41; *wæceþ* 25, 13; *wæccaþ* 24, 42; 26, 38; *wæcende* 24, 43. *onsaecest* 26, 34; *onsækeþ* 10, 33.

In earlier Mercian, for example in the Psalter, there were two distinct verbs, *aweccan—awæhte* "to awake" and *wæcian—wæcade* "to watch." All forms in the Mercian portions of the *Rushworth Gospels* apparently belong to the first, but all have the vowel of the second. Either the *æ*-spellings are analogical, or Farman was up to his usual trick of substituting *æ* for *e*. We should expect to find *e* by *i*-umlaut in the two forms of *onsacan*, but the *æ*'s in these words may be due to analogy with other forms of the same verb, in which the *æ* results from smoothing of *ea* before a palatal consonant plus a back vowel.

Four of the Latin loan-words have also been segregated. The *æ*-spellings are:

bædzere (from Church Latin *baptizo* or *baptizator*, with the suffix -*ere*) 16, 14; 17, 13; *bæzere* 11, 11; *baezere* 14, 2; *bæzeres* 11, 12. *cælc* (from *calix—calicem*) 10, 42; *cælic* 26, 27; 26, 42; *kælic* 20, 22; 20, 23; *cælces* 23, 25; *cælcæs* 23, 26.

The *e*-spellings are *bezera* 3, 1, *bezere* 14, 8, *esules* (from Popular Latin *asilus*) 18, 6, *ecedes* (from *acetum*) 27, 48. In the forms of *bædzere* and *cælc*, the root vowel can be explained in different ways. Perhaps we have here another instance of Farman's confusion of *e* and *æ*. Such an explanation would be sufficient in view of what we have already seen of his orthography; however, both words are learned or semi-learned, and the Latin *a* may have been re-introduced analogically after certain sound changes had taken place in Mercian. Or we may have multiple borrowing. The *e* in *bezere*, for example, may reflect a very early borrowing; the *æ* in *bæzere* and *cælic*, a later reborrowing; and the *a* in *calic* 26, 39, a still later reborrowing. The Psalter has only *celc* and *calic;* hence there is little opportunity for comparison with earlier stages of Mercian.

The use of *æ* for umlauted *a* preceding a nasal is rare in all of the Old English dialects, especially rare in the *Vespasian Psalter*, which contains but two examples.[46] Farman uses *æ* only 27 times, *e* about 260 times. Although this proportion of *æ*'s would seem high in many Old English texts, it is clear that Farman confused *e* and *æ* less before nasals than elsewhere. His *æ*-spellings are these:

[45] For Sievers' explanation of WS. *gemæccea, wæccende, weccan,* and similar forms, see *An Old English Grammar*, p. 56.
[46] *Ængel* 34, 6 and *męnn* 36, 37.

ængel 28, 2; *ængla* 26, 53; *ænglum* 16, 27. *begængum* 21, 34; *ungænge* 15, 6. *ge-mænged* 27, 34. *kęmpe* 27, 27. *mængu* 4, 25; 19, 2; 21, 8; 21, 26; 21, 46; *mængum* 13, 34; 15, 10; 26, 55. *mænigu* 21, 36; *mængistu* 11, 20. *næmned* 27, 8; *genæmned* 27, 33. *stængum* 26, 47; 26, 55. *strængra* 3, 11. *swæncende* 26, 10; *geswæncte* Mk. 1, 34. *tostænced* 26, 31. *þwænga* 23, 5.—*forbærneþ* (with metathesis) 3, 12.

Bülbring associates this use of *æ* with southeastern Saxon Patois found on the borders of Kent.[47] It is interesting, therefore, to note that the *Worcester Chronicle* has a considerable number of similar *æ*-spellings: *ablænde, ablændan, acænned, ænde, lænctene, længst, mænn, mænigeo, mænigfealde, -næmnede, sænde, stængum, swæncte, geswænced, utlændisce, Ænglisc, Cænt, Dæniscan, Hængestes,* and others. Worcester, like the West Riding, is a long way from the borders of Kent.

The umlaut of WG. *a* followed by *l* plus a consonant is practically always *æ* in the *Vespasian Psalter* and the *Corpus Glossary*, the exceptions being a few forms of *wælle*, or *welle*, which contain *e*. In Northumbrian also the *æ* is regular; in strict West Saxon *ie, i,* or *y* may appear; in Kentish *e* is frequent. In Rushworth[1], *æ* appears twenty-four times, *e* ten times. There are also five forms in which *æ* is substituted for *a* (or *ea*?) through analogy with the umlauted forms. The following *æ*-spellings occur:

abælgede 26, 8. *ælde* (preterite sg.) 25, 5. *ældra* 15, 2; 21, 28; *aeldra* 26, 3; *ældran* 26, 47; 27, 20; *ældre* 27, 1; *ældru* 26, 57; *ældrum* 16, 21; 28, 12. *aeldingę* 24, 48. *bęldu* 14, 27. *fælle* (pr. opt.) 5, 29; 5, 30; *fælleþ* 18, 8; *afælleþ* 18, 6; *afældæ* 21, 12; *forðfællende* 18, 26; 18, 29. *fælnissum* 18, 7. *gehæld* (noun) 27, 65. *towælede* (with omission of *w* after the *l*) 27, 60; *awælede* 28, 2.

The analogical forms are: *bedælf* 25, 18, *gedælf* 21, 33, *nælles* 21, 21, *nællæs* 26, 5, *twæmfældum* 23, 15. The ten *e*-spellings are: *ahelde* (pr. opt.) 8, 20; *belgas* 9, 17; 9, 17; *beligas* 9, 17; *winbeligas* 9, 17; *cwelmaþ* 10, 21; *eldran* 27, 3; 27, 12; *eldre* 21, 23; *eldrum* 27, 41.

These ten *e*'s may indicate an admixture of Kentish in Farman's dialect, but such admixture is improbable. As we have seen, the use of *e* for WG. *a* is not necessarily Kentish, while the use of *æ* for WG. *e* and for the ordinary *i*-umlaut of *a* results from Farman's imitation of the West Saxon. As we shall see later, the use of *ē* for the *i*-umlaut of WG. *ai*[48] is not exclusively a Kentish feature. Since there is no other good evidence of Kentish influence in Rushworth[1], perhaps we should seek a different explanation of the *e* before *l* plus consonant. It is possible that Farman, while using *æ* for *e* so many times, occasionally substituted *e* for *æ*; however there is another explanation for about half the examples.

[47] *Ae. Elementarbuch*, p. 71.   [48] See section 11.

I have included a number of forms here with the short vowels because my organization has been guided more or less by etymology. It is generally agreed that lengthening took place before *ld*, *nd*, *ng*, and *rn* somewhat earlier than Farman's time. In the above lists the vowels were probably long in all forms of *ængel*, *begængum*, *ungænge*, *gemænged*, *stængum*, *strængra*, *þwænga*, *ælde*, all forms of *ældra*, *aeldingę*, *bęldu*, *afældæ*, *gehæld*, *twæmfældum*, *ahelde*, *eldran*, *eldre*, and *eldrum*. The same is true of the four examples of *geldeþ* in footnote thirty-two, and of sixty-two examples of *e* for the *i*-umlaut of *a* before nasal, among which are the following: *anhende*, *akende*, *begengu*, *bendum*, *breng*, *ellende*, *ende*, *endigan*, *endunge*, *engel*, *frumkendu*, *glendrende*, *kende*, *lendenu*, *lendu*, *leng*, *lengo*, *utgengum*. A few other forms are doubtful. Sievers included *nc* among the lengthening combinations;[49] perhaps we should consider the vowels in *swæncende*, *tostænced*, and *geswæncte* long. If the metathesis in *forbærneþ* took place early enough, the digraph in that word was probably long by Farman's day.[50] Actually, then, a large proportion of the *æ*'s before nasal and of the *e*'s before *l* plus consonant represent confusion of *ē* and *ǣ* rather than confusion of the short vowels.

4. *I*-UMLAUT OF WEST GERMANIC AND LATIN *o*.

Possibilities for *i*-umlaut of *o* are rare, occurring only in early Latin loans or in words to which suffixes containing *i* have been transferred after Primitive Germanic times but before the period of *i*-umlaut. The *New English Dictionary* postulates four different forms of *morn* in Primitive Germanic: **murganoz*, **marganoz*, **murginoz*, and **marginoz*. The usual form in Farman's glosses is *morgen*, evidently derived from the first of the four ancestral forms. *Margen* and *marne* in the Psalter are from the second. There are three umlauted forms in Rushworth[1], derived from WG. **morg-* or **marg-* plus the transferred suffix *-inoz*: *mergenne* 16, 3, *mærgen* 6, 30, and *mærgne* 21, 18. The vowels of these three might be looked upon as containing umlaut of either *a* or *o*, but the latter seems more probable in view of the usual *morgen*. The *o* umlauted to *oe*, then unrounded to *e*, giving us *mergenne*. Then, if Farman substituted *æ* for *e*, the other two forms would result.

The word *sperta*, from Latin *sporta*, occurs twice—15, 37 and 16, 10. Although *ele* (from Latin *oleum*) appears with *oe* unrounded in the Psalter, it is written *oele* in Rushworth[1]. This spelling may be due to Northumbrian influence. There is no substitution of *æ* in either of these words.

---

[49] *An Old English Grammar*, pp. 82–83.

[50] The *g* in *mængu*, *mengu*, etc. (glossing *turba*), and *mængistu* (*plurimae*) represents an earlier *-ig-*; if the vowel of this suffix was lost in pronunciation before the time of lengthening, these words might also be included above.

5. VELAR-UMLAUT OF WEST GERMANIC *a*.

When WG. *a* occurred in an open syllable followed by a back vowel, it nearly always underwent velar-umlaut in the dialect of the *Vespasian Psalter*, becoming *ea*.[51] In West Saxon and Northumbrian, the *a* usually remained *a*, although sporadic diphthongs appear in those dialects, as well as *æ*'s, the latter generally resulting from analogy. The spelling *heage* (acc. sg.) 21, 33 appears in Farman's glosses. If this is from an earlier *heagan* (compare *heagoðorn* in Corpus), it is the only example of velar-umlaut of *a* in the text. *Geafol* Mk. 2, 14 and the various forms of *geat* (*porta*) are, in all probability, West Saxonisms—very good examples of diphthongization after initial palatal. Farman has some *a*'s, as in *fader* 13, 43, *faran* 8, 28, and *leohtfatu* 25, 1, which are probably due to West Saxon or Northumbrian influence; but his usual rendering of WG. *a* in words in which velar-umlaut might occur is the *æ*:[52]

cæfertun 26, 3; 26, 58; *cæfertune* 26, 69. *fæder* (gen. sg.) 5, 45; 7, 21; 10, 20; 12, 50; 16, 27; 18, 10; 25, 34; 26, 29; 28, 19. *færan* (infin.) 2, 22; 16, 21; *færende* 25, 14; Mk. 1, 5; Mk. 1, 16; Mk. 1, 35; Mk. 2, 13; *fereþ* (imper.) 11, 3. *lehtfætu* (nom. pl.) 25, 8. *gæfel* 22, 17; *gæfelgeroefe* 5, 46; 10, 3; *gæfelhroefe* 9, 10; *gæfelgehrefum* 9, 11; *gæfelgeroefena* 11, 19. *gedæfnade* 18, 33; *gedefnade* 23, 23.

With these, we may compare the spellings of the Psalter: *ceafurtunes* and *ceafortune*, *feadur* (gen. sg.), *fearu* (pr. 1 sg.) *and ðorhfearað* (pl.), *fearende*, *featu*, *gedeafenað*. There is no parallel for *gæfel* in the Psalter, but *geabuli* and *geabules* are found in the *Corpus Glossary*.

The absence of the velar-umlaut of *a* in Rushworth[1] is surprising in view of the thoroughness with which that sound change seems to have been carried out in the dialect of the Psalter. It is true that many individual *æ*-spellings can be explained by analogies too obvious to be worth discussing; yet, if this be analogy, it has been carried out with a consistency unmatched in any Old English text with which I am acquainted.

Dialect mixture may also serve as partial explanation, for *æ*-spellings like these occur in Northumbrian and West Saxon texts, and we know that Farman imitated some non-Mercian usages. If West Saxon and Northumbrian influence were solely responsible, however, we should expect to find only occasional *æ*'s beside many more examples of *a*, such as *fader, gafel;* more examples of *ea* in words beginning with palatals, such as *geafel;* and perhaps a few examples of the Northumbrian *oe*, such as *foerende*.

[51] Except, of course, when it was smoothed by a following palatal consonant.

[52] Perhaps *ıswærigaþ* 25, 37 should have been included in this list, for it is written elsewhere in Rushworth[1] with *a*: *ıswarigaþ* 25, 44, *andswarade* 16, 2, etc. The Psalter has a different, though related, verb: *ondsweoriu, ondsweorede*, etc.

Luick maintains that the sub-dialect of the *Vespasian Psalter* was characterized by an almost universal operation of velar-umlaut, that Farman's sub-dialect lacked the sound change entirely, and that certain other Mercian texts were written in a mixture of these two sub-dialects.[53] Luick's view is hard to refute for the obvious reason that it is insusceptible of either proof or disproof. There is no limit to the number of sub-dialects whose existence may be assumed; for example, Luick sees three different varieties of Mercian in the *Corpus Glossary* alone.[54]

A chronological explanation of the phenomena in this section seems to me more reasonable than Luick's hypothesis. Monophthongization of Old English *ea* from breaking before *r* plus consonant must have begun during or shortly after Farman's time. Luick, himself, dates the change in the latter part of the tenth century or the first part of the eleventh.[55] Other authorities are of the same opinion.[56] Farman has five examples of *æ* or *e* (instead of *ea*) for WG. *a* followed by *r* plus consonant. These may or may not reflect the beginnings of monophthongization; I offer them for whatever they seem to be worth: *þærf* 9, 12, *ðærf* 6, 8, *beðærfeþ* 5, 30, *beþærfeþ* 19, 10, *beþerfeð* 5, 29.[57]

Monophthongization of velar-umlaut-*ea* may well have preceded the monophthongization of breaking-*ea*. In the first place, breaking was a much earlier sound change than velar-umlaut; and usage had had more time in which to become fixed, where breaking-*ea* was coccerned. Second, breaking before *r* plus consonant was widespread: even in Northumbria, where it was weakest, it had powerful effects. Velar-umlaut of *a*, on the other hand, was limited almost entirely to Mercia and the little kingdom of Kent. Consequently, any tendency in Mercia toward monophthongization of velar-umlaut-*ea* would be heightened by such contact with non-Mercian speakers as must have occurred after the conquest by Wessex; while a tendency toward monophthongization of breaking-*ea*, if it should begin in Mercia, might even be retarded by outside contact. Finally, the nature of velar-umlaut favored early monophthongization. According to the accepted phonetic explanation of this sound change, (1) the original *a* was raised and fronted in a word like **gaful* to a sound approaching [æ], while at the same time (2) the following back vowel, in this case *u*, modified the pronunciation of the intervening consonant *f*, whereupon (3) a glide sound developed between the fronted vowel and the modified consonant, producing a diphthong [æ ɑ] or [æ ə], which was

---

[53] *Hist. Gram.*, pp. 165, 211.   [54] *Ibid.*, p. 34.   [55] *Ibid.*, pp. 331–333.

[56] Richard Jordan, *Handbuch der mittelenglischen Grammatik* (Heidelberg, 1925), p. 79; H. C. Wyld, *A Short History of English* (New York, 1927), p. 64.

[57] Apparently there is no *i*-umlaut in any of these forms, cf. *þearfe* 14, 16, *beðearfeþ* 15, 5, etc. See also F. Holthausen, *Altenglisches etymologisches Wörterbuch* (Heidelberg 1932).

usually spelled *ea*. If the back vowels causing this change became fronted or disappeared, it is natural to assume that the consonants would return —through analogy with their pronunciation in other positions—to their original values. We know that the monophthongizing tendency was present in late Old English, and we can see that, once the consonantal pronunciations which were the original causes of the diphthongs had been removed, this tendency would work unimpeded. Now, note that, in the examples from the *Vespasian Psalter* cited above, the original back vowels which produced velar-umlaut are present in all of the words except *gedeafenað* and *fearende*.[58] But in Farman's glosses the back vowels have disappeared or fronted to *e* in all of the examples except *færan* and *lehtfætu*. Even in these two words, the *a* and the *u* had probably lost most of their original quality by Farman's time.[59]

6. Velar-umlaut of West Germanic *e*.

Velar-umlaut of WG. *e* was a thoroughgoing sound shift in the dialect of the *Vespasian Psalter*, for that text has *eo* in nearly all forms in which WG. *e* was followed by a single consonant—other than *c* or *g*—plus a back vowel. Northumbrian was similar to Mercian in this respect, although *ea* appears frequently instead of *eo* in the *Lindisfarne Gospels* and some other Northumbrian texts. In West Saxon the sound change was much less complete, occurring with any frequency only when the intervening consonant was a liquid or a labial. A following *a* had little or no effect in strict West Saxon, and the present-first-singular ending *e* (corresponding to Anglian *u* or *o*) naturally did not cause umlaut. Farman has numerous examples of *eo: ageofu* (pr. 1. sg.) 18, 29, *forgeofan* Mk. 2, 7, *beoran* 7, 18, *cweoþaþ* 16, 13, *cweoþan* 23, 39, *heofunum* 5, 12, *ongeotað* 13, 13, *weoras* 15, 38, and many others. These correspond phonologically with the us-

---

[58] In *fearende*, the *ea* is probably not the direct result of velar-umlaut anyhow, but the result of analogy with other forms of the same verb, e.g. *fearu, fearað*.

[59] If it were otherwise, Farman would hardly have substituted one vowel for another with such frequency in his inflectional endings. Note these substitutions of *a*, *o*, and *u* for *e*: strong nouns, *aldorsacerdos* (gen. sg. masc.) 26, 51, *deaða* (dat. sg. masc.) 15, 4, *geofu* (acc. sg. fem.) 23, 19, *heofunas* (gen. sg. masc.) 13, 24, *mængu* (nom. pl. fem.) 4, 25, *restedægas* (gen. sg. masc.) 28, 1, *tintergu* (acc. sg. neut.) 25, 46, etc.; present third singulars, *awerdað* 5, 13, *cerraþ* 24, 18, *cweþaþ* 12, 32, *cymaþ* 23, 35, *sellaþ* 13, 44, *sprecaþ* 10, 20, *weorþaþ* (of *weorþan*) 24, 21, etc.; present optative plurals, *biddan* 6, 8, *cuman* 27, 64, *cweoþan* 23, 39, *etan* 6, 25, *forstælan* 27, 64, *flugan* (preterite?) 3, 7, *geheran* 13, 15, etc. Farman also substituted *u* for *a* and *a* for *u*: weak nouns and adjectives, *ærestu* (nom. pl. masc.) 20, 10, *aldru* (nom. pl. masc.) 26, 57, *begengu* (nom. pl. masc.) 21, 38, *eorðu* (gen. sg. fem.) 5, 13, *forþmestu* (acc. pl. masc.) 23, 6, *godu* (voc. sg. masc.) 25, 23, *næhstu* (acc. sg. masc.) 5, 26, etc.; preterite indicative plurals, *blewan* 7, 25, *coman* 21, 1, *cwoman* 17, 42, *eodan* 21, 9, *feallan* 15, 30, *feollan* 17, 6, *foeddan* 25, 37, etc. For substitution of *e* and *æ* for the back vowels, see section 17.

ages of the Psalter and of some Northumbrian texts, for example the Northumbrian portions of the *Rushworth Gospels*.

Many words in Farman's glosses have *e* instead of *eo*:

agefe (pr. 1 sg.) 18, 26. *beranne* 3, 11. *cweþe* (pr. 1 sg.) 5, 34; 6, 25; 8, 9; *cweðe* 8, 9; 13, 30. *cweðaþ* (plural indicative) 15, 5; 21, 26; *cweþað* 7, 22; 11, 17; 17, 10. *cweþaþ* (imper. pl.) 10, 27. *cwepan* (infin.) 3, 9; 4, 17; 11, 7; 26, 22; Mk. 2, 9. *cweþanne* Mk. 2, 9; *cweþane* 9, 5; *gecweþanne* 9, 5. *efalsung* 12, 31; *efulsung* 12, 31; *efalsunge* 26, 65; *hefalsunge* 15, 19; *hefalsaþ* 9, 3; *efalsade* 26, 65; *hefalsadun* 27, 39. *enlefan* 28, 16. *etaþ* (pl. indic.) 6, 19; 15, 27; 15, 32; 23, 14; *etað* 15, 2; *geetaþ* 6, 31. *etæþ* (imper. pl.) 26, 26. *etan* (infin.) 14, 16 ; 25, 35; 25, 42; *ete* (infin.) 15, 20. *etanne* 12, 4; 26, 17. *etende* 8, 30; 11, 18; 11, 19; 24, 38; *etendra* 14, 21; *etendum* 26, 21. *forstelaþ* 6, 19; 6, 20. *hefonum* 18, 19. *hlengendes* 26, 7. *metaþ* 7, 2. *ongetað* 15, 17; *ongetaþ* 7, 16; 7, 20; 13, 14; 13, 19; 13, 51; 16, 9; 16, 11. *ongeteþ* (imper. pl.) 15, 10. *begetaþ* 5, 7. *ongetende* 14, 35; 22, 18. *setule* 23, 2; *setulas* 23, 6. *welerum* 15, 8. *weras* 12, 41; 14, 35. *wesaþ* 10, 16; *wesa* (infin.) 3, 14.

In addition to the forms listed, there are about sixty examples of *cweþende* and its various inflectional forms. Probably, about sixty examples of *henu* and one of *þenu* (3, 10) should also be added. Some of the words are doubtful, but nearly all are paralleled by umlauted forms in other Anglian texts. The forms of *efalsian* and *efalsung* may be compared with the umlauted *heofolsaþ* of Mark 2, 7, and with *eofulsunge* and *eofulsadun* in the Northumbrian portions of the *Rushworth Gospels*. *Hlengendes* suggests *hlionade* and *hliongende* of the *Lindisfarne Gospels*. As for *þenu*, it is apparently formed on the analogy of *henu*, which is paralleled by *heonu* in Lindisfarne.

Farman is too early for the late Old English monophthongization of *eo*, which is thought to have occurred in the eleventh century. Moreover, although there are four clear examples of *e* for *eo* before *r* plus a consonant,[60] which are comparable to the examples of *æ* before *r* plus consonant already noted, the abundant examples of velar-umlaut-*eo* present a picture very different from that in section five.

Farman's imitation of West Saxon accounts for most of the *e*-spellings satisfactorily, as most of the *e*'s precede a nasal or a dental, precede a consonant followed by *a*, or appear in present first singulars ending in *e*. Even forms like *hefonum* and *welerum*, while irregular in West Saxon, occur rather frequently in early West Saxon texts. In *agefe*, *ongetað*, and *begetað*, we see spellings which resemble neither strict West Saxon nor

---

[60] These are *awerþ* (imper. sg. of *aweorþan*) 5, 29, *cwern* 18, 6, *werþe* (pr. opt. of *weorþan*) 24, 20, and *werþeð* (pr. 3 sg.) 9, 16. The last may be compared with *geweorþað* 21, 21 and *forweorðeð* in the Psalter, both present third singulars. WG. *i* broke to *io* before *r* plus consonant, *io* fell together with *eo*, and then *e* was substituted for *eo* to produce *werþeð*. Note also the one substitution of *æ* for *e* in *gewærþe*, section 2.

the usage of the Psalter. It is true that occasional examples of *geld, sceld,* and similar forms without palatal-diphthongization are found (beside *gield, scield,* and the like) in texts which are considered pure West Saxon,[61] but Farman is more likely to have encountered the commoner forms in *ie, i,* or *y.* It is possible that Farman was led through imitation of the official West Saxon to use *e* in words like *cwepe* and *etap,* and then through analogy to transfer the *e* to *agefe* and *ongetap.*[62]

The *e* probably represents Farman's natural pronunciation in *setule, setulas,* and the present participles *cwepende, etende,* and *ongetende.* The *u* in the first pair is parasytic, as we may see by comparing it with *settlas* 21, 12; 23, 6; and *hehsettle* 27, 19.[63] The fact that Farman substituted *æ* for *e* in *sætil,* listed in section two, is further evidence that his pronunciation was that of *e.* The *eo* which appears in Mercian participles, such as *cweoðende* and *eotende* of the *Vespasian Psalter,* is purely analogical. However it was pronounced by the Psalter scribe, it was apparently an *e* in Farman's pronunciation. His substitution of *æ* in the many examples of *cwæpende* listed in section two indicates as much.

7. SMOOTHING OF OLD ENGLISH *ea.*

Farman's uses of *e* and *æ* for the smoothing of *ea* are, generally speaking, similar to those of the Psalter. In the latter we find *e* before *rc* and *rg;* usually *æ,* but occasionally *e,* before *h* and *g.* Farman has *e* in *gemerkade* 27, 66, and eight examples of *e* before *h*:

ehtu (pr. 1 sg. of *æhtigan*) 11, 16. *exlan* 23, 4. *gereht* (pt. ppl. of *reccan*) 1, 23. *geseh* (pt. sg.) Mk. 1, 10. *gepehtunge* 12, 14. *wehton* 8, 25. *wexan* 13, 30; *wexep* 13, 32.

The *e* in *wexep* may be due to *i*-umlaut, of course; but the infinitive, in which there was certainly no umlaut, also contains *e.* Four of these nine spellings, Bülbring attributes to late West Saxon influence, i.e., to the shift of *ea* to *e* in that dialect: *ehtu, gepehtunge, exlan,* and *wexan.*[64] Bülbring may be correct; however we find examples of *geðeht* and *wex* (*cera*) in the Psalter, beside the more frequent *æ*-spellings. The Psalter also contains several examples of *gerehte, awehte,* and the like.

The following *æ*'s before *c, g,* and *h* appear in Farman's glosses:

æchir 12, 1. *bepæht* 6, 29. *flæx* 12, 20. *mæht* (pr. 2 sg.) 5, 36; 8, 2; *mæhtest* (pt. 2 sg.)

---

[61] P. J. Cosijn, *Altwestsächsische Grammatik* (Haag, 1888), p. 18.

[62] Palatal-diphthongization of short *e* to *ie* is the only important WS. feature which Farman's glosses lack.

[63] Cf. also *sedle* 19, 28; 23, 22; 25, 31; *sedlum* 19, 28; and the form *seld* in the *Vespasian Psalter.*

[64] *Ae. Elementarbuch,* p. 130.

26, 40; *mæhte* 8, 28; 22, 46; 26, 9; Mk. 1, 45; Mk. 2, 2; *mæhton* 17, 16; 17, 19; *mæhtun* Mk. 2, 4; *mæh* (pr. 2 sg.) Mk. 1, 40. *mæht* (*potestas*) 7, 29; 21, 23; 28, 18; *mæhte* 9, 6; 9, 8; 20, 25; 21, 23; 21, 24; 21, 27; Mk. 1, 27; Mk. 2, 10; *mæhti* 8, 9; *mæhtæ* 10, 1; *hæmæhte* Mk. 1, 22. *næht* 28, 13; *nęht* 12, 40; *næhta* 4, 2; Mk. 1, 13; *næhte* 26, 31; *næhtes* 14, 25. *onsaece* (pr. 1 sg.) 10, 33. *restedægum* 12, 5; 12, 11. *sæh* 21, 19; *gesæh* 3, 7; 4, 18; 8, 14; 9, 9; 9, 23 12, 22; 14, 14; 20, 3; 22, 11; 26, 71; 27, 24; Mk. 1, 16; Mk. 1, 19; Mk. 2, 5; Mk. 2, 14; *gesæg* (with *g* from plural) 3, 16; *gesægh* 4, 21. *þæhtunge* 27, 1; *gepæhtunge* 27, 7; 28, 12; *gepæhtungę* 26, 4; *gepæhtungæ* 22, 15. *waexaþ* 6, 28; *wæxeþ* Mk. 1, 6.

Among Farman's other spellings are *geseah* with unsmoothed diphthong, *dagum* with *a*, and several examples of *niht*—all of which look like Saxonisms. He has no *e*-spellings for *næht* such as the occasional *neht*'s of the *Vespasian Psalter.*[65]

8. SMOOTHING OF OLD ENGLISH *eo*.

As in the Psalter, Farman' regular spelling for *eo* before *rc, rg, c, g,* and *h* is the smoothed *e*. The Psalter has a few diphthongs before *c*, for example *spreocan, spreocu.* Farman has *spreocan* 6, 7.[66] He also has *syxta,* some examples of *riht,* and a number of unsmoothed *eo*'s in *feoh, feorh,* and *weorc*—all of which may be West Saxonisms.[67] We need not suppose that these forms were copied from an exemplar, of course; they could have been picked up from West Saxon speakers or from documents written in that dialect. The regular *e*-spellings in Rushworth¹ are the following:

bergaþ (*cauete*) 16, 11. *brecanne* 5, 17; *breccane* 5, 17. *cneht* 2, 9; 2, 11; 2, 13; 2, 13; 2, 14; 2, 20; 2, 21; 8, 6; 8, 8; 8, 13; 12, 18; 17 18; 18, 4; *cnehtes* 2, 20; *cnehtas* 2, 16; 18, 3; *cnehtum* 11, 16; 14, 21; 15, 38. *ercnastan* 13, 46; *ercnanstanas* 7, 6; 13, 45. *feh* 27, 6. *ferh* 2, 20; 6, 25; 10, 39; 10, 39; 16, 26; 20, 28; *fere* (dat. sg.) 6, 25. *gesech* (imper. sg. of *geseon*) 8, 4. *reht* 12, 36; 20, 4; *rehtæs* 25, 19; *rehte* Mk. 1, 3; *unreht* 13, 41; 24, 12; *unrehthæmeþ* 5, 32. *sex* 17, 1; *sextan* 20, 5; *sextig* 13, 8; 13, 23. *sprecan* 12, 34; Mk. 1, 34; *gesprecaþ* 10, 20; *sprece* (pr. 1 sg.) 13, 13; *sprecende* 9, 33; 15, 31; 17, 3; Mk. 2, 2. *tinterga* 18, 34; *tintregum* 4, 24; *tintergu* 25, 46; *tinterga* (infin.) 8, 29. *werc* 11, 2; 26, 10.

The forms of *tintreg* are very doubtful. According to Holthausen, the

---

[65] Bülbring attributes *neht, mehtigra*, etc., of the Psalter to *i*-umlaut. *Ibid.*, p. 76

[66] Such sporadic examples of unsmoothed diphthongs before palatal plus back vowel hardly indicate Kentish influence. In addition to the *eo*'s in Rushworth¹ and the Psalter, I note *hreacan* in the latter, *heage* in the former, *onseacan* and *borðδeaca* in the *Corpus Glossary.* Girvan apparently considers such sporadic spellings evidence of Kentish or Southeastern origin, however—*Handboek*, pp. 87–89.

[67] Luick looks upon these as characteristic of Farman's sub-dialect of Mercian—*Hist. Gram.*, p. 215.

metathesis in the *rg*-forms took place after the time of breaking but be-fore the period of velar-umlaut and smoothing.[68] It is also possible that we have here a weakening in the second element of a compound.

There are, in addition to the words listed above, a few *æ*-spellings:[69]

cnæhte 18, 5; *cnęhte* 2, 8; *cnæhtas* 18, 2; 21, 15. *gefæht* (noun) 24, 6; *gefæhta* 24, 6. *wærc* 23, 5; *wærcum* 23, 3.

These last may be due to Farman's tendency to substitute *æ* for *e*. Or they may be borrowed spellings. Bülbring treats *cnæhtas* and *gefæht* as Northumbrian forms, brought about by smoothing of the Northumbrian *ea* (from earlier *eo*).[70] Both *wærc* and *wærcum* gloss *opera* and should not be confused with Anglian *wærc* (*dolor*).[71]

9. ISOLATIVE DEVELOPMENT OF WEST GERMANIC *ā*.

WG. *ā*, when unaffected by neighboring sounds, became *ǣ* in West Saxon, *ē* in the other Old English dialects. Farman's glosses contain both *e*- and *æ*-spellings, the proportion being about *ǣ*:*ē*::7:10. The examples of *e* are too numerous for complete listing, but the following forms ap-pear:[72]

agefe (pt. opt.), *bede* (pt. 2 sg.), *bedun, bedon, bede* (pt. opt.), *abeden* (pt. opt.), *gebedun, gebede* (pt. opt.), *bere* (pt. opt.), *beron, cwedun, cwedon, cweden* (pt. opt.), *efen* (vesper), *efenne, et* (pt. sg.), *etun, eton, forgetun, ongeton, ongetun, gefegon, herum (pillis), lecnade, let* (imper.), *forlet, letaþ, leteþ, letan, forlete* (pr. 1 sg.), *forletes, forleteþ, forleteð, forletaþ, forlete* (pr. opt.), *forletae, forleten, forletan, forletenne, forletende, forletendæ, forletendre, forletne* (pt. ppl.), *forletnae, forletnisse, merne (insignem), mersung, merðo, gemerdon, nedle, nedra, nedrana, ondred* (imper.), *ondredeþ, ondredaþ, scep, scepa, scepum, sed, seda, segon, segun, gesegon, gesegun, sel, setun* (pt. pl. of *sittan*), *gesetun, slep* (noun), *slepe, slepade, slepte, sleptun, slepeþ, slepað, slepende, sprecun, sprece* (pt. opt.), *þer, ðer, wede, ge-wedum, gewedad* (pt. ppl. of *gewedigan—vestire*), *wepned, wepenu, were, weron, werun.*

Perhaps *gefetun*—13, 7 and 13, 8—should be added. Although Schulte treats these as scribal errors for *gefeollun*,[73] Holthausen refers them to a Strong V verb *fetan*, meaning "to fall."[74] I omit the noun *sprece* 6, 7

[68] See *Wörterbuch*.

[69] The proportions of *e* and *æ* are not so important here as in some other sections, yet they may be of interest. The proportions are approximately *æ*:*e*::7:1 for smoothing of *ea*, and *æ*:*e*::1:7 for smoothing of *eo*.

[70] *Ae. Elementarbuch*, pp. 85–86.

[71] For explanation of the latter, see Jordan's *Eigentümlichkeiten*, pp. 51–53, or Holt-hausen's *Wörterbuch*.

[72] All repetitions and some inflectional variants are omitted.

[73] *Glossar.*   [74] *Op. cit.*

advisedly; although the vowel of West Saxon *spræc* and *gespræc* seems to have been *ǣ*, the form *gespreocu* in the *Vespasian Psalter* suggests that the vowel may have been short in Mercian.

Farman has 165 *æ*-spellings:

æfen Mk. 1, 32; *æfenne* 27, 57. *æriste (resurrectionem)* 22, 23; 22, 28; 22, 30; 22, 31; *æristæ* 27, 53. *agæfe* (pt. opt.) 18, 30. *cræd* (pr. 3 sg. of *crawan*) 26, 34; 26, 75. *cwæde* (pt. 2 sg.) 26, 25; 26, 64; *cwædon* 2, 5; 9, 28; 12, 23; 15, 33; *cwædun* 13, 10; 16, 14; 19, 7; 20, 7; 20, 22; 20, 33; 21, 16; 21, 27; 21, 31; 21, 41; 22, 21; 22, 23; 22, 42; 26, 5; 26, 35; 26, 61; 26, 66; 26, 73; 27, 4; 27, 21; 27, 23; 27, 40; 27, 49; Mk. 1, 37. *forstælen* (pt. opt.) 28, 13. *frætun* 13, 4. *gesæge* (pt. opt.) 22, 11; 26, 58; *gesægon* 2, 9; 12, 2; 15, 31; 26, 8; *sesægan* 20, 34; 27, 55. *hwær* 2, 2; 2, 4; 24, 28; 26, 13; 26, 17; *wær* (without *h*) 8, 20. *læces* 9, 12. *læt* (imper.) 8, 21; *gelaet* 6, 13. *mærsige* Mk. 1, 45; *gemæred* 28, 5. *rędę* (pr. opt.) 24, 15. *scæp* (*oues*) 25, 33. *swær* 25, 26. *ungeþwære* 5, 42; 26, 5; *monnŏwære* 21, 5. *wæda* 28, 3. *wære* (pt. opt.) 1, 22; 2, 4; 2, 15; 2, 23; 3, 13; 4, 1; 4, 14; 12, 17; 14, 26; 16, 20; 20, 28; 21, 4; 24, 22; 26, 24; 26, 24; 26, 56; Mk. 1, 45; Mk. 2, 1; *węre* 8, 17; 13, 35; *węre* (pt. 2 sg.) 25, 21; 25, 23; *wæron* 12, 4; 25, 10; *węron* 12, 3; 18, 31; *wærun* 11, 20; 14, 21; 23, 30; 23, 30; 26, 22; 27, 38; Mk. 1, 20; Mk. 1, 27; Mk. 1, 36.

Besides the forms listed, there are sixty-two *æ*-spellings of *þær* (spelled *þær*, *ŏær*, *þęr*, *ŏęr*). This is the appropriate point at which to mention *swæ* 18, 14; 19, 8; 26, 40. The regular use of *swe* in the Psalter suggests that in Mercian this lengthened *a* fell together with WG. *ā*. In Rushworth the usual form is *swa*, probably through West Saxon influence. *Swæ* or *suæ* is common in Northumbrian. The *-þwære*-forms above are paralleled by *monŏwære* and *monŏwęrnis* in the Psalter;[75] otherwise the latter has *e* in all words containing WG. *ā*.

Several explanations of Farman's mixture of *æ* and *e* for WG. *ā* have been offered. Luick is very dubious in the matter, apparently hesitating between the hypothesis that both *ē* and *ǣ* belonged to Farman's sub-dialect and the long-discarded view that he was a West Saxon copying a Northumbrian orginal:[76]

Ob Ru.¹ die Sprache eines mercischen Gebietes aufweist, in welchem *ǣ* und *ē* aufeinanderstießen und sich mischten (ein Sprachzustand, der sich auch im Frühmittelenglischen bei Orrm findet), oder ob der Glossator Farman aus einem *ǣ*-Gebiet stammte und teils seiner nordhumbrischen Vorlage folgte, teils seine heimischen *ǣ* einfließen ließ, ist unsicher.

My objections to the sub-dialect hypothesis have been stated elsewhere.[77]

Menner argues that both *ē* and *ǣ* were variants of Farman's own dia-

---

[75] These forms are doubtful, but probably contain WG. *ā*. They appear to be related to the third principal part of *geþweran* "to mix. stir," Strong IV. See Fr. Klaeber's *Beowulf* (Boston, 1936), p. 343.

[76] *Hist. Gram.*, p. 129.   [77] See section 5.

lect, adducing as proof the fact that the glossator used some *æ*-spellings even in his gloss to parts of Mark and John, in which he was following a Northumbrian gloss containing *e*-spellings.[78]

These instances show clearly that the *wær*- forms in Matthew are not copied Saxonisms, but Farman's own, and that *wer*- forms are perfectly natural to him. In using both forms Farman seems to be following variants of his own dialect.

Such substitution of *æ* for *e* is clearly incompatible with the view that the Saxonisms in Matthew and elsewhere in Rushworth[1] were mechanically copied from an archetype. It certainly indicates that Farman knew and consciously approved both spellings. Thus far Menner is correct, but the use of both *æ* and *e* may not prove that both pronunciations, [e:] and [æ:], belonged to Farman's native Mercian.[79] Familiarity with the usages of both Mercian and West Saxon would be sufficient, I believe, to produce the mixture of spellings which we have seen.

Others have attempted to explain Farman's spelling through phonetic tendencies within Mercian. Henry Sweet noted that a large proportion of the *æ*'s for WG. *ā* appear before *r* or after *w*.[80] That is true, but why? What other Mercian text possesses this feature? What have *r* and *w* in common that would cause a shift of *ē* to *æ* or prevent a shift of *æ* to *ē*? Sweet neglected to explain. As far as I can see, the abundance of *æ*-spellings before *r* and after *w* is due, not to any phonetic tendencies, but to the frequency with which Farman used the adverb *þer* (or *þær*) and the preterite forms of two common verbs, *wesan* and *cweþan*. Moreover, he did not use *æ* at all consistently before *r* or after *w*, as one may see by consulting the first list in this section. Brown held that Farman never adopted a West Saxon usage unless it happened to coincide with some speech tendency of his own:[81]

Innerhalb dieses Schwankens aber sind allerlei feine Sprachtendenzen gut durch-

---

[78] "Farman Vindicatus," pp. 15–16.

[79] Perhaps I am misrepresenting Menner's view. Sometimes he seems to use the term *dialect* in the sense of the speech of a tolerably homogeneous group of people who share certain special speech habits differing from those of other groups. At other times he broadens the meaning of the term until it includes all the personal speech habits of an individual as well, e.g. "The whole history of modern dialectology, with its doctrine that every individual may, in a sense, have a dialect of his own, points to the possibility that Farman's variations in Matthew may be natural to himself."—*op. cit.*, p. 18. If this is what Menner has in mind, there is nothing to be gained by arguing about definitions. We can agree that Farman's inconsistent spellings are variants of his own "dialect," in the sense in which that word is sometimes used by modern dialectologists, but of course Farman's "dialect" was a mixture of the Mercian dialect (in the older sense of the term) and the West-Saxon and Northumbrian dialects.

[80] *History of English Sounds* (Oxford, 1888), p. 126.

[81] *Die Sprache*, I, 80.

geführt. So steht jenes æ für westg. â fast ausschliesslich bei r, w und mit w wechselndem g.

But Brown, like Sweet, failed to explain how and why these consonants produced this effect, unparalleled elsewhere in Mercian. One suggestion, not a very good one it is true, has been overlooked by the seekers after *Sprachtendenzen*. Possibly Farman's usage is comparable to the West Saxon use of *ā* instead of *ǣ* before *w*, *p*, *g*, *c*, *r*, or *l* plus back bowel.[82] If these consonants tend to shift *ǣ* back to *ā* in West Saxon, might they not shift *ē* to *ǣ* in Mercian? The *æ*-spellings in *gesægun*, *wæron*, and a number of other forms could be accounted for in this way, and a few others like *gesæge* could be attributed to analogy. There are three objections, however: (1) we should still have to find an explanation for *æfen*, *agæfe*, *cwædun*, and other forms; (2) we should have to account for the near absence of this tendency in other Mercian texts;[83] and (3) we should have to find an explanation of the fact that *a*-spellings of the sort under consideration are much less frequent in West Saxon than the *æ*-spellings are in Rushworth[1].

Bülbring attributes *æ* for WG. *â* in Farman's glosses to Saxon influence,[84] rightly I am sure. Farman was imitating the official West Saxon. If he could substitute *æ* for his native *e* in words containing WG. *a*, and even for WG. *e* and umlaut-*e*, his use of *æ* for his native *ē* from WG. *â* should not surprise us. The fact that he sometimes substituted *æ* for *e* while following a Northumbrian original in Mark and John indicates, not that both sounds were natural to his native dialect, but that he considered the *æ*-spelling an acceptable variant.

We note that the *æ*-spelling is employed for the long vowel less frequently than for the short. Compare the proportion *ǣ*:*ē*::7:10 with the *æ*:*e*::25:2 of section one. The difference is probably due to Northumbrian influence. The West Riding, or most of it, had been a part of the old Mercian kingdom, yet it had been held by Northumbria at various periods prior to the tenth century, had changed hands several times in fact.[85] Farman was in contact with men who spoke Northumbrian, of whom Owun, his fellow glossator, was evidently one. He was familiar with at

---

[82] Sievers, *An Old English Grammar*, p. 38; Bülbring, *Ae. Elementarbuch*, pp. 52–53; Luick, *Hist. Gram.*, p. 155; Girvan, *Handboek*, pp. 49–50.

[83] Examples are very few: *monŏuaeran* and a few others in the *Vespasian Psalter*, *naep* from Latin *napus* in the *Corpus Glossary*, sporadic examples in other Mercian texts. Examples from the *Life of St. Chad*, the Tanner MS. of Bede, and the *Worcester Chronicle* prove nothing of course, for these texts are known to contain a strong West Saxon element.

[84] *Ae. Elementarbuch*, p. 38.

[85] The best discussion of the boundaries of Mercia is probably in J. Brownbill's article "The Tribal Hidage," *English Historical Review*, xxvii (1912), 625–648.

least one Northumbrian text, the *Lindisfarne Gospels*.[86] Since Northumbrian agreed with West Saxon in the use of *æ* for WG. *a*, Farman's tendency to imitate the latter dialect went unchecked. On the other hand, the Northumbrian *ē* for WG. *ā* opposed the West Saxon usage and partially counteracted its effects upon Farman.[87]

10. Isolative development of West Germanic *ē*.

WG. *ē*, including *ē* in Latin loans and *ē* in the preterites of Class VII verbs, shows great regularity in Farman's glosses. The following forms appear:[88]

ahengon, fellun, feng, fengon, ondfeng, ondfengon, ɪfengon, onfeng, onfengon, onfengun, onfenge, gefeng, gefenge, heht, geheht, her (adverb), *let* (pt. sg.), *forlet, forletun, forlete, forleten.—fefer* (from Latin *febris*).

There are seventy-three examples of *e*, none of *æ*. The absence of the latter may be due to the restraining influence of Northumbrian, pointed out in the preceding section. We shall see, however, that Farman occasionally used the *æ* for *ē* from other sources. It is also interesting to note that the *Worcester Chronicle* contains a number of *æ*-spellings, some of which occur several times: *hæt* (pt. sg.), *hæton, gehæton, læt* (pt. sg.), *læton, forlæt, forlæton, alæt*. Perhaps it is unnecessary to point out that Northumbrian could have had little inhibiting influence upon a Worcester scribe.

11. *I*-umlaut of West Germanic *ai*.

The umlaut of Old English *ā* from West Germanic *ai* appears in West Saxon and Northumbrian as *æ*, in Kentish frequently as *e*. The ordinary spelling of the *Vespasian Psalter* is *æ*, but there are *e*-spellings in some forms of *gebreded, aledde, lereð, flesc, forðrestan, clene*, and *enne*, which seem to reflect the pronunciation of the Psalter scribe. Farman also has *e*-spellings—thirty-six of them:

---

[86] Skeat, *Holy Gospels*, IV, xii–xiii.

[87] The influence of Nthb. was not merely negative. The list of features in Farman's glosses which are common in Nthb. but not in the Psalter is rather long, although some of them are represented by only a few examples: 1. *a* for WG. *a* followed by *r* plus consonant—*arþu* 11, 3, *forwarþ* Mk. 1, 39, etc.; 2. *eo* for WG. *a* before *r* plus consonant—*eorfeþe* 7, 14; 3. *ea* for WG. *e* before *r* plus consonant—*bearma* 16, 11, *wearþe* (pr. opt.) 5, 30, etc.; 4. *ea* for WG. *a* after palatal—*geatt* 7, 13, *ceastre* 21, 10, etc.; 5. *ā* for contraction of *a* plus *a*—*ofslan* 21, 38, *thuað* 15, 2, etc.; 6. *ɪ* for Anglian *ē* after palatal—*scipa* (*oves*) 18, 12, etc.; 7. *ɪo* for WG. *au*—*bebeod* (pt. sg.) Mk. 1, 25; 8. *ēa* for OE. *ēo*—*eade* 24, 38, *hread* 12, 20, etc.; 9. *ei*-diphthongs—*geceigde* Mk. 1, 20, *ðreiga* 16, 22, etc.; 10. loss of final inflectional *n*—*lichoma* (gen. sg.) 6, 22, *gehera* (infin.) 13, 17, etc. In addition, Nthb. is like WS., in that it has *æ* for the isolative development of WG. *a* and seldom shows velar-umlaut of WG. *a*.

[88] The *heht*-forms may have had short vowel.

enne 17, 8; 18, 6; 18, 10; 27, 15; 27, 16. *erran* (comparative of *ær*) 12, 45; *erestu* 20, 16. *femnan* 25, 1; 25, 7; 25, 11. *geclensige* Mk. 1, 40; *geclensad* 8, 3; Mk. 1, 42; *unklene* 8, 16; 12, 43; *unclenra* 10, 1; *unclennisse* 23, 25. *helend* 12, 25; 13, 57; 14, 12; 14, 13; 14, 16; 14, 25; 14, 27; 14, 31; *helende* 14, 29; *gehelde* 14, 14. *hemende* 24, 38. *hwete* 13, 29; 13, 30. *ledað* 21, 2. *lessa* 11, 11. *sneddun* 21, 8. *to delanne* 10, 35. *ðem* 2, 8. *unaduescendlice* 3, 12.

Probably *gemerum* (*finis*) 8, 34 also belongs here.

The *æ*-spellings are so numerous and so commonplace that I shall not list them completely. The following forms occur:[89]

adwæsced, adwæscet, æ, ae, ælaruw, æghwelcum, æghwilc, ægwilc, æghwonan, æhte, ænig, ænigum, ængum, nænig, nængum, nænegum, nænigne, nænegu, ænne, ær, ærne, ærran, ærrum, ærest, æreste, ærestu, æræst, æringe, ærþon, ærðon, æswic, æswiceþ, æswicað, æswicende, awæged, blæcern, brædaþ, onbræddon, clæne, clænsigaþ, clænsade, geclænsige, clænsunge, unclæne, dæghwæmlice, dæghwæmlicu, dæle, eastdæle, westdæle, gedælaþ, gedældun, fæmne, gefætted, gemænes, genægeþ (without *h*), *gesælde, unsæleþ, getæceþ, hælon* (infin.), *hælo* (pr. 1 sg.), *hæleþ, hæl* (imper.), *hælde, hælende* (pr. ppl.), *gehæle, gehæleþ, gehælde, gehæled, gehælen* (infin.), *hælend* (noun), *gehæl* (interj.), *hælo* (noun), *gemęru, gemærum, gemaerum, hæme, hæmeþ, hæmde, hæmed, hætu, hæþne, hwæm, hwæte, hwætes, kægen, lædeþ, lædde, læded, lædenne, gelæde* (infin.), *gelædde* (pt. ppl.), *læfde* (*reliquit*), *læfed, lærest, lærde, læran, forlæreþ, gelærde, læsesta, mæste, næfre, ræcep, (þorriget), ræsed, stæna* (adj.), *stænęst* (pr. 2 sg.), *stændun, twæm, þæm, ðæm, þæm, þære, wæled* (cf. O. Icel. *veill, veilindi*), *wælid, gewælde, wræð* (*grex*).—*ælmesse* (Pop. Lat. **alimosina*), *ælmes, ælmisse.*

The proportion of *e* is small, about *ǣ*:*ē*::20:1. Because of the examples of *e* in the Psalter, the *Corpus Glossary*,[90] and other Mercian texts, we are hardly justified in calling Farman's occasional use of *e* for *ǣ* a Kentish feature.

12. *I*-UMLAUT OF OLD ENGLISH *ō*.

The chief sources of Old English *ō* are WG. *ō* and the WG. *ā* followed by nasal. Both regularly umlauted to *ōē* in all of the dialects. In West Saxon the *ōē* was unrounded at an early date; in Northumbrian it remained rounded until relatively late. While the *ōē*-spelling is almost universal in the Psalter and fairly frequent in Rushworth,[1] Luick sees evidence of unrounding even in the former.[91] Farman, in addition to his

---

[89] I do not include certain forms. The comparative adverb *mae* or *mæ* (cf. *mae* in the Psalter) occurs ten times. In these, WG. *ai* has not become *ǣ*, but the adverbial ending *e* has been added to the adjective *ma*. The form *wæ* 23, 15 glosses Latin *væ;* it is a scribal error, influenced no doubt by the *æ* of the Latin, for Farman wrote *wa* everywhere else. Perhaps *lære* (dat. sg. of *lar*) Mk. 1, 22 has *æ* by analogy with *lærende* in the same verse.

[90] Corpus contains *gelestunne, scultheta, stictenel*, and *uuegið*.

[91] *Hist. Gram.*, p. 169.

oe-spellings, has the following examples of *e* for the *i*-umlaut of West Germanic *ō*.[92]

bledsade 14, 19; *bletsade* 26, 26; *gebletsade* 25, 34. *eadmedaþ* 18, 4. *feran* 8, 18; *ferde* 8, 34; *forðfere* 14, 22. *gehrefun* 9, 11. *gemette* 20, 6; 26, 40; 26, 43; *gemettun* 22, 10. *wepan* (infin.) 9, 15; *wepaþ* 24, 30; *wepende*, 2, 18. *westen* Mk. 1, 12; Mk. 1, 13; *westenne* Mk. 1, 3; Mk. 1, 4; *westinne* 3, 3; *westige* Mk. 1, 35; *westigum* Mk. 1, 45.

On the basis of these *e*-spellings, we might conclude that the unrounding of Mercian *ōē* was well advanced by Farman's time. West Saxon usage probably influenced the glossator here as elsewhere, but we have definite evidence that Farman's own pronunciation was an unrounded one, in seven examples of *æ*: *blęd* (*fructus*) 7, 17; 7, 18;[93] *gedræfde* 24, 6; *ræccet* (*regat*) 2, 6;[94] *wæstenne* 11, 8; 15, 33; *węstene* 24, 26. His substitution of *æ* for his native *ē* from WG. *ā* led him to substitute *æ* for his native *ē* from *i*-umlaut of *ō*. It is not likely that he could have made the substitution if his own pronunciation had not been *ē* rather than *ōē*.

Farman's glosses contain examples of *e*, as well as *oe*, for the *i*-umlaut of WG. *ā* before a nasal:

wen (noun) 11, 23; *wenest* 18, 1; 24, 45; 26, 53; *wenaþ* 5, 17; 10, 34; 24, 50; *wendon* 20, 10. *ehtende* (**anhtj-*) 10, 23; *ehtendum* 5, 44; *hehtende* 5, 11.

———

Three examples of *æ* indicate that this *ōē*, like the other, was in an advanced stage of unrounding: *cwæmdon* 12, 10, *cwaen* 12, 42, and *hwæne* 26, 39.[95]

[92] The numerals *twegen*, or *twægen*, and *begen* are obscure but probably belong here. According to *Girvan, Handboek*, pp. 41–42, WG. **twaii* received an analogical *ō* from the neuter **twō*, the *ō* umlauted to *ōē*, and then unrounded to *ē*. The Psalter has one example each of *twoega* and *twegen*. Farman has sixteen examples of *ē*: *twegen* 4, 18; 4, 21; 8, 28; 10, 29; 14, 17; 18, 16; 18, 16; 18, 19; 24, 40; 24, 41; 25, 15; 25, 22; *twege* 5, 41; 18, 20; *twegra* 21, 31; 27, 21; and sixteen in which *æ* has been substituted for *ē*: *twægen* 11, 2; 14, 19; 19, 5; 19, 6; 20, 21; 20, 30; 21, 1; 21, 28; 25, 17; 25, 17; 25, 22; 25, 22; 26, 37; 26, 60; 27, 38; 27, 51. There is a remote possibility that the *æ*-forms are directly descended from **twaii* and contain *i*-umlaut of WG. *ai*, but Farman's tendency to use *æ* for *ē* makes the other alternative seem more probable. *Begen* 13, 30 and 15, 14 may be explained in the same manner as *twegen*—Girvan, *op. cit.*, p. 267.

[93] Not to be confused with *blǣd* meaning "renown," which is related to *blāwan*. This *blǣd*, or rather *blēd*, is related to *blōwan* and contains *i*-umlaut of *ō*. See J. R. Hulbert, *Bright's Anglo-Saxon Reader* (New York, 1936), p. 258.

[94] Schulte associates this form with *rǣcan* "reach." That is an error, for the verb is clearly *rēcan* "heed, care for, i.e. rule."

[95] *Hwæne* glosses *pusillum*, cf. modern Scottish *wheen*. Schulte, in his *Glossar*, mistakenly treats it as a form of *hwa*.

13. *I*-UMLAUT AND SMOOTHING OF OLD ENGLISH *ēa*.

The effects of *i*-umlaut and smoothing upon *ēa* are almost identical in the Anglian dialects[96] and can, therefore, be treated together. The two types of *ēa* can also be grouped for this discussion.

The Old English *ēa* which resulted from breaking of West Germanic *ā* was umlauted to *ē* in the *Vespasian Psalter* and in Northumbrian, to *īe* in West Saxon. In Farman's glosses it appears as *e* five times—*nehsta* 21, 37, *nexstan* 5, 43, *nehsto* Mk. 1, 38, *nehstum* 19, 19, and probably *geneleccende* (**genāhe-*) 4, 3—and as *æ* eleven times:[97]

nærra 21, 31; *næhsta* 20, 14; *næhstu* 5, 26; 19, 30; 19, 30; 20, 12; 20, 16; 20, 16; 22, 39; *næhstum* 20, 8; *ætnæhste* 26, 60.

Since the ordinary forms in West Saxon and Northumbrian were *niehsta* and *nesta* respectively, it is apparent that Farman was substituting *æ* for *ē* rather than directly copying non-Mercian spellings. His actual pronunciation was probably [e:].

The breaking-*ēa* smoothed to *ē* in the Psalter and in Northumbrian, usually remained *ēa* in West Saxon.[98] Farman has *e* in *neh* 16, 27; 24, 32; 26, 18.

The *ēa* from West Germanic *au* was umlauted to *ē* in the Psalter and generally in Northumbrian; in West Saxon it became *īe*, later *ī* or *ȳ*. Farman's glosses contain about 140 *e*-spellings, among which the following forms occur:

ætece ("to increase"), *geeced*, *alefed* ("permitted"), *anlepum*, *begende*, *beginge*, *beman*, *cegan*, *ceganne*, *cege*, *cegde*, *cegende*, *gecegende*, *tocegende*, *degles*, *degullice*, *degulnisse*, *depu*, *depiδ*, *depte*, *deped*, *depid*, *gedeped*, *epre*, *unepe* (by analogy with preceding), *ewis-*, *ewisade*, *gemnis*, *gemung*, *gemunge*, *gemungæ*, *gemunglic*, *gemunglice*, *heran*, *herdon*, *geherest*, *gehereþ*, *geheraþ*, *geherde*, *gehere*, *geheran*, *gehera*, *geheranne*, *geherende*, *gehered*, *hernisse*, *gehernisse*, *lefaδ* ("believe"), *gelfeaδ*, *gelefæþ*, *gelefde*, *gelefdest*, *gelefdun*, *gelefdan*, *gelefed*, *gelefan*, *gelese*, *toleseþ*, *alesnisse*, *leget* (*fulgor*), *ned*, *nede*, *recils*, *scetan*.

The form *edmodaδ* Mk. 1, 27 looks like a mere scribal error for *eadmedaþ*. Two forms, *ceigde* 20, 25 and *geceigde* Mk. 1, 20, may be due to Northumbrian influence, although *geceigo* occurs in the Psalter. There are sixteen *æ*-spellings:

---

[96] The two sound changes were very similar although one took place considerably later than the other. In each case, a following palatal sound caused the velar second element of the diphthong to disappear.

[97] *H* in the superlatives is analogical, cf. *nesta* in the Psalter. The *h* of the positive *neh* found its way into *nehsta*, etc., but apparently the analogy did not affect the comparative *nærra*.

[98] In late WS., the *ēa* was frequently reduced to *ē* by palatal-umlaut. This *ē* also appears, through analogy, in late WS. superlatives, e.g. *nehsta*, etc., in the *West Saxon Gospels*.

æwis- 21, 31. *alǣfed* (*is alǣfed* glosses *licet*) 20, 15; 22, 17; *gelǣfed* 12, 4. *cægeþ* 15, 23; *cęgde* 25, 14; *acægde* 2, 7; 2, 15; *gecægde* 4, 21; 18, 32; 22, 14; *cæcæged* 20, 16. *gehęraþ* 8, 27. *gelǣfende* (*credentes*) 21, 22. *lǣget* 24, 27. *nǣddun* 27, 32.

Old English *ēa* from *au* smoothed to *ē* in the Psalter, except in *ðæh*, which always appears with *æ*. Northumbrian usage was approximately the same as that of the Psalter. In West Saxon this smoothing did not take place, although in late West Saxon the *ēa* was frequently reduced to *ē* by palatal-umlaut. Farman's glosses contain forty-two examples of *ec* or *ek* (usually *eac* in West Saxon) and thirty-three other *e*-spellings:

ceke 5, 39. *ege* 5, 29; 5, 38; 5, 38; 6, 22; 6, 22; 6, 23; 7, 3; 7, 3; 7, 4; 7, 4; 7, 5; 7, 5; 13, 16; 18, 9; *egan* 9, 29; 9, 30; 17, 8; 20, 15; *egna* 20, 33; *egum* 13, 15; 20, 34; 21, 42; *egu* 13, 15. *forbecun* 24, 24. *heh-* 4, 5; 4, 8; 12, 5; 27, 19; Mk. 2, 15. *to ekan* (*extra*) 15, 38; *to eke* 25, 20; *eknum* 24, 19.

One form, *ðreiga* (infinitive) 16, 22, looks Northumbrian, while unsmoothed forms resembling West Saxon are rather frequent. In addition to five examples of *þæh*—15, 20; 21, 21; 24, 26; 26, 33; 26, 35—and two with Saxon unsmoothed diphthong—*þeah* 24, 23 and *ðeah* 16, 26, Farman has *æc* 24, 27 and *bæg* 27, 29. No doubt *hæmæhte* (older **heahmeahte*) Mk. 1, 22 should also be included with the *æ*-spellings.

14. SMOOTHING OF OLD ENGLISH *ēo*

Old English *ēo* from WG. *eo-eu* smoothed to *ē* in the *Vespasian Psalter*, as did *ēo* from breaking of WG. *i* before *h*. Most of Farman's spellings, except for his use of *k* and some confusion in the inflectional endings, are like those of the Psalter: *flega* (*culicem*) 23, 24; *leht-* 4, 16; 6, 23; 25, 4; 25, 8; Jn. 18, 3; *monsek* 17, 15; *monsekae* 4, 24; *wexon* (pt. pl.) 13, 7. No *æ*-spellings appear, but there are several examples of West Saxon unsmoothed *eo*.

15. CONTRACTED FORMS CONTAINING *ē* AND *ǣ*.

For contraction after loss of *j*, Farman's practice was similar to that of the Psalter scribe, although his proportion of *ǣ* is much greater. There are four examples of *æ* in *æce* (**ajukja*) and three of *e*;[99] *æce* 19, 16; 19, 29; 25, 46; 25, 46; *ece* 25, 41; *ecce* 18, 8; *eknisse* 21, 19.

For contraction after loss of *w*, Farman has *ē* in *edæs* (Gothic *awēþi*) 26, 31. The form *næht* (*nihil*) 23, 16 is not clear. The usual spelling in the Psalter is *nowiht* without loss of *w* or contraction. Farman usually has *nawiht*. Possibly *næht* has been influenced by *nænig* or perhaps by the Northumbrian *næniht*, which occurs occasionally in Lindisfarne. *Nellaþ*

---

[99] For Bülbring's explanation of this word as it appears in the Psalter, see *An English Miscellany*, pp. 43–45.

23, 8, contraction of *ne willaþ*, may be mentioned here, although the *e* was probably short.

Both *ē* and *ǣ* appear for contraction after loss of *h*. In *seon* and *geseon* there are ten examples of *e* and two of *æ*, in forms which would have *ēo* or *ie* in either the Psalter or West Saxon:[100]

geseeþ (pr. pl.) 11, 5; *geseende* 5, 1; 8, 34; 9, 2; 9, 4; 13, 13; 13, 14; *gesene* (pt. ppl.) 6, 18; *to geseenne* 11, 8; *to seenne* 11, 9; *gesænæ* 6, 5; 23, 5.

There are no examples of *ē* in the various forms of *slean*, or *slan;*

slæ (pr. 1 sg.) 26, 31; *slae* (pr. opt.) 5, 39; *slæþ* (pr. 3 sg.) 5, 21; *ofslæþ* 23, 34; *slægst* (with analogical *g*) 23, 37; *ofslægþ* 17, 23; *slæhþ* (pr. pl. with analogical *h*) 10, 28; 24, 9.

Here again, we may have examples of Farman's tendency to substitute *ǣ* for *ē*; or, in view of the *æ*-spellings of this verb which appear in the *Lindisfarne Gospels*, perhaps we should attribute Farman's *ǣ*'s to Northumbrian admixture. There are no examples of *ǣ* in *ten* (**tehan*): *ten* 18, 24; 25, 1; 25, 28; *tene* 20, 24; *feowertene* 1, 17; 1, 17; 1, 17.

The verb *gan* shows contraction of another type. WG. **gai-is*, **gai-iþ* appear as *gǣst*, *gǣð* in the present second and third singulars of both the *Vespasian Psalter* and West Saxon. Farman has *ǣ* in these forms and also, evidently through analogy, in plurals and various other forms of *gan*:

gæst 8, 19; *gæs* 5, 26; *gæþ* 2, 6; 5, 30; 7, 21; 8, 9; 12, 43; 12, 45; 13, 44; 15, 11; 19, 23; 26, 24; 28, 7; *gæþ* 7, 21; *gæþ* (plural) 13, 49; 18, 3; 21, 31; 23, 13; *gæð* 15, 18; *gæ* (pr. opt. sg.) 18, 9; *gæn* (pl.) 13, 28; *gæ* (imper. sg.) 5, 24; *gæþ* (pl.) 2, 8; 9, 13; 10, 5; 11, 4; 20, 4; 24, 26; 25, 6; 25, 9; 26, 18; 27, 65; 28, 10; 28, 19; *gaeþ* 8, 32; *begæþ* 20, 25; *forþgaeþ* 4, 4; *ingaþ* 15, 11; *ingæð* 15, 17; *ingæn* (pr. opt.) 10, 11; *ofergæþ* 15, 2; 15, 3; *utgaeþ* 12, 43; 15, 19; *utgæþ* 24, 27; *utgæn* 10, 11.

The comparative and superlative forms of *neh* listed in section thirteen should be mentioned here. They are examples of *i*-umlaut, but they also represent contraction. In the Anglian dialects, **nēahira* and **nēahista* lost the *h* before the *i* was syncopated; hence such forms as *nesta* appear in the Psalter. After examining so many of Farman's deviations from the usage of that text and finding that all of the important ones can be adequately explained through West Saxon and Northumbrian influence, or through Farman's tendency to substitute *æ* and *ǣ* for *e* and *ē*, or through the difference in date between the two manuscripts, I believe we are safe in assuming that Farman's dialect was basically a later development of the

---

[100] *Gesænæ* and *gesene* correspond to WS. *gesiene*, which is usually classified as an adjective. Girvan, *Handboek*, p. 296, states that the word is used for the past participle of *seon* in the *Lindisfarne Gospels* and some other northern texts. At any rate, the connection with *geseon* is clear.

dialect of the Psalter. The form *nehsta* may, therefore, have been derived from the earlier *nesta* with the addition of an analogical *h; næhsta* is the same, plus substitution of *æ* for *e;* and *nærra* is from earlier **nēra*, with substitution of *æ* for *e* and with an extra *r*.[101]

16. Diphthongs followed by *w*.

Before *w*, the diphthongs *ēa* and *ēo* occasionally appear as *e*. *Streaw* is written *streu* three times: 7, 3; 7, 4; 7, 5. According to Bülbring, the pronunciation was that of *ēuw* in such forms.[102] The diphthong *ēo* plus *w*, in addition to numerous *eow-* and *euw*-spellings, shows the following examples of *ew* (or *eu*):

blewan (pt. pl. of *blawan*) 7, 25. *ewer* (for *eower*) 7, 11. *geheu* (pt. sg. of *geheawan*) 27, 60. *hreunisse* 3, 2; 3, 8; 3, 11; 12, 41; *hrewnisse* 4, 17. *lareu* 17, 24; 22, 16; 22, 36; 23, 7; 23, 10; 23, 10; 26, 18; 26, 25; 26, 49; *larewas* 23, 8. *latewas* 23, 16. *sewe* (preterite of *sawan*) 25, 24. *ðewige* (beside *ðeowige* 6, 24) 4, 10.

Bülbring is of the opinion that *eu* and *ew* in this group represent an *ēuw*-pronunciation.[103]

17. Unaccented *e* and *w*.

Since Farman's uses of *e* and *æ* in unaccented syllables seem to be well understood and have never been subject to much controversy, they may be dealt with briefly. A few illustrations of Farman's usages should suffice.

The glossator substituted *æ* for *e* in words having slight stress in the sentence. Although the *ē* (from Germanic *iz*) in *me, þe, he, we,* and *ge* is usually written *e* in Rushworth[1], there are three examples of *æ*: *wæ* 6, 31; 6, 31; *wę* 23, 30. The relative *þe* appears as *ðæ* once—Mk. 1, 24. There is one example of *þęs* (*hic*) 9, 3. The final *e*'s of pronoun forms are frequently written *æ*:

hinæ 5, 41; 21, 46; 22, 15; 26, 16; 27, 38; 27, 44; 27, 54; 28, 13; *hinae* 8, 31. *hiræ* 23, 37; 26, 13. *þæræ* 16, 25; *þaræ* 28, 2. *þissę* 10, 42.

The second element of the diphthong in *hie* is affected; *hiae, hię,* and *hiæ* occur altogether more than one hundred times. The spelling *næm* for *ne eam* appears once—3, 11, and nineteen final *æ*'s occur in the optative of the same verb:

siæ 4, 3; 5, 29; 16, 22; 18, 8; 21, 19; 22, 42; 23, 5; 24, 17; 26, 2; 27, 19; 27, 23; 27, 40; *się* 14, 28; 16, 13; 18, 6; *siae* 10, 13; 10, 13; *syæ* 27, 42; *sięn* 7, 1.

The unstressed adverb *ne* appears as *næ* once, 26, 53; and *gæ* for *ge* (*etiam*) also occurs once, 17, 25.

---

[101] False gemination is extremely common in tenth-century Anglian texts.
[102] *Ae. Elementarbuch*, p. 41. [103] *Ibid.*, p. 42.

Unaccented elements of compounds often appear reduced to *e*. Among the *e*-spellings are the following forms.

berern (*-*razn*) 3, 12; 6, 26; 13, 30; *blæcern* 5, 15; 6, 22; *carcern* 5, 25; 14, 3; 18, 30; *carcerne* 14, 10; *carkern* 25, 43; *quartern* 25, 39. *enlefan* (*ain-) 28, 16; *elleftan* 20, 9. *forþmestu* (*-*maista*) 23, 6. *geonrettæ* (*-*orhaitj*-) 22, 6. *geneleccende* (*-*laikj*-) 4, 3; *nealehctun* 21, 1; *tonealehte* 21, 34. *hlaferd* (*-*ward*) 22, 44; *hlaferde* 15, 27; *laferd* 10, 24. *ondetu* (*andhaitj-) 7, 23; 11, 25; *ondeto* 10, 32; *ondeteþ* 10, 32; *ondetende* Mk. 1, 5; *ondentende* 3, 6. *þyles* (*-*laisiz*) 4, 6; 6, 18; 7, 1; 7, 6; 13, 15; 13, 29; 17, 27; 26, 5; 27, 64; ðyles 15, 32; 25, 9.

The following compounds appear with *æ*: *ællefta* 20, 6; *carkærn* 25, 36; *carcrænnæ* 25, 44; *þylaes* 5, 25; *ytmæst* 22, 13; *ytmæste* 8, 12; 12, 45.

Prefixes and suffixes show few irregularities in the use of *e* or of *æ*, and these have been dealt with fairly thoroughly elsewhere.[104]

In his inflectional endings, Farman substituted *e* for *a*, *o*, or *u* rather frequently.[105] A few specimens will serve as well as a multitude. The masc-plur. nominative and accusative ending is usually -*as*, but often -*es*; *bokeres* 23, 25, *fisceres* Mk. 1, 16, *gastes* 12, 45, *hlafes* 4, 3, *sacredes* 12, 5, *stanes* 27, 51. The genitive plural usually ends in -*a*, occasionally in -*e*: *bokere* 5, 20, *hlaferde* 15, 27, *synne* 26, 28, and *ðeode* 10, 5. Masculine *n*-stem nouns often end in -*e*: *doeme* (nom. sg.) 5, 25, *doeme* (nom. pl.) 12, 27, *geleafe* (gen. sg.) 6, 30, *geroefe* (gen. sg.) 27, 27, *lamwyrhie* (gen. sg.) 27, 7, *wille* (acc. sg.) 7, 21. There are numerous -*eþ* endings for the present plural, indicative and imperative: *ascakeþ* (imp.) 10, 14, *asceadeþ* (ind.) 13, 49, *behaldeþ* (imp.) 6, 1, *bideþ* (ind.) 11, 3, *cumeþ* (imp.) 11, 28, *doemeþ* (ind.) 7, 2, *falleþ* (ind.) 15, 27. Infinitives frequently end in -*en* or -*e*: *bebyrgen* 8, 21, *bodige* Mk. 1, 45, *forleten* 1, 19, *ingangen* 23, 13, *mærsige* Mk. 1, 45, *swerige* 26, 74. The older -*u* or -*o* ending appears on present indicative first singulars, but the -*e* is more frequent: *ahsige* 21, 24, *cume* 8, 7, *cweþe* 5, 34, *sæcge* 26, 29, *sende* 10, 16. Preterite indicative plurals usually end in -*un* or -*on*, occasionally in -*en*: *arisen* 27, 52, *bleowen* 7, 27, *comen* 20, 9, *flugen* 26, 56, *stoþen* 28, 9.

Farman apparently felt free to substitute *æ* for *a*, *u*, *o*, or *e* in the inflectional endings. The masculine and neuter genitive singular is usually -*es*, but often -*æs*: *cælcæs* 23, 26, *fiscæs* 7, 10, *folcæs* 21, 23, *gæflæs* 9, 9, *husæs* 15, 24, *melwæs* 13, 33, *monnæs* 10, 23. Strong dative singulars end in -*e* or in -*æ*: *æristæ* 27, 53, *domæ* 12, 41, *folcę* 27, 24, *londæ* 24, 18, *stanę* 24, 2, *yflæ* 5, 37. The oblique singulars of strong feminine nouns end in -*e* or -*u*, sometimes in -*æ*: *aeldingę* 24, 48, *cneorissę* 23, 36, *gepæhtungæ* 22, 15, *hreuwnissę* 11, 20, *mintæ* 23, 23. In strong plurals, the substitution of *æ*

---

[104] Brown, *op. cit.*, Part II—*The Language of the Rushworth Gloss* (Göttingen, 1892), pp. 3–8.

[105] For his substitution of back vowels for *e*, see footnote 59.

for *a* is rare, but several interesting forms occur: *aldursacerdæs* (acc. pl. masc.) 26, 14, *sacerdæs* (nom. pl. masc.) 26, 59, *mynetræ* (gen. pl. neut.) 21, 12. Oblique cases and plurals of the *u*-stems often end in *-æ: hondæ* (acc. sg.) 12, 13, *sunę* (gen. sg.) 24, 39, *sunæ* (dat. sg.) 2, 15, *sunæ* (nom. pl.) 20, 21. The same is true, to a lesser degree, of the oblique cases and plurals of the *n*-stems: *circae* (acc. sg. fem.) 16, 18, *geroefæ* (dat. sg. masc.) 27, 2, *hiwæ* (acc. pl. neut.) 10, 25, *lamwyrhtæ* (gen. sg. masc.) 27, 10. A few specimens will show how the *æ* is used in adjectival forms:

alnę (acc. sg. masc.) 24, 14; *medmiclæs* (gen. sg.) 16, 8; *formæ* (dat. sg.) 26, 17; *miclæ* (instrumental) 27, 46; *monsekae* (acc. pl. masc.) 4, 24; *winstrae* (wk. nom. sg. fem.) 6, 3; *iungæ* (wk. nom. sg. masc.) 19, 20; *blindę* (wk. voc. sg.) 23, 26; *yterræ* (comparative) 22, 13; *marae* (comp.) 5, 47; *læsæst* (superlative) 2, 6.

The *æ* frequently replaces the vowels of common adverbial endings, as in *sonæ* 21, 19, *innæ* 24, 26, *utæ* 12, 46, *næfræ* 7, 23, *nallæs* 7, 21, and *nællæs* 26, 5. Among verb endings the picture is much the same. A few examples will indicate the varied uses of the *æ:*

stænęst (pr. 2 sg.) 23, 37; *geseęs* 7, 3. *gearwæþ* (pr. 3 sg.) 6, 30; *gesitæþ* 25, 31; *sweræþ* 23, 16. *forlæræþ* (pr. pl.) 24, 5; *frętwæþ* 23, 29. *astigæ* (pr. opt. sg.) 27, 42; *geweorþæ* 23, 16. *ðyncæ* 22, 17. *alucæ* (pr. opt. pl.) 13, 29; *wuldrigæ* 5, 16. *fylgæ* (imper. sg.) 9, 9; *locæ* 27, 4. *abidęþ* (imper. pl.) 26, 38; *clænsigæþ* 10, 8; *gebycgæþ* 25, 9. *gefylldæst* (pt. 2 sg.) 21, 16; *wistęs* 25, 26. *getahtæ* (pt. 3 sg.) 3, 7; *geherdæ* 4, 12. *brustæn* (pt. pl.) 27, 51. *gegearwæd* (pt. ppl.) 11, 8; *gefongnae* (acc. pl. masc.) 4, 24; *gecorænæ* (nom. pl. masc.) 22, 14. *bycgæ* (infin.) 20, 1. *cymendę* (pr. ppl.) 16, 28; *fylgænde* 9, 9; *gangænde* 22, 15.

Clearly, the great weakening of English inflections which helps to differentiate Middle English from Old English was already in an advanced stage in tenth-century Mercian.

CONCLUSION

Farman's personal speech habits must remain a mystery, no doubt; at present I see no way of determining whether the inconsistencies of his spelling reflect a mixed type of speech or merely a mixed orthography. Nevertheless, if we have succeeded in distinguishing the non-Mercian features of his text and especially those features in which he seems to have been imitating the official West Saxon of the tenth century, we should be able to restore the general outlines of the glossator's native speech— his pronunciation as it would have been without the influence of non-Mercian speakers and writers.

Farman's native pronunciation was probably a short *e*-sound of some sort in the following groups of words: (1) those containing the isolative development of WG. *a*, for example *efter—æfter;* (2) those having the isolative development of WG. *e*, such as *stefn—stæfn;* (3) those with ordinary *i*-umlaut of *a*, *hefiglice—hæfige;* (4) those with *i*-umlaut of *a* before a nasal, *genemde—genæmned;* (5) verbs in which analogical *e* had been substituted for WG. *i*, *agefeþ—agæfeþ;* (6) a few forms containing the *i*-umlaut of WG. or Latin *o*, *mergenne—mærgen;* (7) some of the forms which would have appeared with velar-umlaut of *e* in the *Vespasian Psalter*, for example *cweþende—cwæþende;* (8) words containing the smoothing of *ea* before *r* plus a palatal, *gemerkade;* and (9) those which have the smoothing of *eo*, *cnehtas—cnæhtas*. Possibly breaking *-eo* was occasionally reduced to an *e*-sound (or perhaps ø) as spellings like *awerþ* and *cwern* seem to suggest; however the evidence is insufficient for safe generalization. There may have been an *e*-sound for the *i*-umlaut of *a* before *st*, as in *befest—fæste*, and for the double-umlaut of *a*, as in *ætgædre*, but here again we have too few examples.

Farman's native dialect probably had a *æ*-sound in the following groups: (1) words which had formerly contained *ea* by velar-umlaut, such as *cæfertun* and *færan;* (2) words containing a smoothed *ea* before *h*, *mæht* and *waexaþ;* (3) some of the words which had *i*-umlaut of West Germanic *a* before *l* plus consonant, for example *abælgede* and *fælleþ*. Perhaps the same sound occurred in a few forms which had formerly contained the breaking-*ea*, as *þærf* and *beþærfeþ*. The few *e*-spellings for (2) and (3) should not be taken too seriously. The former—*geseh*, *wexeþ*, and six others—are comparable to the rare *e*-spellings of the same kind in the Psalter. In both texts they may indicate a slight tendency to raise and front the *æ* before *h*, or they may be purely analogical. Of the latter—*eldran*, *beligas*, and the rest—five occur before lengthening combinations and probably reflect the Mercian tendency to shift *ǣ* to *ē*,[106] while the remaining five hardly justify any generalization.

A long *e* of some sort was apparently Farman's native pronunciation for: (1) West Germanic *ā*, as in *let—læt;* (2) West Germanic *ē*, as in *her* and *feng;* (3) the *i*-umlaut and smoothing of *ēa*, as in *nehsta—næhsta*, *ec—æc, geheraþ—gehẹraþ;* (4) the smoothing of *ēo*, as in *monsek* and *leht-;* (5) the *i*-umlaut of *ō*, as in *westenne—wæstenne, wenaþ* and *cwaen;* and (6) the *e* lengthened before *nd* and similar combinations, as in *ende, engel—ængel*, and *stenceþ—tostænced*.[107] I am not aware that anyone has ever questioned the [e:] in (2), (3), (4), or (6); and the unrounding of *ōē* in (5) seems to be generally accepted despite Farman's use of *oe-* as well as *e*-spellings. As for West Germanic *ā* in (1), Farman's fluctuation between *e-* and *æ*-spellings probably resulted, like his use of both *e* and *æ* for the

[106] Cf. treatment of the *i*-umlaut of WG. *ai* in both Rushworth[1] and the Psalter.
[107] See section 3.

West Germanic short *a*, from imitation of West Saxon. His use of *æ*- as well as *e*-spellings for the *i*-umlaut of *ō* tends to confirm this view, for [æ:] in those words seems just as improbable as [æ] in words containing West Germanic *e*. Some of the contracted forms are not easy to interpret. The sound was probably [e:] in *ece—æce, edæs*, and *ten*. But in forms like *geseeþ* and *geseende*, the pronunciation may have been [e:], or it may have been a diphthongal [e:ə] pronunciation resulting from juxtaposition of the root vowel with the weakened vowel of the ending. Since Farman did not ordinarily use *ee* to indicate a long *ē*, the latter interpretation seems more probable. There is no good reason for supposing that the sound in *slægst* and *slæþ* was [æ:]. More probably it was [e:], as in *sles* and *sleð* of the Psalter. Farman's tendency to substitute *æ* for *ē* was strengthened, in this instance, by his acquaintance with Northumbrian usage. The *æ*-spellings found in the other forms of this verb may be analogical.

The long *æ* [æ:] was evidently Farman's usual pronunciation of the sound resulting from *i*-umlaut of West Germanic *ai*. As in the work of the Psalter scribe, however, we find a tendency to shift the sound toward [e:] in a few forms, especially before *d, l, m, n, r*, and *s*.[108] Probably [æ:] was Farman's native pronunciation in contractions like *gæst* and *gæþ;* and other forms of this verb may have had the same sound by analogy, although here again we may have a diphthongal [a:ə], similar to the [e:ə] mentioned above.

As we have seen in section sixteen, Farman may have represented the pronunciations [æ:ʊ] and [e:ʊ] by *e*-spellings when those diphthongs preceded *w*.

Weakened vowels, very close to [ə], must have been present in most of Farman's inflectional endings. There is no other way to account for his indiscriminate use of *e, æ, a*, and *u* in the various forms noted in section seventeen and footnote fifty-nine.

Most of the pronunciations enumerated above are the same as those which scholars have inferred from the spellings of the *Vespasian Psalter*, but not all. We should hardly expect the Mercian dialect to be exactly the same in the tenth century as it had been in the ninth. Farman's spellings seem to indicate the following changes: (1) monophthongization of velar-umlaut-*ea* to *æ*, which had not begun at the time the Psalter was glossed but which was far advanced, if not complete, by Farman's time;[109] unrounding of *oe* and *ōē* to *e* and *ē*, which had begun early enough to leave traces in the Psalter and which was virtually complete when Rushworth[1]

---

[108] For explanation of the effect of these consonants, see Bülbring, *Ae. Elementarbuch*, p. 69; Luick, *Hist. Gram.*, p. 172.

[109] The monophthongization of breaking-*ea* may have begun in Farman's time, cf. *þærf*, etc., in section 5.

was glossed; (3) weakening, almost to [ə], of the vowels in the inflectional syllables, which hardly appears in the Psalter but seems to have proceeded very rapidly in the Mercian dialect; (4) use of *e* for West Germanic *i* in the second and third singulars of strong verbs belonging to classes III, IV, and V; and (5) lengthening before *ld, nd,* and similar combinations, which is commonly believed to have occurred in the ninth and tenth centuries.

Other spellings differ from those of the Psalter because of West Saxon or Northumbrian influences.[110] In three uses of the *æ* the glossator was apparently influenced by both West Saxon and Northumbrian: (1) *æ* for isolative development of West Germanic *a*, (2) *æ* for *i*-umlaut of *a* before *st,* and (3) *æ* for double-umlaut of *a.* In two usages he seems to have been influenced by West Saxon alone: (4) *e* for West Germanic *e* originally followed by dental or nasal plus back vowel, and (5) *ǣ* for the isolative development of West Germanic *ā.* It is significant, I believe, that the proportions of non-Mercian spellings are much larger for (1), (2), and (3) than for (4) and (5). In two of his usages, Farman may have been influenced by Northumbrian alone: (6) *æ* for isolative development of West Germanic *e,* a usage which appears only occasionally, however, in Northumbrian texts; and (7) *ǣ* for contraction of *a* plus *e* as in *slæþ.* No important *e-* or *æ*-spelling in Farman's portion of the *Rushworth Gospels* can be definitely identified as Kentish.

A further result of Farman's contact with non-Mercian usages appears in his substitution of *æ* and *ǣ* for *e* and *ē* in words which would normally contain *e* and *ē* in any of the Old English dialects: (1) *æ* for isolative development of West Germanic *e,* (2) *æ* for ordinary *i*-umlaut of West Germanic *a,* (3) *æ* for *i*-umlaut of *a* before nasal, (4) *æ* for smoothing of *eo,* (5) *ǣ* for *i*-umlaut of *ō,* (6) *ǣ* for *i*-umlaut and smoothing of *ēa.* Although Northumbrian usage may have affected the first of these features to some extent, the regular usages in all of the dialects could have had no direct effect. Perhaps we should call these features the indirect effects of dialect mixture.

Although this article has been concerned primarily with Farman's uses of *e* and *æ,* some of the conclusions have more general implications. First, the dialect of Rushworth,[1] if we subtract from it all differences which are due to later date and all differences due, directly or indirectly, to non-Mercian influences, is essentially the same as the dialect of the *Vespasian Psalter.* It is not necessary to suppose, with Luick, that Mercian was a chaotic hodge-podge of loosely related sub-dialects, most of them bearing

---

[110] For other non-Mercian usages, see footnotes 42 and 87.

a closer relationship to non-Mercian dialects than to one another.[111] Second, although dialect mixture accounts for many of the differences between Rushworth[1] and the Psalter, Schulte's extreme view that Farman was copying an archetype is untenable. Where would the glossator find an archetype containing *æ* for West Germanic *e*, or *ǣ* for the *i*-umlaut of *ō*? Certainly not in any variety of early West Saxon now known. Third, while many of Brown's conclusions seem acceptable, his "Sprachtendenzen" are of little value as far as *e* and *æ* are concerned, for they do not manifest themselves in other Mercian texts and they are not necessary to an understanding of Farman's usages. Two of Brown's statements are not supported by the evidence. Velar-umlaut of *a* does not appear "stark entwickelt" in all of the Mercian texts;[112] in Farman's glosses, the examples of *ea* from this source are very rare and very doubtful. West Germanic *e* did not become *æ* in Mercian,[113] but the opposite shift occurred, *æ* becoming *e*. Fourth, Menner is correct in contending that Farman was not a Mercian who made a careless copy of a West Saxon gloss—that Farman's work has linguistic value of its own. But we shall learn little about the dialect by treating all of Farman's contradictory, sometimes fantastic, spellings as though they represented bona fide Mercian pronunciations. Instead we must compare these usages with those found in other Mercian texts and with West Saxon and Northumbrian usages as well. After eliminating borrowed features, we can examine the residue for indications of what tenth-century Mercian was like.

SHERMAN M. KUHN

Oklahoma A. & M. College

[111] One would expect to find local variations in speech within an area so large as Mercia' and I would not deny for an instant the possibility that such variations existed. But they will be found, if at all, through study of the minor features of the extant texts, rather than in the broad, general features with which Luick has dealt.

[112] *Die Sprache*, p. 81.

[113] *Ibid.*

SYNONYMS IN THE OLD ENGLISH BEDE

A NOTABLE FEATURE of the Old English version of Bede's *Ecclesiastical History* is its frequent use of synonymous pairs of words or phrases to translate single expressions in the original Latin. J. M. Hart called attention to this peculiarity in an article entitled "Rhetoric in the Translation of Bede,"[1] in which he maintained, first, that the rhetorical device known as amplification was familiar to Old English writers and, second, that King Alfred could not have translated Bede. In support of his contentions, Hart presented a long, though only partial, list of synonymous pairs accompanied by the single expressions found in the corresponding Latin. His views are summed up as follows:[2]

Even these few [examples] ought to satisfy any one that the process of rhetorical amplification was known in England long before the Conquest and quite apart from the needs of alliterative verse. Further. I would ask those who still adhere to the Alfredian authorship of the *Bede* translation, if they can discover anything like this 'doubling' in the *Pastoral* or the *Orosius*.

The present study is not intended as a refutation of either argument. There is sufficient evidence in Old English literature to prove, without recourse to the Bede translation or to the poetry, that amplification through the use of synonyms was known to Old English writers. The view that Alfred personally translated Bede's work seems to be in disfavor at the present time, although the challenge in Hart's second sentence has been met—had been met, in fact, even before his article was published.[3] If any portion of his discussion invites refutation, it is the assumption that the synonyms of the Old English Bede must be rhetorical in nature, that they reflect a conscious and deliberate application, on the part of the translator, of a rhetorical principle. The purpose of this article is to point out certain resemblances between the synonyms of the Bede and the double and triple glosses found in manuscripts of the ninth and tenth centuries.

Multiple translations of the Latin appear frequently in the interlinear glosses to the *Vespasian Psalter*, the *Rushworth Gospels*, and the *Lindisfarne Gospels*. Some of these synonymous groups result from an effort to adapt the translation to two different dialects. Others appear to spring from an attempt on the part of the glossator to clarify the meaning by offering as many translations of the Latin as he can call to mind. For example, a free and general rendering may be combined with one which is more specific and literal, or a Latinate translation may be clarified by a purely native synonym or explanation. It would appear that considerations of clarity and accuracy, rather than any striving after rhetorical elegance, motivated the work of the glossators.[4]

[1] *An English Miscellany, Presented to Dr. Furnivall* (Oxford. 1901), pp. 150–154. The synonymous pairs had previously been noted by August Schmidt, who included a list of examples in his dissertation, *Untersuchungen über König Ælfreds Bedaübersetzung* (Berlin, 1889), pp. 37–39.

[2] *Op. cit.*, p. 151.

[3] Henry Sweet. *King Alfred's West-Saxon Version of Gregory's Pastoral Care*, Part II, EETS, OS, L (London. 1872), xli; Gustav Wack, *Über das Verhältnis von König Aelfreds Übersetzung der Cura Pastoralis zum Original* (Greifswald, 1889), pp. 18–21; Albert Dewitz, *Untersuchungen über Alfreds des Grossen westsächsische Übersetzung der Cura Pastoralis Gregors* (Bunzlau, 1889), pp. 34–36.

[4] It is true that accuracy and clarity are essential qualities of *rhetoric* in the best sense, but Hart's discussion indicates that he used *rhetoric* in the popular sense of artifice and rhetorical ornament.

Reprinted by permission from *Journal of English and Germanic Philology*, 46 (1947), 168-76.

[73]

The *Vespasian Psalter* is a good example of a text with glosses in two dialects. Originally glossed throughout by a ninth-century Mercian, it later passed into the hands of scribes who added second glosses here and there during the tenth or eleventh century.[5] These second glosses, usually preceded by *uel* or the abbreviation *l*, are clearly in the West Saxon dialect. In Psalm 142, verse 3,[6] *obscuris* is glossed *degulnissum* in the ninth-century hand, *uel þystrum* in a much later hand. If the palaeographical difference were absent, one might still guess the origin of this doublet. The Mercian root *degul*- corresponds to West Saxon *diegel,' digel, dygel*, while the suffix -*nis*- (very rarely -*nes*- in Mercian) is almost always -*nes*- in West Saxon. The second gloss, *þystrum* (Mc. ðeostrum, aðiostrade), is West Saxon in its phonology. In Psalm 2, verse 11, *tremore* has the Mercian *cwaecunge*, with typical smoothed vowel, plus the West Saxon *byfunge*. The verb *dormierunt* 75, 6 is glossed by *hneapedon*, showing the Mercian velar-umlaut of *a* to *ea*, and by the later *uel slypton*. with West Saxon unstable *y*. *Adheserunt* 101, 6 is glossed *ætfeiun*, with Mercian *è* for West Germanic *ā;* in addition, it has the later gloss *ætclofodon*, resembling West Saxon, in which most Weak II preterites were formed in -*od*-, rather than Mercian, in which -*ad*- was the usual suffix.

Other doublets contain one gloss which may be identified dialectally, coupled with a form which might belong to either dialect. *Immolabo* 26, 6 is glossed by *ageldu* (WS. usually *agylde*) and later *offrige*. In the same verse, *iubilationis* is glossed *wynsumnisse* (WS. -*nesse*) and *lofes*. *Constringe* 31, 9 is glossed *geteh* (WS., Kentish *geteoh*) *uel gewriþ*. *Magna* 37, 17 is glossed by *ða miclan* of indeterminate dialect and by West Saxon *fela* (Mc., Kent. *feola*). *Usquequaque* 37, 9 has *a hu lenge swiður uel agehwær;* the former gloss is phonologically uncertain, although the suffix -*ur* is typical of early Mercian, but the latter gloss (Mc., Kent. -*hwer*) is clearly West Saxon. *Uerum* 31, 6 was first rendered *hweðre*, to which a later hand has added *þeah* (Mc. ðæh).

Many of the synonymous pairs of the Psalter contain only general Old English forms which cannot be assigned to any dialect by phonological criteria. The handwritings, however, provide conclusive evidence. Of this sort are *getelde uel on eardungstowe* for *tabernaculo* 26, 6; *lust uel gewilnung* for *desiderium* 37, 10; and a number of other pairs.

Synonymous pairs with dialectal differentiation are of frequent occurrence in the Old English translation of Bede. Each of the following examples contains a Mercian form joined by the abbreviation *z*, for *et* or *ond*, with a West Saxon synonym:[7]

70, 11–12. is to *forbeorenne z* to *forlætenne* (debet abstinere 51, 3)
72, 25. hafa ðu . . . *sprece z geþeahte* (debet agere 53, 3)

---

[5] Henry Sweet, *Oldest English Texts*, EETS, OS, LXXXIII (London, 1885), 188, 191, 220, 227, 238, 239, 293, 319, 331, 360, 361, 392. In the British Museum MS. *Cotton Vespasian A. I* or in MLAA Rotograph No. 332, these second glosses appear on fols. 12ʳ, 13ᵛ, 31ʳ, 35ʳ, 40ᵛ, 41ʳ, 41ᵛ, 72ᵛ, 88ʳ, 95ᵛ, 96ʳ, 116ʳ, 116ᵛ, and 135ʳ.

[6] For convenience of reference, I use Sweet's verse numbering although it is inaccurate and was adopted by Sweet only to facilitate comparison with Stevenson's edition.

[7] Numbers at the left refer to page and line in Thomas Miller. *The Old English Version of Bede's Ecclesiastical History of the English People*, Part I, EETS, OS, Vols. XCV, XCVI (London. 1890). Latin equivalents in parentheses, with their page and line references, are from C. Plummer. *Venerabilis Baedae Historiam Ecclesiasticam Gentis Anglorum*. etc., Vol. I (Oxford, 1896). I have not attempted to indicate which examples are borrowed from Hart or from Schmidt and which are of my own collecting.

134, 7. *gesprec*	ː *geþeaht* (consilio 111, 14)
158, 29. se cyning him *gef*	ː *sealde* (donabantur munere regio 132, 20–21)
184, 34. *song* . . .	ː *rædde* (dicebat 150, 1)
288, 29 *ofgefen*	ː *forlæten* (destituta 222, 33)
368, 31. *cegde*	ː *laðode* (uocabat 273, 16–17)
422, 5–6. *salde* him	ː *forgeaf* (donauit . . . ei 303, 7)
428, 8. of *ðere* niolnesse	ː of *ðære* witestowe (de abysso 306, 23)
430, 29. þu *sceawadest*	ː *gesawa* (uidisti 308, 9)

It is true, of course, that almost any Anglian form may be matched by sporadic forms in Saxon texts. Velar-umlaut of *e* before a liquid occurs in Saxon Patois. Unbroken *a* before *l* plus consonant, *o* for *a* before nasal, and *-ad-* for *-od-* in Weak II preterites are all occasionally found in early West Saxon. Monophthongization of *ea* to *e* occurs in late West Saxon. Nevertheless, the normal forms in strict West Saxon would be *forberanne*, *spræce*, *gespræc*, *geaf*, *sang*, *ofgiefen* (or *ofgifen* or *ofgyfen*), *ciegde* (*cigde*, *cygde*), *sealde*, *þære*, and *sceawodest*. Similarly, the regular, though not universal, spellings in Mercian would be *forletenne*, *geðæhte*, *geðæht*, *salde*, **redde*, *forleten*, **leaðade*, *forgef*, *ðere*, and *gesege*. Two of the forms do not occur in the Mercian texts, but the normal phonological developments are those indicated.

The pairs listed below contain a West Saxon form followed by a Mercian synonym:

32, 6. *bæd* hine	ː *halsade* (obsecrans 16. 6)
34, 18. *gesawen*	ː *gemildsad* (respectus 18, 15)
168, 7. *sealdon*	ː *gefon* (donauerunt 139, 26–27)
236, 9. *feaht*	ː *wonn* (pugnaturis ductor exstiterat 178, 9)
312, 30. *fæstnodon*	ː *underwreoton* (subscribimus 240, 25)
370, 22. *geara*	ː *longe* (iamdudum 274, 10)
422. 24. hioscipes *fæder*	ː *higina aldor* (pater familias 304, 1)
424, 31–32. þæs *byrnendan* fyres	ː ðæs unadwæscedan *leges* (flammarum inextinguibilium 305, 10–11)
426, 21. *geseah* ic	ː *sceawode* (cerno 305, 33)
432, 25–26. *gesawe*	ː *sceawadest* (cernis 309, 6)

The typical Mercian forms would be *bed*, *gesegen*, *saldun* (or *-on*), **fæht*, *festnadun* (or *-on*), *gera*, *feder*, *bernendan*, *gesæh*, and *gesege*. The West Saxon forms corresponding to those in the second column would be *halsode*, *gemiltsod*, *geafon*, *wann*, *underwriton*, *lange*, *ealdor*, *lieges* (*liges*, *lyges*), *sceawode*, and *sceawodest*. The *-on* of *gefon* and the *-or* of *aldor* may be tenth-century Mercian; in the eighth- and ninth-century texts, these suffixes are usually *-un* and *-ur*.

In the group below, a Mercian form is followed by a synonym which may be either West Saxon or Mercian:

64, 18. to *edneowunge*	ː to *bote* (reparandis 48, 25)
74. 1. *gerehte*	ː *gebette* beon scylen (corrigantur 53, 4)
76. 25. to *gebeorenne*	ː to *gefremmenne* (offerenda 55, 2)
78, 10. we *weotan*	ː *leorniað* (nouimus 55. 22)
212, 14. *geficoto*	ː *gewinn* (certamina 165, 2–3)
368, 30. *moningum*	ː *larum* admonitionibus 273. 16)
374. 29. *onwalhne*	ː *gesundne* (integrum 276. 18)
412. 21. *bodade*	ː *lærde* (praedicabat 298. 21)
418. 5. *gesegon*	ː *beheoldon* (intuentibus 301, 1)
420. 23–24. þet is . . . *geceged*	ː *nemned* (uocatur 302, 25)
426, 15–16. wæron *fallende*	ː *gewitende* (decidentes 305, 29)

The West Saxon forms of the words in the first column would be *edniwunge,* *gereahte* (later *gerihte*), *geberanne, witon, gefiitu, manungum, onwealhne,* *bodode, gesawon, gecigeð* or *gecieged,* and *feallende.*

In the following group, a form of indeterminate dialect is followed by a Mercian form

38, 2. ða *oncneow*	ꞇ *þa ongæt* (persensit 20, 3)
40, 25–26. *geworht*	ꞇ *getimbrad* (extructa 21, 29)
56, 2. ða ongunnon heo *forhtigan*	ꞇ *ondredan* him (perculsi timore 42, 22)
70, 6. *oncneowon*	ꞇ *ongeton* (didicimus 50, 32)
94, 6. *heold* he	ꞇ *rehte* (rexit 79, 1)
168, 7–8. *eardungstowe*	ꞇ *biscopseðl* (sedem episcopalem 139, 28–29)
182, 2. *astod*	ꞇ *awunade* (remansit 147, 22)
390, 14. he scolde . . . *hælan*	ꞇ *lecnian* (sanandae . . . curam adhibere 284, 23–24)
400, 30. *tobrocen* wæs	ꞇ *tolesed* (solueretur 290, 20)
422, 26–27. *gehrinen*	ꞇ *gestonden* (tactus 304, 3)
438, 29. *heowe*	ꞇ *ondwliotan* (uultu 312, 9)

The West Saxon forms corresponding to those in the second column would be *ongeat, getimbrod, ondrædan, reahte* (or *rihte*), *ongeaton, bisceopsetl,* *awunode, læcnian, tolysed* or *toliesed, gestanden,* and *andwlitan* or *ondwlitan.* The preterite singular *ongæt* is late Mercian with the same substitution of *æ* for *e* which we find in Farman's glosses and in the Worcester version of the *Anglo-Saxon Chronicle.*

Synonymous pairs in which a West Saxon word is followed by a form of indeterminate dialect have no great significance in a text which is predominantly West Saxon, but a few specimens will help us complete our comparison of the Bede with the *Vespasian Psalter:*

36, 32. *tealde*	ꞇ *wende* (autumans 19, 32–33)
44, 13. *hyrnysse*	ꞇ *underþeodnysse* (subiectionem 26, 6)
88, 26–27. to *geþeahtunge*	ꞇ to *frignesse* (ad consulta 62, 3–4)
234, 30. wuton we þam *syllan*	ꞇ *bringan* (offeramus ei 177, 23)
352, 24–25. *gesyhst*	ꞇ *sceawast* (cernis 264, 20)
416, 8. ðæt *fyht*	ꞇ *þæt gewinn* (bello 300, 3)

The Mercian forms would be *getalde, gehernisse, geðæht, sellan, gesist,* and *gefeht.*

In many pairs a West Saxon form follows an indeterminate form:

54, 27. *heold*	ꞇ *reahte* (rexit 42, 14)
70, 7. *growan*	ne *weaxan* (succrescere 50, 33)
416, 4. *gewinnes*	ꞇ *gefeohtes* (belli 299, 32)
418, 17–18. *wuldre*	ꞇ *wyrðmyndum* (gloria 301, 13)

The Mercian forms would be *rehte* or *ræhte, wæxan, gefehtes,* and *weorð-* *myndum.*

The examples given in these six lists by no means exhaust the doublets of the Bede translation which show dialectal differences. They have been selected with a view to illustrating as many dialect features as possible and, at the same time, avoiding controversial forms, which would necessitate complicated explanations without throwing much additional light on the problem. The similarity of these pairs to the double glosses of the Psalter should be obvious. A translator, especially an inexpert one, might well lean upon an earlier interlinear gloss, changing *l* to ꞇ and altering some words to fit his own dialect while leaving others very much as he found them.

Similar pairs of synonyms are found in those parts of the *Rushworth Gospels*[8] which Farman copied from the *Lindisfarne Gospels*, but with this difference: whereas the Saxon scribe who second-glossed the *Vespasian Psalter* left the original Mercian glosses untouched,[9] Farman usually transliterated the Northumbrian glosses and then added his synonyms. As a consequence, the dialectal differences tend to fade out in Farman's version, and it is only by comparison with the original that we can see how some of his doublets arose. In Mark 1, 7, for example, *Lindisfarne* has *undoa* for *soluere*, which Farman alters to *undon* before adding *ł loesan*. In Mark 1, 17 he has changed *gesie* (*fieri*) to *gebeoþan ł geseon*. In Mark 1, 40, *Lindisfarne* has *mið cnew beging* for *genu flexo*, while *Rushworth* has *mid cneu begende ł beginge* for *genu flexu*. In Mark 1, 44, *Lindisfarne* has *ðu coeðe* (*dixeris*), Farman *sæcge ł cwepe*. When the *Lindisfarne Gospels* contain a synonymous pair of their own, Farman may adopt one word and make a substitution for the other, as in Mark 1, 45, Li. *ingeonga ł incuma*, Ru. *ingangan ł ineode* (*introire*). Or he may accept both Northumbrian words, merely altering the spellings: Mark 2, 2, Li. *ne maehte foa ł nioma*, Ru. *ne maehte foan ł nioman* (non caperet); Mark 2, 7, Li. *forgeafa ł forleta*, Ru. *forgeofan ł forletan* (*dimittere*).

It seems quite probable that a translator working with a gloss would proceed after Farman's manner, at least a part of the time. In this way, the translator or translators of the Old English Bede may have obliterated many of the dialectal features of some earlier gloss.

We cannot detect such alterations since the gloss itself is no longer in existence, but we can see something very similar by comparing the readings of the various manuscripts of Bede's history.[10] For example, the first list of synonymous pairs given above contains eight Mercian forms from MS. *Tanner 10* of the Bodleian Library, the earliest manuscript of the Old English version: *forbeorenne*, *sprece*, *song*, *ofgefen*, *cegde*, *salde*, *ðere*, *sceawadest*. Seven of the pairs appear in MS. *41* of Corpus Christi College, Cambridge, a later independent copy of the archetype of *Tanner 10*. The spellings are altered, however, to conform to the dialect of a West Saxon scribe: *forberenne*, *tospræce*, *sang*, *ofgyfen*, *gecigde*, *þære*, *sceawodest*. The eighth Mercian form, *salde*, occurs in a clause which the late manuscript omits. Two of the Mercian forms, *gesprec* and *gef*, occur in MS. 279 of Corpus Christi College, Oxford. In both cases the doublets are preserved in MS. *Kk. 3. 18* of the Cambridge University Library, a direct copy of the preceding, but in both cases the Mercian forms have been Saxonized: *gespræce*, *geaf*.

Not all the doublets or synonymous pairs in the glosses are of dialectal origin. Skeat suggested that Aldred, who glossed the *Lindisfarne Gospels*, might have been revising an older gloss in the first three Gospels but that his work in John was independent.[11] Without either accepting or rejecting Skeat's interpretation of Aldred's note, we shall take most of our examples

[8] W. W. Skeat, *The Holy Gospels in Anglo-Saxon, Northumbrian, and Old Mercian Versions* (Cambridge, 1871–1887), Part II.

[9] This statement is apparently true. There are many erasures and minor alterations in the Mercian gloss, but most of them appear to be contemporary.

[10] See Miller, *op. cit.*, Part II, EETS, OS, Vols. cx–cxi (London, 1898); or Jacob Schipper, *König Alfreds Übersetzung von Bedas Kirchengeschichte*, Bibliothek der angelsächsischen Prosa, IV (Leipzig, 1897–1899).

[11] Skeat, *op. cit.*, IV, ix and 188.

from John. Aldred's frequent doublets in this Gospel, in which his independence has never been questioned, indicate either that he was groping for the right word or that he wished to supply as many possible translations of crucial words as he could. A few examples will serve: 4, 10, *uæter cuic ł lifwelle uæter (aquam uiuam)*; 4, 12, *ahne ł hueðer (numquid)*; 5, 1, *doeg halig ł symbeldoeg (dies festus)*; 5, 9, *awarð ł geuorden uæs (factus est)*; 6, 16, *ofstigon ł foerdon (descenderunt)*; 6, 22, *floege ł lyttel scipp (nauicula)*; 7, 4, *in degle ł in deigelnise (in occulto)*; 7, 44, *uældon ł uilnadon (uolebant)*.

That Aldred was truly racking his brains for synonyms is evidenced by a number of his glosses in John. Not satisfied with a pair, he frequently found three or four renderings of one Latin word. In 3, 7, *oportet* is glossed *geriseð ł behofað ł gedæfneð*. Other examples are: 11, 2, *geðuog ł smiride ł leðrede (unxit)*; 16, 33 *getreuað ł gelefeð ł getryccað (confidete)*; 18, 4, *feoll ł cuom ł forðeode (processit)*; 18, 28, *ðæs giroefa halle ł motern ł sprecern (praetorium)*. In Matthew 1, 18, *desponsata* has four glosses: *biwoedded ł beboden ł befeastnad ł betaht*. Aldred frequently added *ł* after a gloss as though he were searching for further equivalents: for example, John 4, 44, *uorðscip ł aare ł (honorem)*; 18, 43, *gecidon ł getugon ł (litigabant)*; 9, 22, *geondetate ł (confiteretur)*; 14, 8, *genog is ł (sufficit)*; 14, 22, *ðu ædeauas ł ðu eauande arð ł (manifestaturus es)*.

Although he was evidently striving for variant renderings for their own sake, one can see special reasons for some of the synonyms. When the Latin word was well known or when it was a proper name without a native equivalent, he would sometimes use it, perhaps in abbreviated form or perhaps with an English termination, as his gloss. Then he would often add the closest approach to a native equivalent or an explanation in English. *Portam* in Matthew 7, 13 is rendered *port ł dure ł gæt*. Examples from John are: 11, 48, *romane ł romuaro (romani)*; 19, 2, *of ðornum ða corona ł ðæt sigbeg of ðornum (coronam de spinis)*; 1, 43, *of ðær byrig ł of beðsaida (a bethsaida)*; 1, 28, *iordanen ðone stream (iordanen)*; 19, 39, *se ðegn nicodemus (nicodemus)*; 21, 2, *sunu zabedei .i. iacob ł iohannes (filii zebedaei)*. In one instance, a Latin word of the gloss is not taken directly from the Latin text: John 19, 13, *lapide stratus . . . ł . . . mið stane gebræded (lithostrotus)*.

Sometimes in the glosses, a general term is supplemented by one which is more specific, or a figure is linked with a literal translation. In Matthew 5, 27, *non moechaberis* has the general rendering *ne gesynnge ðu* and the specific *ne serð ðu oðres mones wif*. Both meanings of *piscinam* are glossed in John 5, 4: first the general and secondary *uoel*, then the specific and primary *fiscpol*. *Panem* in John 6, 31 is rendered *hlaf ł fostrað*. *Cohors* in John 18, 12 has the gloss *compuearod roemisce* with the added explanation, *fif hund cempo*. In John 1, 1, the figurative *Uerbum* is glossed *uord* with the literal explanation, *þæt is godes sunu*. *Magis* Matthew 2, 16 is glossed by both *dryum* and *tungulcræftgum*.

Most of the peculiarities of the glosses also appear in the translation, often with very awkward results.

Triplets similar to those used by Aldred occur in the translation of Bede. They are rather rare, but the following examples are hard to account for except on the assumption that the translation was based upon an interlinear gloss:

46, 21. *ehtan ł slogan ł on wæll fyldon (insequitur 28, 5–6)*
102, 31. *heora sacerdas ł biscopas ł munecas (sacerdotes eorum 84, 5)*

104, 3–4. heo us mid heora *wiðerwordum onbenum* : *wyrgnessum* ehtað (aduersis nos *inprecati-*
    onibus perse quuntur 84, 21–22)
216, 27, *grim* : *cald* : *fyrstig* : mid hiise gebunden (*acerrimum* et glacie constrictum 167, 19–20)
422, 22–23. þara sume we her hredlice *areccan* : *aasecgan* : *aawritan* willað (e quibus hic
    aliqua breuiter *perstringenda esse* putaui 303, 28–29)

Miller translates the second example[12] "they assail us with their adverse
imprecations and curses," interpreting *wiðerwordum* as an adjective, *wiðer-*
weardum "against, adverse," and as the Old English equivalent of *aduersis*.
It seems probable that the scribe read and translated *aduersis nos* rather
than *aduersis inprecationibus* and that he felt *ehtað us* to be a satisfactory
rendering of *persequuntur aduersis nos*. Moreover, the prefix *on-* (*ond-*)
of *onbenum* has the meaning "adverse, against, opposed to." If *wiðer-*
wordum is an adjective, it must be paired with a synonymous prefix—a
type of doublet hard to duplicate either in the glosses or in the Bede translation.

The foreign-plus-native type of doublet used by the glossators also
appears in the Bede, as a few examples will illustrate:

48, 3. *consul* : *cyning* on Rome (consulatum 28, 21)
48, 13–14. *Constantinopolim Creca ealdorburh* (Constantinopolim 29, 7)
346, 6–7. *Genesis* þæt is *seo æreste Moyses booc* (Genesis 261, 1)
422, 1–2. *þære halgan fæmnan* : *martires Sče Cecilian* (sanctae martyris Ceciliae 303, 3)
442, 27–28. *Satanan þone ealdan feond moncynnes* (Satanan 314, 15)

As in Aldred's glosses, there are instances in which the foreign member of
the doublet is not merely a repetition of the original word. For example,
English *heafde beslegen* and the loan-word *gemartyrad* (40, 11–12) render
decollatus (21, 15). *Scriptura sancta* (360, 1) is translated by *þæt halige ge-*
writ and by *se canan* (486, 1–2). Some of the explanatory amplifications in
the translation were undoubtedly suggested by double glosses or marginal
notes; for example, *paralysis langore depressam* (278, 13) is explained *mid*
þa aðle geslægene beon, þe Crecas nemnað paralysis : *we cweðað lyftadl* (378,
23–24).

The general-specific and literal-figurative combinations are fairly frequent in the Bede translation. Representative examples follow:

34, 18. *gesawen* : *gemildsad* (respectus 18. 15)[13]
40, 5–6 *beah* : *sige eces lifes* (*coronam* uitæ 21, 10–11)
46, 23. *from wulfum* : *wildeorum* (a *feris* 28. 7)
68, 24. *ðis mot beon swa* : *eallum gemetum þat is alyfed* (hoc fieri modis omnibus licet 50, 23)
74, 25. *usse ealdres* : *þa ærestan men* (primi parentes nostri 54, 9)
78, 13–14. *hire untrymnes onweg gewat* : *heo wæs hal geworden* (ab ea . . . sua infirmitas recessit
    55, 24–25)
80, 32. *broða* : *Godes þeowa* gesomnunge (congregationi *fratrum* 57, 22)
116, 20–21. *forðferde* : *þat heofonlice rice gestah* (regnum caeleste conscendit 93, 27)
168, 7–8. *eardungstowe* : *biscopseðl* (sedem episcopalem 139, 28–29)
286, 27. *deaðe* : *forðfore* (morte 221, 25)
338, 8–9. *þyssum mynstre* þæt is *æt Streonesheale* (huic monasterio 256, 12)
404, 7–8. *mid ða liflestan yðe* þæt is *mid fulwihte bæðe* (uitale . . . unda 291, 28)
412, 21. *halo word* : *godcundre lare* (uerbum salutis 298, 20–21)
424, 11. : he þer *Godes þiohade* : *scare* onfeng (acceptaque *tonsura* 304, 22)

The foregoing comparisons warrant certain conclusions. First, the arche-

---

[12] *Op. cit.,* 1, 105.
[13] The Latin reads "subito diuina gratia respectus." the Old English "þa wæs he semninga
mid þam godcundan gyfe gesawen : gemildsad." What we really have here is a translation
which renders both the primary and the secondary meanings of *respectus*.

type of the Old English translation of Bede's *Ecclesiastical History* was either a gloss or an adaptation of a gloss. The maker or makers of the version which has come down to us leaned heavily upon the original, copying much of it without change, the rest with minor changes, chiefly in spelling. No other hypothesis will account for certain of the double and triple renderings of the Latin, particularly those in which members of the same pair are derived from different dialects. An independent translator might conceivably resort to clumsy and unidiomatic amplifications for the sake of clearness, but to suppose that he would supply correct variants from two different dialects is to credit him with a scientific knowledge of linguistics unknown in tenth-century England. A man with an old gloss before him would be very apt to copy such variants, and if he were careless or in a hurry or afflicted with excessive reverence for his exemplar, he would often neglect to transliterate into his own dialect. There is corroborative evidence for this hypothesis in the fact that several partial glosses of Bede manuscripts are still in existence, an indication that these works were rather frequently glossed in Old English times.[14]

Second, the Bede gloss used in the translation must have contained second glosses similar to those of the *Vespasian Psalter*. A number of these were copied without alteration in the Old English Bede. One may assume either that the original glossator was a Mercian and the later scribe a West Saxon or that a West Saxon original received second glosses in Mercian. Of the two assumptions, the former seems more probable. The abundance of Anglian glosses and glossaries based on glosses, ranging in date from the *Corpus Glossary* of the eighth century to the *Rushworth Gospels* of the late tenth, coupled with the relative scarcity of West Saxon glosses, suggests that interest in such matters developed late in Wessex. When the West Saxons finally began to gloss manuscripts, their glosses were apt to be derivative and based on Anglian originals.[15]

Miller observed that the existing manuscripts of Bede's history, while predominantly West Saxon in dialect, contain a strong Mercian element, which is most striking in the oldest of the group, Bodleian MS. *Tanner 10*.[16] He noted also a decided pro-Mercian bias in the translator's accounts of the early conflicts within the Church. These features he explained by supposing that the archetype of all the existing manuscripts was produced in Mercian territory.[17] Obviously there is no real conflict between Miller's views and the one presented here. We may account for the Mercian element merely by localizing the original gloss, rather than the later translation, in Mercia. That the translation was a West Saxon product is suggested by the fact that most of the actual Old English translations, as distinguished from glosses, were produced by West Saxons or under West Saxon direction.

[14] Glosses to parts of two MSS. of the *Hist. Eccl.* and to six MSS. of the *Vita Sancti Cuthberti* are given by H. D. Meritt, *Old English Glosses (A Collection)*, MLAA, General Series, XVI (New York, 1945), 6–21. Other Bede glosses appear in Sweet's *OET*, pp. 180–182, and in A. S. Napier, *Old English Glosses* (Oxford, 1900), pp. 198–200.

[15] Take, for example, the Psalters. Uno Lindelöf, *Die Handschrift Junius 27* (Helsingfors, 1901), pp. 43–44, 47.

[16] Miller, I, xiii–xv, liv. In this connection, I should like to point out that a large proportion of the examples cited in this article are from the Tanner MS., which is generally recognized as most faithful of all existing MSS. to the common archetype. Anyone who wishes, however, may, by checking my examples in Miller or Schipper, see that all of the MSS. contain at least a few of the dialectally differentiated pairs—an indication that such pairs derive from the archetype rather than from the scribes of the existing MSS.

[17] Miller, I, lviii–lix.

Third, while this study offers nothing conclusive on the subject of Alfredian authorship, it may reopen the question to further discussion. If the Mercian original underlying the Old English Bede was a gloss, and if the translation made from it was the work of a West Saxon, why may not that West Saxon have been Alfred himself? Of Alfred's works, the one which most resembles the Bede in this matter of synonymous pairs is his translation of the *Cura Pastoralis*. Both translations are characterized, moreover, by a literalness and a rather timid dependence upon the Latin text, very unlike the freedom of treatment found in the Boethius and the Orosius. The older view was that the first two were early works, written while Alfred was still a novice and lacked confidence in his own capacities as a translator. What expedient could be more natural for an inexperienced scholar than that of using earlier glosses to guide him in his work?

Fourth, the rhetorical importance of the synonymous pairs has probably been exaggerated. They are to be regarded, not as a species of ornamentation introduced by an independent translator, but as a rhetorical accident growing out of the manner in which the translation was made.

SHERMAN M. KUHN

Oklahoma A. & M. College

A DAMAGED PASSAGE IN THE *EXETER BOOK*

A GOOD example of what can be done toward recovering the text of damaged manuscripts is furnished by lines 22–25a of *Christ I*, on folio 8ʳ of the *Exeter Book*. Direct examination of the manuscript, aided to some extent by the use of ultra-violet light, made possible the following transcription:[1]

> huru we for þearfe   þas w(or)d spreca∂
> . . . . . gia (∂)   þone þe mon gescop
> þæt he ne hete . . . (ce)ose . . . . can
> c(e)arfulra þing

Each dot, in this system of transcription, represents space for one letter; and the combination of parentheses with underscoring indicates that the letter so marked is uncertain but can be inferred from the neighboring letters. Ultra-violet photography enabled G. P. Krapp and E. V. K. Dobbie to verify most of the doubtful letters and to recover a few more:[2]

> huru we for þearfe   þas word spreca∂
> 7 m . . . gia∂   þone þe mon gescop
> þæt he ne .ete . . . ceose weor∂an
> cearfulra þing

Three of the new readings require comment. In 24b, *weor∂an* seems hard to reconcile with the *c* recorded by earlier transcribers, but the apparent *c* can be explained as a fragment of the loop of ∂, the rest of the letter being invisible except in the ultra-violet print. The *c* of *ceose*, which Chambers and Flower regarded as purely inferential, is dim in their facsimile, and its outline differs from that of a normal *c*. To the present writer, it looks more like *t*. The lower strokes of *c* and *t* are indistinguishable in the script of the *Exeter Book*, but the upper stroke, as far as it can be seen at all, suggests the cap stroke of a *t*. It seems possible, therefore, that the *c* which Krapp and Dobbie read may be a *t* with the left side of the cap stroke obscured. The first two letters of *.ete* present further difficulties. Like all preceding editors, Chambers and Flower read *hete*. Krapp and Dobbie remark that "the *h* of *hete* is by no means certain and looks rather like a *b*." Claes Schaar, the most recent investigator, suggests a third possibility. He believes that Krapp and Dobbie "may have been mis-

[1] R. W. Chambers, Max Förster, and Robin Flower, *The Exeter Book of Old English Poetry* (London, 1933), p. 70.
[2] *The Exeter Book* New York, 1936), pp. 3, 247.

Reprinted by permission from *Journal of English and Germanic Philology*, 50 (1951), 491-93.

led by a slight crease in the parchment" and argues for *læte*, rather than *bete*, as the true manuscript reading.[3]

Schaar's reading is by no means impossible. The disputed letters are visible in the Chambers facsimile; they have not been obscured by stains or knife cuts in the manuscript, as so many of the words on folio 8ʳ have been. We can see a tall upright stroke, which may belong to a normal *h*, a normal *b*, or an awkward *l*. Projecting from the base of the upright and extending to the right, is a mark which does not belong to an *h*, cannot be the curl of a normal *l*, and seems too firm and definite to be an accidental mark or crease in the parchment. Another mark appears above and to the right of the first; its position, direction, and curvature indicate that it is part of *b* rather than *h*. If extended, these two marks would form the bow of a normal *b*. Three light marks proceed from the upper fragment of the bow and extend to the right. If these are disregarded as accidental, the manuscript reading is *be*. If only the uppermost, the faintest and least regular of the three, is ignored, the lower two combine with the upper bow fragment and the following *e* to form *æ*—a crude *æ* but recognizable. The letters in question look as though original *be* had been roughly altered to *læ* by partial erasure of the bow of *b* and addition of the connecting strokes. Whether the alteration is to be regarded as a hasty correction or as stupid tampering by a later hand, depends upon how one deals with 24b.

The latest reconstruction preserving *hete* is that of Ferdinand Holthausen: *þæt he ne* [*his cwealm*] *hete* [*ge*] *ceose* [*wre*] *can*.[4] This is, in effect, an admission that the line is hopeless and must be rewritten. Schaar emends less thoroughly, but he is forced to substitute *forlore* for *ceose* in order to provide *læte* with sense and alliteration: *þæt he ne læte to forlore weorðan.*

The following reconstruction is rather plausible if *bete* and *teose* are accepted as manuscript readings: *þæt he ne bete*[*o to*] *teose weorðan.* The form *beteo* is the present optative of *beteon*, in its legal, or quasi-legal, sense, "to assign, bestow, grant, bequeath." Its object, *cearfulra þing*, is an undesired gift. This "*thing* of the sorrowful ones" may be either a court (a judicial assembly, a judgment), before which the sorrowful ones are arraigned, or a sentence (a legal decree, a judgment) passed upon the sorrowful ones. Elsewhere in Old English, *beteon* appears only occasionally in the legal sense, and is used of the

---

[3] *Critical Studies in the Cynewulf Group* (Lund, 1949), pp. 71–72.
[4] "Zum ae. Crist I," *Beiblatt zur Anglia*, LIV (1943), 31–32.

giving of an estate, an office, a favor. The lines in *Christ I* would seem to afford the sole example of an unfavorable, perhaps ironical, use. *Teose* is a form of *teosu* (or *teso* or *tæso*), "injury, damage, ruin." The inflection is unusual, for we should expect an oblique case to be *teosu* or *teoso*. Leveling with other feminine nouns, due possibly to the late (tenth- or eleventh-century) scribe of the *Exeter Book*, would account for the final *e*. If *beteo* and *teose* are correct, and if the syntax of the line is conventional, the two remaining letters should be *to*, in the sense "as a, for a."

The hiatus in line 23 can be filled without too much difficulty. Holthausen would read *ond myndgiað*, "and we remind" or "and we exhort"; while Krapp and Dobbie suggest *ond monegiað*, "and we admonish" or "and we exhort."[5] Both reconstructions satisfy linguistic and metrical requirements, but there may be stylistic reasons for preferring *ond monegiað*. The poet represents mankind as prisoners addressing God, their judge. As we have seen, two legal terms appropriate to the situation occur in lines 24–25. *Monian* (or *manian*) also has a legal sense at times, "to make a claim upon" or "to present a claim to" someone. It is rather likely that the poet would prefer this word for its legal overtones.

As finally reconstructed, lines 22–25a would read:

> Huru, we for þearfe,   þas word sprecað,
> 7 m[one]giað   þone þe mon gescop,
> þæt he ne bete[o,   to] teose weorðan,
> cearfulra þing

We may interpret as follows: "Truly, we for necessity (or because of distress) speak these words, and we present our claim to (or we petition) him who created man, that he assign (or bestow) not—to become as ruin (to us)—a judgment (a court? a sentence?) of the sorrowful ones." Or, for those who dislike the parenthetic style, this would be better:

> Truly, for our woes,   these words we speak
> and to the molder of man   we make our petition,
> that he bestow not   destruction upon us,
> a judgment of the sorrowing.

SHERMAN M. KUHN

University of Michigan

⁵ Earlier guesses are disregarded here, because the Chambers facsimile demonstrated their impossibility.

ON THE SYLLABIC PHONEMES OF OLD ENGLISH

SHERMAN M. KUHN

University of Michigan

1. The phonemic system of Old English has become a matter of increasing interest to linguists in recent years. Twenty years ago, structural linguists seldom concerned themselves with the phonemes of a 'dead' language, while traditional linguists and philologists generally regarded phonemes as something exotic, something outside the purview of normal language activities and studies. Since 1939, however, we have seen a fair number of publications dealing with the Old English phonemic system or portions of it, written either from a structural viewpoint or in a manner which indicates an awareness of the structural problems of the language.[1]

Very few of these studies deal with more than a small segment of the Old English phonemic system; most of them attack some portion of something which is described as the 'traditional interpretation' or the 'traditional view'. To my knowledge, no one has yet given us an account of all the Old English phonemes from the viewpoint of the traditional linguists. There are several reasons for this

[1] Marjorie Daunt, Old English sound changes reconsidered in relation to scribal tradition and practice, *Transactions of the Philological Society 1939* 108–37 (1940); J. W. Watson, Northumbrian Old English *ēo* and *ēa*, *Lg.* 22.19–26 (1946); id., Non-initial *k* in the North of England, *Lg.* 23.43–9 (1947); Herbert Penzl, The phonemic split of Germanic *k* in Old English, *Lg.* 23.34–42 (1947); W. F. Twaddell, The prehistoric Germanic short syllabics, *Lg.* 24.139–51 (1948); Norman E. Eliason, Old English vowel lengthening and vowel shortening before consonant groups, *Studies in philology* 45.1–20 (1948); A. S. C. Ross, Old English *æ* ~ *a*, *English studies* 32.49–56 (1951); R. P. Stockwell and C. W. Barritt, Some Old English graphemic-phonemic correspondences—*ae*, *ea*, and *a*, *Studies in linguistics: Occasional papers*, No. 4 (Washington, D. C., 1951); Karl Brunner, The Old English vowel phonemes, *English studies* 34.247–51 (1953); Sherman M. Kuhn and Randolph Quirk, Some recent interpretations of Old English digraph spellings, *Lg.* 29.143–56 (1953); Alfred Reszkiewicz, The phonemic interpretation of Old English digraphs, *Biuletyn Polskiego Towarzystwa Językoznawczego* 12.179–87 (1953); M. L. Samuels, The study of Old English phonology, *TPS 1952* 15–47 (1953); Daunt, Some notes on Old English phonology, *TPS 1952* 48–54 (1953); C. E. Bazell, rev. of Stockwell and Barritt (1951), *Litera* 1.75–7 (1954); W. G. Moulton, The stops and spirants of early Germanic, *Lg.* 30.1–42 (1954); Stockwell and Barritt, The Old English short digraphs: Some considerations, *Lg.* 31.372–89 (1955); Kuhn and Quirk, The Old English digraphs: A reply, *Lg.* 31.390–401 (1955); Gerd Bauer, The problem of short diphthongs in Old English, *Anglia* 74.427–37 (1956); Hans Kurath, The loss of long consonants and the rise of voiced fricatives in Middle English, *Lg.* 32.435–45 (1956); The binary interpretation of English vowels: A critique, *Lg.* 33.111–22 (1957); Seymour Chatman, The *a/æ* opposition in Old English, *Word* 14.224–36 (1958); C. F. Hockett, *A course in modern linguistics* 372–9 (New York, 1958); J. A. Nist, Phonemes and distinctive features in *Beowulf*, *SIL* 13.25–33 (1958); James Sledd, Some questions of English phonology, *Lg.* 34.252–8 (1958); Stockwell, The phonology of Old English: A structural sketch, *SIL* 13.13–24 (1958); Hockett, The stressed syllabics of Old English, *Lg.* 35.575–97 (1959); Kemp Malone, Diphthong and glide, *Mélanges de linguistique et de philologie: Fernand Mossé in memoriam* 256–66 (Paris, 1959); Stockwell and Rudolph Willard, Further notes on Old English phonology, *SIL* 14.10–13 (1959); Stockwell and Barritt, Scribal practice: Some assumptions, *Lg.* 37.75–82 (1961).

silence. In the first place, there is no single 'traditional view', because traditional linguists differ concerning many details of Old English phonology; and if a scholar takes sides on any point against one of the better known grammars or handbooks, many of his fellow-traditionalists will conclude at once that his work is unsound. Many of the structuralists, on the other hand, will be inclined to view him with suspicion merely because he defends traditional views. A more important reason is probably that the traditional linguist has little to say that is new or startling. For the most part, he can only restate well known facts and interpretations in phonemic terminology.

I believe, nevertheless, that such a restatement is desirable, if only that we may have a better understanding of what is being attacked. In the sections that follow, I shall first attempt to reconstruct the Old English syllabics as they were about 700 A.D., shortly before the appearance of the first written records. I shall then show the development of this system in each of the OE dialects in which any writings survive: Mercian (Merc.), Northumbrian (Nhb.), West Saxon (WS), and Kentish (Kt.).[2] An account which is as inclusive as this must necessarily be general. Only a small part of the evidence on which it is based can be given. Many facts which concern the incidence of phonemes rather than their existence in a given dialect must be passed over briefly or omitted. Individual works and scholars can be mentioned only when they are especially pertinent to the discussion.[3]

OLD ENGLISH SYLLABICS ABOUT 700

2. The table below presents the OE phonemes at a period for which we have no written records. The phonemes must be inferred from data in later MSS and from developments in cognate languages. The system is an abstraction—as though the living language had been frozen at a particular point in time. In some ways it may be inexact; for example, it shows an independent phoneme /ȳ/, although in the year 700 the sound in question may have been further advanced in the direction of /e/ than the table suggests.

The principal texts used in this reconstruction are three early Latin-English glossaries: the *Epinal Glossary* (8th century), the *Corpus Glossary* (8th), and the *Erfurt Glossary* (early 9th).[4] The first is most conservative in its spellings and seems to be the earliest linguistically, although it may not be the earliest MS. The second represents a revision, with additions and much modernization, of the original glossary (now lost) from which *Epinal* was derived. The third is closely related to *Epinal* and very similar, but was copied by a scribe familiar with High German and shows a few un-English features. Some additional evidence will be

---

[2] Linguistic analysis normally proceeds from the individual and specific to the general. The order of the analysis itself is reversed here for clarity of presentation.

[3] For the earlier studies, see A. G. Kennedy, *A bibliography of writings on the English language from the beginning of printing to the end of 1922* (Cambridge, Mass., and New Haven, 1927). For more recent work, see the various annual bibliographies and those in recent grammars, such as K. Brunner's *Altenglische Grammatik nach ... Eduard Sievers*[2] (Halle, 1951) and A. Campbell's *Old English grammar* (Oxford, 1959).

[4] Henry Sweet, *The oldest English texts* = *EETS OS* 83.35–121 (1885); W. M. Lindsay, *The Corpus Glossary* (Cambridge, 1921).

| | FRONT VOWELS | | BACK | | UNACCENTED |
	UNROUND	ROUND	VOWELS	DIPHTHONGS	VOWELS
HIGH	/i/ [ɪ] /ī/ [iː]	/y/ [ʊ̈] /ȳ/ [üː]	/u/ [ʊ] /ū/ [uː]	/io/ [ɪɒ, ɪɛ] /īo/ [iɒː, iɛː]	[ɪ]
MID	/e/ [ɛ] /ē/ [eː]	/œ/ [ö] /œ̄/ [öː]	/o/ [ɒ] /ō/ [oː]	/eo/ [ɛɒ] /ēo/ [eɒː]	/ə/
LOW	/æ/ [æ, æɹ] /ǣ/ [æː, ɛː]	/ɔ/ [ɔ]	/a/ [ɑ, ɔ] /ā/ [ɑː]	/æa/ [æɒ, æɒ] /ǣa/ [æɒː, æɒː]	[ə]

TABLE I

found in three early Northumbrian fragments (*Caedmon's Hymn, Bede's Death Song, Leiden Riddle*) and in the proper names of the earliest MSS of Bede's history.[5] For much of our understanding of these earliest surviving texts, we are indebted to H. M. Chadwick, whose *Studies in Old English* appeared in 1899.[6] By comparing items common to two or more of the early glossaries, he was able to reconstruct most of the scribal practices[7] of the original (Archetype I), which is generally thought to have been written late in the seventh century. Although Arch. I, like the three glossaries derived from it, was basically Mercian, the dialect was much less differentiated from other dialects of Old English than it later became.

This table obviously owes something to Hockett 576 (1959). I use one symbol, /ɔ/, for a phoneme outside the scope of his article. In place of some of his other symbols, I prefer symbols somewhat closer to the graphs used for them in Old English texts: /œ/ for his /ø/; /a/ for his /ɑ/ (although there are several shapes of this grapheme in the MSS, modern printed texts have settled upon the one I use); /io, eo, æa/ for his /i, ə, a/; and /ə/ with allophones [ɪ, ə] for sounds in unaccented syllables. I prefer a macron to Hockett's dot for the phoneme of length, partly because it is used in the printed texts, partly because it makes possible the indication of stress within a vowel cluster, as /ēo/ (falling) versus /eō/ (rising). I do not treat long vowels as self clusters, or use /h, w, y/ for either length or glide, for reasons that will appear below. I treat vowel plus length as a complex phonemic unit in order to avoid certain difficulties which arise when the phonemic system must be treated diachronically;[8] thus, /ǣ/ is not merely /æ/ plus length, but a higher and more fronted sound, which became /ē/ (long open *e*) in Middle English while the /æ/ without length became a lower, more retracted sound commonly written *a* in Middle English. There was a similar qualitative difference between the members of most short–long pairs; the difference is

---

[5] Sweet, *OET* 132–47, 149–51; A. H. Smith, *Three Northumbrian poems* (London, 1933); E. V. K. Dobbie, *The Anglo-Saxon minor poems* 104, 107, 109 (New York, 1942); Charles Plummer, *Venerabilis Baedae historiam ecclesiasticam* (Oxford, 1896).

[6] *Transactions of the Cambridge Philological Society* 4.87–265.

[7] I agree with Hockett 578 (1959) that any analysis of OE phonemes must account satisfactorily for scribal practices. To be more specific, I am certain that the OE writing system (or any other alphabet system used for a language before the invention of dictionaries) was roughly phonemic; otherwise it would have been like an elaborate cipher, unintelligible to anyone who did not possess a special key. I am equally certain that the graphemes were roughly phonetic; otherwise how would anyone identify the phonemes?

[5] I agree with Kurath 114 (1957).

important historically but was not sufficient to keep the scribes from writing both sets of phonemes with one set of graphemes.

2.1. It should be clear from the table that the short syllabics of prehistoric English about 700 had advanced well beyond the prehistoric Germanic stage outlined by Twaddell (150). The allophones [æ, a], [y, u] and [ø, o] had become separate phonemes, and a new series of diphthongal phonemes had arisen. Some of the new phonemes in their turn had developed allophones which would later become significant. There were also dialectal differences, in the incidence of phonemes and the preference for certain allophones, which do not show up in the table but which will be noted in the discussion of individual phonemes.

2.2 /i/ < Gmc. /i/ in *fisc, biden* (pppl. of *bīdan*), etc.; Gmc. /e/ before nasal plus consonant in *bindan*, etc.; Gmc. /e/ before /m/ in *nimen* (pr. opt. pl. of *niman–nioman*), etc.; Lat. or Gk./i, y, e/ in *ċiriċe, ġim*, etc. There was already a tendency to diphthongize /i/ in an open syllable followed by a back vowel (velar umlaut); this would later produce an allophone [ɪu], which would fall together with /io/ and ultimately with /eo/. But the tendency cannot have been far advanced by 700; cf. Epinal *sifun-*, Corpus *sibun-*, later OE *siofon, seofon*.[9] Only after /w/ was the change noticeable enough to be reflected in spelling; e.g. Corpus *uudu-*, Epinal *uuidu* (but also *uudu*), Erfurt *uuydu*, later OE *wudu, wiodu*.

2.3. /ī/ < Gmc. /ī/ in *bīdan*, etc.; Gmc. /im, in/ in *fīf, swīþe*, etc.; Lat. /ī, ē, oe/ in *wīn, pīn*, etc. Before /h/, this sound had developed in the WS and Kt. dialects a diphthongal allophone [iuː] or [ioː], falling together with the reflex of Gmc. /iu/. Very likely, the same 'breaking' took place in the Anglian dialects (i.e. Merc. and Nhb.); but if so, the diphthong had been reduced to a monophthong by 700 ('smoothing'); cf. Ep. *bituicn*, Erf. *bituichn*, later WS *betwēoh, betwēonum*.

2.4. /e/ < Gmc. /e/ in *weġ, sweltan*, etc.; Gmc. /a/ with fronting and *i*-umlaut in *bed, hebban*, etc. Like /i/, this vowel tended to diphthongize in an open syllable followed by a back vowel, but velar umlaut had scarcely affected scribal practices by 700; cf. Ep., Corp., Erf. *bebr* (later OE *beofor*) and early Nhb. *hefen-, hefaen-*, later OE *heofon, heofen*.[10]

2.5. /ē/ < Gmc. /ē/ in *hēr* adv., etc.; Gmc. /e/ final under the accent in *sē* pron., etc.; Gmc. /iz/ in *mē*, etc. This phoneme existed in all of the dialects but was relatively infrequent in WS.[11] In the other three dialects, Gmc. /æ/ (WGmc. /ā/, WS /ǣ/) had become /ē/ in words like *dēd, lētan, wēpen* (WS *dǣd, lǣtan, wǣpen*); cf. Ep., Erf. *meeġ*, Corp. *meiġ*, etc. Similarly, Latin /ā/ had become /ē/ in *strēt* (WS *strǣt*), etc.[12] In Merc. and Nhb., /ē/ had also resulted from smoothing of Gmc. /eo/ before /c, ċ, g, ġ, h/; e.g. Merc. *flēge, þēh*, WS (and Kt.) *flēoge, þēoh*. This process was advanced but not yet complete in the basically Merc. Archetype I.[13]

[9] Chadwick 226–8, 250.

[10] Ibid.; see also Hilmer Ström, *Old English personal names in Bede's history* 117 (Lund, 1939).

[11] This must be inferred from later WS, for there are no surviving WS texts comparable in date to the glossaries and early Nhb. texts.

[12] Chadwick 206–10, 250.

[13] Ibid. 219–20, 225.

2.6. /æ/ < Gmc. /a/ in closed syllable or in open syllable followed by an originally front vowel ('fronting'), cf. WS, Nhb. *dæg, dæges, fæder, fæt, æfter,* etc.; Gmc. /a/ with secondary *i*-umlaut, cf. WS *æpeling, hærfest, gædeling* (< *apyling, *harybist, *gadyling < *apuling, *harubist, *gaduling),* etc. A raised and fronted allophone, a sound somewhere between [æ] and [ɛ] which I now indicate [æ⊥],[14] existed in Merc., in Kt., and to a limited extent in Nhb.; cf. Merc. (*Vespasian Psalter*) *deg, deges, jeder, jet, efter,* etc. The evidence of the early glossaries indicates that this allophone was of minor importance, certainly not yet a phoneme, in the Merc. of Arch. I.[15] The spelling in this MS must have been normally *ae,* occasionally *e*; cf. Ep. *uuaeter-,* Corp. *uueter,* Erf. *uaeter* (and at least twenty-nine other instances in which all three have some allograph of *æ*), but Ep., Corp., Erf. *reftras* (and eight other instances in which all three have *e*). Another source of /æ/ in Anglian was the [æ] from smoothing of /æa/, dealt with under that diphthong. Although /æ/ originated as an allophone of /a/, it was certainly an independent phoneme in Old English.[16]

2.7. /ǣ/ < Gmc. /ai/ with *i*-umlaut in *hǣlan, hǣþ,* etc. The incidence of this phoneme was greatly increased in WS by the reflex of Gmc. /æ/ in that dialect (see /ē/ above). In Merc. and Nhb., /ǣ/ also arose from the smoothing of Gmc. /au/ before /c, ċ, g, ġ, h/. This change was well advanced but not yet complete by 700, and the resulting monophthong was commonly spelled *æ* in Arch. I; cf. Ep. *-bēag,* Corp., Erf. *-bǣg* (later Merc. *bēg,* WS *bēag,* later *bēah*) and Ep. *-lēċ,* Corp. *-leec,* Erf. *-lēc* (WS *lēac*).[17] There was also a tendency for /ǣ/ (< Gmc. /ai/) to become raised and fronted to [ɛː] in the Anglian dialects, especially before dentals; and this sound later fell together with /ē/; cf. Ep. *tāēnil,* Erf. *tēnil,* Corp. *tāēnil* (but elsewhere *-tēnil*), later OE *tænel, tēnel.* In Kt., the shift of /ǣ/ to [ɛː] to /ē/ went much further than in Anglian. This tendency was probably present but still in its earliest stages when Arch. I was written.[18]

2.8. /y/ < Gmc. /u/ with *i*-umlaut in *cyning, byċġan,* etc.; Latin /o/ before nasal with *i*-umlaut in *mynstre,* etc.; Lat. /u/ with *i*-umlaut in *pyt,* etc. This sound was clearly distinct from /u/ by 700. It was still relatively stable if the spellings of the early glossaries are to be trusted. There is no evidence of un-rounding to /i/ or of the Kt. shift to /e/ before the ninth century.

2.9. /ȳ/ < Gmc. /ū/ with *i*-umlaut in *mȳs, fȳr, ontȳnan,* etc.; Gmc. /un/ with *i*-umlaut in *cȳþan, ȳst,* etc.; Gmc. /wō/ with *i*-umlaut in *cȳe,* etc. This sound, like the preceding, was an independent phoneme and relatively stable around 700.

2.10. /œ/ < Gmc. /o/ with *i*-umlaut, cf. Merc. *doehter* dat. sg., etc.; Lat. /o/ with *i*-umlaut in Anglian *oele,* etc. This must always have been a rare pho-

[14] I once tried using Bülbring's [æᵉ] for this, but I find this symbol often misinterpreted as a diphthong. — The diacritic here is intended to indicate a vowel simultaneously raised and fronted.

[15] Chadwick 190–5.

[16] For WS, see Ross 49; Stockwell and Barritt 37–8 (1951). For Merc., see Chatman 229–36. The proofs for WS can be extended to Nhb., those for Merc. to Kt.

[17] Chadwick 223–5.

[18] Ibid. 212.

neme because Proto-Gmc. /u/ did not become /o/ before /i, j/, and the umlaut could take place only when an /o/ was introduced into umlaut position through analogy or borrowing. There was a tendency to unround /œ/ to /e/ in all dialects. The evidence of Archetype I is not clear as to how far the unrounding had gone, but the survival of *soęrgęndi* in Ep., *ōroehtig* in Corp., *doehter* and *oexen* in the *Vespasian Psalter*, suggests that there was probably such a phoneme around 700.

2.11. /œ̄/ < Gmc. /ō/ with *i*-umlaut in *fōēt* nom. pl., *dōēman*, etc.; Gmc. /am, an/ with *i*-umlaut in *sōēftc*, *tōēþ* nom. pl., *gōēs* nom. pl., *ōēhtan*, etc.; Gmc. /æ/ before nasal with *i*-umlaut in *cwōēn*, *wōēnan*, etc. This phoneme eventually unrounded to /ē/, but much more slowly than its short counterpart. It was spelled *oe* in Arch. I; cf. Ep. *ģirōēfan*, Corp., Erf. *ģcrōēfan*, later WS *ģerēfan*. It was spelled either *oe* or *oi* in early Nhb.; cf. *Cōēnrēd*, *Cōīnrēd* in Bede.[19]

2.12. /ȫ/ < Gmc. /a/ before nasal with *i*-umlaut; cf. Ep., Erf. *dopaenid*, Corp. *doppaenid* (later OE *dopcnid*), Ep., Erf. *aemil*, Corp. *emil*, etc.; *Haengest* beside *Hcngist*, *Middilaengli* beside *Middilengli*, etc., in the early Bede MSS.[20] The regular spelling in Archetype I was probably *ae*. During the course of the eighth century, this phoneme fell together with /e/, except in a part of the Southeast Midland area (Essex and part of Middlesex), where it held its ground until some time in the Middle English period.[21] It is a question whether this sound should be regarded as a phoneme in prehistoric Old English. It began as an allophone of /a/ and ended in most dialects as an allophone of /e/; hence there is a period in which it belonged to neither of these phonemes. It could be regarded as an allophone of /æ/ during the transition, but it did not develop like /æ/. The latter normally became WS, Nhb. /æ/, Merc., Kt. /ɛ/; /ȫ/ became /e/ in all the dialects except the small subarea already mentioned. On the whole, the analysis of OE phonology is simplified for us if we treat /ȫ/ as a phoneme about 700.

2.13. /u/ < Gmc. /u/ in *hund, dulfun, -on* (pt. pl. of *delfan*), etc.; Gmc. /o/ in *fugul, -ol, hunig*, etc.; Lat. /o/ before nasal in *munt*, etc. In unaccented syllables, there was a tendency to lower /u/ to /o/ in all of the dialects.

2.14. /ū/ < Gmc. /ū/ in *mūs, brūcan*, etc.; Gmc. /un/ in *ūs, mūþ, þūhte*, etc.; Gmc. /u/ in *fūre* (gen. sg. of *furh*), etc.; Gmc. /wō/ in *cū, hū*, etc.

2.15. /o/ < Gmc. /o/ in *dohtor, morgen*, etc.; Lat. /o/ in *offrian*, etc.; Gmc. /ō/ shortened in *godspel*, etc.

2.16. /ō/ < Gmc. /ō/ in *dōm, grōwan*, etc.; Gmc./am, an/ in *fōn, gōs, sōfte, tōþ*, etc.; Gmc. /o/ in *hōles* (gen. sg. of *holh*), etc.; Gmc. /æ/ before nasal in *mōna*, etc.

2.17. /a/ < Gmc. /a/ in open syllable before back vowel in *faran, dagas* nom. pl., *fatu* nom. pl., *clawan*, etc.; Gmc. /a/ in closed syllable before certain long consonants in *habban*, etc.; Gmc. /a/ before nasal in *man, ram*, etc.; Lat. /a/ in *carcern, salm*, etc. Phonetically, this sound was probably low back unround. Stockwell and Willard, although using the symbol /ɔ/, say that it may

---

[19] Ström 97.

[20] Chadwick 204-6, 250; Ström 93.

[21] K. Luick, *Historische Grammatik der englischen Sprache* 349-50 (Leipzig, 1921); cf. ME *pani* 'penny', *pans* 'pence', etc.

have been 'phonetically ... low back unround [ɒ]'.[22] Hockett represents it as /ɑ/, places it among the rounded vowels, but says that it was not necessarily 'rounded in the physiological sense'.[23] The treatment of borrowed words containing Lat. /a/ and /o/ seems to me significant. The earliest borrowings with Lat. /a/ develop like words with Gmc. /a/; e.g. *condel, candel,* and *ceaster, cæster, cester.* Late borrowings are spelled with *a,* as though OE /a/ were identical with Lat. /a/; e.g. *capellān, caric, cat, catte, castel, cwatern* 'four-spot', *canceler, canon, cantere, cantic.* Lat. /o/, certainly a rounded vowel, is commonly *o* (not *a*) in late borrowings; e.g. *ācordian, coliandre, columne, corōna, copel, comēta, consolde, consul.* Lat. *chronica* appears in late WS as *cranic,* but this *a* precedes a nasal and may merely indicate that the allophone [ɔ] survived in late WS, although generally spelled *a.*

There were probably dialectal differences in the incidence of /a/ as early as about 700. This phoneme was more frequent in Merc. and Nhb., where it occurred before /l/ plus consonant; e.g. *ald* (WS, Kt. *eald*). It was most frequent in Nhb., where it seems to have occurred also before /r/ plus consonant; e.g. *arm* beside *earm, eorm* (Merc., WS, Kt. *earm*).[24]

There were two important allophones of /a/ in all of the OE dialects: [ɔ] before nasal, [a] elsewhere. The former must have existed from very early times, for when lengthened it fell together with /ō/ in all dialects, as in *gōs,* etc. In metathesized forms like *orn* 'ran', it eventually fell together with /o/ in most dialects of Middle English. The [ɔ] was much more important in Anglian than in WS and Kt.; cf. Merc., Nhb. *mon, rom,* etc., early WS *man, mon, ram, rom,* late WS *man, ram.* In Anglian /ɔ/ became phonemic for a time in the ninth and tenth centuries but later (probably early in the ME period) fused with /a/. The early glossaries vary in spelling practices: Ep. shows nearly all *a* before nasal, while Corp. has *o* about five times as often as *a.* Arch. I apparently had *a* rather consistently.[25] The early Bede MSS fluctuate between *a* and *o.*[26] We may conclude, I think, that [ɔ] was still an allophone at the end of the seventh century.

2.18. /ā/ < Gmc. /ai/ in *hāl, hātan,* etc.; Gmc. /æ/ before /w/ in *cnāwan,* etc.; Gmc. /a/ final under the accent in *swā* (but also *swē* in Anglian), etc. In WS, Gmc. /æ/ before /p, g/ plus back vowel also became /ā/; e.g. *slāpan, māgas* nom. pl., etc. This phoneme was rounded to /ō/ in ME (long open *o*),[27] but in OE and early ME it is spelled *a* with no suggestion of rounding.

2.19. Length in OE vowels calls for additional comments. Length was clearly phonemic, as Reszkiewicz has demonstrated by means of minimal pairs.[28] Doubling of the vowel is also an indication of length in some OE texts, e.g. in the *Corpus Glossary.* Although a long vowel is not invariably doubled in Corp., the following instances may be noted: *briiġ, criid, fiil, liim, miil, piic, tiiġ, wiin-*;

[22] Page 10 (1959).

[23] Page 576 (1959).

[24] For *a* and *ea* in the early Bede MSS, see Ström 92, 103–4.

[25] Chadwick 200–3.

[26] Ström 92.

[27] Except in the Northern dialect.

[28] Page 181. His set of minimal pairs are all WS, but similar pairs can be adduced for all dialects except Kt., in which the surviving texts contain insufficient materials.

breer, -leec, eil, deid; bruun, cuu, ġebuur, luus, muus, tuun; ānmood, boog, flooc, flood, foor, fornoom, forsooc, ġemoot, good, goor, goos, hood, hool, loob, roopnis, stool, wooð; aac, aam, aar, baan-, baar, baat, braad-, faag, faam, flaan, gaad, gaar-, ġemaad, haal-, haam, laac, laam, paad, waar. Length was rarely indicated by doubling when the vowel or diphthong was spelled with a digraph, but it was phonemic here also. Malone notes minimal pairs in WS: *heoru* 'sword' : *hēoru* 'pleasant', *sċeat* 'money' : *sċēat* 'corner'.[29] One may add *heofon* 'heaven' : *hēofan* 'to lament' : *hēofon* 'lamentation', *ġear* 'creaked' : *ġēar* 'year', *steor-* (in *steorglēaw* 'clever at astronomy') : *stēor-* (in *stēorlēas* 'uncontrolled'), *mæġ* 'can' : *mǣġ* 'kinsman'.

The OE 'lengthening' of Gmc. /æ, iu, eo, au/ is sometimes misunderstood. In Gmc., this series stood alone, there being no corresponding series, either longer or shorter; hence, these phonemes were neutral, neither long nor short.[30] In pre-historic OE, they became /æ, io, eo, æo/, the last > /æa/; e.g. **dæd, *þiustru, *ċeosan, *heafud.* Through fronting, breaking, and other sound changes, a parallel series arose; e.g. **dæġ, *iorrja, *heorte, *bearn.*[31] The new sounds were shorter than the old; hence, quantity became significant. Without any phonetic change in themselves, the older series became phonemically /ǣ, īo, ēo, ǣa/.

The fact that long vowels in OE are often doubled in writing should not lead us to suppose either that they were self clusters or that a long vowel was neces-sarily equal in quantity to two short vowels. The self-cluster concept is precluded by the later history of the sounds; e.g. WS /a/ became southern ME /a/, but WS /ā/ became ME /ō/ (long open *o*); WS /æ/ fell together with ME /a/, but WS /ǣ/ became ME /ē/ (long open *e*); WS /e/ became ME /e/, when lengthened (in ME) /ē/, but WS /ē/ became ME /ẹ/ (long close *e*). There was clearly a qualitative as well as a quantitative difference, although it was not great enough in OE to prevent the scribes from writing both long and short vowels with the same set of graphemes. As for absolute quantity in OE, this is something which we do not know and may never know. The metrical evidence of OE poetry indi-cates that a long vowel (or a long diphthong) was longer than a short vowel (or a short diphthong), but it does not tell us how much longer.[32] Hitherto, most at-tempts to solve this problem have been based on introspection rather than evi-dence.

2.20. /io/ < Gmc. /i/ before /r/ plus consonant in *iorre, iorsian*, etc. This phoneme (complex phonemic unit, if you prefer) appears to have been distinct from /eo/ at the end of the seventh century. It fell together with /eo/ in Merc. during the ninth century, in Nhb. and Kt. late in the OE period or early in the ME period. In early WS, its [ɪʊ] allophone fell together with /eo/, while its [ɪɛ] allophone became phonemic. Originally, /io/ is thought to have been phonetically [ɪʊ], and this pronunciation may be reflected in early Anglian *iu*-spellings;[33] cf. *uuiurthit* in *Bede's Death Song*. This allophone has been omitted from Table I

[29] Page 260.
[30] They are customarily left unmarked, as though short.
[31] According to Samuels 43, the short diphthongs became phonemic in the seventh cen-tury. /æ/ must have become a phoneme considerably earlier through the loss of inflectional endings, etc.
[32] See also Samuels 24.
[33] Chadwick 216–8; Ström 106–7.

because it was probably rare at 700 and because it has little importance for the later history of OE.

The allophone [ɪɛ] was due in some instances to the weakening of the second element of /io/ to [ɛ], perhaps to [ə]. There are occasional *ie*-spellings in the early glossaries and in later Anglian texts, which suggest that this allophone existed in Anglian. In early WS it became the dominant allophone; hence, I write the early WS phoneme /ie/ rather than /io/. In late WS, /ie/ monophthongized to /i/, and then rounded to /y/ unless prevented from rounding by a palatal consonant; e.g. *ierre, iersian, siehþ*, etc. (later *yrre, yrsian, sihþ*, etc.). Another source of early WS /ie/ was Gmc. /a/ with breaking and *i*-umlaut (Angl. /æ/ or /e/) in *ierfe, fiellan, hliehhan, sliehþ, ġiest*, etc. A further source was Gmc. /e/ with diphthongization by initial palatal in *ċiele, ġiefu, sċieran*, etc. There is no WS text comparable in date to the early glossaries, and the evidence of the latter does not suggest that [ɪɛ] was as yet an important allophone when Archetype I was written. We should probably assume, however, that [ɪɛ] was important in WS as early as about 700; for palatal diphthongization and *i*-umlaut had certainly taken place before this date.

2.21. /io/ < Gmc. /iu/ in *þiostru, ġeþiodan*, etc.; Gmc. /i/ by breaking in *lioht*, etc.; Gmc. /ijō, iju/ in *þrio*, etc. The diphthong in words like *lioht* was generally smoothed to /ī/ in the Anglian dialects by 700; it survived in Kt., fell together with /ēo/ during the ninth century in WS. The phoneme /io/ was originally [iʊ:] phonetically, and this pronunciation may be reflected in occasional *iu*-spellings of the eighth century; e.g. Corp. *ðiustra* (later Nhb. *ðiostro*, later Merc. *ðeostru*, WS *ðiestre*). The pronunciation [iʊ:] was undoubtedly dominant about 700. The phoneme fell together with /ēo/ in OE, but more slowly than its short counterpart fell together with /eo/. An allophone [iɛ:] existed in all dialects and is reflected in later Merc. by spellings like *sie* (nom.sg. fem. of *sē*). In WS, [iɛ:] was, or soon became, the dominant allophone; hence, in early WS, the phoneme must be written /ie/ rather than /io/. In this dialect, the phoneme (like its short counterpart) had several sources: Gmc. /iu/ with *i*-umlaut in *liehtan*, Gmc. /au/ with *i*-umlaut in *hieran*, etc. Like the short diphthong, it was rounded in late WS to /ȳ/.

2.22. /eo/ < Gmc. /e/ before /r/ plus consonant in *heorte*, etc. In Anglian this phoneme also resulted from /e/ before /lf/ in *seolf* (late Nhb. *solf, sulf*; WS *self, sylf*). In Nhb., /eo/ was confused with /æa/ from an early period; cf. *Earpualdo* (for *Eorp-*) in the Moore MS of Bede, etc.[34] In the tenth-century Nhb. gloss of the *Lindisfarne Gospels*, *ea* is frequently written for /eo/, as in *hearte*. In the Nhb. portions of the gloss to the *Rushworth Gospels*, the opposite is true, and *eo* frequently appears for /æa/. The confusion of the short diphthongs may have been purely orthographic and due to the parallel confusion of their long counterparts.

2.23. /ēo/ < Gmc. /eo/ in *þēof, ċēosan*, etc.; Gmc. /ew, eww/ in *trēo* 'tree', *trēow* 'trust', etc.; Gmc. /e/ in *fēores* (gen. sg. of *feorh*), etc.[35] Falling together of

---

[34] Ström 104.

[35] There is doubt, however, about the lengthening of vowels after loss of /h/ in the clusters /lh, rh/; see Randolph Quirk and C. L. Wrenn, *An Old English grammar* 137 (1955).

/īo/ with /ēo/ was just beginning when Archetype I was written.[36] An [eʊː] allophone in early OE may be reflected in a few *eu*-spellings of the eighth and early ninth centuries: *Hrēutford*, etc., in the Bede MSS,[37] *flēutas* in the *Erfurt Glossary*. The orthographic confusion of /eo/ and /æa/ in Nhb. has already been mentioned. A similar confusion of /ēo/ and /ǣa/ appears in the late Nhb. texts; e.g. *behēald* (for -*hēold*), *ēade* (for *ēode* pt. sg.), *ōēajas* (for *ōēof-*), etc., in the Lindisfarne gloss; *fīcbēome* (for -*bēam-*), *dēode* (for *dēad-*), *hēonissum* (for *hēa-*), etc., in the Nhb. portions of the Rushworth gloss. The early Bede MSS show this confusion to some extent; e.g. *Eodbaldo* (beside *Ead-*, *Aeod-*), *Strēanæshalch* (beside (*Strēonæs-*.)[38] Without more evidence, we cannot say whether Nhb. /ēo/ and /ǣa/ had fallen together phonemically by the beginning of the eighth century.

2.24. /æa/ < Gmc. /a/ before /r/ plus consonant in *hcard*, *bearn*, etc.; Gmc. /a/ before /h/ in *seah* pt. sg., etc. Breaking before /h/ probably took place in all dialects; it is difficult otherwise to account for Merc. *slēan* (Nhb. *slēa*, beside *slǣ*, *slā*) from Gmc. **slahan* and other contracted forms. In noncontract forms, /æa/ before /h/ was smoothed to /æ/ in the Anglian dialects; cf. *sæh* pt. sg. (WS, Kt. *seah*). This Anglian smoothing was not complete until some time in the eighth century, but was well under way by 700. In WS and Nhb., the incidence of /æa/ was increased by palatal diphthongization, which must have preceded 700; e.g. *ċeaster*, *ġeat*, *sċeaft* (also spelled with *æ*, *e*, in Nhb., with *e* in late WS) as compared with Merc., Kt. *ċester*, *ġet*, *sċeft*. There is no real evidence of palatal diphthongization in Archetype I.[39] The early Bede MSS show *Ceadda* but *cæstir*.[40] In WS and Kt., /æa/ also resulted from Gmc. /a/ before /l/ plus consonant; e.g. *eald*, *healtian* (Anglian *ald*, *haltian*).

2.25. /ǣa/ < Gmc. /au/ in *hēafod*, *ċēas* pt. sg., etc.; Gmc. /a/ in *slēan*, *mēares* gen. sg., etc.; Gmc. /aw*, *awu*, *aww/ in *clēa*, *hrēa*, *hēawan*, etc. In WS, Gmc. /æ/ broke to /ǣa/ before /h/; e.g. *nēah* (Merc., Nhb. *nēh*). The diphthong was further augmented in WS by palatal diphthongization of Gmc. /æ/ in *ċēace*, *ġēar*, *sċēap*, etc.; cf. Anglian *ċēce*, *ġēr*, Merc. *sċēp*, Nhb. *sċīp*.

2.26. /ə/. The vowels and diphthongs of unaccented syllables are very difficult to pin down. If long, they were usually but not invariably shortened. If short, they were weakened in various ways, sometimes apparently to /ə/. Variation in spelling (*heofon*, *heofan*, *heofen*) suggests the existence of /ə/. Alternations like *stefn* ~ *stefen*, *heofnas* ~ *heofenas* are a further indication. The /ə/ must also be assumed in prehistoric English as an intermediate stage between **cwipiþ* and *cwiþ* (pr. sg. 3 of *cwepan* ~ *cweoþan*) and similar forms. Parasitic vowels must have begun as /ə/; cf. *berct*, *berect*, *berict* (WS *beorht*) in the early Bede MSS. At the present time, it would be rash to generalize about the distribution of /ə/ in OE, but its existence as a phoneme seems certain. It probably varied considerably in pronunciation, but I have been content with suggesting two allophones: [ɪ], in-

[36] Chadwick 216-8.
[37] Ström 101.
[38] Ibid. 99-101, 147. Similar confusion of /eo, æa/ and /ēo, ǣa/ occurs to a limited extent in the *Vespasian Psalter* gloss and other Merc. texts.
[39] The apparent examples given by Chadwick 228 are actually due to velar umlaut.
[40] Ström 107-8.

clining to high front articulation and generally derived from front vowels in un-accented syllables, and [ə], inclining to a lower, more retracted articulation and generally derived from back vowels in unaccented syllables.

2.27. The OE diphthongs require further comment. As far as the diphthongs of OE about 700 are concerned, I find myself in rather close agreement with Hockett. The sounds represented by *io* (or *ie*), *eo*, *ea*, long and short, were pho-nemically distinct from the other syllabics of OE; they were certainly no mere allophones of the phonemes represented by *i*, *e*, *æ*.[41] Germanic had diphthongs /iu, eo, au/ (Hockett's /iw, ew, aw/), which entered early OE as phonetic diphthongs /ĭo, ēo, æ̆a/ (Hockett's /iw, ew, æw/).[42] In view of his argument for parallel de-velopment of the long and short syllabics, Hockett would perhaps agree that the short *io, eo, ea* also represented phonetic diphthongs in the early period. If so, there is, thus far, no disagreement between Hockett's views and those of the traditional type.

Hockett believes that later (perhaps by the time the *Vespasian Psalter* was glossed) the diphthongs of early OE were phonetically [ɪ, ə, a], long and short. I can see no possibility, at present, of reconciling this view with the findings of traditional linguistics or comparative linguistics.[43] If we agree (as Hockett does, 596) that OS *liudi*, OHG *liuti*, OFris. *liŏde* contained diphthongs, why should we assume that OE *līode* (later *lēode*) contained a monophthong? If the digraphs in OS *diop*, OHG *tiof*, OFris. *diăp*, OIc. *diūpr* represented diphthongs, why should the digraph in OE *dēop* be interpreted differently? If OHG *stroum* and OIc. *straumr* have diphthongs spelled as though diphthongal, and OS *strōm*, OFris. *strām* have monophthongs spelled as though monophthongal, why should OE *strēam* have a monophthong spelled as though diphthongal? English missionaries had a large share in converting all of these other peoples and in transmitting to them the written Scriptures and the art of writing. One would expect more parallelism in the development of scribal practices.

The development of twin forms in ME is hard to explain except on the as-sumption that there were diphthongs and that stress shift could occur in those diphthongs; i.e. there existed twin pronunciations in OE, [ẹ́oː] beside [ɛóː], etc. Hockett notes OE *čēosan* > ME *chẹsen, chọsen* (597). Further examples are OE *lēosan* > ME *lẹsen, lọsen*; OE *scēawian* > ME *shẹwen, shọwen*; OE *fēawe* > ME *fẹwe, fọwe*; OE *ģeond* > ME *yẹnd, yọnd*; WS, Kt. *weald* > *wẹald, wọld*; WS *ģeomor* > southern ME *yẹmer, yọmer*; WS *scēadan* > sth. ME *shẹden, shọden*; WS *čeald* > sth. ME *chẹld, chọld*; WS *ģeong* > sth. *ME yeng, yo(u)ng*.[44]

Finally, I do not venture to use /h, w, y/ to represent the second elements of diphthongs or to indicate vowel length. Even experts in the use of these symbols

[41] Hockett 575–7 (1959). This view is attacked by Stockwell and Barritt (1961).

[42] Hockett 596 (1959). The spellings cited by Hockett as reflections of early pronunciation are from the eighth-century glossaries and the early Bede MSS.

[43] I do not have space to discuss Hockett's five orthographical principles (590–1). They are admirably set forth, but I see no necessity for explaining *io, eo, ea* by principle 5; his principle 4 would explain them equally well.

[44] Malone distinguishes between true diphthongs and 'glides' (256). He holds that OE *io, eo, ea, ie* represented true diphthongs until almost the end of the OE period (258–61).

| | FRONT VOWELS | | BACK | | UNACCENTED |
	UNROUND	ROUND	VOWELS	DIPHTHONGS	VOWELS
HIGH	/i/ [ɪ]	/y/ [ʊ̈]	/u/ [ʊ]	/io/ [ɪɒ]	
	/ī/ [i ꞉]	/ȳ/ [ü꞉]	/ū/ [u꞉]	/īo/ [ɪɒ꞉, ɪɛ꞉]	[ɪ]
	/e/ [ɛ]	/œ/ [ö]	/o/ [ɒ]	/eo/ [ɛɒ, ɛə]	
MID	/ē/ [e꞉]	/ōͤ/ [ö꞉]	/ō/ [o꞉]		/ə/
	/ɛ/ [æ˕]		/ɔ/ [ɔ]	/ēo/ [eɒ꞉, eə꞉]	
LOW	/æ/ [æ]		/a/ [ɑ]	/æa/ [æɒ, æə]	[ə]
	/ǣ/ [æ꞉, ɛ꞉]		/ā/ [ɑ꞉]	/ǣa/ [æɒ꞉, æə꞉]	

TABLE II

frequently err when introducing them into OE phonemic transcriptions.[45] How could a traditionalist like myself hope to use them correctly? I am also deterred by the objections raised by Hans Kurath,[46] even though these are partially met by James Sledd.[47]

THE SYLLABICS OF MERCIAN

3. The *Corpus Glossary* represented a mid stage between Chadwick's Archetype I (*c*700) and the full development of Mercian in the gloss of the *Vespasian Psalter* (*c*825). In Corp., some of the newer allophones noted in Table I are better reflected in the spellings, but there is no apparent change in the phonemic structure of the dialect.[48] The syllabics of ninth-century Merc. are presented in Table II. The analysis is based on the gloss to the *Vespasian Psalter* and a contemporary fragment called the *Lorica Prayer*.[49]

Changes in the incidence of phonemes can be dealt with briefly, since most of the allophones, as well as the sound changes which produced them, have already been described. The incidence of /æ/ had been greatly reduced by the operation of the second fronting in the eighth century. Except in a few positions, e.g. before /h/ in *mæht*, [æ] had moved to [æ˕] and was a new phoneme. The short /œ/ was a relic phoneme, having almost completely fallen together with /e/. The long /ōͤ/ was more stable, but this also was beginning to unround. The incidence of /a/ had been reduced by the splitting off of /ɔ/ and by the combined operation of velar umlaut and the second fronting, which caused /a/ in open syllable followed by back vowel to become /æa/. The diphthong /io/ was by this time a relic, surviving only in velar-umlaut position (*nioman*, etc.). Breaking-/io/ had fallen together with /eo/. The long /īo/ was rapidly falling together with /ēo/.

3.1. /ő/ was no longer a phoneme, having unrounded to /e/ in *ende, wemman*, etc.

3.2. /ɛ/ is a misleading symbol for the new phoneme from the second fronting

---

[45] See Stockwell and Barritt 388 (1955); Stockwell 23 (1958).

[46] Pp. 111–2, 121 (1957).

[47] Pp. 253–4 (1958).

[48] My article, The dialect of the Corpus Glossary, *PMLA* 54.1–19 (1939), presents the data, which can readily be interpreted in structural terms.

[49] Both are available in Sweet's *OET* 174, 188–420. Errors, chiefly in Sweet's Latin text of the Psalter, do not materially affect the general phonemic analysis.

of /æ/ from Gmc. /a/. Phonetically, the sound must have been somewhere between [æ] and [ɛ], for in ME times it coalesced with the reflexes of /æ/, /ɔ/, and /a/, not with the reflex of Merc. /e/.[50] It is spelled e too regularly in the Vespasian gloss to be regarded as an allophone of /æ/, from which Hockett correctly separates it. A few minimal pairs contrasting /e/ and /ɛ/ are probably concealed by the e-spelling: wes (imp. sg. of bīon) : wes (pt. 1 and 3 sg.), cweð (imp. sg. of cweoðan) : cweð (pt. 1 and 3 sg.), bed (nom. sg.) : bed (pt. 1 and 3 sg. of biddan), hel (nom. sg.) : hel (pt. 1 sg. of helan). Pairs to illustrate the distinction /æ/ ~ /ɛ/, which no one appears to question, are much rarer, but perhaps æt (prep.) : et (adv.) will serve.

3.3. /ɔ/ < Gmc. and Lat. /a/ before nasal is consistently written o, and Hockett rightly separates it from /a/. That /ɔ/ was no longer a mere positional variant in Merc. is indicated by the shape of Late Lat. borrowings in the Vespasian gloss: plant, geplantade, (?)organe, etc. Moreover, /ɔ/ can appear before a consonant other than a nasal; cf. born (pt. 3 sg. of beornan), orn (pt. 1 sg. of eornan). That /ɔ/ did not fuse with /o/ is indicated by its falling together with /a, æ, ɛ/ in ME.

3.4. In later Merc. of the tenth century, /œ, ō̄, io, īo/ fell together with /e, ē, eo, ēo/ respectively. In the late tenth and eleventh centuries, /eo, ēo, æa, æa/ monophthongized to /ö, ȫ, æ, ǣ/. These appear in early ME: /ö, ȫ/ spelled eo, oe, o, u, ue, etc.; /æ/ spelled a, æ, ea; /ǣ/ spelled e, æ, ea, etc. They became /e, ē, a (æ), ē/ earliest in the eastern parts of the old Merc. area. The late Merc. texts, of which Farman's gloss to portions of the Rushworth Gospels is the most important, are difficult to analyze because of the strong influence of WS, the standard dialect in the tenth and eleventh centuries. But much can be learned from them if due precautions are taken.[51]

THE SYLLABICS OF NORTHUMBRIAN

4. The Nhb. dialect closely resembles Merc. in some respects, probably because the two kingdoms were closely associated from the fifth century to the seventh. Mercia seems to have been a dependency of its northern neighbor until the rise of King Penda in the second quarter of the seventh century. The early Nhb. fragments have been mentioned. The principal texts of later Nhb. are the ninth-century Liber Vitae of Durham,[52] and the tenth-century glosses of the Lindisfarne Gospels, the Durham Ritual, and portions of the Rushworth Gospels.[53] The vowels and diphthongs appear in the table below.

Most of the sound changes affecting Nhb. syllabics have been mentioned in connection with the prehistoric period. We may note here the survival of /y, ȳ, œ, ōē/ as phonemes until the tenth century. In the Northern dialect of ME, they

[50] Hockett would not use later historical evidence in a synchronic article. Since this article is both synchronic and diachronic, I have no scruples about using any valid evidence that I can find.

[51] E and Æ in Farman's Mercian glosses, PMLA 60.631–69 (1945).

[52] Sweet, OET 153–66.

[53] W. W. Skeat, editions of the four Gospels in WS, Merc., and Nhb. (Cambridge, 1871–87); Uno Lindelöf, Rituale Ecclesiae Dunelmensis, Surtees Society, Vol. 140 (1927).

| | FRONT VOWELS | | BACK | | UNACCENTED |
	UNROUND	ROUND	VOWELS	DIPHTHONGS	VOWELS
HIGH	/i/ [ɪ] /ī/ [iː] /e/ [ɛ]	/y/ [ʏ] /ȳ/ [üː] /œ/ [ö]	/u/ [ʊ] /ū/ [uː] /o/ [ɒ]	/io/ [ɪɒ, ɪə] /īo/ [ɪɒ!, ɪə!] /eo/ [ɛɒ, ɛə,	[ɪ] /ə/
MID			/ō/ [oː]	æa, æə]	
LOW	/ē/ [eː] /æ/ [æ, æ˕] /ǣ/ [æː, ɛː]	/œ̄/ [öː]	/ɔ/ [ɔ] /a/ [ɑ] /ā/ [ɑ!]	/ēo/ [ɛɒ!, ɛə! ɛɒ!, ɛə!]	[ə]

TABLE III

appear unrounded to /i, ī, e, ē̦/. The phonemes /io, īo/ remained distinct from /eo, ēo/ in the tenth century. In ME of the fourteenth century, however, the same fusion appears as that which we have noted in Merc.

4.1. /ɔ̄/ fell together with /ē/, as in most OE dialects.

4.2. /ɔ/ became phonemic in Nhb., as in Mercian. [æ˕], however, remained an allophone.

4.3. The spellings *ea* and *eo* are confused in late Nhb., as already noted. I have indicated phonemic fusion with a wide range of variant pronunciations as one means of reconciling the scribal practices of the tenth century with the various and inconsistent developments of later times. Unfortunately there are no further texts from the old Nhb. area until the fourteenth century, and by that time several sound changes had occurred which make the evidence hard to interpret. The short diphthongs /eo, æa/ apparently split between 1000 and 1300 A.D. (or perhaps they were not truly fused in the tenth century), for they appear generally to be /e/ and /a/ in the *Cursor Mundi*.[54] The long diphthongs show more evidence of fusion than the short. There are several views as to what happened.[55] Watson points out a Northern dialect of modern English in which the reflexes of OE /ēo/ seem to have fallen together with those of OE /ǣa/.[56] There are rimes in the *Cursor Mundi* which suggest that fusion had taken place: *leme* (OE *lēoma*) : *bem* (OE *bēam*); *leue* (OE *lēaf*) : *leue* (OE *lēof*); *leue* (OE *lēaf*) : *thef* (OE *þēof*); *ded* (OE *dēad*) : *yede* (OE *geēode*); etc.[57] In general, the reflexes of OE /ǣa/ in the *Cursor Mundi* show a tendency to rime with ME /ē̦/ (long close e): *dede* (OE *dēad*) with *red* (Anglian *rēd*, WS * rǣd*), etc. This might suggest that Nhb. /ǣa/ fell together with /ēo/, rather than the reverse. With our present knowledge, it seems to me hazardous to say anything more positive. The frequency with which expected ME /ē/ and /ē̦/ rime in the *Cursor Mundi* led Strandberg to assume that northern ME /ē/ had become close /ē̦/ in a number of contexts in which we should not normally expect this change. Possibly the rimes of this text are not dependable as evidence for the reflexes of OE /ē, ǣ, ēo, ǣa/. The modern dialects,

---

[54] The MSS are of the late 14th century, and some of the spellings probably reflect the late ME shift of /er/ > /ar/.

[55] For a summary, see Watson 19–20 (1946); see also Campbell 117–20.

[56] Op.cit. 21–6.

[57] Otto Strandberg, *The rime-vowels of Cursor Mundi* 106–7, 118, 145, etc. (Uppsala, 1919). I omit studies of later Northern texts for lack of space.

| | FRONT VOWELS | | BACK | | UNACCENTED |
	UNROUND	ROUND	VOWELS	DIPHTHONGS	VOWELS
HIGH	/i/ [ɪ]	/y/ [ʉ]	/u/ [ʊ]	/ie/ [ɪɛ, ɪə]	
	/ī/ [iː]	/ȳ/ [ʉː]	/ū/ [uː]	/īe/ [ɪɛː, ɪəː]	
MID	/e/ [ɛ]		/o/ [ɒ]	/eo/ [ɛɒ, ɛə]	[ɨ] /ə/
	/ē/ [eː]		/ō/ [oː]	/ēo/ [ɛɒː, ɛəː]	[ə]
LOW	/æ/ [æ]		/a/ [ɑ, ɔ]	/æa/ [æɑ, æə]	
	/ǣ/ [æː]		/ā/ [ɑː]	/ǣa/ [æɑː, æəː]	

TABLE IV

also, are in need of further clarification, which may come with the publication of the linguistic atlases of England and Scotland now being prepared by Harold Orton and Angus McIntosh. For the present, I believe that my phonemicization can serve as a working hypothesis.

THE SYLLABICS OF WEST SAXON

5. As the dialect in which most of OE literature has survived, WS is well known and can be treated briefly. The principal texts in early WS are the Parker MS of the *Anglo-Saxon Chronicle* (as far as A.D. 901) and King Alfred's translations of Orosius' history and of Gregory's *Pastoral Care*.[58] The MSS used were written about 900 and are basically early WS, although some of their spelling practices suggest Merc. influence and others point to the onset of sound changes which are regarded as characteristic of late WS.[59] The vowels and diphthongs of early WS are given below.

Most of the phonetic features of early WS have already been noted. As in the other dialects, the second elements of diphthongs tended to become [ə]. The question whether the short *ie, eo, ea* represented diphthongs has been rather fully discussed elsewhere.[60] The incidence of /eo/ and /io/ was reduced in WS by the manner in which dental consonants, palatals, velars, and nasals hindered velar umlaut; e.g. WS *cwepan* (Merc. *cweoðan*), *niman* (Merc. *neoman*, Nhb. *nioma*), WS *brecan* (Merc. *ǵebreocan*), etc.

5.1. The phonemes /œ, ǣ/ had probably disappeared from the spoken dialect by the late ninth century, although sporadic *oe*-spellings occur in the early WS texts.[61]

5.2. As in Merc. and Nhb., the phoneme /ō/ fused with /e/.

5.3. The phonemes /ie, īe/ were rapidly becoming monophthongs at the close of the ninth century, as is indicated by spellings like *fird, irfe, ǵehīran, ǵestīran*, and by reverse spellings like *briengan, ǵegrīepð*.

---

[58] C. Plummer and J. Earle, *Two Saxon chronicles parallel*, 2 vols. (Oxford, 1892, 1899); Sweet, *King Alfred's Orosius* = *EETS OS* 79 (1883); Sweet, *King Alfred's West Saxon version of Gregory's pastoral care* = *EETS OS* 45, 50 (1871-2; repr. 1909).

[59] For a useful analysis, see P. J. Cosijn, *Altwestsächsische Grammatik*, 2 vols. (The Hague, 1883-6).

[60] Daunt, Samuels, Stockwell and Barritt, Barritt, Bazell, Reszkiewicz, Malone, Kuhn and Quirk; see fn. 1.

[61] Cosijn 1.71, 76.

	FRONT	BACK	DIPHTHONGS	UNACCENTED
HIGH	/i/ [ɪ] /ī/ [iː]	/u/ [ʊ] /ū/ [uː]	/ĭɒ/ [ɪɒ, ɛɒ, ɪɒ, ĭə]	[ɪ]
MID	/e/ [ɛ] /ē/ [eː]	/o/ [ɒ]	/īɒ/ [ɪɒː, eɒː, ɪɒː, ĭə:]	/ə/
	/ɛ/ [æ⊥] /ɛ/ [æ]	/ō/ [oː]		[ə]
LOW	/æ/ [æ] /ǣ/ [ǣː, eː]	/a/ [ɑ, ɔ] /ā/ [ɑː]	/æɑ/ [æɑ, ĭɑ, æə] /ǣɑ/ [æɑː, ĭɑː, æəː]	

TABLE V

5.4. The late WS phonemes were the same as those in Table IV, with a few exceptions. /i, ī/ had a tendency, at least in some parts of the WS area, to round to /y, ȳ/ except in the neighborhood of palatal consonants. /y, ȳ/ tended to unround to /i, ī/ before palatal consonants. /ie, īe/ monophthongized to /i, ī/ and then rounded to /y, ȳ/ except in the neighborhood of palatal consonants. Thus the older phonemes /ie, īe/ probably disappeared from the spoken dialect, although occasional *ie*-spellings occur as archaisms in the late WS texts.[62] The other diphthongs remained and even survived in early ME with a diphthongal pronunciation, at least in some parts of the Southern area.[63] The effects of palatal umlaut (*meaht* > *miht*) and other late WS sound changes are dealt with in all of the standard grammars and handbooks of OE. The late WS texts are too numerous to list even selectively. Generally, the works of Aelfric and Wulfstan and the *West Saxon Gospels* are regarded as major texts.

THE SYLLABICS OF KENTISH

6. The Kt. dialect of the OE period survives only in a few fragments, and these are mixed with other dialects, the early ones with Merc., the later with WS. Only by comparing their features with those of Kt. texts of the ME period[64] can one arrive at any conclusions as to the sounds of Kt. in the older period. The following table fairly represents the views of many traditional linguists.

The tendency of /æ/ to develop a higher, more fronted allophone in Anglian is paralleled by a similar development in Kt., but the tendency was stronger in Kt., shifting /æ/ toward /ē/ in almost any context. The allophone [ɔ] did not become phonemic. The first elements of the phonemes /æɑ, ǣɑ/ underwent some degree of raising and fronting in late Kt. Frequently they are spelled with *ia* or other digraphs suggesting this pronunciation, and even in middle Kentish we find spellings like *dyaþ*, *dyeaþ*, which suggest the survival of a diphthongal /ĭə/ or /īə/ as late as the fourteenth century.

6.1. The new phoneme /ɛ/ arose in Kt., as in Merc. The fact that Merc. and

[62] According to Brunner 249–50 (1953), /ie/ acquired a 'palatoguttural pronunciation' in late WS. Although not actually rounded, the sound was often confused with /y/ and hence written *y*. He concedes that 'a rounded [y] may have been substituted for it by some speakers or in some areas.'

[63] Henning Hallqvist, *Studies in Old English fractured ea* 9–77 (Lund, 1948).

[64] Especially *Dan Michel's ayenbite of inwyt*, ed. by R. Morris, = *EETS OS* 23 (1866); and *William of Shoreham's poems*, ed. by M. Konrath, = *EETS ES* 86 (1902).

Kt. share this and some other features may be due to the fact that Kent was under Merc. rule during most of the eighth century and the first part of the ninth.

6.2. Kt. was the first dialect (of those in which any writings have survived) to lose all of its front rounded vowels. /y, ȳ/ shifted to /e, ē/ during the ninth century. /œ, œ̄/ unrounded to /e, ē/, as in Merc. and WS. /ɔ̄/ unrounded to /e/, probably at the same time as in Merc.

6.3. Spelling evidence suggests that /eo, ēo/ fell together with /io, īo/ in late Kt. The middle Kt. evidence is not clear, but some of the spellings suggest a raised and fronted articulation of the first element (cf. *chiese* < OE *ćēosan*, etc. in *Ayenbite*). On the other hand, *heuene* (OE *heofon*), etc., in the same text suggest that /eo/ did not completely fall together with /io/ in late Kt. of the OE period. As with the Nhb. diphthongs, I have chosen a compromise phonemicization.

7. This discussion has been an attempt at description rather than argument. It represents the views of many traditional linguists, but by no means all. To introduce all the theories which conflict with my schematization would swell the article to great length and defeat its purpose, which is to present the OE syllabics structurally in a form easily grasped and understood. If there is any one inference which might be regarded as a structural conclusion, it is that the OE dialects were surprisingly alike in their structure. The differences produced by the numerous sound changes affected chiefly the incidence of phonemes and the variety of allophones. The early loss of the old front rounded vowels in Kt. only anticipates a similar loss in the other dialects. The new phonemes /ie, īe/ in WS resulted from the rise to dominance of allophones which were present in the other dialects also. The new phonemes, /ɔ/ in Merc. and Nhb., /ɛ/ in Merc. and Kt., were comparatively short-lived. The latter is probably the source of the modern English [æ] pronunciation of the sound written *a*, but that is a matter too complicated to be introduced here.

Beowulf and the Life of Beowulf:
A Study in Epic Structure

It is a well known fact that the epic[1] poem *Beowulf*, while concentrating on two high points of its hero's career, provides enough additional biographical material, in its digressions and asides, to enable us to reconstruct most of Beowulf's life. It is also no secret that the composer of *Beowulf*, like Shakespeare, was not interested in telling a plain, unadorned tale. He chose to interweave many strands into one and to enhance his central plot with sub-plots, songs, oratory, wit, poetic allusions—the sort of literary accoutrements which make the difference between a *Beowulf* or a *Hamlet* and the typical non-adult Western. The data examined in this paper have been dealt with, wholly or in part, countless times; and many of the ideas which I shall discuss have become so familiar as to seem the common property of scholars and critics.[2] If I have anything new to offer, it is to be found in the rearrangement of old facts and old ideas into a fresh synthesis. For my purpose is not to establish the facts of Beowulf's life, which are reasonably well understood, nor to defend the poet's unstraightforward narrative method, which has already found able champions.[3] My goal is a better understanding of the way in which the poet selected biographical details and wove them into the fabric of his poem.

For this purpose, the facts of the poem, insofar as they are directly related to Beowulf, may be divided into five parts: I, the early life; II, the expedition to Denmark; III, the middle life; IV, the dragon killing; and V, the aftermath. I and III are woven into II and IV, while V appears only in IV, chiefly in the latter part.

I.

The early life of Beowulf has twelve sections:[4]

1. 2813–2816. Beowulf was descended from the Wægmundings, a family

[1] This study is not concerned with definitions of the epic. I am well aware of those definitions which are contrived so as to exclude all epics except the Homeric and which even relegate the *Odyssey* to a second-rate, 'corrupt' status.

[2] I can give credit for borrowed ideas only in special cases; if I were to do otherwise, my notes would become unmanageable.

[3] For one of the ablest, see James R. Hulbert, '*Beowulf* and the Classical Epic,' *Modern Philology*, XLIV (1946), 65–75.

[4] The line numbers are those used in most editions. There are assumed to have been 3182 lines, although it is impossible to be certain as to precisely how much has been lost in the badly damaged folio 198ᵛ.

Reprinted by permission from *Studies in the Language, Literature, and Culture of the Middle Ages and Later*, ed. E. Bagby Atwood and Archibald A. Hill (Austin: University of Texas Press, 1969), pp. 243-64.

harshly dealt with by Wyrd. At the close of Beowulf's reign, he and Wiglaf were the only surviving members.[5]

2. 262–266. Beowulf's father was the noble warrior Ecgþeo, the point-leader (*ordfruma*),[6] who lived to a ripe old age and whose fame lived after him.

3. 372–375a. Beowulf's mother was the only daughter of Hreðel, king of the Geats.[7] During his boyhood, Beowulf visited Denmark.[8]

4. 459–472. Ecgþeo carried out the greatest of blood feuds when he killed Heaþolaf among the Wylfings and escaped alive. But his own tribe dared not shelter him for fear of war with Heaþolaf's people.[9] He fled to Denmark, where the new king Hroðgar welcomed him, paid the wergild for Heaþolaf, and so made peace. After swearing oaths of friendship to Hroðgar, Ecgþeo returned to the land of the Geats.

---

[5] The nationality of the Wægmundings is not clear. Beowulf was obviously a Geat, but his father may have been a Wylfing (see note 9); Wiglaf, whose father fought for the Swedes (2611–2625), is called *leod Scylfinga* (2603), which would link him to the Swedish royal family. Two explanations seem to me possible: (a) the descendants of Wægmund split into two sub-clans, one of which united with the Swedes while the other united with the Geats; (b) the Wægmundings were professional warriors who had no nation of their own but were adopted by any tribe with which they happened to serve for a generation or two. In support of (b), we may note that Beowulf is called *freca Scyldinga* (1563) after his adoption by Hroðgar; in support of (a), however, Wiglaf is called a Scylfing while serving the Geats and after his family had presumably severed relations with the Swedes.

[6] This interpretation takes *ord-fruma* to be a literal and transparent compound. It accepts the view that the Geats, like some other Scandinavian tribes, used a wedge formation in battle with the strongest men at the point which would first come into contact with the enemy.

[7] Hroðgar may seem to be uncertain who Beowulf's mother was in 942b–946, but his language here is probably conventional; cf. Luke 11, 27. Beowulf is clearly Hygelac's nephew in 2170b.

[8] He no doubt accompanied his father in exile. It must have been in Denmark that he gained the name *Beowulf*, a nickname due to some resemblance to Beowulf of the Scyldings, Hroðgar's grandfather. The hero's original name, presumably alliterating with Ecgþeo, has been forgotten. R. W. Chambers suggested that Beowulf was an 'intruder' in the Wægmunding genealogy because his name does not alliterate—*Beowulf* (with a supplement by C. L. Wrenn, Cambridge, 1959), p. 11. This remark loses sight of the importance of nicknames among the Anglo-Saxons; e.g. Aldwine, bishop of Lichfield, was also called Wor; Æðelred, Mercian aldorman of the Gaini, was better known as Mucel. Many other examples, Anglo-Saxon and Scandinavian, could be cited.

[9] Whether Ecgþeo was a Geat himself, who entered the land of the Wylfings to achieve his feud, or whether he was a Wylfing by birth, does not greatly concern us in a study of epic technique. The former view is the one commonly held, but Kemp Malone has made a good case for the latter in 'Ecgtheow,' *MLQ*, I (1940), 37–44 (reprinted in Kemp Malone, *Studies in Heroic Legend and in Current Speech*, Copenhagen, 1959, pp. 108–115). Both interpretations involve emending *gara cyn* in line 461.

5. 2426–2443, 2462b–2471. At the age of seven, Beowulf was back in Geat-land, living at the court of King Hreðel, where he was treated like one of Hreðel's own sons. The second son, Hæðcyn, killed his elder brother, Here-beald, with an arrow. Whether the killing was deliberate or accidental, it was an unspeakable grief to Hreðel and one which could not be alleviated by re-venge or wergild.[10] Hreðel died of sorrow, and Hæðcyn ascended the throne of the Geats.

6. 2183b–2189. Beowulf had an undistinguished boyhood, being regarded as lazy and receiving little in the way of gifts from the king.[11] Later, all this changed.

7. 2682b–2687. The hero's great strength caused him to overtax any weapon which he used:

> Him þæt gifeðe ne wæs
> þæt him irenna   ecge mihton
> helpan æt hilde.[12]

8. 506–524. A report, circulated by Breca no doubt, had it that he and Beo-wulf had risked their lives in a swimming match in the wintry sea. It was a foolhardy venture, which wiser men had tried to prevent. After seven days, Beowulf had been beaten. Breca emerged on the coast of the Heaþoræmas and returned home to the land of the Brondings, having made good his boast against Beowulf.

9. 530–581a. According to Beowulf's account, which we are led to accept as the true one, there was no swimming match at all. He and Breca were boys at the time; they boasted that they would swim out in the sea, and they fulfilled their boast. Both were armed when they risked their lives in the sea, and Beowulf at least wore his coat of mail. They remained together for five days, until the coldest of storms separated them in the night. Beowulf was dragged

---

[10] Beowulf, the speaker at this point, interrupts his narrative with the famous elegiac passage (2444–2462a), in which Hroðgar is compared to the old man whose son has been hanged.

[11] I suspect that the boy hated King Hæðcyn and hence was uncooperative. For a different explanation, which would place the inglorious period somewhat later in Beowulf's youth, see Malone, 'Young Beowulf,' *JEGP*, XXXVI (1937), 21–22. The case for putting the inglorious period early is restated with fresh arguments by Adrien Bonjour, *The Digressions in Beowulf*, Medium Aevum Monograph, V (Oxford, 1950), 24–28. The exact placing of the period is not essential to the present discussion.

[12] This passage seems incompatible with the several accounts of Beowulf's successes with weapons, but we should probably pay special heed to the word *gifeðe* 'granted, vouchsafed by a higher power.' The same, or a related, expression is apt to occur when the successes are reported; i.e., when Beowulf's weapon does not fail him, a piece of special good fortune has been granted him. I take it that the poet did not regard the few exceptions as sufficient to invalidate the general rule.

to the bottom by a sea monster, but it was granted him (*me gyfeþe wearð*) to kill the beast with his sword. Other monsters attacked him, but it was granted him (*me gesælde*) to slay nine of these nicors. With morning, Beowulf went ashore in the land of the Finnas.

10. 418–424a. In early youth, the hero performed other feats against monsters, overcoming five jotuns and killing nicors by night. (No chronology is given us, but these exploits seem related to 9 and no doubt belong to the same period in Beowulf's life.)

11. 2472–2500. The first account of the Battle of Ravenswood follows immediately after the story of the deaths of Herebeald and Hreðel (5), but it seems probable that some time, perhaps a few years, intervened. The strife between the Geats and the Swedes was begun by the sons of the Swedish king Ongenþeo. These princes led many bands of raiders over the sea to plunder Geatland around the place called Hreosnabeorh. Beowulf's kinsman, Hæðcyn, avenged these injuries with a raid against the Swedes but was himself killed in the battle. The next morning, it was reported (*þa ic on morgne gefrægn*)[18] that another kinsman (Hygelac) renewed the fight, and Ongenþeo was killed by a Geat named Eofor. Beowulf's part in the battle was far less brilliant than Eofor's, it would seem, but he repaid all of the gifts of Hygelac, as it was granted him (*swa me gifeðe wæs*) with the feats of his bright sword. Hygelac granted him land and lordship. Thereafter Beowulf was the foremost man in Hygelac's army, the warrior who fought at the point of the phalanx (*ana on orde*). It was not necessary for the king to seek an ordfruma outside the tribe of the Geats.

12. 2922b–2998. The second account of the Battle of Ravenswood omits the events leading up to the battle and begins with the statement that Ongenþeo killed Hæðcyn at Hrefnawudu. Hæðcyn's attack from the sea had been a suc-

---

[18] This may suggest that Beowulf was not present at the battle—a view held by a number of scholars, e.g. Fr. Klaeber in *Beowulf and the Fight at Finnsburg* (Boston, 1936), p. xlv. It is possible, however, that Beowulf was merely using a poetic formula (cf. *Exodus* 98a). Such formulas cannot always be taken literally. In 1969b, *gefrunon* probably does not mean that Beowulf and his band merely heard reports of Hygelac; they came to his burg and found him there. In 2952, *hæfde . . . gefrunen* does not indicate that Ongenþeo and his men had merely heard of Hygelac's might; they had just experienced it. The way in which lines 2490–2493a immediately follow the account of the battle and seem to continue the narrative without interruption (with no break indicated in the MS and with no adverb or phrase indicating lapse of time in the text) suggests that the poet regarded Beowulf as having been present. Moreover, Beowulf, in order to become Hygelac's ordfruma, must have proved himself in battle, for the position was not one to be given to an untried warrior. No battle is mentioned except the one at Ravenswood. The messenger's failure to mention Beowulf in his account of the battle could mean only that the young man performed well in his first battle but did not distinguish himself in single combat, as did Wulf and Eofor.

cess: he had captured a great deal of booty and had carried off Ongenþeo's wife, the mother of Onela and Ohthere. But the raiders were overtaken by the Swedish king and his troops. After the defeat and death of the Geatish king, the survivors of his party took refuge in the wood called Hrefnesholt, where they were surrounded by the Swedes. All through the night Ongenþeo regaled them with accounts of what he would do in the morning, how he would slay some with the sword and hang the rest from the trees. At dawn, the fugitives heard the war horns of Hygelac sounding in the distance, and presently the main body of the Geatish army arrived and routed the Swedes. Ongenþeo and his personal retainers sought shelter within an earthen rampart, and there Wulf Wonreding brought the Swedish king to bay. Ongenþeo was wounded but struck down his assailant. Wulf's brother continued the fight, killed Ongenþeo, and bore his armor to Hygelac. The new king of the Geats rewarded the brothers with land and gold, and gave his only daughter to Eofor in marriage.

Certain features of this part of the biography stand out clearly. We may observe first that it is remarkably full. Condensed as it is into 247½ lines, it provides more facts than we can dig up about the early years of most of the historical figures of the Middle Ages. Some important details are obviously missing; for example, we do not know the name of Beowulf's mother. Omissions like this are probably due to gaps in tradition, the poet's imperfect knowledge. There may be other omissions due to the process of selection; that is, the poet may have considered some details unimportant or irrelevant to his purpose. The one thing which should be clear to us is that he intended to include in his poem as complete an outline of the hero's life as his knowledge and his notions of epic structure would permit.

Most of the passages containing biographical matter are short. Six of them (1, 2, 3, 6, 7, and 10) are less than ten lines in length. Only three run over twenty lines: the second account of the swimming exploit, the second account of the Battle of Ravenswood, and lines 2462b–2500 (11 and part of 5, continuation of the Hreðel story and first account of the Battle of Ravenswood). Apparently the poet did not intend that his biographical matter should impede the narrative unduly. The long speech of the Messenger, which includes passage 12 and other matters (128 lines in all) is exceptional, but even this is not so lengthy as the digression in which Beowulf gives an account of his trip to Denmark and of the affairs of the Danish court (lines 1999–2151).

Only two passages (6 and 7), twelve lines in all, represent the poet speaking in his own person. The other nine passages, 235½ lines, are put into the mouths of the characters, much as the antecedent action of an Ibsen play is woven into the dialogue. Beowulf, who is the star of course, has 123½ lines in six passages (1, 2, 5, 9, 10, 11); Hroðgar has 17½ lines in two passages (3, 4); Unferð has nineteen lines in one passage (8); and the Messenger has 75½ lines in one passage (12). It seems fairly clear that the poet ocntrolled his materials consciously, that he planned the biographical passages as organic parts of the poem rather than as excrescences upon it.

When we examine the passages closely, we find that all are generally appropriate to their speakers, and that several of them would be inappropriate to anyone else. The first four are mainly concerned with Beowulf's parents and ancestry. Who could be better informed in such matters than Beowulf (1, 2) and Ecgþeo's friend Hroðgar (3, 4)? Passages 8, 9, and 10 have to do with Beowulf's youthful exploits; and of these, 10 comes most naturally from the hero himself, as he explains his mission to the Danes and sets forth his special competence in the field of extermination of monsters. So much has been written about the poet's artistic handling of 8 and 9 that I can have little to add[14]; more appropriate spokesmen than Unferð and Beowulf could hardly be found. Passages 6 and 7 deal with matters slightly discreditable to Beowulf, and therefore unlikely to be introduced by his friends, but hardly discreditable enough to be cast up by an Unferð. The poet himself mentions them briefly. The remaining passages (5, 11, 12) are mainly historical, Beowulf's part in them being a small one. Passage 5 on the affairs of Hreðel and his family comes most naturally from the mouth of Beowulf, the only survivor of Hreðel's household at the time the story is narrated; 11 is very appropriate to Beowulf if he was a participant, less appropriate if he was not. The Messenger is a nameless, shadowy figure, probably created by the poet to serve as his own mouthpiece. He is like some of the messengers in Greek tragedy (e.g., those in *Oedipus* or *Hippolytus*) or even comparable to the tragic chorus.[15] Once he has been created, however, one can hardly say that the speech (12) which he was created to speak is inappropriate to him.

The narratives of past events are not lumped together, as in classical epic, but are distributed at various spots in *Beowulf*, wherever they are appropriate to the occasion. Seven of them, 106 lines, appear in part II, the Danish expedition: 2, 3, 4, 6, 8, 9, and 10. All but 6 are concerned with the hero's parents, boyhood, and youthful victories over non-human antagonists. They are the sort of thing which Hroðgar's Danes would be impatient to know, also the things which the poet's audience[16] might be interested in hearing or seeing near the

[14] I mention only a few of the most recent discussions bearing upon this subject: A. G. Brodeur, *The Art of Beowulf* (Berkeley, 1959), pp. 142–157; James L. Rosier, 'Design for Treachery: The Unferð Intrigue,' *PMLA*, LXXVI (1962), 1–8; Norman E. Eliason, 'The þyle and Scop in *Beowulf*,' *Speculum*, XXXVIII (1963), 267–284; J. D. A. Ogilvy, 'Unferth: Foil to Beowulf?' *PMLA*, LXXIX (1964), 370–375.

[15] If there were any evidence that the *Beowulf*-poet was familiar with Greek or Roman tragedy, we might suppose that he had borrowed this device of the messenger. In the absence of such evidence, we can only assume that his Messenger was independently invented.

[16] In the broadest sense, not necessarily excluding either listeners or readers.

outset of the poem. Their logical place is rather early in part II, and that is where they appear. Passage 6 is a very general comment on Beowulf's undistinguished boyhood, which could have been introduced early. Instead, the poet brings it in immediately after a passage praising Beowulf's excellent qualities at the time of his return from Denmark, thus using the former ignominy as a foil to present glory. Since sharp contrasts and reversals of fortune provide the poet with one of his favorite rhetorical devices,[17] we can be fairly certain that he considered this the most appropriate spot for 6.

Five passages, 141 ½ lines, appear in part IV, the dragon killing: 1, 5, 7, 11, 12. Of these, the first has to do with the ancestry of Beowulf and Wiglaf. It is very appropriately brought in as the last two survivors of the Wægmundings are by themselves, after sharing the fight with the dragon and as Beowulf bestows the heirlooms of his family on the younger man. Passage 7 is general and is used to explain why Beowulf's sword breaks on the dragon's head. As far as logic goes, the hero's bad luck with weapons could have been introduced into the account of the fight with Grendel's dam or even into the swimming digression. Artistically, however, the passage is more effective where it is. Both of the earlier narratives are replete with detail and circumstance as they stand; they are certainly not in need of an additional aside. In both places, moreover, the poet would have been under the necessity of explaining why, if swords were useless to Beowulf, the hero managed to use a sword so effectively on a particular occasion. Such an explanation could easily be lame and awkward. In its present position, the comment tends to be taken for granted; the sword lies there shattered and useless, and for the moment one forgets all about the swords which had not failed Beowulf on other occasions. Passages 5 and 11 are included in Beowulf's speech to his retainers as they pause before the attack upon the dragon. The lines form a prelude to Beowulf's last boast, which they help to motivate.[18] Through them, we see his last single-handed venture against heavy odds, as part of the man's life and part of a heroic tradition. It is no rash or desperate act for this man, in this tradition, but the natural and inevitable consequence of all that he is and all that he has been in the past. At any other spot in the poem, this passage would lose most of its effect. Passage 12 is an important part of the Messenger's prophetic speech, in which he foretells the doom of the Geats. The poet could perhaps have underscored the danger from the Swedes more briefly, but I think that there is some-

---

[17] For example, lamentation after feasting, *þa wæs æfter wiste wop up ahafen* (128); Heremod versus Sigemund and Beowulf (898–915); Offa's bride versus Hygd (1925–1943); Offa's bride before and after her marriage (1931b–1954).

[18] From Beowulf's own standpoint, the lines had the purpose of strengthening the spirits of his retainers. Their effect seems to have been negligible except, perhaps, on Wiglaf.

thing to be said for the circumstantial account of ancient hatreds renewed in one generation after another, of heroes who consider their lives a small price to pay for the revenge of a former defeat, of wars in which the vanquished regularly expect no mercy and receive none. The danger to the Geats is no ordinary danger.

In view of the way in which the twelve passages are scattered through the poem, it is remarkable that we find so little repetition. The poet seems never to forget what he has said earlier or what he plans to say later on. The first seven passages are unique or virtually unique. The first contains matter alluded to nowhere else in the poem; the next three share only the mention of Ecgþeo and Beowulf,[19] but mention of the father and son is hardly to be avoided in any of these; the fifth shares very few details with other parts of the poem; the sixth and seventh are unique. In passage 10, the slaying of nicors may be a repetition of one detail in 9, but this is not certainly the case. Only in 8–9 and 11–12 do we find the same matter dealt with twice.

The repetition of the swimming adventure is well motivated, for Beowulf is correcting an erroneous report. Inevitably both Beowulf and Unferð mention the two participants, the fact that they swam in the ocean until separated, and the hardships of cold and storm which they encountered (515–516, *geofon ypum weol, wintrys wylmum*; 546, *wado weallende, wedera cealdost*). It would be hard to tell the story at all without these basic facts. Beowulf's claim that Breca could not swim away from him and that he would not leave Breca (541–543) is a direct answer to Unferð's gibe in 517–518 (*he þe æt sunde oferflat, hæfde mare mægen*), but the reply is managed without any actual repetition. Beowulf does not mention that the conduct of the swimmers was considered foolhardy nor that anyone attempted to dissuade them from the venture. Nor does he mention Breca's coming ashore and returning to his home. Nearly all of Beowulf's narrative is new, of course—facts not to be found in Unferð's version. Some of the differences between the two accounts are no doubt due to the poet's awareness that Beowulf and Breca were separated by the storm and probably knew little of each other's adventures thereafter, but most of the differences must stem from the poet's conscious avoidance of repetition. Verbal resemblances are few. We find *þa git on sund reon* (512b) paralleled by *þa wit on sund reon* (539b), very likely a deliberate echo. The poetic formula *aldrum nepdon* (510a) is repeated in *aldrum neðdon* (538a); something like this seems to have been almost routine in accounts of this sort.[20] There may be an echo of *holm up ætbær* (519b) in *ða mec sæ oðbær* (579b); in this case, a formula may have been deliberately changed to avoid exact repetition. Other verbal resemblances can be found, but they are too indefinite to be significant. Obviously there is no mechanical repetition of

---

[19] Beowulf is not mentioned by name.

[20] Cf. *aldre geneþan* (1469b) and *ealdre geneðde* (2133b).

formulas on even a small scale, although both passages deal with the same event.[21]

Lack of repetition in the two accounts of the Battle of Ravenswood is even more remarkable, for the two passages are more than 400 lines apart in the poem. Again, there are some inevitable restatements of basic facts: the conflict was between the Swedes and the Geats; the principal actors were Ongenþeo, Hæðcyn, Eofor, and Hygelac; the attacks on both sides were made over the sea (2477a, *ofer heafo*; 2954a, *sæmannum*, 2955a, *heaðoliðendum*, etc.); Hæðcyn and Ongenþeo were killed. But the second account omits the raiding by Ongenþeo's sons, which was the cause of the conflict, as well as Beowulf's repayment of Hygelac's generosity. On the other hand, the first account makes no mention of the place Ravenswood, the initial success of Hæðcyn's raid, the plight of the Geats in the grove, the onslaught of Hygelac's army and route of the Swedes, the earth-walled enclosure, the part of Wulf Wonreding in the fight, the despoiling of Ongenþeo's armor, or the rewards given to the sons of Wonræd. In fact, the two accounts are so different as to preclude accidental dissimilarity. The poet must have designed them to supplement each other with a minimum of overlapping. There are no extensive verbal resemblances: *Sweona ond Geata* (2472b, 2946b); *gomela Scylfing* (2487b), *gomela Scilfing* (2968a); *Geata dryhtne* (2483a, for Hæðcyn), *Geata dryhten* (2991b, for Hygelac). These formulas are of the inevitable sort, given the subject matter. Other resemblances are too indefinite to be considered repetition.

II.

The expedition to Denmark is obviously an important part of Beowulf's life, but the central incidents of *Beowulf* are not the main concern of this

---

[21] May I introduce two passages from an English ballad to illustrate the sort of repetition of theme and formula which never occurs in *Beowulf*?

> But vpp then rose that lither ladd,
> And did on hose and shoone;
> A coller he cast vpon his necke,
> Hee seemed a gentleman.
> And when he came to that ladies chamber,
> He thrild vpon a pinn;
> The lady was true of her promise,
> Rose vp and lett him in.
> ****************
> But vp then rose good Glasgeryon,
> And did on both hose and shoone,
> And cast a coller about his necke;
> He was a kinges sonne.
> And when he came to that ladies chamber,
> He thrild vpon a pinn;
> The lady was more then true of promise,
> Rose vp and let him in.

Glasgerion, st. 9–10, 15–16, in *English and Scottish Popular Ballads* (selected from F. J. Child's edition by G. L. Kittredge; Boston, 1932), pp. 136–137.

discussion. The expedition is in twelve sections,[22] which will be summarized with a minimum of comment:

1. 1–193. Prologue: The Scyldings and Heorot.
2. 194–261, 267–371, 375b–381a. Voyage and arrival of the Geats.
3. 381b–417, 424b–458, 473–490. Council in Heorot.
4. 491–505, 525–529, 581b–661. Feast in Heorot.
5. 662–836. Fight with Grendel: cleansing of Heorot.
6. 837–990. Morning after the fight; the ride to the mere.
7. 991–1201, 1214b–1250. Second feast in Heorot.
8. 1251–1398. Attack of Grendel's dam and morning after.
9. 1399–1650. Killing of Grendel's dam: cleansing of the mere.
10. 1651–1887. Beowulf and Hroðgar.
11. 1888–1976. Return of the Geats to Geatland.
12. 1977–2183a, 2190–2199. Beowulf and Hygelac.

A total of 2080½ lines is devoted to the fighting,[23] feasting, oratory, songs, and philosophy of this part. This total, of course, excludes the passages of part I but includes all other digressions.

III.

The middle life of Beowulf has eleven sections:

1. 2913b–2921. At some time after the Danish expedition, Hygelac invaded the northern coast of Europe with a fleet of ships. He was defeated and slain through the courage and superior numbers of the Hetware. The enemy included Hugas, Frisians, Hetware, and the Merovingians.

2. 1202–1214a. The collar given by Wealhþeo to Beowulf, and by Beowulf to Hygelac, was worn by the king when he guarded the spoils of his last raid. Pride led him over the sea to be killed by the Frisians and the Franks. The collar, with Hygelac's armor, passed into the possession of the enemy.

3. 2501–2508a. Beowulf killed Dæghrefn, champion of the Hugas, with his bare hands. By no means did the Huga carry off the armor to present it to the Frisian king.[24]

---

[22] Any appearance of symmetry arising from the number 12 in I and II is an illusion: the sections are for convenience of presentation only. There are nine continuous passages here, which could have been cut up and labeled in several different ways.

[23] Critics who are distressed by (a) the amount of violence in *Beowulf* or (b) the amount of folklore material in the poem should examine the passages above to see how small these things bulk in relation to the Danish expedition as a whole.

[24] Although Hygelac's raid and death are not mentioned, the Hugas and the Frisians are enough to indicate that the occasion is the same as that of 1 and 2. It is generally assumed, I believe, that the armor (*frætwe, breostweorðunge*) refers to Beowulf's

4. 2354b–2368. When Hygelac was slain in the land of the Frisians, Beowulf escaped by swimming to the land of the Geats with thirty suits of armor. The Hetware had no cause to exult, for few who faced Beowulf lived to see their homes.

5. 2369–2396. Queen Hygd offered Beowulf the throne of the Geats, for she doubted her son's ability to defend the country, now that Hygelac had fallen. Beowulf refused to take the kingdom from Heardred but instead became a sort of regent.[25] The sons of Ohthere, fleeing the wrath of their uncle, King Onela of the Swedes,[26] sought refuge with the Geats. Onela pursued the fugitives, Heardred was killed in battle, and Beowulf became king of the Geats. As king, he befriended Eadgils, one of the sons of Ohthere, and after a time invaded the land of the Swedes, killed Onela, and presumably put Eadgils on the Swedish throne.[27]

6. 2611–2625a. Weohstan killed Eanmund, the exiled son of Ohthere, in battle.[28] As a reward, King Onela gave him his nephew's sword and armor. He said nothing about any blood feud, although Weohstan had killed his brother's son. Later, Weohstan went to live among the Geats.[29] After many years he died, leaving Eanmund's sword to his son, Wiglaf.

7. 2200–2209a. After the fall of Hygelac and the killing of Heardred by the Swedes, Beowulf ruled the kingdom ably for fifty years.

8. 2732b–2743a. Beowulf reigned honorably for fifty years, protected his people, refrained from treachery, honored his oaths, slew no kinsmen.

9. 2397–2400. Beowulf survived all dangers until he went against the dragon.

10. 2633–2646a. He entertained his warriors suitably in the mead hall. He was generous to his retainers with gifts of gold and arms. Apparently he continued to perform heroic deeds.

---

armor, which the Huga hoped to strip from him. It seems to me possible that this is a reference to the thirty suits of armor (2361–2362) which the Geats had captured and which Dæghrefn tried to recover.

[25] There is no indication that Beowulf was present when Onela attacked the Geats. We should assume, perhaps, that when Heardred came of age, Beowulf retired from the court to his own estate.

[26] Onela is not mentioned by name in this passage, nor is the fact that the fugitives were his nephews, but cf. passage 6.

[27] The idea that Beowulf sent his people to assist Eadgils while he stayed at home seems to me inherently unbelievable. The syntax of lines 2391–2396 also makes it probable that *he* in 2395 refers to Beowulf.

[28] No doubt the battle in which Heardred fell.

[29] This is nowhere stated, but it seems likely; when Eadgils returned and Onela was killed, the land of the Swedes was not a safe place for the killer of Eanmund.

11. 2729–2732a. Beowulf had no son.[30]

The middle life of Beowulf is handled much less fully than the early life; there are 127 lines in part III, slightly more than half the number devoted to I. The materials of III show less variety than those of I, seven of the passages being concerned with only two incidents (the fall of Hygelac and the second Swedish war) and four being in the nature of general commentary on Beowulf's reign. If we look for the cause of the relative barrenness of III, we may find it in passage 8, where we are told that no king among the neighboring tribes dared attack the Geats while Beowulf reigned, that Beowulf for his part kept his oaths and sought no quarrels with anyone, and that his reign was free from unnatural killings (and no doubt from other sensational or scandalous events). If he continued to fight with monsters (as 9 and 10 may suggest), it is unlikely that he exterminated any during his long reign which would not pale in comparison with Grendel or his dam, or even in comparison with the nicors and jotuns disposed of in his early years. Either the poet's sources recorded nothing between the second Swedish war and the dragon fight, or the events recorded did not appeal to the poet as epic material.

The passages are generally short, as in I: 4, 5, and 9 are one continuous passage of 46 ½ lines; 8 and 11 are also continuous (14 ½ lines); 1, 3, and 7 are under ten lines; 2, 6, and 10 are under twenty lines. The poet himself accounts for a much greater proportion than in I, 83 lines (2, 4, 5, 6, 7, 9); while speeches by the characters account for only 44 lines: Beowulf 22 (3, 8, 11), Wiglaf 12½ (10), and the Messenger 8½ (1).

The appropriateness of passages to speaker and occasion is still generally above reproach. Passages 8 and 11 are spoken by the dying king as he looks back upon his reign. Their tone and the manner in which they blend with the rest of Beowulf's speech to Wiglaf make them appropriate only to Beowulf, although their content could no doubt have been adapted to the mouth of some other character had the poet so chosen. The third passage is part of Beowulf's speech to his retainers before the dragon fight. It seems appropriate that the old man should recall the heroic past, not only to hearten his retainers but also to strengthen his own spirit and prepare the way for his last audacious boast. The tenth belongs to Wiglaf's rebuke to the retainers who had deserted their king. A reminder of Beowulf's kingly qualities seems inevitable at this point and is most appropriately brought in by one who was himself a member of the

---

[30] Like nearly everyone of my generation, I was brought up to believe that Beowulf married Hygelac's widow, Hygd, but I can find no evidence that Beowulf was married. The woman (*meowle*) of 3150, who lamented for him at his funeral, is not represented as his wife. Probably this is a singular with plural sense, and *meowle* stands for all the mourning Geatish women. Kenneth Sisam calls her 'a typical Geatish woman,' *The Structure of Beowulf* (Oxford, 1965), p. 56, an explanation which makes good sense but seems to me less probable than my own.

comitatus. Passage 1 is part of the Messenger's prophetic speech. Without it, his forebodings of strife with the Franks and the Frisians would fall flat. Of the passages delivered by the poet in his own person, one is inevitable and two others reflect an important feature of the poet's style. Passage 7 opens the dragon killing division of the poem;[31] the lines are transitional and necessary to bridge a gap in time. In order to put them into the mouth of any character, the poet would have had to postpone them and begin the dragon killing much more abruptly than he began the Danish expedition. Passages 2 and 6, on the later history of the golden collar and the earliest history of Wiglaf's sword, respectively, are digressions of a sort which the poet apparently considered essential to heroic poetry.[32] Their places in the poem are determined by the points at which the collar and the sword are mentioned. The longest passage (4, 5, 9) is the only one which could have been given to someone other than the poet without any real awkwardness. It follows rather naturally, however, after the poet's allusion to the fights with Grendel and his dam. It is introduced by the rhetorical *No þæt læsest wæs*, which looks like a poetic formula,[33] and certainly suggests that the poet deliberately chose this point for an important biographical digression.

Moreover, the poet was restricted in his handling of the middle-life passages. It would have been difficult to put them into the mouths of the actors in the Danish portion without giving his characters supernatural prophetic powers. Only one passage of 12½ lines (2) is placed in II, and this is taken by the poet himself. All others are in IV, and this arrangement in turn has the effect of restricting the use of the characters of part IV as narrators. In part II, the poet could use several devices (the arrival of distinguished guests at a royal court, feasts, councils, a fliting) which might be out of place in IV, since they would probably detract from the somber tone of this part. In spite of some individual misfortunes, the terror of Grendel, and some forebodings of disaster to the Scyldings, the tone of II is joyous. The poet makes no attempt to conceal the fact that Beowulf, with the assistance of the Almighty, is more than a match for the forces of evil. Even Wyrd can be overruled (1056). The tone of the dragon fight, on the other hand, is gloomy.[34] We know almost from the begin-

---

[31] I.e., lines 2200–3182 of *Beowulf*. I hope that my references to 'parts' of the life of Beowulf and 'divisions' of the poem are clear enough to prevent confusion.

[32] Cf. the digressions on Hrunting (1525b–1528), on the origin of the dragon's hoard (2233–2270a), on the burning of Heorot (81a–85), and many others.

[33] I do not find it elsewhere in OE poetry, although *Guðlac* 769a has a similar pattern and function.

[34] I cannot go so far as to call it tragic. After a long and glorious life, Beowulf died heroically and victoriously, in a manner befitting a member of the warrior aristocracy to which he belonged. His passing meant sorrow and hardship for the Geats, but the loss was no greater than if he had lived a few years longer and died in his bed.

ning that Beowulf is going out to meet his death. The songs and feasting and rough good humor of the Danish expedition have no place here.

As we have already noted, the biographical passages forming part III are limited to three topics. Passages 1, 2, 3, and 4 deal with Hygelac's last raid. The first gives the basic facts: (a) Hygelac's raid was by sea (2915a, *faran flotherge*); (b) he was killed in this raid (2916–2919a, *þær hyne Hetware hilde gehnægdon, elne geeodon mid ofermægene þæt se byrnwiga bugan sceolde, feoll on feðan*); (c) the enemy are referred to as Hugas, Frisians, Hetware, and Merovingians. Fact (a) is mentioned in different terms in 2 (1208b, *ofer yða ful*) and in 4(2367a, 2368b, *Oferswam ða sioleða bigong . . . eft to leodum*). Fact (b) is repeated, but in different words and with emphasis on different details, in 2 (1205b, *hyne Wyrd fornam*; 1209b, *he under rande gecranc*) and in 4 (2355b, *þær mon Hygelac sloh*; 2358–2359a, *Hreðles eafora hiorodryncum swealt, bille gebeaten*).[35] Of the enemies, the Hetware are mentioned again in 4, but not in 2 or 3. The Hugas are called Franks in 2, and Dæghrefn is a Huga in 3, though the Frankish dynasty is mentioned only in 1. The Frisians are indicated in four ways in the four passages: *on Fresna land* in 1 (2915b); *fæhðe to Frysum* in 2 (1207a); *Frescyninge* in 3 (2503b); and *Freslondum on* in 4 (2357b). It is interesting to see how carefully the poet avoided sameness in the expression of these details, even though the passages are widely separated in the poem.

Apart from basic facts, passage 2 is all fresh matter. The capture of Hygelac's collar and armor is not mentioned in the other accounts, nor the fact that he had captured booty and was guarding it when he was killed, nor that his fall was attributed to excessive pride (1206, *syþðan he for wlenco wean ahsode*). Passage 3 duplicates nothing in the other accounts except the names of some of the enemy tribes; in fact, if it were not for the mention of a champion of the Hugas and a king of the Frisians, we should probably never have guessed that this passage is connected with the fall of Hygelac. Most of passage 4 has to do with the thirty coats of mail, possibly alluded to in 3, and Beowulf's escape by swimming, which is not even hinted at in the other passages.

Verbal similarities, other than references to men and tribes, are not very striking. The word *frætwe* appears in 1 (2919b, *nalles frætwe geaf*), 2 (1207b, *He þa frætwe wæg*), and 3 (2503a, *nalles he ða frætwe*); but the meaning and use are different in the three places. This is no mechanical repetition of a poetic formula, but it could be an echo-device. There may be a link between passages 7 and 1 in *niða genægdon*, used of the killing of Heardred (2206a) and *hilde gehnægdon* (? for *genægdon*), used of the killing of Hygelac (2916b).

Passages 5, 6, and 7 have to do with the second war with the Swedes. Here we cannot find much duplication of even the basic facts. The pieces fit together

---

[35] Also mentionel, only to establish chronology, in 7 (2201b, *syððan Hygelac læg*).

almost perfectly, each supplying details essential to a comprehension of the others. We know that Heardred was Hygelac's son, that he became king of the Geats, and that the sons of Ohthere sought refuge in Geatland—we know these things only from passage 5 (2369–2384a). One of the exiled princes, Eadgils, is named in 5 (2392b); the other, Eanmund, is named only in 6 (2611b). Onela is named and his relationship to the sons of Ohthere made clear only in 6 (2616b, 2619a), although the Swedish king is indicated in 5 by a 'kenning (2381b, *helm Scylfinga*) and by an epithet (2387b, *Ongenðioes bearn*). That Heardred's foes were Swedes is unmistakable only in 5 (2383a, *Swiorice*; 2381b, *Scylfinga*), although the fact is clear enough in 7 (2205b, *Heaðo-Scilfingas*) for those who are versed in the tribal names. That the Swedes invaded Geatland is suggested in 5 but expressly stated only in 7 (2204–2205). Heardred is killed in both 5 and 7, although language and details differ:

2384b–2388.   Him þæt to mearce wearð;
    he þær for feorme   feorhwunde hleat,
    sweordes swengum,   sunu Hygelaces;
    ond him eft gewat   Ongenðioes bearn
    hames niosan   syððan Heardred læg.
2202–2206. ond Heardrede   hildemeceas
    under bordhreoðan   to bonan wurdon,
    ða hyne gesohtan   on sigeþeode
    hearde hildefrecan,   Heaðo-Scilfingas,
    niða genægdon   nefan Hererices.

Weohstan's killing of Eanmund is known only from 6, as are Onela's gifts and the later history of Weohstan. If it were not for the mention of Onela and the exiled son of Ohthere (2612a, 2616a), we should have difficulty connecting this passage with the second Swedish war. Beowulf becomes king of the Geats in 5 (2389–2390a, *let ðone bregostol Biowulf healdan, Geatum wealdan*) and in 7 (2207–2208a, *syððan Beowulfe brade rice on hand gehwearf*). The befriending of Eadgils and the slaying of Onela are found only in 5 (2391–2396).

There are a few verbal similarities in this group of passages. The formula *uferan dogrum* of 5 (2392a) reappears in *ufaran dogrum* of 7 (2200b); and *syððan Hygelac læg* in 7 (2201b) suggests *syððan Heardred læg* in 5 (2388b). Passages 5 and 6 may be linked by *suna Ohteres* in the former (2380b, referring to both sons) and *suna Ohteres* in the latter (2612a, referring to Eanmund only).

The remaining passages (8, 9, 10, 11) characterize Beowulf's reign. Passages 9 and 11 share no details with each other or with 8 or 10. They are so general that they could be taken as applying to Beowulf's life as a whole, but in the contexts in which they are placed, they seem to have a narrower application to his life as king of the Geats. Passage 10 exhibits Beowulf's relationship with his retainers, showing him in this, as in everything else, an exemplary ruler by the standards of the heroic age. The only element in this passage which is not unique is the mention of Beowulf's famous acts and audacious deeds (2645–2646a), a comment so general in nature as inevitably to have several parallels in other portions of the poem. Passage 8 shows no overlapping with 9, 10, or 11, but the references to the length and stability of Beowulf's reign (2732b–2733a, *Ic ðas leode heold fiftig wintra*; 2737b, *heold min tela*) are shared with 7 (2208b–2209a, *he geheold tela fiftig wintra*). This overlap is probably inevitable, for 7 is transitional, its primary purpose being to place the dragon killing chronologically, that is, after the deaths of Hygelac and Heardred and fifty years after Beowulf's accession. Verbal echoes of 7 in 8 are obvious enough. Such similarities within 8, 9, 10, and 11 are lacking, although *ellenweorca* (2399a) and *ellenweorc* (2643a) form a link, possibly intentional, between 9 and 10.

IV.

The dragon killing is central to the plot of *Beowulf* and will be outlined briefly. It falls into eleven sections:[36]

1. 2209b–2286. The theft from the dragon's hoard.
2. 2287–2323. The land of the Geats laid waste.
3. 2324–2354a. Preparations for the dragon fight.
4. 2401–2425. Journey to the dragon's barrow.
5. 2508b–2610. Beowulf enters the barrow, and the fight begins.
6. 2625b–2632, 2646b–2660. Wiglaf and the retainers.
7. 2661–2682a, 2688–2711a. The dragon fight continued.
8. 2711b–2728, 2743b–2801, 2809–2812, 2817–2883. Death of Beowulf.
9. 2892–2910a, 3007b–3017, 3028–3136. Preparations for the funeral.
10. 3137–3168. Funeral of Beowulf.
11. 3169–3182. Epilogue: Estimate of Beowulf by his people.

There are 689 lines in this part, excluding biographical passages of parts I, III, and V, but including the non-biographical elegy on the father of the hanged (2444–2462a).

V.

The aftermath of Beowulf's last exploit and death has six sections:

1. 2884–2891. When the cowardice of Beowulf's retainers became known,

---

[36] I find that I have also arranged part III in eleven sections, but the passages of IV could be split up or combined in many ways; cf. note 22.

their professional careers came to an abrupt end. No ruler wanted their services.

2. 2910b–2913a. Upon hearing of Beowulf's death, the Franks and the Frisians renewed their ancient strife with the Geats.

3. 2922–2923a. The Swedes also repudiated their treaties with the Geats.

4. 2999–3007a. Beowulf had been gone but a short time when the Swedes made war on his people.

5. 3018–3027. Geatish women went ihto slavery in foreign lands. The wolf and the black raven feasted on the bodies of fallen Geats.[37]

6. 2802–2808. One reminder of past glories remained to the subjugated people: the tomb of Beowulf. Seamen from afar could see it long afterward, overlooking the sea, high on the crags of Hronesnæs.

These six passages are evidently drawn from traditions about the history of the Geats which were known to the poet. He makes the speeches of his characters foreshadow[38] events which have already taken place. The passages are short, the longest being ten lines, the total for all six 38 lines. All are spoken by the actors of part IV: 23 by the Messenger, who predicts wars with the neighboring nations and the fall of the Geats (2, 3, 4, 5); eight by Wiglaf, who forecasts the disgrace of the retainers (1); and seven by Beowulf, who orders the construction of his barrow on the headland (6). The appropriateness of each passage to the speaker and the occasion seems too obvious for extended comment. As the only loyal member of the comitatus, and as Beowulf's heir, Wiglaf is in the best possible position to foretell the disgrace of the disloyal retainers. Beowulf's orders for his funeral and his tomb are most appropriate to the dying king. The four passages from the Messenger's long speech could hardly be removed without destroying the effect of the speech, since it is his predictions of the future which give his historical accounts their chief motivation.

There is little repetition in these passages. The belief that Beowulf's death will bring disaster to the Geats is variously expressed by the Messenger in 2, 4, and 5. This is in the nature of an inevitable repetition—in any case, one which gives the idea an emphasis evidently desired by the poet. Also inevitable perhaps are the three references to the spread of the bad news in 1, 2, and 4:

---

[37] This does not necessarily imply that the Geats were exterminated, absorbed into another tribe, or even permanently subjugated.

[38] My references to prophecy are intended in a natural, human sense. The prophecies are rather indefinite and may be only an approximation of the calamities of the Geats as the poet knew them. In this connection, we should consider carefully Brodeur's comparison of Beowulf's predictions concerning Ingeld with the version in Saxo Grammaticus' *Gesta Danorum*, Book VI, and its implications for those who would interpret the poem— *op. cit.*, pp. 174–180.

2888b–2890a.	syððan æðelingas
	feorran gefricgean fleam eowerne,
	domleasan dæd.
2911b–2913a.	syððan under*ne*
	Froncum ond Frysum fyll cyninges
	wide weorðeð.
3002–3003a.	syððan hie gefricgeað frean userne
	ealdorleasne.

Verbal resemblances, *syððan* and *gefricgean—gefricgeað*, have little significance, if any.

SOME CONCLUSIONS

In this survey of Beowulf's life, I have tried to improve our understanding of some of the techniques used by the poet, especially in his handling of the lesser events included in the biography. Certain qualities in his presentation seem to me to stand out most clearly.

The first of these is fullness—one might even say, completeness. The record of lesser events comprises twenty-nine passages, 412½ lines, more than one-eighth of the poem.[39] It would seem that the poet was trying to include all of the traditions about Beowulf that he knew and considered relevant. That this fullness is deliberate and due to art rather than chance is indicated by the treatment of the other characters. Hygelac figures only in scenes which involve Beowulf. The events of Hroðgar's life which do not involve Beowulf directly are concerned with his father, Ecgþeo, or furnish background for Beowulf's exploits. Other characters, like Unferð and Hroðulf, are the subjects of allusive comments which suggest that the poet, and his audience no doubt, knew much more about them than the poet saw fit to tell. It is only in his treatment of Beowulf that he appears to have aimed at completeness. He has not given us as detailed a life as we of the twentieth century would like to have, but the twenty-nine passages contain all of the facts necessary for a reasonably good condensed biography of a great man against the background of his times.

The second quality appears in the distribution of the passages. Instead of gathering them together and presenting them in chronological order, the poet has introduced them at various points in his work, wherever they seemed to him most appropriate to the context. I can see nothing haphazard in the arrangement. There is an obvious lack of symmetry between the two major divisions of the poem: the first, or Danish, division (2199 lines) contains eight of the biographical passages, totaling 118½ lines (a little over five percent);

[39] One might, of course, expand the record somewhat by including passing allusions, references to Beowulf as *sunu Ecgþeowes*, etc. Or one might reduce it materially by eliminating both accounts of the Battle of Ravenswood on the assumption (probably mistaken) that Beowulf was absent from the battle.

whereas the second, or dragon, division (983 lines) contains twenty-one passages, totaling 294 lines (something over thirty percent). As long as the passages are appropriate to speaker and occasion, however, this lack of symmetry need not disturb our conception of the poet's art. The Anglo-Saxons did not especially prize exact symmetry, as we can readily see in the irregular strophes of *Deor* (7, 6, 4, 3, 7, and 15 lines) or the asymmetry of *Christ* II and III (427 and 798 lines, respectively)[40] or the irregular lengths of the various parts of *Widsið*.

The third quality is one which we may call inseparability. Most of the biographical passages are short, under twenty lines. One of them (I, 1) is a speech by one of the characters. More often the passage is part of a speech which is otherwise concerned with the immediate action and, hence, cannot be removed without damage to the plot: I, 2, 3, 4, 5, 8, 10; III, 8, 10, 11; V, 1, 5, 6. Or the passage may be a brief aside by the poet himself: I, 6, 7; III, 2, 6, 7. Such passages, totaling 294 lines (approximately thirty percent). But as we have noted at the outset, the poet was not averse to interrupting the action when it seemed to him desirable to do so. There are four long stretches of biographical matter. is One the poet's digression (*No þæt læsest wæs*) of 46½ lines, containing passages III, 4, 5, 9. Another is the Messenger's speech of 128 lines, which is concerned with the immediate action; i.e., it announces Beowulf's death and directs the building of his funeral pyre. It contains a 97-line sweep of biography, history, and prophecy, which includes passages V, 2, III, 1, V, 3, I, 12, and V, 4 in that order. The other two long passages are spoken by Beowulf. His 77-line reply to Unferð is very much concerned with the immediate action but also contains I, 9 (51½ lines). His 84-line speech to the retainers is concerned with the immediate action, although more subtly than the preceding, and is diversified by the non-biographical elegiac passage. It contains a stretch of 46 lines, which include part of I, 5, plus I, 11 and III, 3. It seems clear that the poet intended the lesser events of Beowulf's life to form an inseparable part of the epic rather than an excrescence upon it.

The fourth quality is economy. The poet repeats little, even when he gives two or more accounts of the same incident. Exact verbal repetition is practically non-existent in the biographical passages. It would seem, not only that the poet planned his work carefully, but that he was able to see (or hear) his poem as a whole, so that he knew as he reached line 1202 precisely what he would be saying in lines 2354–2368. The widely scattered sections of biography fit into one another like the pieces of a jigsaw puzzle, without any noticeable gaps and

---

[40] Naturally, I have in mind the arrangement and divisions in the *Exeter Book*, which seem to be due to an intelligent and perceptive compiler. Whether he regarded the *Christ* as one long poem in three parts or as an anthology in three parts is a question which does not bear upon the dissymmetry.

with hardly more duplication than is absolutely necessary if we are to fit the pieces together.

The fifth quality, which really includes all of the others, is conscious artistry. This may not be obvious as one reads or listens to the poem. The poetry seems to flow freely like the work of a man interested only in the affair of the moment: the apt kenning, the bold turn of a phrase, the vivid bit of description, or the rush of the narrative. It is only after painstaking analysis that the poet is fully revealed as the artist that he is, one who obtains his best effects by meticulous planning.

The present study bears upon several important critical problems. I do not wish to enter into a detailed consideration of any of these at this time, but I can indicate briefly what the problems are. First, there is the question of composition. Was *Beowulf* composed by a poet who worked slowly, perhaps with pen and parchment, or was it put together extemporaneously by a scop standing before his audience with a rough outline of the story to guide him and a great store of formulas and themes at his command? No doubt, an oral composer could work into his narrative all that he remembered of the hero's life by a mechanical reproduction of themes: a blood feud, a battle, the fall of a chief, and so on. The difficult question is whether, composing in this manner, he could introduce the twenty-nine pieces of the jigsaw puzzle in such a way as to form a harmonious whole without any avoidable repetition of details and without mechanical repetition of poetic formulas. If this question could be affirmatively answered, the theory of oral composition would be measurably closer to general acceptance.

The prevailing opinion today seems to be that *Beowulf* is not two or more older poems patched together, but a unified whole. As I see it, the argument for unity is strengthened by what we have seen of the arrangement of the biographical materials. The early life of Beowulf as reported in the first division of the poem is inadequate without the account of the Wægmunding family, the boyhood at Hreðel's court, and the Battle of Ravenswood, all of which are in the second division. Similarly, the early life as recorded in the second division is deficient without the accounts of Beowulf's parents and his youthful exploits in the first division. The one passage dealing with the middle life in the first division means much more to us when supplemented by the three additional accounts in the second. Above all, the avoidance of repetition, in the second division, of biographical details found in the first, suggests composition by one poet with a comprehensive master plan for the poem as a whole.

The third problem is a general one involving sources. The theory that *Beowulf* was pieced together out of a number of older ballads seems now generally discredited. Certainly, if the poem derives from popular ballads of the type represented by *Glasgerion*, its structure, especially in its economy, shows no relationship to the sources. We shall also encounter difficulties if we regard

Beowulf as a translated and versified Norse saga.[41] Although there are variations in the structure of the sagas which have come down to us, the typical saga dealing with the life of a single hero proceeds chronologically, very much in the manner of my own arrangement of the life of Beowulf: ancestors, early life, middle life, old age (if the hero lives so long), death, vicissitudes of the hero's family and friends after his death. I can recall no saga in which past, present, and future are woven into one pattern as in *Beowulf*. If such a saga exists, it would furnish strong support for a view once held by very distinguished scholars.

On the other hand, any view of *Beowulf* which regards the poem as purely fictitious will meet with problems in the biographical matter. The fullness of the record which we have noted above is understandable if the poet was incorporating ancient traditions which he believed to be true. If he was merely inventing a fiction for some such purpose as religious or political allegory, some of the details 'invented' might seem useless or even incongruous. To take one example, if *Beowulf* is interpreted as an allegory of Salvation, why is the Central Figure provided with an uncle and a grandfather? What is signified by the death of Ecgþeo before the opening of the poem? Why must the Messenger predict servitude for Beowulf's people after, and apparently as a result of, his death? Such questions as these would inevitably have to be answered, unless we assume that the composer of *Beowulf* was working with traditional sources of some kind.

The fourth and last of the problems which I should like to mention is that of models. Eminent scholars have held the view that the *Beowulf*-poet modeled his work after the classical epics.[42] Again, the handling of the biographical matter offers difficulties. If the poet had been imitating the *Iliad*, would he not have omitted most of the biographical and historical digressions, leaving it for medieval counterparts of Ovid, Euripides, and the rest to tell us how Beowulf became the hero he was and what sort of life he led when not involved in the central actions of the plot? If he had been imitating the *Odyssey* or the *Aeneid*, would he not have introduced Beowulf's origin and early adventures and battles in one lump, probably upon his arrival at Hroðgar's court? The Scylding would be the obvious substitute for Alcinoüs or Dido as Beowulf recounted his past. I suppose that an imitator of the classics could easily have brought in all of

---

[41] The ballads as we know them and the sagas which have survived are much later than the poem. We suppose that things comparable to the sagas and ballads existed in the seventh century, but we cannot be positive in the matter.

[42] An Irish model for *Beowulf* is suggested by James Carney, *Studies in Irish Literature and History* (Dublin, 1955), pp. 77–128. A comparison of *Beowulf* with the *Táin Bó Fraích* is given on pp. 116–127. I would point out that the earlier and later life of the Irish hero are not woven into the fabric of *TBF*; in fact, they are scarcely mentioned.

Beowulf's middle life together in Part IV, much as the history of Latium is introduced in the seventh book of the *Aeneid: Nunc age, qui reges, Erato, quae tempora rerum,* etc. The aftermath passages could have been combined into one and presented as a prophecy following obvious models in the sixth book of the *Aeneid* or the eleventh book of the *Odyssey*. Instead, the *Beowulf*-poet weaves the biographical elements into the structure of his epic, a bit here and a bit there—not like the figures on a Grecian vase, neatly arranged in a simple order, but like the interwoven motifs on one of the cruciform pages of the *Lindisfarne Gospels* or one of the intricate initials of the *Vespasian Psalter*, disappearing for a time to reappear, always in the right place and with a consistent shape but always with an element of surprise.

SHERMAN M. KUHN

The University of Michigan
January 1966

ON THE CONSONANTAL PHONEMES
OF OLD ENGLISH

1. Some years ago I attempted a brief description of the Old English vowel system.[1] Writing from the viewpoint of the traditional linguists, I sought to transpose their ideas into structural terms. The few innovations introduced seemed to me necessary to a sound structural description and, at the same time, not incompatible with the traditional methodology. The present study is designed as a roughly parallel treatment of the Old English consonant system.[2]

1.1. At the outset, I wish to point out that the task of describing the consonantal phonemes is considerably more difficult than that of describing the syllabic phonemes. Three factors contribute to this increased difficulty. First, the OE spelling practices show at least as great a variety in the representation of consonants as in the representation of vowels; but the variant graphs are often widely differing symbols (in free variation) for a single phoneme (*e.g.*, *f*, *b*, and *u* for /f/), while real phonemic distinctions are often ignored almost completely (*e.g.*, *g* for the velar /g/, the semivowel /ǧ/, and the voiced affricate /ǧ/). Second, the problems of interpreting the consonantal spellings are often less obvious than those presented by the vowel symbols. As a consequence, the traditional linguists have tended to overlook some of the facts; for example, they have generally been content to regard /ǧ/ simply as a long or geminated /ǧ/, leaving it for a structuralist to observe that these are two contrasting sounds regardless of quantity. Third, while structuralists have made significant contributions to the description of the OE consonants, they tend to attack the problem piecemeal, each fitting his new analysis of a few phonemes into a general system which is still essentially the traditional one. This practice leads to frequent clashes between structuralist and structuralist, which must be resolved somehow by anyone who attempts to state the traditional views (with their own omissions and contradictions) in structural terms.

1.2. The consonant system which I present is that of about A.D. 700. It is basically

---

[1] "On the Syllabic Phonemes of Old English", *Language*, XXXVII (1961), 522-538.
[2] To avoid confusion, I make no mention of other schools than the Structuralist; *e.g.*, the Tagmemic and the Generative-transform schools. I believe, however, that the system presented here could be converted into tagmemic or generative-transform terms rather easily.

Reprinted by permission from *Philological Essays: Studies in Old and Middle English Language and Literature in Honour of Herbert Dean Meritt*, ed. James L. Rosier (The Hague: Mouton, 1970), pp. 16-49.

[124]

Mercian, but the sparse evidence of eighth-century Northumbrian points to a very similar system for that dialect, and the West Saxon and Kentish systems (judged by their earliest written records, which are of the ninth century or later) probably differed from this one only in the incidence of certain phonemes and allophones. In reconstructing the system of *c* 700, I have used three early manuscripts: the CORPUS GLOSSARY (Corpus Christi College, Cambridge, MS 144), the EPINAL GLOSSARY (Bibliothèque Municipale, Épinal, MS 72), and the ERFURT GLOSSARY (Amplonian Library, Erfurt, MS 42). All three are glossaries of difficult Latin words and phrases, with explanations or synonyms usually in Latin but occasionally in English. The body of Old English material provided in this way is small,[3] but it constitutes the most extensive that we have for the earliest period. Of the three texts, the latest is Erf., an early ninth-century copy of an English exemplar. It was made by a scribe with a High German background, which causes him at times to substitute Old High German words for the OE, and at other times to write hybrid forms which are basically OE but contain one or more graphs used in the OHG manner. There are compensations, however: when the OE gloss did not suggest any OHG equivalent, this scribe copied very cautiously, often it would seem preserving the archaic spellings of his exemplar exactly as he found them. The earliest of the three texts orthographically is Ep., which preserves many archaic spellings and seems to be closer linguistically to A.D. 700 than either of the other MSS. There are lacunae in Ep., a large part of the *c*-section, a little of *u-v*, and all of *d, e, x, y,* and *z* having been lost from the MS. Corp. is approximately twice as long as Erf. It contains nearly all of the matter found in the other two glossaries, plus extensive additions, and all of the items have been rearranged in a more nearly alphabetic order. The compiler of Corp. was an innovator, and his innovations extend to the spellings, which he frequently modernized. In other words, his text is the latest of the three, linguistically and orthographically. Both Ep. and Corp. are eighth-century MSS.[4]

1.3. The relationship of the three glossaries can be shown, with the aid of two hypothetical MSS (Archetype II, the ancestor of Ep. and Erf., and Archetype I, the ancestor of Arch. II and Corp.), as in Table I. If this stemma is correct (and it is supported by abundant evidence),[5] any form in which all three glossaries agree, or

---

[3] Ep. contains only about 951 English entries, about 149 having been lost through destruction of one leaf of the MS. Erf. fills this gap, but its approximately 1186 English entries include about 186 that are in supplementary sections not paralleled in either Ep. or Corp. Corp. contains about 2176 English entries, but nearly half are not paralleled in the other glossaries and represent material added to the original, presumably when Corp. was compiled. Allowing for corrupt forms, accidental omissions of individual words, *etc.*, we have only about 900 English words available as evidence of the state of the language when Arch. I was written.

[4] The exact dates of Ep. and Corp., as well as their relative dates within the century, are controversial. Since these matters are not essential to the problem in hand, I shall not enter into a lengthy palaeographical digression at this time.

[5] See H. M. Chadwick, *Studies in Old English*, in *Transactions of the Cambridge Philological Society*, IV (1899), 87-265; Henry Sweet, *The Oldest English Texts*, EETS, OS, LXXXIII (1885), 1-34.

are in substantial agreement, may be assumed to go back to Arch. I; *e.g.*, *anguens*: *breer* (Corp. 161, Ep. Erf. 68), *accearium*: *steli* (Corp. 55, Ep. 49 *steeli*, Erf. *steli*).[6] A form in which only Ep. and Erf. agree may be an innovation in Arch. II, but one in which Corp. agrees with either of the other two is likely to have descended from Arch. I.[7]

TABLE I.

*Arch. I (c 700 or earlier)

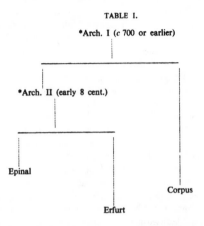

*Arch. II (early 8 cent.)

Epinal

Corpus

Erfurt

2. *Table II* is a somewhat modified traditional arrangement of the OE consonants, with their most important allophones. It may not be completely logical at certain points; for example, /n/ is not a dental in all positions, and /g/ is not a stop in all positions. The rule followed here is one sanctioned by custom; namely, that the allophone which occurs in initial position is regarded as primary and determines the designation of the phoneme and its place in the table. After leaving the stops and spirants, the table is decidedly asymmetrical; but for this I offer no apology, since it reflects the system of an asymmetrical language.[8] Allophones are indicated sparingly. According to the findings of modern acoustic phonetics, every phoneme is so modified by neighboring sounds that it might even be said to have a separate allophone for

[6] Citations, unless otherwise indicated, are from Sweet, *OET*, pp. 35-110. There are better editions of individual glossaries, but for our purposes Sweet has two advantages: he includes only those Latin lemmata which have OE (or possibly OE) equivalents, and he has arranged the texts in parallel columns with convenient cross-references between Corp. and Ep. Erf.

[7] There are possible exceptions, of course; *e.g.*, two scribes working independently could conceivably substitute an ð for an archaic *d* (= ð) in their archetype or make some similar modernization, or they might correct an obvious blunder in the same way if there were only one obvious correction.

[8] The symmetry of my vowel tables may even be misleading in some instances. For example (Table I, *Lg.*, XXXVII, 524), /a/ was a back vowel as compared with /i/, /e/, /æ/, *etc.*, and its effect in producing velar umlaut in Mercian was certainly that of a back vowel, but phonetically /a/ and /ā/ were probably central rather than back. In this case, the pressure of symmetry and a desire to avoid an extra column in the table led me to oversimplify. I hope that no one was misled.

every environment in which it occurs. No doubt, a similar state existed in OE times, but for the purposes of this discussion, it seemed best to include only those secondary allophones which either became independent phonemes at a later date or which give rise to spelling problems in the OE texts.

2.1. TABLE II.

Old English Consonants, c 700.

	Labial	Dental	Palato-velar-glottal
Voiceless stops	/p/ [p]	/t/ [t]	/c/ [k, k']
Voiced stops	/b/ [b, ƀ]	/d/ [d]	/g/ [g, ɡ, g']
Spirants	/f/ [f, v]	/þ/ [þ, ð]	/h/ [h, x. x']
Liquids	/l/ [l, ḷ]	/r/ [r, ɽ]	
Nasals	/m/ [m, ṃ]	/n/ [n, ṇ, ŋ]	
Sibilants		/s/ [s, z]	/š/ [ʃ]
Semi-vowels	/w/ [w]		/ǵ/ [j]
Voceless affricate		/č/ [tʃ]	
Voiced affricate		/ǧ/ [dʒ]	

Length: Usualy indicated by doubling of the consonant, /pp/, etc.

Later changes and dialectal variations in the OE consonants will be noted in the discussions of individual phonemes, but a systematic treatment dial·ct by dialect is probably unnecessary, inasmuch as dialectal variatiƆns in the consonants are much less significant and much harder to determine precisely than are those in the vowels.[9]

2.2. Structuralists who have dealt with OE consonants sometimes differ from this table, as well as from one another, in the symbols used for transcribing the phonemes. There should be no misunderstanding if the following variant usages are kept in mind: /k/ for /c/ — Penzl, Moulton, Stockwell, Hockett; /θ/ for /þ/ — Stockwell, Hockett; /x/ for /h/ — Stockwell; /sc/ for /š/ — Stockwell; /sk/ for /š/ — Hockett; /j/ for /ǵ/ — Moulton, Stockwell; /ỿ/ for /ǵ/ — Hockett; /k'/ for /č/ — Penzl; /c/ for /č/ — Stockwell; /ḳ/ for /č/ — Hockett; /ǧ/ for /ǧ/ — Moulton; /jj/ for /ǧ/ — Stockwell; /ĝ/ for /ǧ/ — Hockett.[10] These differences in transcription do not seem to reflect any basic difference in the interpretation of the consonant system. I piefer /c/ for the palato-velar stop [k, k'] because this phoneme is normally spelled c in the MSS and in the printed texts, k being a very infrequent graphic variant. A symbol which is readily identified has some advantage over one which might be misunder-

---

[9]   E.g., in my Table II (Lg., XXXVII, 533 : the Mercian syllabics), independent phonemes appear which are not present in Table IV (p. 536 : West Saxon syllabics) or in Table V (p. 537 : Kentish syllabics). The consonants present no comparable differences from dialect to dialect.

[10]   Herbert Penzl, "The Phonemic Split of Germanic k in Old English," Language, XXIII (1947), 34-42; W. G. Moulton, "The Stops and Spirants of Early Germanic," Lg., XXX (1954), 1-42; C. F. Hockett, A Course in Modern Linguistics (New York, 1958), pp. 372-379; R. P. Stockwell, "The Phonology of Old English : A Structural Sketch," Studies in Linguistics, XIII (1958), 13-24.

stood. On similar grounds, one might regard /þ/ as preferable to /θ/ for the dental spirant [þ or θ, ð]; /ġ/ as preferable to /j/ or /ʝ/ for the palatal semi-vowel [j] (usually spelled g, in many printed texts ġ); /ċ/ as preferable to /k'/ or /ķ/ for the voiceless dental affricate [tʃ] or [tš]; and /ǧ/ as preferable to /jj/ or /ǧ/ for the voiced affricate [dʒ]. The symbol /š/ does not represent the usage of MSS or printed texts, and /ǧ/ is only partially representative,[11] but I believe that we gain something by reserving /sc/ for the cluster [sk] in words like *scolere* 'learner' (Medieval Latin *scholārius*), and by indicating that /ǧ/, although a cluster phonetically and a geminate etymologically, was a phonemic unit in OE. Lastly, it is customary in dealing with OE consonants to take the initial allophone as primary; hence, one would prefer /h/ to /x/ for the palato-velar-glottal spirant [h, x, x'].

2.3. There are four important areas of disagreement in the analysis of the OE consonant system: (1) /g/, /h/, in which Moulton and Hockett are in agreement against Stockwell, whose views coincide rather closely with those of the traditional linguists; (2) /l/, /r/, in which Samuels and Reszkiewicz are in opposition to Hockett, Stockwell, and the traditional linguists; (3) /hl/, /hr/, hn/, /hw/, in which Hockett, Stockwell, and probably most traditional linguists hold views differing from those of A. Campbell, himself a traditionalist; and (4) the semi-vowels, in which Stockwell is at odds with Hockett, Kurath, and the traditional linguists.[12] These controversies will be taken up at appropriate points: (1) after the phoneme /h/, (2) after the phoneme /r/, (3) after the phoneme /w/, and (4) after the phoneme /ġ/.

2.4. The distributions of the phonemes are generally presented in terms of Moulton's twelve environments:[13] (1) post-junctural position,[14] C—; (2) lengthened or geminated, CC or C:; (3) after nasal and before vowel, NCV; (4) pre-junctural after nasal, NC+; (5) after /l/ and before vowel, lCV; (6) pre-junctural after /l/, lC+; (7) after /r/ and before vowel, rCV; (8) pre-junctural after /r/, rC+; (9) between vowels, VCV; (10) pre-junctural after vowel, VC+; (11) after vowel and before /s/, VCs; (12) after vowel and before /t/, VCt. For some of the consonants which were not included in Moulton's study, additional positions must be noted: for liquids and nasals, (13) pre-junctural after consonant; for /n/ and /s/, (14) after vowel and before /c/ or /g/. In treating the phonemes /c/, /g/, and /h/, I find that I must divide several of Moulton's positions into two, an (a) and a (b). Blanks due to incompleteness of the shared glossary data will be filled, when such a procedure

---

[11] Perhaps /šċ/ and /ċġ/ would have been better.

[12] See note 10 and also M. L. Samuels, "The Study of Old English Phonology," *Transactions of the Philological Society, 1952* (1953), pp. 18-19, 42-43; Alfred Reszkiewicz, "The Phonemic Interpretation of Old English Digraphs," *Biuletyn Polskiego Towarzystwa Językoznawczego*, XII (1953), 180-184; Hans Kurath, "The Binary Interpretation of English Vowels : A Critique," *Lg.*, XXXIII (1957), 111-122; and A. Campbell, *Old English Grammar* (Oxford, 1959), pp. 20, 186.

[13] *Op. cit.*

[14] Several types of juncture are recognized. As used here, post-junctural means word initial, initial in the second element of a compound, or initial after a prefix which was still productive in OE; pre-junctural means word final, final in the first element of a compound, or immediately preceding a derivational suffix which was still productive in OE.

appears safe, with forms from a single glossary or with forms from slightly later texts in the same dialect, *i.e.* Mercian,[15] or from rougly contemporary texts in other dialects. Such substitute forms will always be indicated.

3. Voiceless Stops

3.1. /p/ [p]: (1) *pic* 'pitch' 1593;[16] *paad* 'cloak' 1654; *spoed* 'success' 1663. (2) *yppe* 'upper chamber' (Ep. *uppae*) 1114; *stoppa* 'bucket' (Ep. †*stappa*) 309. (3) *cempan* 'warriors' (Ep. *caempan*) 984; *ampre*[17] 'sour dock' (Ep. *amprae*, Erf. *omprae*) 2077. (4) *gelimp-lice* 'suitable' (Ep., Erf. out) 548; *lemp-halt* 'lame' (Ep. *laempi-*, Erf. †*lemphi-*) 1250. (5) *elpendbaan* 'ivory' (Erf. *elpendes ban*, Ep. out) 712; *gelpende* 'boastful' (Ep., Erf. out) 1940. (6) †*gelp-lih* 'boastful' (Corp. *wlonclice*, Ep. *uulanclicae*) Erf. 112; *cf. hwelp* 'cub' (VPs.). (7) *wondeuueorpe* 'mole' (Ep. *uuandaeuuiorpae*, Erf. *uuondæuuerpe*) 1975; cf. *hearpe* (VPs.). (8) *wearp* 'warp' (Ep., Erf. out) 1928; *scearp-nis* 'sharpness' (Ep., Erf. out) 50. (9) *scipes* 'of a ship' 1748. (10) *naep* 'turnip' (Erf. *nep*) 1363; *þrop* 'thorp' (Erf. *ðrop*, Ep. out) 557. (11) *uaeps* 'wasp' (Corp. *waefs*, Ep. out) Erf. 255. (12) *geuaerpte* 'recovered' (Ep., Erf. out) 572.[18]

The /p/ presents no real phonemic problems. On the basis of its history and the evidence of Germanic cognates and Latin borrowings, it was a voiceless bilabial stop with but one important allophone. It is written p.[19]

3.2. /t/ [t]: (1) *tiig* 'Mars' 1293; *tasul* 'a die' (Ep. *tasol*) 2000; *stig* 'path' (Ep. out, Erf. *stiig*) 651. (2) *gesette* 'he set' (Ep. *gisettae*, Erf. *gisette*) 505; *meottoc* 'mattock, trident' (Ep. *maettoc*, Erf. *mettoc*) 2047. (3) *minte* 'mint' (Ep., Erf. out) 23; *cf. muntas* 'mountains' (VPs.). (4) *flint* 'flint' 1561; cf. *munt* 'mountain' (VPs.). (5) *milte* 'spleen' (Ep., Erf. *milti*) 1896; *fultum* 'aid' (Erf. *fulteam*, Ep. out) 743.[20] (6) *helt* 'hilt' (Ep., Erf. out) 359; *malt* 'malt' 322. (7) *cf. wyrte* 'plant' (VPs.); *wearte* 'wart' (Ep. *uueartae*, Erf. *uearte*) 1485. (8) *walhwyrt* 'foreign plant' (Erf. *uualhuyrt*, Ep. out) 714; *steort* 'tail' (Ep., Erf. out) 404. (9) *teter* 'tetter' 262; *fleotas* 'estuaries' (Erf. *fleutas*) 95. (10) *huæt* 'brisk' (Ep. *huet*, Erf. *huaet*) 1223; *hnut-beam* 'nut tree' 1394. (11) *gitsung*

---

[15] Forms cited from the *Vespasian Psalter* gloss (VPs.) will be found in the glossary to my edition, Ann Arbor, 1965.

[16] Line numbers, unless otherwise indicated, are those of Corp. A form from Ep. or Erf. is given only when it varies from that in Corp.; *i.e.*, when Corp. alone is cited, the other glossaries have an identical form. An obvious misspelling or the use of a different word is marked with a dagger. It is usually assumed that the reader will know when an inflected form of a word (*e.g.*, the dat. sg. of a noun) is cited instead of the uninflected form. Readings of Corp. and Ep. have been checked in W. M. Lindsay, *The Corpus Glossary* (Cambridge, 1921); J. H. Hessels, *An Eighth-Century Latin-Anglo-Saxon Glossary* (Cambridge, 1890); Sweet, *The Epinal Glossary*, EETS, OS, LXXIXb (1883, repr. 1936); and my own microfilm of Corp.

[17] Between nasal and liquid, an environment similar to NCV.

[18] Examples for (11) and (12) are open to question. Earlier /fs/ shifted to /ps/, and the cluster /ps/ may not have occurred in Arch. I. The /pt/ cluster in *geuaerpte* straddles a morpheme boundary, but the same is true of Moulton's *cepte*, p. 22.

[19] The use of *p* for /f/ is treated under /f/ below.

[20] The /lt/ straddles an old morpheme boundary in *fultum*, but it seems probable that the word was no longer felt as a compound.

'greed' (Corp. *gidsung*) Ep. 82; cf. *geunrotsad* 'sad' (VPs.).[21] (12) See (2). The /t/ was probably a pure dental, although it would be difficult to prove that it was not an alveolar like its Modern English reflex. There was a tendency in Mercian to shift pre-junctural /d/ and /þ/ to /t/, as in *raefsit* 'reproved' (Ep. *raebsid*, Erf. *repsit*) 1084; *borẹttit* 'he brandishes' (Corp. *borettið*, Erf. *boretit*) Ep. 1092.[22] In West Saxon, the incidence of /t/ was increased by syncopation and assimilation in the sg. 2 and 3 of many verbs; *e.g.*, WS *rĭt* 'he rides', beside Merc. and Nhb. *rídeð*.

3.3 /c/ [k]: (la) *cempan* 'warriors' (Ep. *cæmpan*) 984; *kaelið* 'he cools' (Ep. *caelith*, Erf. *cælid*) 1119; *kylle* 'wine skin' (Ep., Erf. out) 231; *cynedoom* 'royal authority' (Ep., Erf. *cynidom*) 1719; *cf.* *ceafurtun* 'vestibule' (VPs.). (2a) *-sticca* 'stick' (Erf. †*-stecca*) 171; *cf.* *ðiccum* 'thick' (VPs.). (3a) *stincendi* 'stinking' (Ep., Erf. out) 895. (4a) *cf.* *geswinc* 'trouble' (VPs.). (5a) *cf.* *ylcum* 'all' (VPs.). (6a) *cf.* *milc* 'milk' (VPs.). (7a) *spærca* 'spark' (Ep., Erf. out) 1827. (8a) *berc* 'birch tree' 285; *-gewerc* 'work' (Ep. *-giuueorc*, Erf. *-giuerc*) 1040. (9a) *gẹces*[23] 'cuckoo's' (Ep. *geacaes*, Erf. *gecaes*) 58. (10a) *laec* 'leek' 154; *cuic-* 'alive' (Erf. out) 368. (11a) *cf.* *ricsað* 'he rules' (VPs.). (12a *cf.* *geecte*[24] 'he increased' (VPs.).

[k']: (1b) *cop* 'cope, vestment' (Ep. out) 757; *quiða* 'womb' (Erf. out) 1290; *chroa*, *croha* 'pot' (Ep. *crocha*, Erf. *chroca*) 461. (2b) *loccas* 'locks of hair' 160; *fingirdoccana* 'of the finger-muscles' (Erf. *-doccuna*, Ep. out) 687. (3b) *cf.* *ðoncas* 'thanks' (VPs.). (4b) *wlonc-lice* 'proudly' (Ep. *uulanc-*, Erf. †*gelp-*) 85. (5b) *asolcen* 'torpid' (Ep. *asolcaen*, Erf. *asolcæn*) 1092. (6b) *calc* 'lime' 345. (7b) *orceas* 'demons' (Ep., Erf. out) 1080; *cf.* *carcerne* 'prison' (VPs.). (8b) *storc* 'stork' (Ep. out) 465; *orc* 'pitcher' 1454. (9b) *tacur* 'brother-in-law' (Ep., Erf. *tacor*) 1204; *draca* 'dragon' (Ep. †*droco*, Erf. *draco*) 2027; *cf.* *gebreocu* 'I break' (VPs.). (10b) *aac* 'oak' 1749; *aqueorna*[25] 'squirrel' (Erf. *aquorna*) 1811. (11b) *box* 'box tree' (Ep., Erf. out) 332.[26] (12b) No early evidence.

3.31. The /c/ represents one result of a phonemic split in proto-English, the other result being the voiceless affricate /č/. Germanic /k/ in very early times developed positional variants: a palatal allophone [k] in words like */kinnuz/ 'chin', OE *cin*, Gothic *kinnus*, and a velar allophone [k'] in words like */kornaz/ 'corn', OE *corn*, Got. *kaurn*. At first, the difference was probably no more noticeable to untrained ears (of which there many in those days, no doubt) than that between the MnE sounds in *kin* and *coal*. The two allophones also occurred in medial and pre-junctural positions in accordance with patterns which can best be seen by comparing the examples

---

[21] The cluster in *gitsung* was originally /ds/, and the form in Corp. may be that of Arch. I, the Ep. Erf form being an innovation in Arch. II or even an independent innovation in the two MSS. The cluster /ts/ is rare in OE and usually derived from something else.
[22] For evidence of the same shift in Bede's English names, especially those in the early Merc. MS, Cotton Tiberius C. ii, see Hilmer Ström, *Old English Personal Names in Bede's History* (= *Studies in English*, VIII, 128-138), Lund, 1939.
[23] So MS; Lindsay *gaeces*.
[24] The /ct/ straddles a morpheme boundary.
[25] *I.e.*, *āc-weorna*.
[26] In native words in the earliest period, *x* has the value /hs/, and /cs/ is spelled *cs*; but in this borrowing from Latin, we should probably assume the Latin value of *x*.

given for /c/ above and for /č/ below. These allophones became independent phonemes before the time of the earliest surviving written records in English. According to Penzl,[27] the split grew out of the workings of *i*-umlaut, which caused front vowels to occur after the velar allophone, thus making [k'] no longer a positional variant but a phoneme /c/ in contrastive distribution with the palatal consonant. For example, Merc. *caelf* /cælf/ 'calf' (*cf.* Got. *kalbō*) has an initial phoneme which contrasts with that of *cese* /čēse/ 'cheese' (*cf.* Lat. *cāseus*).[28] *I*-umlaut is commonly thought to have been complete in proto-English at some time in the sixth century;[29] hence, Penzl's explanation would enable us to date the emergence of the /c/ and /č/ phonemes near the close of the sixth century or relatively early in the seventh. Moulton attributes the split to the loss of the /i/ and /j/ in words like *benc* 'bench' (Gmc. */bankiz/) and *streccan* 'to stretch' (*/strakjan/), which left the /č/ and /čč/ in contrastive position with the /c/ and /cc/ of words like *dranc* 'he drank' and *hnecca* 'neck'.[30] Since this loss of /i/ and /j/ probably occurred early in the seventh century,[31] Moulton's explanation narrows the time span during which the plonemic split can be dated; *i.e.*, it can hardly have taken place earlier than the beginning, or later than about the middle, of the seventh century.

3.32. A second sound change, assibilation, affected the palatal phoneme /č/, shifting it from [k], through some such stage as [kj], to [tʃ]. There is some uncertainty as to the time at which assibilation occurred. I suggest that the change could not have been very far advanced at the time when medial unaccented /i/ was lost in the preterites of Weak I verbs. For example, OE *drencan* [drɛntʃan] has the preterite *drencte* [drɛnktɛ], in which an /i/ had originally stood between a palatal [k] and the /t/. The effect of bringing the dental into contact with the palatal was to shift the latter to [k'], so that instead of becoming [tʃ], phonemically /č/, it remained with the velar phoneme, OE /c/. Such a shift of the palatal is very difficult to account for if the two sounds were as far apart at the time of the shift as [k'] and [tʃ]. Since loss of the medial /i/ is generally placed in the first part of the seventh century, it would appear that assibilation began at approximately the time that Moulton sets for the phonemic split of /c/ and /č/.[32]

3.33. When linguistic history repeats itself, the result is apt to be confusing even to linguists; witness the confusion of the late eighteenth century produced by similarities between the Gmc. and the High German consonant shifts. The OE velar /c/ developed positional variants paralleling those of the earlier Gmc. /k/; that is, a palatal [k] in some positions, a velar [k'] in others. The evidence of the new palatal

---

[27] *Op. cit.*, p. 42.
[28] For WS examples, see Penzl's article.
[29] See, for example, Karl Luick, *Historische Grammatik der englischen Sprache* (Leipzig, 1929), p. 266.
[30] *Op. cit.*, p. 24.
[31] Luick, p. 321.
[32] The palatal [kk] also split from the velar [k'k'] and was assibilated at about the same time, *e.g.* *flicci* beside -*sticca*.

[k] is found chiefly in the Mercian and Northumbrian dialects, in which diphthongs underwent the sound change called smoothing before /c/, /g/, and /h/, or a cluster containing one of these preceded by a liquid.[33] For example, early Merc. *lǣc* 'leek' (later *lēc*, WS *lēac*), Merc. *milc* 'milk' (WS *meolc*, from */mioluc/*), and Merc. *werc* 'work' (WS *weorc*) have lost the velar off-glides of their diphthongs. It is hardly possible that a palatalizing change like this could take place before a velar consonant; hence, we must assume a palatal [k] in *lǣc*, etc., which would be in complementary distribution with the velar [k'] after back vowels, as in *bōc* 'book', etc. From the evidence provided by smoothing, we can be fairly certain that [k] occurred medially and finally after all diphthongs whose stressed element was front; *i.e.*, after /ĭo/, /ĕo/, /ǣa/,[34] and in the clusters /lc/ and /rc/ after such diphthongs. Presumably [k] also occurred after the front vowels themselves, /ĭ/, /ĕ/, /ǣ/, and in the clusters /lc/, /rc/, and /nc/ after those vowels. Arguing from the analogy of the earlier Gmc. [k], we might also assume this new [k] in post-junctural position before front or front round vowels and before diphthongs whose first element was front; *e.g.*, in *cempan, kaeliđ, cynedoom, ceafurtun*.[35] We should probably assume the velar [k'] in all other positions. We can do little more than assume (except where the evidence of smoothing appears), for the scribes rarely differentiated between [k] and [k'] or /c/ and /ċ/. In WS and Kentish, the two allophones are impossible to pin down with any certainty.

3.34. If the velar /c/ had developed an allophone [k] while /ċ/ was still pronounced [k], the new allophone would have fused, fallen together phonemically, with /ċ/; and MnE *leek, work, milk* would be **leech, *worch* or **werch, *milch*.[36] The new positional variants of /c/ must, therefore, have arisen after /ċ/ had undergone assibilation and become a sound approaching [tʃ]. Since smoothing of the diphthongs from Gmc. and of the short diphthongs from breaking was far advanced by 700,[37] it seems reasonable to place assibilation about the middle of the seventh century. The relative chronology of the sound changes mentioned in §§ 3.31-4 is as follows: (1) *i*-umlaut (? sixth century); (2) loss of /i/ and /j/ (? early seventh century); (3) phonemic split of /c/ and /ċ/ and assibilation of /ċ/ (? mid-seventh century); (4) rise of new [k] and [k'] and onset of smoothing (? later seventh century).

3.35. The incidence of /c/ is decreased in later Mercian by the substitution of /h/

---

[33] Comparable evidence for WS and Kentish is not easily found. It is possible, of course, that palatal and velar allophones of /c/ existed in those dialects unaccompanied by smoothing. Speech sounds may make sound changes possible, but they do not cause sound changes. Even when we use an expression like 'umlaut-producing,' we should remember that this is merely a sort of shorthand, used only to avoid a more accurate but very cumbersome locution. If an /ĭ/ or a /j/, of itself, caused *i*-umlaut, we should not be able to pronounce *army* or *arduous* today without fronting the /a/.

[34] Evidence for /ĕe/ is lacking.

[35] The *-ea-* reflects velar umlaut of /a/, a sound change which was still in progress in the eighth century and not fully reflected in the spellings of the early glossaries; *cf. caebrtuun* (Ep. *cebǫr-*, Erf. *caeber-*) 2094; *cleadur* 'a rattle' (Ep. *claedur*, Erf. *cledr*) 599.

[36] The rare MnE *milch*, as in *milch cow*, is a different, though related, word.

[73] See *Lg.*, XXXVII, 525, 531.

for /c/ in *ah* 'but' (WS, Kt., Corp. *ac*); in Northumbrian, by the substitution of /h/ in *ah* and in other words, especially in the unstressed pronouns *ih, meh, usih, etc.* (beside *ic, mec, usic, etc.*). The incidence of /c/ was increased in some portions of the Nhb. area by the failure of Gmc. /k/ in certain positions to become /ċ/.[38] In Merc. after 700, the distribution of the allophones [k] and [k'] was affected by the operation of velar umlaut, as reflected for example in Corp. *borð ̇eaca* 'shield-roof, testudo' (Ep. † *borohaca*, Erf. †*brodthaca*) 1999 or VPs. *hreacan* 'throat' (WS *hracan*), *spreocað* 'they speak' (WS *sprecaþ*). A velar off-glide could hardly have developed after the palatal vowel in these forms unless the [k] had become velar through the influence of the following back vowel. On the other hand, Merc. forms like *draecena* 'of dragons' (VPs.) and *sprecu* 'I speak' (VPs.) may be due to the continuing operation of smoothing[39] or, in some cases at least, to analogy with forms in which the /c/ was followed by a front vowel. Unsmoothed diphthongs in Kentish are attributed to the fact that velar umlaut occurred in that dialect, but not smoothing.

3.36. I have said that OE scribes rarely differentiated /c/ and /ċ/ in spelling. This is true, but some exceptions to the rule may be seen if one compares the tabulation for /c/ above with that for /ċ/ below. The spelling *k* is used rarely for /c/, never apparently for /ċ/. There are instances of *qu* for /cw/, a usage lifted bodily from Latin, but *q* for /ċ/ is negligible.[40] Rare *ch* for /c/, as in *chroa*, may be due to the influence of Latin words of Greek origin; *ch* normally represents /h/, not /c/ or /ċ/. A complete account of usage in later OE is hardly feasible here, but I should like to mention two texts which are later than those which we have been considering. The early WS (late ninth-century) Hatton MS of King Alfred's translation of the *Pastoral Care* contains many examples of *k* for /c/: *kelnesse* 'cooling', *kok* 'cock', *kokke* (dat.), *ankor* 'anchor', *æker* 'field', *geoke* 'yoke', *ceak* 'basin', *etc.*[41] Farman's glosses in the *Rushworth Gospels* (tenth-century mixed-Mercian) show *k* for /c/ about 130 times: *kining* 'king', *kasere* 'Caesar', *kneorisse* 'generation', *kræftgum* 'skillful, learned', *besenked* 'sunk, drowned' (with /c/ by analogy with pret. *-sencte*),

---

[38] J. W. Watson, "Non-initial *k* in the North of England," *Lg.*, XXIII (1947), 43-49.

[39] If smoothing was still operative in the eighth century, its effect upon velar-umlaut diphthongs was obviously partial and almost sporadic. This explanation will account for the lack of smoothing in *borð ̇eaca, etc.*, but some other diphthongal forms present greater difficulties : Ep. *geacaes* (Gmc. /au/) and *-giuueorc* (breaking), Erf. *teag* (see /g/ below), Ep. *fleah* and *leax* (see /h/ below), *etc.* These latter might be attributed to uncertainty in scribal practice due to the fact that smoothing was a recent sound change, but they could also be explained as forms taken without respelling from other dialects, *e.g.* West Saxon. The materials of Arch. I and the additional matter in Corp. were apparently collected from scattered interlinear and marginal glosses found in older MSS, some of which may have come from non-Mercian areas. For the best analysis of the heterogeneous origins of the glossary items, see W. M. Lindsay, *The Corpus, Epinal, Erfurt and Leiden Glossaries*, Oxford, 1921.

[40] The second *qu* in Ep. *quiquae* is an obvious scribal error, as may be seen by comparison with the forms in Corp. and Erf.

[41] For further examples in EWS, see P. J. Cosijn, *Altwestsächsische Grammatik* (The Hague, 1883), I, 152-153.

wolken 'sky', *carkern* 'prison', *ciken* 'chicken', *seake* 'sick', *ek* 'also', *etc.*[42] Nei ther of these texts contains any clear example of *k* for /č/.

4. Voiced stops

4.1. /b/ [b]: (1) *beer* 'bier' 264; *baar* 'boar' 287. (2) *ribbe* 'ribwort' (Ep., Erf. *ribbae*) 356; *cf. habbað* 'they have' (VPs.). (3) *cimbing* 'joint' (Ep. out) 554; *ambaect* 'servant' (Ep. *ambect*, Erf. †*ambaet*) 1706. (4) *ymb-ðriodung* 'deliberation' (Erf. †*ymbdritung*, Ep. out) 644; *hymb-licae* 'hemlock' (Erf. †*huymblicae*, Corp. *hymlice*) Ep. 185; *camb* 'comb' 355. (5-9) Becómes [b]. (10) *unsib* 'enmity' (Ep. *unsibb*) 1836; *rib* 'rib' (Ep., Erf. out) 585. (11), (12) Does not occur.

[ƀ]: (1-4) Becomes [b]. (5) *aelbitu* 'swan' (Erf. †*ebitu*) 1439; *halbae* 'side' (Erf. *halbe*, Corp. *halfe*) Ep. 51. (6) *halb-clungni* 'half-congealed' (Corp. *half-*) Ep. 931; *salb* 'ointment' (Corp. *salf*) Ep. 635. (7) *huerbende* 'turning' (Ep., Erf. out) 764; *sinuurbul*[43] 'round' (Corp. †*siunhuurful*, Erf. †*sinuulfur*) Ep. 1047; *cf. hwerfeð* 'it returns' (VPs.). (8) *huerb* 'whorl of a spindle' (Ep., Erf. out) 2108; *tyrb* 'turves' (Ep., Erf. out) 452. (9) *haebern* 'crab' (Ep. *habern*, Erf. *hafern*) 1370; *sceaba* 'plane' 1755; *clouae*[44] 'buckle' (Ep. *clofae*, Erf. *clofæ*) 1327. (10) *endistaeb* 'end' (Erf. †*steb*, Ep. out) 785; *staeb-plegan* 'letter-game' (Corp. *staef-*, Erf. †*scæb-*) Ep. 577; *gloob* 'glove' (Erf. *glob*, Corp. *glof*) Ep. 631. (11), (12) Does not occur.

4.11 The voiced bilabial stop allophone of /b/ is derived from proto-Gmc. /ƀ/, from Indo-European /bh/ in positions (1-4). This [b] alone survived the eighth century to become the /b/ of most OE texts. In pre-junctural position, [b] is due to simplification of older geminates. The bilabial spirant [ƀ] has two sources: IE /bh/ in positions other than (1-4) and proto-Gmc. /f/ (from IE /p/) in accordance with the operation of Verner's Law. The evidence of the early glossaries indicates that /b/ [b, ƀ] and /f/ [f, v] were carefully distinguished in Arch. I, the former being written *b*, the latter *f*.[45] It seems likely that a bilabial spirant pronunciation was current around 700, or had recently been current. That this pronunciation was shifting, or about to shift, to labiodental is indicated by the frequent use of *f* for [ƀ] and of *b* for /f/[46] in the individual glossaries, especially in Corp.[47] In the course of the eighth century, [ƀ] in positions (5, 7, 9) fell together with [v], while [ƀ] in positions (6, 8, 10) fell together with [f]. We may also observe that, in the speech represented by Arch. I, it was apparently possible for [b] and [ƀ] to contrast in position (10). Even though this contrast would rarely occur in speech or writing, it would nevertheless tend to

---

[42] For further examples, see E. M. Brown, *The Language of the Rushworth Gloss to the Gospel of Matthew*, II (Göttingen, 1892), 30-31.
[43] Altered from *sinuurful* ; *b* above *f*.
[44] The *u* is probably an error for *f* or (more probably) *b*. In the Latin text of Corp., *u* appears occasionally for *f*, nearly twice as often for *b* ; see Hessels, pp. xxxvii-xxxviii.
[45] Chadwick, pp. 232-240.
[46] See /f/ below.
[47] For similar confusion in eighth-century Nhb., see Ström, pp. 132-133.

make the phonemic system unstable at this point. Indeed, we are not completely certain that the phoneme /b/ had not already split apart, its apparent identity being an illusion produced by archaic spelling conventions.[48]

4.2. /d/ [d]: (1) *disc* 'dish' 1490; *durhere* 'folding door' 1948. (2) *geddi* 'a lay' (Ep. out) 733; *cf. Adda* (early Bede MSS). (3) *windil* 'basket' (Erf. †*pindil*) 348; *sondę* 'sending' (Ep. †*scandae*,[49] Erf. *sondae*) 502. (4) *lind* 'linden' 2019; *brond* 'firebrand' (Ep. *brand*) 2018. (5) *salde* 'he gave' (Ep. *saldae*, Erf. †*saltae*) 1089. (6) *feld-* 'field' 323; *hold* 'carcass' 853. (7) *wyrde* 'fate' (Ep., Erf. *uuyrdae*) 1480; *-geardas* 'enclosures' 1998; *uuordes* 'of a word' (Ep., Erf. out) 2115. (8) *seglgęrd* 'sail-yard' (Ep., Erf. *segilgaerd*) 165; *uueard* 'guardian' 1783; *brord* 'point' (Erf. *broord*, Corp. †*brond*) Ep. 782. (9) *gredig* 'greedy' 1046; *sadol* 'saddle' (Erf. †*satul*) 1839. (10) *colðred* 'plumb line' (Ep. *colþred*, Erf. *coldraed*) 1548; *hood* 'hood' 369. (11) *gidsung* 'greed' (Ep., Erf. *gitsung*) 184; *cf. bledsung* (VPs.). (12) Does not occur.

The /d/ presents no difficult phonemic problems. From the ninth century on, we find texts in which the graphs *d* and *ð* are frequently confused; this is an orthographic confusion due to the fact that *ð* is merely an OE *d* with a short stroke through the upright. The tendency for /d/ to become /t/ has already been mentioned under /t/, and the shift of /þ/ to /d/ in a few words will be noted under /þ/.

4.3 /g/ [g]: (1) *gyrdils* 'girdle' 1244; *goos* 'goose' 172. (2) *earwicga* 'earwig' (Ep. *earuuigga*, Erf. †*aeruuica*) 240; *sugga* some kind of small bird (Erf. *sucga*) 878. (3) *hringe* 'ring' (Ep. †*hringiae*, Erf. *hringae*) 874; *þungas* 'aconite' (Ep., Erf. *thungas*) 45. (4) *hringfaag* 'ring-streaked' (Erf. †*thrnigfaag*) 1612; *pung* 'purse' (Ep. out) 391; *uulatunc* 'nausea' (Ep. *uulatung*, Erf. *uulating*) 1357. (5-12) Does not occur.

[g]: (1-4) Becomes [g]. (5a) *suelgendi* 'whirlpool' (Ep., Erf. out) 2160. (6a) No clear early evidence. (7a) *duergedostle* 'pennyroyal' (Ep. *duuergaedostae*, Erf. *duergaedostae*) 1686. (8a) *duerg* 'dwarf' 1362; *merg* 'marrow' (Ep., Erf. out) 1308. (9a) *egan* 'eye' (Erf. *ægan*) 2133; *egur* 'high tide, flood' (Erf. *aegur*, Ep. out) 702. (10a) *taeg* 'cord, tie' (Ep. *teac*, Erf. *teag*) 1821. (11a) No clear early evidence. (12a) Does not occur.

[gʹ]: (1-4) Becomes [g]. (5b) *cf. gehalgade* 'hallowed' (VPs.). (6b) *cf. forswalg* 'it swallowed' (VPs.). (7b) *morgenlic* 'of the morning' (Erf. †*morgendlic*) 1535. (8b) *borg* 'security' 2080. (9b) *bogan* 'bow, arch' 901; *cf. weogum* 'ways' (VPs.). (10b) *crog* 'pot' (Ep., Erf. *croog*) 1171. (11b) No clear early evidence. (12b) Does not occur.

4.31. The /g/ has a more complicated history than the other voiced stops. The Gmc. palato-velar spirant /g/ became a stop [g] in post-junctural position, after a nasal, and in gemination;[50] elsewhere it remained a spirant. The spirant allophone developed, or already possessed, positional variants, a palatal [g] and a velar [gʹ],

---

[48] Anyone familiar with Old Irish will note the striking similarity between the OIr. use of *b* and that of Arch. I.

[49] ? *c* expuncted.

[50] A great deal has been written about the age and origin of the geminations which occurred in *earwigga*, *sugga*, etc. Suffice it here to say that the geminations did indeed occur and that the results were not the same as those of the gemination in words like *brycg*.

whose distributions roughly paralleled those of the allophones of Gmc. /k/.[51] In West Gmc., [g] was geminated to [gg] before Gmc. /j/. In proto-English, prior to the period of *i*-umlaut, [g] became palatal [g] before front vowels and diphthongs whose first element was front, and also when preceded by a nasal and followed by Gmc. /j/. At this point, there were three allophones [g, g, g'] and two geminates [gg, gg]. The phonemic split and assibilation of [g] and [gg] took place at about the same time as those of [k] and [kk], resulting in: a new [j], which fused with the old Gmc. /j/ to produce the phoneme which I label /ġ/, as in *ieces, byrgen*, etc.; and a [dʒ], which became an independent phoneme /ǧ/, as in *brycg, fenge*, etc. Only [g], [gg], and [g'] remained with the phoneme /g/.

4.32. After the split, /g/ developed new allophones much like those already described for OE /c/. The [g] remained a stop in post-junctural position, in gemination, and after a nasal, probably with palatal and velar variants which we need not indicate here since they had no observable effect upon the spelling or the later history of the language. The [gg] remained a long palatal or velar stop. The [g'] remained in the neighborhood of back vowels but became palatal before and after front vowels or diphthongs whose stressed element was front. In the Merc. and Nhb. dialects, this new [g] made smoothing possible in *egan, duerg, etc*.[52] The Merc. dialect provides one exception to this last process: the [g'] must have remained or been restored in forms like *weogum* (VPs.), which show velar umlaut and no smoothing of the diphthong. In pre-junctural position, [g] and [g'] had a tendency to become unvoiced, as is indicated by sporadic *h*-spellings in early OE. Later, perhaps in the tenth century, this unvoicing was so general that final [g, g'] must be regarded as having split from /g/ and fused with /h/.[53] Sporadic OE examples like *uulatunc* and more frequent examples in later English seem to reflect a tendency to unvoice final [g] after /n/. Forms like *teac* in Ep. are exceedingly rare; they are difficult to explain, unless we suppose that *c* represents /h/, *i.e.* [x, x'].

5. Voiceless spirants

5.1. /f/ [f]: (1) *þorh-ge-feht* 'through-fight' (Ep. †*þorgifect*, Erf. *dorhgifecilae*) 1537; *falu* 'fallow' 970; *gron-uisc* some kind of fish (Ep., Erf. out) 66. (2) *maffa*[54] 'cawl,? entrails' (Erf. †*naffa*) 1443; *cf. Offa* (early Bede MSS), *ofriu* 'I offer'[55] (VPs.). (3), (4) Nasals were lost before /f/. (5) Became [v]. (6) *wylf* 'she-wolf' (Ep., Erf. out) 1260; *wulf* 'wolf' (Ep., Erf. out) 1259. (7) Became [v]. (8) *cf. acearf* 'he cut off' (VPs.). (9) Became [v]. (10) *hrof-* 'roof' 2020; *uuf* 'owl' 334. (11) *uuaefsas* 'wasps' (Ep. †*waeff-*

---

[51] Their distribution may be observed in a general way by a comparison of the examples for /g/ above with those of /ġ/ and /ǧ/ below.

[52] For rare unsmoothed forms like Erf. *teag.*, see note 39.

[53] For a discussion of Moulton's differing analysis, see /h/ below.

[54] Possibly an error for Lat. *mappa*, according to Lindsay.

[55] From Lat. *offerre*, with the geminate simplified either in pronunciation or merely in spelling.

sas, Erf. †*uuaeps* sg.) 2098; *raefsit* 'reproved' (Ep. *raebsid*, Erf. *repsit*) 1084.[56] (12) *reftras* 'rafters' 150; *gepofta* 'comrade' (Ep. *gidopta*, Erf. †*gidogta*) 503; *scaept-* 'shaft' (Erf. out) 1005; *lybt* 'air' (Ep., Erf. out) 1961.

[v]: (5) *wulfes* 'wolf's' (Ep., Erf. *uulfes*) 355; *scalfur* 'diver' bird (Ep., Erf. *scalfr*) 1304. (7) *cf. ceorfeð* 'he carves' (VPs.). (9) *cefer* 'chafer' (Ep., Erf. *cefr*) 326; *ceber* (Ep., Erf. out) 214; *hofer* 'hump' (Ep., Erf. *ofr*) 2074.

5.11. The labiodental spirant /f/ had two allophones, which became separate phonemes in Middle English: a voiceless [f] in post- and pre-junctural position, in gemination and before a voiceless consonant; and a voiced [v] in other medial positions. At the close of the seventh century, /f/ was wholly a reflex of Gmc or Lat. /f/. During the next century, [b] split from /b/ and fused with /f/ in the manner described above. The [f] allophone was then augmented by reflexes of Gmc. [b] as follows: (6) *halb—half salb—salf* and similar words; (8) *huerb—*hwerf*,[57] *tyrb—tyrf*,[58] etc.; (10) *staeb—stæf, glob—glof, etc.* The [v] allophone was similarly augmented: (5) *aelbitu—*ælfetu*,[59] *halbe—halfe, etc.*; (7) *sinuurbul—siunhuurful, huerbende—*hwerfende, etc.*; (9) *haebern—hæfern, sceaba—*sceafa*,[60] *clouae—clofe, etc.* Evidence for the long /ff/ is weak in earliest OE, but *snoffa* 'nausea', *pyffan* 'to puff, *offrian* 'to offer', *etc.*, turn up in later OE.

5.12. The spelling *b* for /f/ became rare after the eighth century, but it turns up occasionally in ninth-century Merc. and Kt. charters, in early WS texts, in the Nhb. gloss of the *Lindisfarne Gospels*, in Farman's mixed-Merc. glosses, and in the twelfth-century mixed-Kt. gloss of the *Eadwine Psalter*. The spelling *u* for /f/ became even rarer until ME times, but it appears sporadically and unexpectedly in various texts throughout the OE period. If post-junctural /f/ was voiced in Southern England in late OE times, this change is not reflected in the spelling until ME. The spelling *pt* for /ft/ practically disappeared in OE after the eighth century.

5.2. /þ/ [þ]: (1) *þearm* 'gut' (Ep., Erf. *thearm*) 1058; *ðinga* 'of things' (Erf. †*hadga*) 1442; *þinga* (Erf. *dinga*) 1701; *þixlum* 'wagon poles' (Ep. †*dislum*, Erf. *dixlum*) 2007; *ðorh* 'through' (Ep. *þorch*, Erf. *dorh*) 1547; *þu-ðistel* 'sowthistle' (Ep. *þuþistil*, Erf. †*popistil*) 1179; *thrauuo* 'rebuke' (Ep. *thrauu*, Erf. †*trafu*) 200; *ðhuehl* 'washing' (Erf. *thuachl*, Ep. out) 641. (2) *cynewiððan* 'diadems' (Ep., Erf. *cyniuuithan*) 1743. (3), (4) A nasal was lost before /þ/. (6) *spilth* 'ruin' 1544. (8) *mearð* 'marten' (Ep. *mearth*, Erf. *meard*) 937; †*forht* 'forth' (Ep. *fordh*, Erf. †*forthe*) 1090. (10) *mið* 'with' (Erf. *mid*) 1591; *gefremið* 'he makes, perfects' (Ep. *gifraemith*, Erf. *gifremit*) 1629;

---

[56] Original /fs/ became /ps/ ; see Karl Brunner, *Altenglische Grammatik nach der angelsächsischen Grammatik von Eduard Sievers* (Halle, 1951), p. 167.
[57] Not spelled with *f* in the early glossaries, but *cf.* VPs. *hwerfan*, WS *hwierfan* ; LWS *kweorfa*, etc., are from the same root without *i*-umlaut.
[58] Spelled with *f* in later OE.
[59] *Cf.* LWS *ylfete*.
[60] *Cf.* WS *scafa*.

lath 'hateful' (Ep. *laath*) 1113. (11), (12) No occurrence before /s/ or /t/ because of assimilation.[61]

[ð]: (5) *halði* 'sloping' (Corp. *haldi*, Erf. †*thahdi*) Ep. 754. (7) *corthr* 'troop' (Ep. †*cortr*, Erf. *cordr*) 2099; *heorðe* 'hearth' (Ep., Erf. out) 906. (9) *sueðelas* 'swaddling bands' (Ep., Erf. *suedilas*) 1060; *quiða* 'womb' (Erf. out) 1290; *nethle* 'needle' (Ep. *naeðlae*, Erf. *nedlæ*) 1591; *aethm* 'breath' (Ep. *ethm*, Erf. out) 130; *loða* 'cloak' (Ep., Erf. *lotha*) 1237; *hleoþrendi* 'crying out' (Ep. *hlaeodrindi*, Erf. †*thleodendri*) 1065; *wodhae* 'eloquence' (Ep., Erf. out) 583.

5.21. The dental spirant /þ/, from Gmc. /þ/, had two allophones, a voiceless [þ] or [θ] and a voiced [ð], with distributions roughly parallel to those of the allophones of /f/. In a few words, /þ/ was retained until some time in the eighth century and then shifted to /d/. The preposition *mið* is one example; cf. VPs. *mid*, ninth-century WS *mid*, but tenth-century Nhb. *mið*. Other examples involve the clusters /þl/ and /lþ/, which shifted to /dl/ and /ld/; *e.g. halði* and *nethle*.[62]

5.22. The most frequent spellings for /þ/ in the glossaries are *th*, þ, *ð*, and *d*; rare spellings, possibly errors, are *dh*, *ðh*, *ht*, and *t* (as in *cortr*). Since it is possible that two scribes might independently substitute a þ or an *ð* for an archaic spelling of the phoneme, one cannot reconstruct the spellings of Arch. I with much confidence; I believe, however, that the effort is worthwhile. Many correspondences like those in *thrauuo*, *spilth*, *lath*, *aethm* suggest that *th* was the most popular spelling around 700. Correspondences between Ep. and Erf. like those in *dixlum*, *suedilas*, and *hlaeodrindi* suggest that *d* was used in Arch. II; and from the archaic appearance of some of these words, one might infer that some of the *d*'s go back to Arch. I.[63] If this is the case, the compiler of Arch. I used an English adaptation of Old Irish spelling conventions. In OIr. texts generally, a distinction is maintained between *th* for voiceless /θ/ and *d* for voiced /ð/; in OE texts this distinction was abandoned, and the two graphs were interchangeable.[64] Correspondences between Corp. and Ep., as in *þinga*,[65] suggest that the runic þ was used, at least occasionally, in Arch. I. The error *popistil* in Erf. is also of some interest. OE scribes occasionally confused the letters þ and *p* because of the similarity of their shapes; they did not mistake *d*, *ð*, or *th* for *p*. Hence, the Erf. scribe's mistake would have been unlikely, if not impossible, if anything but Ep. *þuþistil* had appeared in Arch. II. Comparing this with Corp. *þuðistel*, one would suspect that the compiler of Corp. merely substituted an *e* for an archaic *i* and an *ð* for one of the þ's in his exemplar, which was either Arch. I or a

---

[61] Moulton's WS *cwiþst* (p. 22) has þ restored analogically; the usual WS form is *cwist*.
[62] Note also the cluster /rþ/ in Corp. *suearth* 'sward' (Ep., Erf. out) 406.
[63] Some of the *d*'s in Erf. are probably due to Continental German spelling practices.
[64] Even in OIr., the distinction was not carried through with absolute consistency; cf. *peccad* beside *peccath* 'sin,' *búaid* beside *búaith* 'victory,' *etc.* Confusion is most frequent in pre-junctural position; see Rudolf Thurneysen, *A Grammar of Old Irish* (translated and revised by D. A. Binchy and O. Bergin; Dublin, 1946), p. 83.
[65] Other examples are *þorh-* (Ep. *þorh-*, Erf. *dorh-*) 1537; *þingunge* (Ep. *þingungae*, Erf. †*ingungae*) 1093.

copy of it. If þ was used in Arch. I, it was evidently commonest in post-junctural position. Similar conventions, *i.e.* þ preferred in post-junctural position and some other graph (usually ð) preferred in other positions, are reflected in many later texts.[66] The Irish use of *d* for both [d] and [ð] must have been troublesome to the English, for whom these sounds were separate and frequently contrasting phonemes. The solution was to add a short distinguishing stroke through the upright of the *d* and to use the resulting ð for the spirants [ð] and [þ].[67] From correspondences between Corp. and Ep. like those in *ðinga, mið,* and *quiða,* one might suppose that ð was used in Arch. I, although this could be only an assumption, for during the eighth and ninth centuries ð became increasingly popular in Merc. and Nhb. texts for /þ/ in all positions. If ð was used in Arch. I, it was like *th, d,* and þ in having no allophonic significance.

5.3. /h/ [h]: (1) *hearma* 'weasel' 1307; *holegn* 'holly' 53; *aesil* 'hazel' (Corp., Erf. *haesl*) Ep. 50. (5) *cf. salhas* 'willows' (*Leiden Glossary*).[68] (7) *furhum* 'furrows' (Corp. *furum*)[69] Ep. 884. (9) *bituichn* 'between' (Ep. *bituicn,* [70] Corp. †*bitun*) Erf. 546; *suehoras* 'fathers-in-law' (Corp., Erf. *sueoras*) Ep. 1062; *sueor* (Ep. out) 2107; *ryhae* 'blanket' (Corp. *rye*) Ep. 1080; *uulohum* 'fringes' (Corp. *uuloum*) Ep. 1066.

[x]: (2a) *cf. hlæhað* 'they laugh' (VPs.). (3), (4) A nasal was lost before /h/. (6a) *elh* 'elk' (Ep., Erf. *elch*) 443. (8a) *mærh* 'sausage' (Ep. *maerh*) 1249; *faerh* 'hog' 1616. (10a) *thegh* 'thigh' (Erf. *theoh,* Ep. out) 556; *flęh*[71] 'flea' (Ep. *fleah,* Erf. †*floc*) 1684; *haeh-nisse* 'height' (Ep., Erf. out) 1960. (11a) *laex* 'salmon' (Ep. *leax,* Erf. *lex*) 1155; *þixlum* 'wagon poles' (Ep. †*dislum,* Erf. *dixlum*) 2007. (12a) *tyctende* 'inciting' (Ep., Erf. *tyctendi*) 70; *oembecht* 'office' (Ep., Erf. *ambechtae*) 501; *naeht-* 'night' (Ep. *naecht-,* Erf. *nect-*) 1384.

[x']: (2b) *croha* 'pot' (Ep. *crocha,* Erf. *chroca*) 461. (6b) *uualh-* 'foreign' 1075; *salh* 'willow' (Ep. *salch*) 1767. (8b) *horh* 'filth' 888; *ðorh* 'through' (Ep. *þorch,* Erf. *dorh*) 1546. (10b) *flach* 'hostile' 1066; *slagh-* 'sloe' (Ep., Erf. *slach-*) 1380; *slah-* (Ep. *slagh-,* Erf. †*salach-*) 1898; *ðruh* 'trough' (Ep. *thruuch,* Erf. *thruch*) 2067;

---

[66] One of these, a portion of the twelfth-century Laud MS of the *Anglo-Saxon Chronicle*, has been used to cast doubt upon Hockett's statement to the effect that OE þ and ð were not used to make allophonic distinctions; see R. P. Stockwell and C. W. Barritt, "Scribal Practice : Some Assumptions," *Lg.,* XXXVII (1961), 78-79; C. W. Hockett, "The Stressed Syllabics of Old English," *Lg.,* XXXV (1959), 580. In general, the statistics compiled by Stockwell and Barritt show merely that the Peterborough scribe preferred þ over ð in post-junctural position, where it represents [þ]; but ð over þ in pre-junctural position, where it represents, not [ð], but [þ]; and ð over þ in medial position, where it may represent either [ð] or [þ]. It is unlikely that an Irish prototype of Sahagún prescribed this usage, for OIr. has neither of the two symbols.

[67] For the use of *d* and ð for /þ/ in the early Bede MSS, see Ström, pp. 129-131. In some OE texts (*e.g.* the VPs. gloss), *d* and ð are often interchanged merely by the careless omission or addition of the small distinguishing stroke.

[68] *Oldest English Texts,* p. 113; or J. H. Hessels, *A Late Eighth-Century Latin-Anglo-Saxon Glossary* (Cambridge, 1906), p. 19.

[69] Lindsay and Hessels, S 117; Corp. form omitted by Sweet.

[70] From *bituin* ; *c* added above.

[71] So MS; Lindsay *flaeh.*

misthagch 'degenerated' (Ep., Erf. out) 667. (11b) *cf. oxan* 'oxen' (VPs.). (12b) *sohte* 'sought' (Ep. *sochtae*, Erf. †*scochtae*) 1545.

5.31. The glottal spirant allophone [h] occurred in post-junctural position, possibly also between vowels and between a liquid and a vowel. The palatal spirant [x] occurred after a front vowel, or a diphthong whose stressed element was front, in the following environments: in gemination, in pre-junctural position and in the clusters /lh/ and /rh/ when pre-junctural, and in clusters with a voiceless consonant, especially in /hs/, /ht/. The velar spirant [xʼ] occurred in the corresponding environments after back vowels. I can find no satisfactory evidence of a mute *h* in Arch. I, but the early glossaries show *h* omitted in Ep. *aesil* (also in Ep. Erf. *ofr* 'hump' 1046 and a few other instances), excrescent *h* in Corp. *heðir* 'kidney' (Ep., Erf. out) 1731. In some of the later OE texts, omitted and excrescent *h* are much more frequent.[72] Between vowels and between a liquid and a vowel, /h/[73] must have been lost in the late seventh or early eighth century. Forms like *salhas, furhum, bituichn,* and *uulohum* could be explained as having an analogically restored /h/, *i.e.* [x] or [xʼ], from *salh, furh, bitwih, wloh*. Other forms like *suehoras* and *ryhae* do not admit of such an explanation. These indicate either that the /h/ was still pronounced, at least occasionally, when Arch. I was compiled, or that the loss was so recent that spellings with -*h*- did not impress the compiler as serious blunders. The spellings *hlæhað* and *croha*, which are later than Arch. I, illustrate the tendency to simplify geminated *hh*. By the time these forms were written, single intervocalic /h/ was completely lost, so that there was no longer any contrast between short and long /h/ in this position.[74] Diphthongs were smoothed in Merc. and Nhb. before [x], just as before the palatal allophones of /c/ and /g/.[75] In WS and Kt., smoothing did not occur; in LWS, however, the later sound change called palatal umlaut shifted *neaht* /næaht/ to *niht* /niht/, *reoht* /reoht/ to *riht* /riht/, *etc.*, indicating that a palatal allophone [x] had developed in that dialect, beside the velar [xʼ] in *geþoht* 'thought', *etc.* From the precision with which the VPs. gloss uses *x* for /hs/ and *cs* for /cs/, I judge that the shift of /hs/ to /cs/ was considerably later than the eighth century; hence, I place *oxan* for the early period under /h/, but for a later period would place it, like Moulton, under /c/.[76]

---

[72] The best example is probably Farman's tenth-century glosses in the *Rushworth Gospels*, which contain *is* 'his', *us* 'house', *eard* 'hard', *eortum* 'hearts', *æfdon* 'they had', *yngrade* 'hungered', *wilce* 'which', *welpas* 'whelps', *rægl* 'clothing', *næscum* 'soft', *etc.*, and *his* 'is', *heow* 'you', *haþas* 'oaths', *hehtende* 'persecuting', *hwute* 'let us', *hryft* 'cloak', *ge-hroefa* 'reeve', *etc.* For further examples, see E. M. Brown, II, 34. I would suggest that the 'cockney' treatment of initial /h/ is a Mercian feature going back at least to the tenth century. London was, of course, a Mercian city in OE times.

[73] Most linguists assume that /h/ in these positions was [h]. For Moulton's arguments in support of this view, *op. cit.*, p. 26.

[74] When written *ch*, as in *crocha*, the length was not expressed; *cf.* also the long /þ/ in *cyniuuithan* above. Long /hh/ written *h* is much less frequent in WS than in Merc.

[75] For unsmoothed diphthongs, or diphthongal spellings, in Ep. *fleah, leax*, see note 39.

[76] Corp. *box* has probably picked up its *x* from *buxus*, its lemma as well as its etymon. In EWS, *x* for /cs/ is rare, but we find *æx*, beside *æcs*, 'ax' in the *Pastoral Care* ; *cf.* Corp. -*ęcus* (Erf. *aesc*, Ep. out) 703 and VPs. *ęcesum* 'axes'. For frequent *x* representing etymological /hs/ in EWS *weaxan*,

5.32. From the evidence of the early glossaries, it would appear that [h] was written *h* in Arch. I. Spellings like the *ch* in Erf. *bituichn* and the *c* in Ep. *bituicn* may well be analogical [x], as already noted. The *gh* and *gch* in *thegh, slagh-, misthagch, etc.*, are of later origin than Arch. I. I take them to be an indication that pre-junctural /g/ was already beginning to be unvoiced. The palatovelar allophones [x, x'] were probably written either *h* or *ch*, but the latter spelling was much more frequent in Arch. I than in the glossaries descended from it. The spellings *x* for [xs] and *ct* (beside *cht*) for [xt, x't] must also have been in vogue around 700.[77] From the differing treatment of [h] and [x, x'], one might argue that the two were separate phonemes, but I should not take the argument too seriously. Arch. I must have been compiled hardly more than thirty years after the Irish-trained Northumbrian, St. Chad, became the first bishop of the Mercians with a fixed see and a permanent abode. Although Chad does not impress me as having the type of personality from which Sahagúns are made, there was abundant opportunity during his episcopate for the popularizing of Irish spelling conventions in Mercia. The use of *ch* for [x, x'] parallels the Irish use of *ch* for [x] from lenited /c/. In Old Irish, *x* was frequently used for [xs],[78] and *ct* beside *cht* for [xt].[79] The Irish orthographical silent *h*, often used before an initial vowel symbol, was not adopted by the compiler of Arch. I; but the Irish usage no doubt reinforced the runic usage and the rather shaky usage of seventh-century Latin, thereby helping to establish *h* as the spelling for post-junctural [h]. The eventual adoption of *h*, instead of *ch*, as the normal graph for [x, x'] was due to the English themselves, and I take it as a strong indication that they regarded [h] and [x, x'] as one phoneme.

5.33. This seems the appropriate point at which to take up Moulton's analysis of /g/ and /h/. According to that analysis, proto-English /h/ split into two phonemes: /h/ [h], originally occurring in positions (1, 5, 7, 9), later reduced to (1) by the loss of /h/ in the other three environments; and /x/ [x], occurring in positions (2, 6, 8, 10, 11, 12). These two sounds were obviously in complementary distribution and would normally be regarded as allophones. The first had glottal articulation, however, while the latter had velar articulation; and, since both were voiceless spirants, the difference in place of articulation alone distinguished them. On the basis of this articulatory difference, Moulton analyzed them as two phonemes. According to Moulton, proto-English /g/ also split into: [g], which became a separate phoneme /g/ occurring only in positions (1, 2, 3, 4); a [g], which was unvoiced to [x] in positions (6, 8, 10) and fused with the phoneme /x/; and a [g] which remained voiced in positions (5, 7, 9) and became a voiced allophone of /x/. Since the voiced [g] remained in

---

beside *weahsan*, 'to grow', *etc.*, see Cosijn, I, 180. Farman's glosses show *axe* 'ax', *geaxast* 'he asks', *etc.*, with etymological /cs/; *wexan* 'to grow', *sextig* 'sixty', *etc.*, with etymological /hs/.

[77] For usages similar to those of Arch. I in early Nhb., see Ström, p. 131.

[78] But *x* for [ks] is a later, Middle Irish, usage.

[79] OIr. *cs* for [xs] either was not adopted by the English or did not survive long enough to affect Arch. I.

complementary distribution with [g], the two might well be analyzed as allophones of one phoneme. Moulton's arguments for separating [g] from [g] and combining it with [x] were two. First, this solution simplifies OE morphophonemics by making it possible to analyze late OE *dragan* (inf.)—*droh* (pt. 1 sg.) as /draxan—dro:x/ rather than as /dragan—dro:h/, and to analyze some other OE verbs with the same sort of simplification. Second, giving /x/ a voiced allophone makes the voiceless spirants more symmetrical, inasmuch as both /f/ and /þ/ had voiced allophones.[80]

5.34. Stockwell and Barritt rejected Moulton's analysis into /h/, /x/, and /g/.[81] They pointed out that [h] and [x] were spelled alike in most OE texts "except in environments where morphophonemic alternation with /g/ readily explains the use of *g*," that the [h] and [x] were in complementary distribution, and that the two were "phonetically similar." They analyzed [h] and [x] as one phoneme, [g] and [g] as another. I agree, of course, but I should like to supplement their discussion.

5.35. The difference between glottal and velar articulation seems to me an insufficient reason for separating two sounds which are alike in their other phonetic features, which are in complementary distribution, and whose earlier and later history makes it desirable to treat them diachronically as one phoneme.[82] As I see it, the glottal articulation is merely a pushing further back of the velar articulation. The difference between the glottal pronunciation in *horn* and the velar in *scoh* 'shoe' may be greater than that between the velar in *scoh* and the palatal in *stihst* 'he climbs', but I submit that the difference is not sufficient to produce a phonemic split. It seems to me no more unreasonable to combine OE [x, x'] with [h] than it is to combine modern French trilled and uvular /r/. The arguments for a split of /g/ and fusing of [g] with /x/ are also dubious. Morphophonemic irregularities are so abundant in OE that simplifying a few verbs is like taking a bucketful of water out of the ocean. A host of other complications will remain unaffected: *þencan—þohte, dæg—dagas, weorþan—wurdon, feoh—feos*, and many others.[83] Even in cases like *dragan—droh*, Moulton merely postpones the problem to ME times, when his /x/ in *dragan* becomes /w/ and his /x/ in *droh* remains unchanged phonetically and phonemically. The argument from symmetry is open to the objection that the parallelism between /f/ and /þ/ on the one hand and Moulton's /x/ on the other can be only partial at best. The /f/ and /þ/ occur post-juncturally, while the /x/ never does. The allophones of /f/ and /þ/ are not distinguished in spelling, while (as Stockwell and Barritt point out) the supposed allophones of /x/ are usually written differently. Moreover, arguments from symmetry are apt to be dangerous; for example, one might argue that, since MnE has a dental nasal /n/ and a palatovelar nasal /ŋ/, MnE must also have a labial nasal /m/ and a palatovelar nasal phoneme which it obviously does not have.

---

[80] *Op. cit.*, pp. 22, 25-27, 39. Hockett, pp. 376-377, follows Moulton.
[81] *Lg.*, XXXVII, 79-80.
[82] They began as one phoneme in proto-Gmc. (Moulton, pp. 39-40), and they were one phoneme throughout much of the ME period; *cf.* Hans Kurath, *Middle English Dictionary, Plan and Bibliography* (Ann Arbor, 1954), p. 5.
[83] Moulton was aware of this weakness, p. 27.

I should, therefore, regard [g, g, gʹ] as one phoneme and [h, x, xʹ] as another throughout the OE period; and I should regard the unvoiced final [g, gʹ] as having split from /g/ and fused with /h/.[84]

6. *Liquids.*[85]

6.1. /l/ [l]: (1) *lind* 'linden' 2019; *lund-laga* 'kidney' 1712; *plumę* 'plum' (Ep., Erf. *plumae*) 1664; *clate* 'burdock' (Ep. *clatae*) 306; *blaec-* 'black' 1360; *gloed* 'ember' (Ep. out) 396; *flooc* 'flatfish' (Erf. *floc*) 1602; *hlutre* 'clear' (Ep., Erf. *hlutrae*) 1216; *slahðorn* 'sloethorn' (Ep. *slaghthorn*, Erf. †*salachthorn*) 1898; *uulatunc* 'nausea' (Ep. *uulatung*, Erf. *uulating*) 1357. (2) *spelli* 'story' 1720; *bolla* 'bowl' (Erf. *bollae*) 1826. (3) *thumle* 'entrails' (Ep., Erf. out) 2140. (4) An /l/ would become syllabic in this position. (5) See (2). (6) Long /l/ was simplified, *cf.* (10), *stal.* (7) Early evidence lacking, but **ceorlas* no doubt existed in the dialect of Arch. I. (8) *ceorl* 'man' (Ep., Erf. out) 2174. (9) *felu-* 'much' (Ep. *felo-*) 2049; *stalu* 'places, stalls' 2153. (10) *smęl* 'small' (Ep. *smael*, Erf. *smal*) 992; *hool* 'hole' 2159; *stal* 'stall' (Ep., Erf. out) 1905. (11) *gyrdils* 'girdle' 1244; *haelsere* 'soothsayer' (Ep., Erf. out) 253. (12) *smeltas* 'smelts' 1784; *holt-* 'wood' 54.

[l̥]: (13) *netl* 'needle' (Ep., Erf. out) 66; *-adl* 'disease' (Corp. *-ald*) Ep. 999; *scofl* 'shovel' (Erf. *scolf*) 2051; *lebl* 'bowl' (Ep., Erf. *lebil*) 2045; *wefl* 'warp' or 'woof' (Erf. *uuefl*, Ep. out) 482; *tebl-stan* 'a die' (Ep. *tebelstan*, Erf. †*tebiltan*) 349; *wedl* 'poverty' (Ep., Erf. out) 1554; *ðuehl* 'washing' (Erf. *thuachl*, Ep. out) 641; *haesl* 'hazel' (Ep. *haesil*) 536; *hrisl* 'shuttle' (Ep. *hrisil*) 1704; *dixl* 'wagon pole' (Corp., Ep. out) Erf. 1147; *cf. sawl, sawul* 'soul' (VPs.); *segl-* 'sail' (Ep., Erf. *segil-*) 165; *sigl* 'jewel' (Ep., Erf. *sigil*) 331; *snegl* 'snail' (Erf. out) 1283.

6.11. The /l/ had two important allophones: the purely consonantal [l] in most positions and a syllabic [l̥] in pre-junctural position after another consonant. In post-junctural position, [l̥] clustered freely after a labial or velar stop, a labial or glottal spirant, /s/, and /w/.[86] The [l̥] could probably have occurred after consonants other than those in the examples (*cf. æpl* 'apple', *tungl* 'star', *spinl-* 'spindle', *etc.*, in later OE), but the evidence for the earliest period is sparse. Two of the examples are questionable. The form *netl* may be merely an error,[87] or it may represent the same development which we see elsewhere in OE *sepel, setl, seld, etc.*, 'seat'. The second *h* in *ðhuehl* represents an [h] which had probably been lost by the time that Corp. and Erf. were written; it may have been merely an archaic spelling even when

---

[84] See /g/ above.
[85] This is the traditional term, which serves to bring together two consonants which are similar in their articulation and in their effects upon neighboring sounds. I am well aware that the term does not describe these phonemes literally and that there were articulatory differences not indicated by the word 'liquid'.
[86] For Campbell's interpretation of *hl*, see /w/ below.
[87] *Cf.* Corp. *nethle* (Ep. *naeðlae*, Erf. *nedlæ*) 1591.

Arch. I was compiled.[88] The [l] usually resulted from the loss of an earlier vocalic ending, as in *scofl* (from */skoblō/) or *tebl-* (from */tabla/, from Lat. *tabula*). Frequently the syllabic consonant developed into vowel plus [l]. One would assume that the vowel must at first have been /ə/; *i.e.*, [ə] after a syllable containing a back vowel, [ɫ] after a syllable containing a front vowel. The /ə/ could then remain /ə/ or become a full vowel: /u/, /o/, /i/, or /e/. In specific instances, it would obviously be difficult for us to determine whether the compiler of one of these glossaries pronounced [l] or vowel plus [l], but I believe the evidence as a whole points to the existence of [l] at the time that Arch. I was compiled.[89]

6.2. /r/ [r]: (1) *redboran* 'counsellors' 1160; *ragu* 'lichen' 1324; *spryng* 'ulcer' 1492; *treuleasnis* 'faithlessness' (Ep., Erf. *treulesnis*) 1533; *crop* 'top, sprout' 57; *breer* 'brier' 161; *drop-* 'drop' (Erf. †*dro-*) 1914; *gryt:* 'meal, grits' (Erf. *gryt*) 1620; *from* 'bold' (Ep. †*fraam*) 60; *-ŏred* 'thread' (Ep. *-þred*, Erf. *-draed*) 1548; *hrooc* 'rook' 991; *screuua* 'shrew mouse' (Ep. *screuua*, Erf. out) 1344; *wrot* 'snout' (Ep. *uurot*, Erf. *urot*) 327. (2) *sibunsterri* 'Pleiades' (Ep. *sifunsterri*, Erf. †*funsterri*) 1599; *cearricgge* some kind of vehicle (Ep. *cearrucae*, Erf. *œarricae*) 1849. (3) *cf. geamrung* (VPs.). (4) An /r/ would become syllabic in this position. (5) *cf. alre* 'all' fem. dat. sg. (VPs.). (6) An /r/ becomes syllabic. (7) See (2). (8) Long /r/ was simplified in this position. (9) *berecorn* 'barleycorn' 1677; *spora* 'spur' 361. (10) *scir* 'bright' (Ep., Erf. *sciir*) 1952; *baar* 'boar' 287; *fear* 'bull' (Ep., Erf. out) 1985; *heor* 'hinge' (Ep., Erf. out) 423. (11) *first-* 'time' (Ep. *frist-*, Erf. †*frit-*) 1108; *hors-* 'horse' (Erf. out) 1346. (12) *-wyrt* 'plant' (Ep. *-uuyrt*, Erf. out) 1289; *wearte* 'wart' (Ep. *uueartae*, Erf. *uearte*) 1485.

[ṛ]: (13) *otr* 'otter' (Erf. †*octer*) 1246; *ottor* 'otter' (Ep. *otor*, Erf. *otr*) 1945; *tetr* 'tetter' (Corp. *teter*) Ep. 766; *heolstr* 'hiding place' (Ep., Erf. *helostr*) 1838; *cledr* 'rattle' (Ep. *claedur*, Corp. *cleadur*) Erf. 218; *spaldr* 'asphalt' (Corp., Erf. *spaldur*) Ep. 54; *fingr-* 'finger' (Erf. *fingir-*, Ep. out) 687; *cefr* 'chafer' (Corp. *cefer*) Ep. 150; *ofr* 'hump' (Corp. *hofer*) Ep. 1046; *scalfr* 'diver' (Corp. *scalfur*) Ep. 647; *roŏr* 'rudder' (Ep. *rothor*, Erf. †*trohr*) 2031; *thothr* 'ball' (Ep. *thothor*, Erf. †*thorr*) 1584.

The allophones of /r/ roughly parallel those of /l/ in their distribution. The [r] allophone clustered freely after any post-junctural consonant other than a liquid, a nasal, an affricate, /s/, or /ġ/.[90] The [ṛ] was less frequent than [l] and occurred after a more limited range of consonants; it originated as the result of loss of a vocalic ending (*e.g. otr* from */otraz/) and tended to develop into vowel plus [r].

6.21. It is possible that further allophonic variants of /l/ and /r/ existed. In Corp. *ald* 'old', an /æ/ was retracted to /a/ before the /l/-plus-consonant cluster; in the WS cognate of this word, *eald*, /æ/ was broken to /æa/.[91] In Corp. *heard* 'hard',

---

88 *Cf. suehoras, ryhae, etc.*, above.
89 For the views of Samuels and Reszkiewicz, see /r/ below.
90 For further discussion of /hr/, see /w/ below.
91 For a brief account (with bibliographical details) of other views as to what happened, see Sherman M. Kuhn and Randolph Quirk, "Some Recent Interpretations of Old English Digraph

/æ/ was broken to /æa/ by the cluster; but in *tharme* 'entrail', the /æ/ may have been retracted, as it frequently was in Nhb. Some scholars explain these sound changes (merely orthographical differences in the opinion of a few) by assuming different articulations for the /l/ in *ald—eald* and in *lāð* 'hateful', for the /r/ in *heard* and in *wer* 'man'. Although the idea of dual pronunciations for the two consonants is an old one in traditional linguistics, I shall cite only a few examples, drawn from recent writers whose views are structurally oriented. For proto-English, M. L. Samuels describes the /l/ and /r/ of *ald-eald* and *heard* as 'dark', the liquids in *lāð* and *wer* as 'palatal'.[92] Fernand Mossé described the /l/ in *ald—eald* as 'velaire', the /r/ in *heard* as 'retroflexe'.[93] Marjorie Daunt called the /r/ in words like *heard* 'retroflex'.[94] Alfred Reszkiewicz calls the /r/ in *heard* 'preconsonantal' or 'postvocalic' and describes it as "probably... retroflex," contrasting this with the /r/ in words like *wer*, which he calls 'prevocalic' and describes as "probably trilled."[95] Although articulatory differences of some sort probably existed, in the present state of our knowledge, we can only conjecture what they may have been. All of the guesses are legitimate attempts to account for the phonetic effects of /l/ and /r/, but they are only guesses. The allophones in question, whatever their nature, had no effect upon the spellings of the consonants themselves, nor did they become distinguishable phonemes in any dialect of Middle English.

6.22. Reszkiewicz holds that there were two *l*-phonemes and two *r*-phonemes in OE.[96] He sought to prove that WS *ea*, *eo*, and *ie* of the kind traditionally regarded as representing short diphthongs were merely spellings for allophones of /a/, /e/, and /i/, respectively. In order to make his proof, he found it necessary to account for such WS minimal pairs as *ærn* 'building': *earn* 'eagle'. He saw three ways of explaining this pair: (1) "the two words are homophones," (2) "*æ* and *ea* represent two different phonemes," or (3) "the two *r*'s... represent two different phonemes." He rejected (1), rightly I think, on the ground that the consistency with which words like *ærn* and *earn* were differentiated in spelling indicates that they were differently pronounced. "The second explanation is hardly possible," he says, "since a phoneme would have to be postulated which would occur in only a limited number of positions (before *h r l* and after *c g sc*) and contrast contextually only in the position before

---

Spellings," *Lg*. XXIX (1953), 143-156; "The Old English Digraphs : A Reply," *Ibid.*, XXXI (1955), 390-401.
[92] "The Study of Old English Phonology," *Transactions of the Philological Society* (London, 1953), p. 43. The precise meaning of 'dark' is not clear to me.
[93] *Manuel de l'anglais du Moyen-Âge, I. Vieil-anglais* (= *Bibliothèque de philologie germanique*, VIII); (Paris, 1945), p. 34.
[94] "Old English Sound Changes Reconsidered in Relation to Scribal Tradition and Practice," *Trans. Phil. Soc.* (London, 1939), pp. 121-122, 128; "Some Notes on Old English Phonology," *Ibid.* (1953), p. 51.
[95] "Phonemic Interpretation," p. 183. The explanation of the occurrence of a 'prevocalic' phoneme in final position is on pp. 184-185.
[96] *Op. cit.*, pp. 179-187. The article deals with early WS only.

r l and after *c g.*"[97] Hence, only (3) remains, and Reszkiewicz analyzes *ærn* as /ar₁n/ and *earn* as /ar₂n/. His argument against (2) is self-refuting. Contrast in one position, any position, is generally accepted as sufficient to establish a phonemic difference. If, as he says, /æ/ and /æa/ contrast in four positions, most structuralists would have no choice but to classify them as separate phonemes. The argument in favor of (3) is also defective. According to Reszkiewicz, the trilled phoneme /r/₁ was spelled *r* both medially and finally (*e.g. faran* and *fær, weras* and *wer, firen*), but the retroflex phoneme /r/₂ was spelled *rr* medially, either *rr* or *r* finally (*e.g. fearras* and *fearr* or *fear, feorran* and *feorr* or *feor, fierran* and *fierr* or *fier*); hence, *fær* is /far₁/, and *fear(r* is /far₂/, *etc.* All of the spellings cited to prove the existence of /r/₂ are derived from geminated /r/. When Reszkiewicz says that "geminated consonants did not occur finally... in early Germanic languages," he is correct, but he overlooks the fact that OE represents a stage in the language much later than that in which the *r*'s were geminated. *Fear* 'bull', for example, had an inflectional ending at the time of gemination, *i.e.* */farza-/. Much later the ending was lost, the /rr/ became final and was simplified in pronunciation, although it was often spelled with *rr* by analogy with forms like the plural *fearras*, which had retained its ending and its long /rr/. There is a quantitative difference between Reszkiewicz's two *r*'s, but it has nothing to do with trilled versus retroflex articulation.[98]

6.23. Samuels suggests the possibility that /l/ and /r/ split in proto-English into palatal /l/, /r/ and 'dark' /l/, /r/, the latter being the phonemes which caused breaking. Later, according to Samuels, the palatal and dark phonemes fused "to form single, more or less neutral *l-* and *r*-phonemes."[99] As far as OE from about 700 on is concerned, there would seem to be no conflict between the views of Samuels and those which are generally accepted. I am inclined, however, to question the likelihood of two complete phonemic splits followed by two complete fusions, without any residue[100] and without any permanent effect upon the consonants of the language. These pairs of phonemes are not needed as a means of accounting for breaking, which could have been caused (or rather made possible) by the combined effect of the liquid plus consonant rather than by the quality of the liquid alone.

7. Nasals

7.1. /m/ [m]: (1) *megsibbe* 'kinship' (Ep., Erf. *megsibbi*) 103; *mus* 'mouse' 1884; *smeltas* 'smelts' 1784. (2) *-uuemmid* 'corrupted' (Ep. *-uuaemmid*, Erf. *-uemmid*)

---

[97] *Ibid.*, pp. 183-184.
[98] Proof for the two *r*-phonemes is given, but the proof for the two *l*-phonemes, is merely suggested, p. 186.
[99] *Op. cit.*, pp. 42-43.
[100] By way of comparison, when /a/ split into /a/ and /ɔ/ in Merc., and then /a/ and /ɔ/ fused in ME times, there was a small residue; *i.e.*, the vowels in *orn* "he ran," *long* "long," *etc.*, were left (as the result of changes occurring after the split) with phonemes other than the combined /a/ — /ɔ/.

1101; *gremman* 'to irritate' (Ep., Erf. out) 1195; *cf. rommas* 'rams' (VPs.). (3), (4) Does not occur. (5) *selma* 'couch' 1895; *helmes* 'of a helmet' (Ep., Erf. out) 418; *duolma* 'confusion' (Erf. †*dualma*) 457; *cf. salmas* 'Psalms' (VPs.). (6) *elm* 'elm' 2149; *cualm-stou* 'place of execution' (Ep., Erf. out) 2. (7) *orfiermae* 'squalid' (Erf. *orfermae*, Corp. †*orfeormnisse*) Ep. 933; *hearma* 'weasel' 1307; *tharme* 'entrail' (Ep., Erf. out) 2140. (8) *-wyrm* 'worm' (Ep., Erf. *-uuyrm*) 1253; *þearm* 'entrail' (Ep., Erf. *þearm*) 1058; *storm* 'storm' 1378. (9) *gefremid* 'made' (Ep. *gifraemid*, Erf. *gifremid*) 1643; *hęmedo* 'copulation' (Ep., Erf. out) 1036; *leoma* 'light' 1166; *haman* 'crickets' 464. (10) *liim* 'lime' (Ep., Erf. *lim*) 295; *stream* 'stream' 1714; *brom* 'broom' (Ep., Erf. *broom*) 959. (11) *hromsa* 'garlic' (Ep., Erf. *hramsa*) 56. (12) Does not occur.

[m̩]: (13) *ouuaestm* 'sprout' (Ep., Erf. out) 1942; *cf. westem* (VPs.); *aethm* 'breath' (Ep. *ethm*, Erf. out) 130; *faeðm* 'fathom' (Ep., Erf. out) 1510; *-bosm* 'bosom' (Ep., Erf. out) 412.

The labial nasal [m] was, of course, the common allophone. The syllabic [m̩] occurred in pre-junctural position immediately after another consonant; it seems to have been rare except after a dental or sibilant. Like the other syllabic consonants, [m̩] originated as the result of loss of a following vowel and had a tendency to develop into vowel plus non-syllabic consonant, as in VPs. *westem* or later OE *maðm, maðum, madm* 'treasure'.

7.2. /n/ [n]: (1) *nest* 'rations' (Ep. out) 756; *naep* 'turnip' (Erf. *nep*) 1363; *nomun* 'they took' (Ep. *naamun*, Erf. †*noumun*) 247; *cnioholen* 'butcher's broom' (Ep. *cnioholaen*, Erf. †*cniolen*) 1759; *a-gnidine* 'rubbed' (Erf. *agnidinne*, Ep. out) 655; *fnora* 'sneezing' (Erf. †*huora*) 1909; *hnut-* 'nut' 1394; *snel* 'quick' (Erf. †*blidi*) 127. (2) *grennung* 'grinning' (Ep. *graennung*, Erf. †*graemung*) 1738; *scinneras* 'magicians' (Erf. †*scineras*) 1822; *wonnan* 'pale' (Ep., Erf. *uuannan*) 1215. (3) *cf. nemne* 'unless', *gesomnung* 'assembly' (VPs.). (4) An /n/ would become syllabic. (5) No early evidence. (6) An /n/ would probably become syllabic. (7) *þyrne* 'thorn bush' (Erf. *thyrnae*, Ep. out) 710; *eornisti* 'earnestness' (Ep. *eornęsti*, Erf. *eornesti*) 1845; *suornadun* 'coagulated' (Ep. *suornodun*, Erf. *suarnadun*) 518. (8) *isern* 'iron' (Ep. *isęrn*, Erf. *isaern*) 115; *-ðorn* 'thorn' (Ep., Erf. *-thorn*) 1897; *horn* 'whale' (Ep. *hran*, Erf. *hron*) 267. (9) *taenil* 'basket' (Erf. *tenil*) 868; *flanum* 'arrows' 1894. (10) *tin* 'wooden beam' 2023; *bruun* 'brown' 931. (11) *suinsung* 'harmony' (Erf. †*ruinsung*) 1303. (12) *flint* 'flint' 1561; *cf. munt* 'mountain' (VPs.).

[n̩]: (13) *sigebecn* 'trophy' (Ep. *sigbeacn*, Erf. †*beanc*) 2043; *hraefn* 'raven' (Erf. *hraebn*, Ep. out) 553; *stebn* 'voice' (Ep., Erf. out) 2164; *bituihn* 'between' (Ep., Erf. out) 1310; *bituichn* (Ep. *bituicn*, Corp. †*bitun*) Erf. 546; *lybsn* 'amulet' (Ep., Erf. out) 1413; *regn-* 'rain' (Ep. *regen-*) 1253; *segn* 'banner' (Ep. *seng*) 1167; *þegn* 'servant' (Ep. *thegn*, Erf. *degn*) 77.

[ŋ]: (14) *lenctin-* 'springtime' (Ep. †*lectin-*) 2001; *wlonc-lice* 'proudly' (Ep. *uulanc-licae*, Erf. †*gelplih*) 85; *heringas* 'herrings' 1781; *holunga* 'in vain' 1373; *pung* 'purse' (Ep. out) 391.

The [n] was a dental (possibly alveolar) nasal, which clustered post-juncturally after /c/, /g/, /f/, /h/, and /s/.[101] Syllabic [n] occurred after /c/, /b/ (i.e. [b], later /f/), /h/, /s/, and /ǥ/. VPs. *wepen* 'weapons' does not show any spelling indicating [n], but cf. later WS *wæpn*. Later OE *myln, mylen* 'mill' and *stemn* (from *stefn*, from *stebn*) do not appear in early texts.

8. *Sibilants*

8.1. /s/ [s]: (1) *segn* 'banner' (Ep. *seng*) 1167; *sadol* 'saddle' (Erf. †*satul*) 1839. (2) *cressa* 'cress' (Ep. *cressae*) 1860; cf. *assan* 'asses' (VPs.). (4) cf. *wrigelse* 'covering' (VPs.). (6) *bridels* 'bridle' (Ep. *bridils*, Erf. *brigdils*) 261. (8) *baers* 'bass' (Corp. †*brers*) Ep. 592; *hors-* 'horse' (Erf. out) 1346. (10) *saes* 'seat' (Ep., Erf. *ses*) 2050; *mus* 'mouse' 1884. (12) *þistel* 'thistle' (Erf. *thistil*, Ep. out) 384; *ost* 'knob' 1387. (14) *musclan-* 'mussel' (Ep., Erf. out) 593; *musscel* (Ep., Corp. out) Erf. 1117; *malscrung* 'enchantment' (Ep., Erf. out) 838; *aesc* 'ax' (Corp. *ecus*, Ep. out) Erf. 321.

[z]: (3) *hromsa* 'garlic, ramson' (Ep., Erf. *hramsa*) 56; *suinsung* 'harmony' (Erf. †*ruinsung*) 1303. (5) *haelsere* 'soothsayer' (Ep., Erf. out) 253. (7) cf. *horsum* 'horses' (VPs.). (9) *isern-* 'iron' (Ep. *isern-*, Erf. *isaern-*) 272; *tasul* 'a die' (Ep. *tasol*) 2000; *briosa* 'gadfly' 1976; *haesl* 'hazel' (Ep. *haesil*) 536; -*bosm* 'bosom' (Ep., Erf. out) 412; *lybsn* 'amulet' (Ep., Erf. out) 1413.

8.11. The voiceless [s] occurred post- and pre-juncturally and in medial position before or after a voiceless consonant. The cluster /sc/ probably occurred in *muscel* and other borrowings from Latin which were too recent for the cluster to have undergone palatalization and assibilation to /š/. In *aesc*, we may have a metathesized form of *æcs*, in which case the *sc* certainly represents /sc/. One could not be certain about *malscrung* from the OE evidence, but the forms of ME *malskren* and MnE *masker* point to retention of the *sc*-cluster. The cluster was also retained, beside /š/, in some forms of *fisc* 'fish', *tusc* 'tusk', *etc.*; otherwise, later OE metathesized *fixas*, *tux*, ME *tusk* beside *tush*, *etc.*, would be difficult to explain. The voiced [z] occurred medially between vowels or between a vowel and syllabic /l, r, m, n/. Theoretically, it should also occur medially before or after a voiced consonant, but in these positions there was apparently some fluctuation between the voiced and voiceless allophones. Before a voiced consonant, [z] was regular: *raesde* 'he rushed' (Ep., Erf. out) 1120; *osle* 'ouzel' (Ep., Erf. *oslae*) 1306; *besma* 'besom' (Ep., Erf. out) 1794; *lybesne* 'amulets' (Ep., Erf. out) 1930; and *leswe* 'pasture' (VPs.). But *hlysnende*, 'listening' (Ep., Erf. out) 82, acquired a /t/ in ME times, which suggests that a voiceless pronunciation of the /s/ existed in OE.[102] After a voiced consonant, the fluctuation is more obvious. How does one account for the OE change of *bledsian* to *bletsian*, *mildsian* to *miltsian*, *etc.*, if the /s/ was invariably voiced? How shall we account for ME *rampsoun* beside *ramesen*, *etc.*, or the post-OE development of the

---

101 For discussion of /hn/, see /w/ below.
102 The /t/ could also have come through analogy with *hlystan*.

inflected forms of *hors*? Analogy with related forms in which the clusters were pre-junctural might account for these phenomena if they were somewhat rarer; but in view of their frequency, it would seem safer to assume a great deal of fluctuation between [z] and [s] in medial position after a voiced consonant.[103] The [z] in positions (3, 5, 7) should, therefore, be taken with a small grain of salt.

8.2. /š/ [ʃ]: (1) *scel* 'shell' (Ep. out) 716; *scadu* 'shadow '(Ep., Erf. *sceadu*) 1801; *scomo* 'shame' (Ep. *scamu*, Erf. *scoma*) 1679. (3), (4) A nasal in these positions was lost. (5), (6) No clear early evidence. (7) *cf. forscas* 'frogs' (VPs.). (8) *mersc* 'marsh' (Erf. *merisc*, Ep. out) 394; *horsc-lice* 'briskly' (Ep., Erf. *horsclicae*) 1358; *forsc* 'frog' (Ep., Erf. out) 1258. (9) *biscop-* 'bishop' 1021; *frysca* 'kite' bird (Ep., Erf. out) 340. (10) *disc* 'dish' 1490; *edisc* 'park' 324; *flaesc* 'flesh' (Ep., Erf. out) 2135; *tusc* 'tusk, tooth' (Ep. out, ? Erf. *dens:tusc*) 961. (12) *gegiscte* 'closed' (Ep. *gigiscdae*, Erf. †*gescdae*) 1447; *cf. wysctun* 'wished' (VPs.). The contrast between /š/ and /sc/ is difficult to establish in Mercian of around 700, partly because the materials are sparse, partly because palatal diphthongization did not operate in Merc.[104] In WS of the ninth to eleventh centuries, forms like *sciel, sceamu, bisceop*, etc., furnish clues. There are similar clues in Nhb. But it is not until the rise of ME spelling practices, including the adoption of *sh* and *sch* for /š/, that we can have much certainty in specific cases. The fact that a phoneme /š/ existed in the period when Arch. I was compiled seems, however, to be undisputed.

9. Semi-vowels

9.1. /w/ [w]: (1) *uueod-* 'weed' (Ep., Erf. *uuead-*) 1764; *windil* 'basket' (Erf. †*pindil*) 348; *woedeberge* 'mad berry' (Erf. †*poediberga*, Ep. out) 736; *waar* 'seaweed' (Erf. *uar*, Ep. †*paar*, altered to *uaar*) 120; *tuin* 'twine' (Erf. *tuigin*, Ep. †*tuum*) 343; *cuicbeam* 'aspen' (Erf. out) 368; *quiða* 'womb' (Ep. out) 1290; *duerg* 'dwarf' 1362; *þuerh-* 'cross-' (Ep., Erf. *thuerh-*) 1761; *hwaeg* 'whey' (Ep., Erf. *huaeg*) 1847; *suualuue* 'swallow' (Ep. *suualuae*, Erf. *suualuuæ*) 1665. (2) A /ww/ became /uw/, which developed in various ways. (3) No clear early evidence. (4) A /w/ became /u/. (5) *calwer* 'pressed curds' (Ep. *caluuaer*, Erf. *caluuer*) 956. (6) A /w/ became /u/. (7) *gegeruuid* 'prepared' (Ep. *gigeruuid,* Erf. †*gigarauuit*) 1632; *spearua* 'sparrow' (Ep. *spearuua*) 855. (8) A /w/ became /u/. (9) *beowes* 'of grain' (Ep. *beouuas*, Erf. *beouaes*) 1278; *clauuo* 'claw' 211; *pauua* 'peacock' 1509. (10) *iuu* 'yew' 1972. (11) *cf. hreowsade* 'repented' (VPs.). (12) No early evidence.

9.11. The rounded labial spirant /w/ presents no great phonemic problems, but the spellings used for /w/ are of some interest. In the earliest texts, *u* and *uu* are the usual spellings, the former being especially favored in clusters after another consonant. The symbol *v*, a graphic variant of *u*, appears rarely in later OE texts, although it is

---

[103] The phonetic reasons for this fluctuation offer a promising field for further study.
[104] The form *sceadu* above probably contains /æa/ by velar umlaut, not by palatal diphthongization.

rather frequent in a few, *e.g.* the tenth-century Nhb. gloss to the *Durham Ritual*. The *u*- and *v*-spellings were obviously adapted from Latin usage. They were not influenced by Old Irish; for, in the latter, *u* represents a vowel, except in a few *qu*-forms borrowed from Latin. Apparently *uu* was an English innovation, intended to distinguish /w/ from /u/, a distinction which was highly desirable in written English but not absolutely necessary in Latin. Mercian scribes seem to have been the first to introduce the runic *w* (*p*) into texts written in the Latin alphabet. Although the rune was familiar enough to Northumbrians and appears in the seventh-century inscriptions of the Ruthwell Cross and the Bewcastle Column, the personal names of the early Bede MSS have only *u* and *uu*.[105] In MSS of around 700, the runic *w* was probably a rare innovation. Errors like *pindil*, *poedibergæ*, and *paar* indicate that an unwary scribe might mistake it for *p*. It could also be mistaken for þ, as we see in †*þoot* (Erf. †*þuood*, Corp. out) Ep. 444. This last word glosses *facundia*, *eloquentia* (*i.e.* OE *wōþ*) and points to something like **wood* or **wood* in the exemplar. The scribe of the *Corpus Glossary*, who was an innovator, frequently substituted *w* for the older spellings, *e.g.* in *calwer*. The Erfurt scribe (or the English scribe whose MS he copied) preferred *u* or *uu* exclusively, and may have substituted one of these for any *w* which he found in his exemplar, except when he mistook the *w* for a *p*. The Epinal scribe, who was either the earliest or the most conservative of the three, used *w* only nine times, in five instances corresponding to *w* in Corp., four times corresponding to *uu* in Corp. The evidence is admittedly inconclusive, but it seems to point (and this is especially true of the *p* and þ errors) to the use of the runic *w* in Arch. I.[106] The runic symbol increased in popularity, until in the ninth century it became the usual spelling for /w/ in all areas except Northumbria, where *u*, *uu*, and *v* were often used (beside more frequent *w*) as late as the tenth century.

9.12. Now that we have examined the phonemes /l, r, n, w/, the time has come to discuss the clusters which these consonants form with /h/, as in *hlutre*, *hrooc*, *hnut-*, *hwaeg*, etc. During ME times, the first three clusters lost the /h/, while the fourth often appeared (especially in East Midland texts) in the form *wh*, a spelling which is commonly assumed to have represented a voiceless *w*, like the [м] which survives in the speech of some people today. Linguists have naturally been inclined to entertain the possibility that voiceless /w/ and also voiceless /l/, /r/, and /n/ existed in OE times, perhaps as occasional variants of the clusters or perhaps as pronunciations characteristic of certain (not clearly defined) areas. Karl Brunner expressed the thought as follows: "Anlautendes *h*... steht unbeschränkt vor Vokalen, außerdem in der Verbindungen *hl*, *hr*, *hn*, *hw*, die vielleicht nur als stimmlose *l*, *r*, *n*, *w* aufzufassen sind (wie z.T. engl. *wh*)."[107] A Campbell has carried the idea a step further. In his

---

[105] See Ström, p. 128. These MSS also have a *uu*-ligature, which may be called a 'w', but it bears no resemblance to the rune.

[106] This is the view of H. M. Chadwick, *op. cit.*, pp. 242-244, to whom the present discussion is deeply indebted.

[107] *Altengl. Gram.*, p. 195. For earlier expressions of the same idea, see Sievers, *Angels. Gram.*, § 217, and H. Sweet, *A History of English Sounds* (Oxford, 1888), p. 135.

table of consonants, he lists four new simple consonants: voiceless liquids *hl* and *hr*, voiceless nasal *hn*, and voiceless spirant *hw*.[108] Later, in his discussion of the loss of consonants, Campbell says: "In all Gmc. languages, initial *x* became a breathing or glottal spirant. Before *l, n, r, ų*, it disappeared, leaving the consonant voiceless, and *h* is written in OE as a diacritic to indicate this."[109]

9.13. We should take note of the fact that, although Campbell writes in phonetic rather than in phonemic terms, his analysis creates four new consonantal phonemes. If accepted, his *hl* would be in contrast with /l/, his *hr* with /r/, his *hn* with /n/, and his *hw* with /w/. The contrasts can easily be illustrated with minimal pairs (WS) like the following: *hlæw* 'mound': *læw* 'injury'; *hlāf* 'loaf': *lāf* 'remnant'; *hrīm* 'hoar-frost': *rīm* 'number'; *hrūm* 'soot': *rūm* 'space'; *hnifol* 'forehead': *nifol* 'gloomy'; *hnāt* 'he clashed': *nāt* 'he knows not'; *hwer* 'kettle': *wer* 'man'; *hwā* 'who': *wā* 'woe'. There are many more like these; and, for those who are not impressed by minimal pairs, there are the examples in my discussions of /h, l, r, n, w/ above, which clearly show that /hl/, *etc.*, were in contrastive distribution with post-junctural /l/, *etc.*

9.14. I do not believe that we can accept the four new phonemes. They are not supported by the OE spelling evidence. Texts which contain sporadic examples of *l* for /hl/ and *hl* for /l/ also contain sporadic examples of dropped and excrescent *h* before a vowel. A text, like Farman's glosses in the *Rushworth Gospels*, which shows rather numerous spellings like *rægl* for *hrægl* and *gehroefa* for *geroefa*, will also show rather numerous spellings like *eard* for *heard* and *hað* for *að*.[110] The evidence of the OE alliterative poetry is against the new phonemes, for /hl/, /hr/, /hn/, /hw/ alliterate with one another or with any other initial /h/, although /l/, /r/, /n/, and /w/ do not alliterate with one another or with vowels. This argument is weakened by the fact that the poetic tradition was conservative and occasionally followed rules of alliteration which antedated some sound changes and phonemic splits; however, I suppose that we may assume that the *h*-alliterations reflect contemporary speech until someone brings forward evidence to prove that they are only traditional.

9.15. The voiceless-*w* phoneme is hard to reconcile with the evidence of Middle and Modern English. A mere diacritic is not likely to survive massive changes in scribal tradition as the *h* did in several dialects of ME and Middle Scottish, in the combinations *hw, qu, quh, ʒw*, etc. It is even less likely to develop, among mainly non-literate speakers, into a distinctly audible sound [h] and then survive for centuries as it has in the speech of millions of English-speaking people today. Even those who pronounce a voiceless [ʍ] or a voiced [w] in most *wh*-words are apt to have an [h] in *who*.[111] It would seem that the *h* in this word has never been a diacritic.

---

[108] *OE Gram.*, p. 20.
[109] *Ibid.*, p. 186.
[110] See E. M. Brown, II, 34.
[111] Reduction of /hw/ to /h/ must have been rather frequent in ME. I see no other way to interpret reverse spellings, such as those for *hou* 'how' (OE *hū*) which appear in certain ME texts : *hwu, whou, who, qwou, quhu*, etc.

9.16. The voiceless-r phoneme is rendered dubious by the evidence of metathesized forms in OE. If metathesis occurs in a word with *hr*, so that the 'voiceless-r' is no longer post-junctural, what happens? Will not the voiceless *r* either remain voiceless and keep its diacritic, or become voiced and lose its diacritic? OE *hors* 'horse' was metathesized from older */hros-/ (*cf.* OIc., OHG *hross*); it became neither *ohrs*, with voicless *r* and diacritic *h*, nor *ors*, with voiced *r* and no diacritic. Instead, the so-called diacritic became a consonantal phoneme. It may be objected that the metathesis in *hors* could have occurred befor the /h/ was lost in the cluster /hr/; *cf.* OFris. *hors*, OS *hers*. The next example is not open to this objection. The word *hræn* 'wave, sea' occurs in the *Epinal Glossary*, made long after the Anglo-Saxons left the Continent. The original /hr/-cluster is confirmed by OIc. *hrönn*, gen. *hrannar*. Metathesized *hærn* appears in a tenth-century MS (*Andreas* 531 in the *Vercelli Book*) and in an eleventh-century glossary (Cotton Cleopatra A. iii).[112] The metathesized form is neither *æhrn* nor *ærn*. Another example may be disputed, but I think that most scholars will accept it after a little cogitation. The word *hornfisc* occurs in *Andreas* 370, a poem probably composed in the eighth century but preserved in a MS of the tenth. The word is frequently interpreted 'garfish' and compared with a late and very rare word in Old Icelandic (*i.e.*, *hornfiskr* in the *Sturlunga Saga*). From the context in *Andreas*, the garfish seems unlikely. This is probably a metathesized form of *hronfisc* 'whale'; *cf.* *hronfixas* in *Beowulf* 540 and *hronfiscas* in Alexander's letter to Aristotle.[113] So far, I have not been able to find similar test words for the other three clusters, but if *h* represented /h/ rather than a diacritic before /r/, we are probably safe in assuming that it also represented a consonant before /l/, /n/, and /w/.

9.2. /ʒ/ [j] From Gmc. /j/: (1) *gere* 'year' (Ep., Erf. *geri*) 1028; *geoc*- 'yoke' (Ep., Erf. out) 1424; *iesen* 'entrails' (Ep., Erf. out) 797; *cf.* *gugude*, *iuguðe* 'youth' (VPs.). (2) Gmc. /jj/ underwent various developments. (3-6) A /j/ would be lost or vocalized. (7) -*berge* 'berry' (Erf. -*bergæ*, Ep. out) 736; -*beriae* (Ep. -*berię*. Erf. -*bergen*) 59; *styrga* 'sturgeon' (Ep., Erf. *styria*) 1614; *cf.* *swergu* 'I swear' (VPs.); *hergan* 'to praise' (*Caedmon's Hymn*). (8) Became /i/, then /e/. (9) *cf.* *gecegu*, *geceigo* 'I call' (VPs.). (10) *cf.* *heg* 'hay' (VPs.); *ei*, *eig* 'island' (early Bede MSS). (11), (12) Does not occur. From Gmc. /g/: (1) *gaec* 'cuckoo' (Erf. *gęc*, Ep. out) 618; *ieces* 'cuckoo's' (Erf. †*iaces*, Ep. out) 380; *gesca* 'sob' (Ep., Erf. *iesca*) 1865; -*gæt* 'gate' (Ep., Erf. -*gaet*) 1538; *cf.* *iefian* (altered to *gefian*) 'joy' (VPs. 20,6); *hin-iongae* 'departure' (Bede's Death Song). (3), (4) A /g/ bécame /ʒ/ or /g/. (5) *faelge* 'felly' (Erf. *felge*, Ep. out) 390; -*felge* (Ep., Erf. -*felgae*) 1563. (6) -*baelg* 'bag' 910; *tylg* 'more strongly' 1636. (7) *byrga* 'surety' (Ep., Erf. *byrgea*) 1652; *byrgen* 'tomb' (Ep., Erf. out) 1350; *wergendi* 'cursing' (Erf. *uuergendi*, Ep. out) 632. (8) *myrg-nis* 'mirth, music' (Ep., Erf. out) 1352; *cf.* *on byrg* 'in the town' (Charter, Cotton Augustus II. 79, early ninth-cent.). (9) *faegen* 'glad' (Ep. out) 543; *staegilre* 'steep' (Ep. *staegilrae*, Erf. *stegelræ*) 1638. (10) *suoeg* 'noise' 925; *grei* 'gray' 981; *greig* (Ep., Erf. out) 850;

112 Thomas Wright, *A Second Volume of Vocabularies* (London, 1873), p. 33.
113 Stanley Rypins, *Three Old English Prose Texts*, EETS, OS, CLXI (1924), p. 33, line 7.

bodeg 'body' (Ep., Erf. *bodẹi*) 1891; *omei* 'rusty' (Ep., Erf. out) 866; *popæg* 'poppy' (Ep. *popaeg*, Erf. †*papoeg*) 1621; *popei* (Ep., Erf. out) 1516. (11) *cf. egsan* 'fear' (*Leiden Riddle*). (12) Does not occur.

9.21. The above tabulations show the two main sources of the semi-vowel /ġ/. In the earliest written records, *g* is used indiscriminately for the reflexes of both Gmc. /j/ and the palatal allophone which split from Gmc. /g/ in proto-English. The letter *i* is in free variation with *g*, as a minority spelling for /ġ/ from both sources. Rarer graphic variants are *ge* in *geoc* (Corp.), *byrgea* (Ep., Erf.) and *ig* in *greig* (Corp.), *geceigo* (VPs.). All of these variants appear in later MSS throughout the OE period. The preference for *g* over *i* increased greatly, except that in the work of WS scribes *i* rather than *g* became the preferred spelling for the /ġ/ in verbs like *herian, swerian* (generally *hergan, swergan* in Merc. and Nhb. texts). The use of *ge* for /ġ/ increased in later texts, especially WS texts, before back vowels. There can be no real doubt as to the pronunciation of /ġ/: it was a palatal spirant with very weak constriction.

9.22. Stockwell classifies his OE /j/, which corresponds to /ġ/ in this analysis, as a 'stop' and suggests that its pronunciation was similar to that of the palatal spirant in North German *liegen*.[114] There is no evidence in Old or Middle English to support this view. It requires us to assume that Gmc. /j/ became a stop and then reverted to semi-vowel in ME, an assumption which I should not be prepared to make without some kind of supporting evidence.

9.23. So far from being supported by the OE evidence, Stockwell's interpretation of /ġ/ appears to be refuted by the treatment of Scriptural names in OE poetry and by the evidence of vocalization. Names like *Iacob Iudiþ, Hierusalem* (with silent *h*), *etc.*, often alliterate with one another, which suggests that the semi-vowel still had the Latin (sometimes Popular Latin) sound, *i.e.* [j] or, rarely, [ɪ] or [i]. Frequently such names alliterate with native /g/ or /ġ/, just as the native /ġ/ does:[115] *Iared* in *Genesis A* 1174, *Iafeð* in *Genesis A* 1552, *Iosep* in *Exodus* 588, *Hierusalem* in *Daniel* 2, *Iudea* in *Daniel* 707, *Iuliana* in *Juliana* 148, *Iudith* in *Judith* 168, *etc.*[116] Occasionally such names are spelled with *g* or *ge* and alliterate with /g/ or /ġ/: *Gerusalem* in *Daniel* 707, *Geared* in *Genesis A* 1195, *etc.* When /ġ/ from Gmc. /g/ occurred between /i/ and another consonant, it frequently vocalized to /i/, and the two vowels coalesced into /ī/. Early examples are: Corp. *brīdels* 'bridle' (Ep. *brīdils*, Erf. *brigdils*) 261; *iil* 'hedgehog' (Ep., Erf. out) 765; VPs. *brīdels*, *īles* (altered to *igles* 103,17), *hefīe* 'heavy', *weolīe* 'rich', *etc.* The OE stops did not behave in this manner.

9.3. The semi-vowels of OE were /w/ and /ġ/. To the best of my knowledge, there were no others. I am familiar with the phonemic analysis and system of transcription

---

[114] *SIL*, XIII, 18. This is not the view of Moulton, p. 25, of Hockett, p. 376, or of most linguists, traditional or structural.
[115] The alliterative tradition, in this instance, is older than the split of /ġ/ from /g/.
[116] Sometimes the alliteration is with vowels : *Iared* in *Genesis A* 1063, *Hierusalem* in *Paris Psalter* 124, 1, *etc.*

which George L. Trager and Henry Lee Smith Jr. have worked out for some dialects of Modern English.[117] Their system takes full advantage of certain distributional facts of MnE; *i.e.*, that, in most dialects, the consonants /h/, /w/, and /y/ occur only in post-junctural position. These symbols are, therefore, available for the transcription of non-initial phenomena of any sort. It is certainly convenient to be able to transcribe *bite* /báyt/, *bout* /báwt/, *yeah* /yéh/, etc. Whether it is scientifically accurate to give labels like /h, w, y/ to purely vocalic glides and lengthenings after vowels, is another matter. The acoustical researches of Gordon E. Peterson and Ilse Lehiste show that the consonants /h, w, y/ are altogether dissimilar to the glides and lengthenings of MnE and as unrelated to them phonetically as they are historically.[118]

9.31. Stockwell posits the three semi-vowels of Trager and Smith for OE.[119] For WS (and presumably, with some modification, for other dialects), he presents the following complex syllabic nuclei containing his post-vocalic /h/: /eh/ as in *fēt* 'feet', /æh/ as in *hǣlan* 'to heal', /ɔh/ as in *bān* 'bone', and /oh/ as in *scōh* 'shoe'. The /h/ in these nuclei is unrelated to the phoneme spelled *h* in *hǣlan* and *scōh*, which Stockwell phonemicizes as /x/.[120] It is called "an off-glide in the direction of central position"; but in practice it seems to be equivalent to a phoneme of length, added to the vowels /e/, /æ/, /ɔ/ (my /a/), and /o/, and presumably varying in articulation from mid-front-unround to mid-back-round. As far as WS is concerned, this glide is rarely reflected in the writing; but when written, it is an *e* after /e/, an *a* after /ɔ/, and an *o* after /o/. The following nuclei containing Stockwell's /w/ are posited: /iw/ as in *bīetel* 'beetle', *dīofol* 'devil', and *stīward* 'steward';[121] /ew/ as in *brēost* 'breast' and *fēower* 'four'; /æw/ as in *bēam* 'beam' and *fēawe* 'few'; /uw/ as in *fūl* 'foul' and *cnūwian* 'to break'; /ow/ as in *grōwan* 'to grow'; and /ɔw/ as in *clawu* 'claw' and *blāwan* 'to blow'. This /w/ is called "an off-glide in the direction of high back rounded position" but must have varied greatly in articulation. In WS it is written *e*, *o*, or zero after /i/, *o* after /e/, *a* after /æ/, zero after /u/, zero after /o/, and *w* or zero after /ɔ/ (my /a/). Only two of Stockwell's nuclei contain his /y/: /iy/ as in *bītan* 'to bite' and /üy/ as in *fȳr* 'fire'. This /y/ is called "an off-glide in the direction of high front position" but seems to be merely a phoneme of length after /i/ and /ü/ (my /y/). In WS, it is almost never expressed in writing, although we sometimes see *ii* for /ī/.

---

[117] *An Outline of English Structure* (= *Studies in Linguistics : Occasional Papers*, III ; Norman, 1951), pp. 11-52.
[118] Peterson and Lehiste, "Duration of Syllabic Nuclei in English," *Journal of the Acoustical Society of America*, XXXII (June, 1960), 693-703; Lehiste and Peterson, "Transitions, Glides, and Diphthongs," *Ibid.*, XXXIII (March, 1961), 268-277; Lehiste, *Acoustical Characteristics of Selected English Consonants* (Bloomington, 1964), especially pp. 116-140, 181-189.
[119] *SIL*, XIII, 15-17. Kurath, "Binary Interpretation," esp. pp. 111-112, 121, and Hockett, *op. cit.*, p. 376, reject Stockwell's view.
[120] Stockwell is unable to preserve the phonemic model set by Trager and Smith, in which the initial consonant /h/ is equated with the post-vocalic centering glide.
[121] When the glide /w/ precedes a consonantal /w/, Stockwell posits an OE geminate; *i.e.*, *iw* is a spelling for /iww/, *eow* for /eww/, *eaw* for /æww/, *uw* for /uww/, *ow* for /oww/, and *aw* for /ɔww/.

9.32. The /h, w, y/ hypothesis for OE is interesting and ingenious, but I am not sure that it belongs, strictly speaking, in the realm of linguistic science. It cannot be tested by such methods as Peterson and Lehiste have applied to MnE, for there are no native speakers to provide the acoustical data. It cannot be tested by spelling evidence, since the three posited phonemes are generally unrelated to anything in scribal practice. It cannot be tested by comparative evidence, for the same glide phonemes can be posited for any language which is no longer spoken; indeed, I once heard a linguistic speaker posit them for an even half-dozen of languages, and prove their existence to his own satisfaction — in slightly under three minutes. As a method for transcription the scheme would be more useful if it were simpler to apply and less beset with pitfalls. Experience shows that even those scholars who are most familiar with it and who are dealing with carefully selected OE words must devote much of their time and energy to correcting errors in their own carefully considered transcriptions.[122]

10. *Affricates*

10.1. /ċ/ [tʃ]: (1) *cest* 'chest, casket' 365; *ceol* 'ship' 442; *cese* 'cheese' (Ep., Erf. out) 912. (2) *flicci* 'flitch' 1551; *styccimelum* 'piecemeal' (Erf. †*scyccimelum*) 1473; *wraeccan* 'exiles' (Ep., Erf. out) 812; *recceo* 'I narrate' (Ep., Erf. out) 139. (3) *lepeuuince* 'lapwing' (Erf. *laepaeuincæ*, Ep. out) 619; *uulencu* 'pride' (Ep., Erf. out) 846. (4) *finc* 'finch' 921; *benc* 'bench' (Ep., Erf. out) 1895. (5) *milcit* 'he milks' (Ep. *milciþ*. Erf. *milcid*) 1323; *suelce* 'also' (Ep. *suilcae*, Erf. *suilce*) 75; *gehwelci* 'each' (Erf. *gihuelci*, Ep. †*gihuuuelci*) 1700. (6) cf. *hwelc* 'which, what' (VPs.). (7) *birce* 'birch' (Ep., Erf. *birciae*) 1609; *serce* 'shirt' (Ep., Erf. *sercae*) 210. (8) cf. *wirc-nisse* 'occupation' (VPs.). (9) *boece* 'beech' (Ep. *boecae*, Erf. †*boeccae*) 93; *leceas* 'physicians' 1578; *quice* 'couch grass' (Ep. †*cuiquae*, altered to †*quiquae*, Erf. *quicae*) 989; *quicae* (Ep. *cuicae*, altered to *quicae*, Erf. †*cuique*) 2130. (10) *pic* 'pitch' 1593; *broec* 'breeches' 1244; *cryc* 'crutch' (Ep., Erf. *crycc*) 1222. (11), (12) Does not occur.

10.11. The manner in which a palatal [k] split from Gmc. /k/ and, by assibilation, became [tʃ] /ċ/ has been outlined above in the discussion of /c/. It is easy to see that a separate phoneme is present in ME, after the *ch*-spelling, adopted from the Old French, came into regular use for the reflex of OE /ċ/. In OE, the phonemic identity of /ċ/ is less obvious. The use of *k* for /c/ but not for /ċ/ in some texts has been noted above. Further evidence appears from the late ninth century on: *orceard, orcerd, orcyrd*, etc., for older *ort-geard* 'orchard', and *gefeccan*, etc., for older *gefetian*, *-fetigan* 'to fetch'.[123] This shift of /tġ/ [tj] to /ċ/ [tʃ] parallels the later development in words like *nature, feature*, etc., and strongly suggests that /ċ/ was recognized by the scribes as a special sound with an identity of its own. Contrastive distribution

---

[122] See *SIL*, XIII, 23; and the later article by Stockwell and Rudolph Willard, "Further Notes on Old English Phonology," *SIL*, XIV (1959), 10-13.
[123] For additional evidence, see Penzl, *op. cit.*, p. 36.

of /ċ/ and /c/ can clearly be seen by comparison of the tabulations for these two phonemes. Minimal and analogous pairs, chiefly from WS and much later than *c* 700, may be cited. Moulton notes the following: *cēne* 'bold': *cēn* 'pine torch' (dat. *cēne*);[124] *hnecca* 'neck': *reċċan* 'to narrate'; *drincan* 'to drink': *drenċan* 'to give to drink'; *dranc* 'he drank': *benċ* 'bench'. To these one may add: *cwic* 'alive' (pl. *cwice*): *cwiċe* 'couch grass';[125] *beswic* 'deceit' (dat. *-swice*): *swiċe* 'escape'; *weorcum* 'works' (dat. pl.): *Mierċum* 'Mercians' (dat. pl.);[126] *sincan* 'to sink': *senċan* 'to cause to sink'; *swincan* 'to toil': *swenċan* 'to oppress'; *smēocan* 'to emit smoke': *smīċan* 'to fumigate'.

10.2. /ǧ/ [dʒ]: (1), (2) Does not occur. (3) *fenge* 'capture' (Ep., Erf. *faengae*) 1630; *gemęngan* 'to mix' (Ep., Erf. out) 547; *gemengiunge* 'confusion' (Ep. *gimaengi-*) 522. (4) *steng* 'pole' (Erf. *stęng*, Ep. *stegn*) 480; *spryng* 'ulcer' (Ep. *spyrng*) 351; *cf. leng* 'longer' (VPs.), *lencg* (Golden Gospels inscription). (5-8) Does not occur. (9) *asaecgan* 'to say' (Ep., Erf. out) 720; *galdriggan* 'enchanters' (Ep., Erf. out) 1124; *cf. dernlicgende* 'idolatrous' (VPs.), *dernliggað* (VPs.), *to ymbhycggannae* 'to think about' (Bede's Death Song). (10) *saecg* 'sedge' (Ep. *segg*, Erf. *secg*) 977; *ecg* 'edge' (Ep. Erf. out) 50; *mygg* 'midge' (Erf. *mycg*) 1814; *brycg* 'bridge' (Ep., Erf. out) 1623. (11), (12) Does not occur.

10.21. The voiced affricate had a limited distribution, for it could occur only when Gmc. /g/ had been preceded by /n/ and followed by /i/, as in *feng, steng spryng, leng, etc.*; preceded by /n/ and followed by /j/, as in *gemengan, gemengung, etc.*; or preceded by a short vowel and followed by /j/, as in *asecgan, galdricge dernlicgan, ymbhycgan, secg, ecg, mycg, brycg, etc.* It was, nevertheless, an independent phoneme, contrasting with /g/, /ǧ/, and the geminates of those two. I believe that Moulton was the first to demonstrate unmistakably that the OE consonant in words like *ecg* was no longer merely a geminated /ǧ/.[127]

10.22 Spellings vary in the earliest texts: after /n/, usually *g*, rarely *gi* or *cg*; after a vowel, either *cg* or *gg*. There is no reason to suppose that the spelling situation around 700 differed materially from this. In later texts, especially in WS, *ge* and *cge* occur frequently, as in *sengean*, beside *sengan*, 'to singe', *secgean*, beside *secgan*, 'to say'. Pre-junctural *cg* is often simplified to *g* or *c* in the early Bede MSS; *e.g.*, *Egbrect, Ecberht*, beside *Ecgbercht*.[128] Otherwise, final *cg* or *gg* for /ǧ/ was very seldom simplified, an indication that the scribes did not regard it as an ordinary geminate like *bb* or *nn*. We may here note a parallel between /ǧ/ and /ċ/ in the late OE *micgern* 'fat of the kidneys', from an older */mid-ġern/ (or /-ġiern/ or /-ġearn/), *cf.* OHG *mittigarni*. The Scottish and North English use of [g] rather than [dʒ] in

---

[124] *Op. cit.*, p. 24. Around 700 and for some time afterward, *cēne* 'bold' was *cōēne* /cǣne/, and there could be no minimal contrast until after unrounding of /ǣ/ in the ninth century.

[125] *Cf.* above *cuic-* 'alive' : *quicae* 'couch grass' (*c* 700).

[126] *Cf. werc-um* in VPs., *Merċ-iorum* (with Lat. inflection) in early Bede MSS.

[127] *Op. cit.*, p. 25. Moulton notes the contrast as seen in *weg* /weǧ/ 'way' : *wecg* /weǧ/ 'wedge', *etc.*

[128] Ström, p. 133.

words like *brig* 'bridge', *rigg* 'ridge', *etc.*, is probably due to Scandinavian influence rather than to any dialectal usage in Nhb.[129]

11. /:/ Consonant length existed in Old English, and length was phonemic in most of the dialects throughout the OE period, as the following pairs (chiefly ninth-century WS) illustrate: *hopian* 'to hope': *hoppian* 'to hop'; *hāte* 'hotly': *hātte* 'is (was) called'; *seten* 'a shoot': *setten* 'set' (pr. opt. pl.); *scyte* 'shooting': *scytte* 'I shoot'; *baca* 'bake' (imper. sg.): *bacca* 'ridge'; *loca* 'enclosure': *locca* 'locks of hair' (gen. pl.); *gebeda* 'of prayers': *gebedda* 'bedfellow'; *hoga* 'care': *hogga* 'of hogs'; *bile* 'beak': *bille* 'sword' (dat.); *swelan* 'to burn': *swellan* 'to swell'; *sparode* 'he spared': *besparrade* 'bolted, shut' (? from ON); *freme* 'perform' (imper. sg.): *fremme* 'perform' (opt. sg.); *wine* 'friend': *winne* 'struggle' (pr. opt. sg.); *suna* 'son' (dat.): *sunna* 'sun'; *rece* 'stretch', *etc.* (imper. sg.): *recce* (pr. 1 sg.).

11.1. All consonants could occur with length except /š/, /w/, /ġ/, and /ǧ/. Long consonants did not occur post-juncturally. They were simplified in pre-junctural position,[130] but the long consonant was often restored (at least in the spelling), through analogy with inflected forms in which the long consonant was medial. When forming a cluster with another consonant, a long consonant was usually simplified, even if the cluster was a relatively late development due to loss of an intervening vowel: *sende* 'he sent' (*send-de*), wyrtruma 'root of a plant' (*wyrt-truma*), *sibsum* 'peaceful' (*sibb-sum*), *feorcund* 'foreign-born' (*feorr-cund*), *locfeax* 'hair' (*locc-feax*), *stilnes* 'quietness' (*still-nes*), *þrymlic* 'powerful' (*þrymm-lic*), *henfugol* 'hen' (*henn-fugol*), *etc.* Consequently, long and short consonants contrast only in positions (2) and (9). By the close of the OE period, as Hans Kurath has pointed out, long consonants occurred almost exclusively after short vowels.[131] Consonant length may have been non-phonemic, or nearly so, in Northumbria as early as the tenth century. No other explanation would seem to account for the many false geminations in the gloss of the *Lindisfarne Gospels*: *clioppadon* 18, 40; *earlipprica* 18, 10; *eorlippric* 18, 26; *hrippe* (for *ripe*) 4, 35; *uætter* 4, 11; *uittnesa* 8, 18; *aurittéð* 8, 6; *ongeattas* 8, 43; *spreccende* 8, 40; *sprecco* 12, 50; *to bruccanne* 4, 32; *reccone* 18, 27; *huidder* 8, 14; *ðidder* 18, 2; *goddo* 10, 34; *nomma* 17, 12; *frumma* 8, 25; *cymmende* 10, 12; *cuommon* 18, 20; *penninga* 12, 5; *heannissum* 8, 23; and many more.[132]

[129] Richard Jordan, *Handbuch der mittelenglischen Grammatik* (Heidelberg, 1934), p. 172.
[130] Moulton, p. 25.
[131] "The Loss of Long Consonants and the Rise of Voiced Fricatives in Middle English," *Lg.*, XXXII (1956), 435-436. For some exceptions, see James Sledd, "Some Questions of English Phonology," *Ibid.*, XXXIV (1958), 252-258.
[132] These examples are from John's Gospel, but the other Gospels contain many similar spellings.

THE AUTHORSHIP OF THE OLD ENGLISH BEDE REVISITED

A third of a century ago, when I first began to think seriously about the authorship of the Old English translation of Bede's *Ecclesiastical History*, the controversy over this subject had seemingly reached an impasse. There was a strong Alfredian party, drawing its support from irrefutable mediaeval authorities: Ælfric of Eynsham, William of Malmesbury, and an inscription found at the beginning and the end of an eleventh-century manuscript of the Bede translation (Italics below are mine.):

> Manega halige bec cyðað his [Gregory's] drohtnunge and his halige lif, and eac *Historia Anglorum, ða ðe Ælfred cyning of Ledene on Englisc awende*.[1]

> Denique plurimam partem Romanæ bibliothecae Anglorum auribus [Alfred] dedit, opimam prædam peregrinarum mercium civium usibus convectans; cujus præcipui sunt libri Orosius, Pastoralis Gregorii, *Gesta Anglorum Bedæ*, Boetius De Consolatione Philosophiae, liber proprius quem patria lingua Encheridion ... appellavit.[2]

> Historicus quondam fecit me [this book] Beda latinum, *Ælfred*[3] *rex Saxo transtullit ille pius*.[4]

These three witnesses appear to be independent. I can see no close resemblances, verbal or otherwise, which one could use as evidence that any of the three is derived from any other. It seemed in the early twentieth century, and still seems, that King Alfred's authorship of the Bede is much better attested than the authorship of most literary works of the Middle Ages.

There was also a powerful Mercian party, founded by Thomas Miller[5] and supported by some of the best philologists of Europe and America.[6]

---

[1] Ælfric's sermon on Gregory the Great, in Benjamin Thorpe (ed.), *The Homilies of the Anglo-Saxon Church*, II (London, 1846), 116, 118. According to Dorothy Whitelock, Ælfric's phraseology in the homily indicates that he had the extant OE Bede before him; hence, it is hardly possible he was referring to any lost translation – "The Old English Bede," *Proceedings of the British Academy 1962*, XLVIII (1963), 58, 79–80.

[2] William of Malmesbury in William Stubbs (ed.), *Gesta Regum Anglorum*, Rolls Series (1887), I, 132.

[3] Altered to *Alured*, a common spelling in Middle English, in the first occurrence.

[4] Cambridge University Library MS. Kk. 3. 18.

[5] See his edition, *The Old English Version of Bede's Ecclesiastical History of the English People*, Part I, EETS, OS, No. 95, 96 (1890–91), pp. xxvi–lix.

[6] To mention only a few: Max Deutschbein, "Dialektisches in der ags. Uebersetzung von Bedas Kirchengeschichte," *Beiträge zur Geschichte der deutschen Sprache und Literatur*,

Reprinted by permission from *Neuphilologische Mitteilungen: Studies Presented to Tauno F. Mustanoja on the Occasion of His Sixtieth Birthday*, 73 (1972), 172-80.

These scholars had discovered that the Old English Bede is not in the Early West Saxon dialect of King Alfred, but rather in a mixture of West Saxon and Mercian. The West Saxon is predominant, but Mercian is represented by a heavy sprinkling of Mercian spellings, grammatical forms, and lexical items. Of the hundreds of examples available, I have selected a few which illustrate the more important types of Mercianisms found in the earliest manuscript of the Old English Bede.[1]

Phonology: *hefdon* "they had" (WS *hæfdon*); *wonn* "fought" (WS *wann*); *cald* "cold" (WS *ceald*); *rehte* "ruled" (WS *reahte, rihte*); *gef* "gave" (WS *geaf*); *ælding* "delay" (WS *ieldung, yldung*); *bescerian* "to deprive" (WS *bescierian*); *deagum* "days" (WS *dagum*); *beneoman* "to take away" (WS *beniman*); *seolf* "self, himself" (WS *self, sylf*); *lecnian* "to cure" (WS *lecnian*); *gefon* "they gave" (WS *geafon*); *cegde* "called" (WS *?ciegde, cigde*, but more probably a different word); *tolesed* "loosened" (WS *toliesed, -lysed*); *gesegon* "they saw" (WS *gesawon*); *lifgan* "to live" (WS *libban*).

Morphology: *usse* "our" (WS *ure*); *ðere* fem. dat. sg. (WS *þære*); *ðeara* gen. pl. (WS *þara*); *forleort* "was lost" (WS *forlet*); *awunade* "remained" (WS *awunode*).

Vocabulary: *in* "in, on" (WS *on*); *leoran* "to go" (WS *faran, feran, gan*, etc.); *meord* "reward" (WS *med*); *nemne, nymðe* "except" (WS *butan*); *rec* "smoke" (WS *smic*).

XXVI (1901), 169–244; Friedrich Klaeber, "Zur altenglischen Bedaübersetzung," *Anglia*, XXV (1902), 257–315; XXVII (1904), 243–282, 399–435; Richard Jordan, *Eigentümlichkeiten des anglischen Wortschatzes*, Anglistische Forschungen, XVII (Heidelberg, 1906); Otto Eger, *Dialektisches in den Flexionsverhältnissen der angelsächsischen Bedaübersetzung* (Borna-Leipzig, 1910); R. J. Menner, "Vocabulary of the Old English Poems on Judgment Day," *PMLA*, LXII (1947), 583–97. Menner's other articles on dialect vocabulary are somewhat later, as is Jackson J. Campbell, "The Dialect Vocabulary of the OE Bede," *JEGP*, L (1951), 349–372.

[1] Bodleian Library MS. Tanner 10. Some of the items (e.g. *cald* and *ælding*) are general Anglian; i.e., they could be either Mercian or Northumbrian; but the likehood of Nhb. influence in the language of the OE Bede is remote. A few items (e.g. *wonn* and *awunade*) could be regarded as early West Saxon in a sense; there are occasional forms which look like Mercianisms in all of the EWS texts, but no other contains the abundance and variety of Mercianisms found in Tanner 10. The items labeled WS are not all exclusively West Saxon; some are shared with another dialect, and some are general Old English. The geographic distributions of, and the linguistic principles underlying, the forms cited are set forth in numerous grammars and handbooks.

Almost every important feature of the Mercian dialect appears in the Bede. The Mercian party seemed in the early twentieth century, and still seems, unquestionably correct in holding that the translation was made in a mixture of dialects which Alfred could not have used under any kind of normal circumstances. In short, the Irresistible Force had encountered the Immovable Obstacle.

Various philologists had offered explanations of the considerable Mercian element in the work of a West Saxon king, but by 1947 all had been discarded as improbable. In general, philologists went their way, ignoring the evidence of Alfredian authorship, while literary scholars went theirs, forgetting the linguistic evidence. Dorothy Whitelock, in the generally admirable study already mentioned (see fn. 1, p. 172), has adequately summarized the attempts to reconcile the conflicting data, and their failures – with one exception. Jacob Schipper explained the Mercianisms in the Bede as due to the influence of Werfrið, Plegmund, and the other Mercian scholars at Alfred's court.[1] He referred to the king's own account in the preface to the *Pastoral Care*, of the manner in which he made his translations: first consulting with one of his learned helpers, reading and discussing the Latin passage to be translated, and then turning it into English. Schipper further suggested that Alfred might have taken from these learned conferences written notes, and even glossings, made by himself or by an assistant, to guide himself in the final composition.

> Höchst wahrscheinlich ist es, dass er sich dabei zur Erleichterung seiner Arbeit und zur Unterstützung für sein Gedächtnis schriftlicher Aufzeichnungen und Glossierungen bediente, die er sich (oder vielleicht auch ein Anderer für ihn) während des Studiums des Textes gemacht hatte.[2]

Miss Whitelock, inaccurately I think, credits Schipper with anticipating my own suggestion that Alfred possessed a Latin text of Bede's history with an interlinear gloss.[3] As a consequence, her refutation of my argument is

---

[1] I see no objection to this as an explanation of Mercianisms in *all* of the early WS texts or as a *partial* explanation of those in the Bede.

[2] *König Alfreds Übersetzung von Bedas Kirchengeschichte* in C. W. M. Grein (ed.), *Bibliothek der angelsächsischen Prosa*, IV (Leipzig, 1899), xlii. This is a repetition of what he had said in "Die Geschichte und der gegenwärtige Stand der Forschung über König Alfreds Uebersetzung von Beda's Kirchengeschichte," *Sitzberichte der Philosophisch-Historischen Classe der kaiserlichen Akademie der Wissenschaften*, CXXXVIII (Vienna, 1898), Abh. VII, p. 8.

[3] *Op. cit.*, p. 58.

made to serve simultaneously as a refutation of Schipper, whose views come through untouched.

Schipper did not suggest the use of an earlier interlinear translation, comparable to the glosses of the *Vespasian Psalter*, the *Lindisfarne Gospels*, etc.; rather he suggested that Alfred and his helpers made their own little glosses while consulting about passages from the Latin Bede. The main objection to Schipper's view is that it forces us to assume a degree of ineptitude on Alfred's part which is incompatible with what we know of the man. If he was hurriedly revising an old interlinear gloss, to be copied by a scribe, he might well neglect to normalize the dialect at times or forget to turn an unidiomatic expression or an inartistic tautology into more acceptable English. He might, for example, fail to notice that *gesegon* (Miller 266.7) is the Anglian rather than the West Saxon form. But it is hard to believe that he would, himself, mechanically reproduce such a Mercianism merely because the word had been given the Mercian pronunciation in conference and had been so written down by an amanuensis. Or Alfred might let a double translation, consisting of a Mercian word plus a West Saxon or general Old English synonym, stand if it was present in the old gloss; e.g., *cegde & laðode* (266.12–13, both rendering *vocabat*), followed closely by *cegdon & laðodon* (266.30–31). The first tautology could even be explained by Schipper's theory: perhaps someone like the Mercian Werfrið suggested it as a means of clarifying the sense for Mercian readers. But the second occurrence would seem a bit absurd in a text prepared by Schipper's method – as though either Alfred or his Mercian reader were incapable of seeing the linguistic equation, *laðode: cegde: : laðodon: x*, for himself. Such mechanical repetitions of the obvious are common enough, however, in the interlinear glosses. Two more examples, and I shall let Schipper's theory rest. In the synonymous pair *bodedon & lærdon* (158.25), both elements are general Old English and easily understood in the context. There is no reason why Alfred and Werfrið should decide on a double translation, even less reason why they should decide that it must be repeated almost immediately (158.28). Working on his own, Alfred would almost certainly have translated *in eundem modum* as *on þæm ilcan gemete* (or something equally idiomatic), just as Henry Sweet said that he should have done;[1] and it is most unlikely that any Mercian scholar would lead him astray in such a

---

[1] *An Anglo-Saxon Reader* (7th ed.; Oxford, 1894), p. 212.

simple matter of general Old English syntax. If, however, the king's old manuscript had the rendering *in þæt ilce gemet*, which adheres to the Latin syntax as interlinear glosses often did, he might correct it or, if in a hurry, overlook it.

In my article "Synonyms in the Old English Bede," [1] I supposed that I had found a third horn to the dilemma facing scholars in 1947. The assumption that Alfred had used an older Mercian gloss with West Saxon additions would allow them to retain Alfred as the author, leaving the veracity of witnesses like Ælfric and William unimpeached, while at the same time accounting for the obvious Mercian substratum in the translation. My argument was not based, as Miss Whitelock suggests (p. 58), upon the mere existence of synonymous pairs (double translations of the Latin) in the text. There are more tautologies to the page in the Bede than in any other Old English literary work.[2] These tautologies also differ from those of the other works (and this is more significant than the difference in frequency) in having a decidedly more gloss-like character. In the article, I noted: (1) pairs with dialectal differentiation, which suggest an original gloss in one dialect with second glosses in another (pp. 169–171); (2) pairs which combine a foreign borrowing, often hardly more than the lemma minus the Latin inflection, with a native synonym (p. 174);[3] (3) pairs combining a literal with a figurative translation or combining a translation of a general sense of the Latin word with a translation of the specific sense used at the particular point in the text (p. 174); and (4) triple translations of a sort which are common in some of the glosses but exceedingly rare elsewhere (pp. 173–174). Anyone who cares to see the full argument with the evidence is invited to examine the article itself.

I cannot say that my discovery of the third horn had any earth-shaking consequences. J. J. Campbell considered my "basic suggestion . . . plausible and attractive" but found my evidence, "based mainly on the phonology of the word pairs . . . not entirely convincing."[4] More recently, Gerhard Nickel has rejected P. Fijn van Draat's explanation of the tautologies,

---

[1] *JEGP*, XLVI (1947), 168–176.

[2] I was well aware of the tautological pairs in other OE texts, specifically in Alfred's own translation of the *Pastoral Care*. That was the point of my fn. 3, p. 168.

[3] These can occur elsewhere but are most frequent in the interlinear glosses, which have the Latin word right there to suggest one of the renderings.

[4] *Op. cit.*, pp. 349–350.

apparently preferring my explanation or, at least, my explanation of the dialectally mixed pairs.[1] And, of course, Miss Whitelock has examined my argument hastily and refuted it briefly.[2]

Miss Whitelock's discussion (pp. 58–59) begins with the suggestion, dealt with above, that my only reason for postulating an interlinear gloss [3] was the mere existence of double translations. She observes that there are other ways of accounting for this feature but mentions only Van Draat's third article on cursus (p. 80, n. 13).[4] She notes that double renderings of the Latin also appear in the *Pastoral Care* and in Werfrið's translation of Gregory's *Dialogues*. This is true, of course, but the synonymous pairs in those works generally lack anything which could be taken as dialectal differentiation and are far less gloss-like in their nature than those of the Bede. I should not wish to rule out the possibility that the *Pastoral Care* and the *Dialogues* were also based upon, or influenced by, older interlinear

[1] *Die Expanded Form im Altenglischen* (Neumünster, 1966), p. 175.

[2] There is little that I would change in the original article. I may have overstated Alfred's "literalness" and "timid dependence upon the Latin" in the *Pastoral Care* (p. 176), see William H. Brown, Jr., "Method and Style in the Old English *Pastoral Care*," *JEGP*, LXVIII (1969), 667. I had in mind the much greater freedom shown by Alfred in his translations of Boethius and Orosius, which extends far beyond syntax and idiom. I no longer regard *slypton* as WS with unstable *y* (p. 169); see my ed. of the *Vespasian Psalter* (Ann Arbor, 1965), pp. 172, 254. I should certainly have had more to say about Van Draat's views on cursus in the OE Bede, although cursus in OE seemed to be a dead issue in the 1940's. For what I regard as the most significant change in my views, see the conclusion of this article.

[3] On pp. 76–77, she suggests that both Werfrið and the author of the OE Bede "were influenced by the practice of interlinear glossing of a text" and that the latter author was "unable to shed the habits of a school of interlinear glossing." There is no evidence that either man was a practicing glossator; hence, I infer that Miss Whitelock supposes them to have possessed and used old MSS containing glosses. Were those glosses, by any chance, in MSS of Gregory's *Dialogues* and Bede's *Ecclesiastical History*? And if so, is there any reason why Anglo-Saxon authors would refrain from using those glosses in their work? It seems to me that Miss Whitelock has somewhat compromised the position taken earlier in her article.

[4] "The Authorship of the Old English Bede: a Study in Rhythm," *Anglia*, XXXIX (1915–16), 319–346. In my opinion, Van Draat's conclusions were vitiated by faulty handling of the evidence and lack of rigor in his methodology. His conclusions in the Bede article are also confuted, in large part, by his findings in another of his articles, "The Cursus in Old English Poetry," *Anglia*, XXXVIII (1914), 377–404. For my own views on the so-called cursus in OE, see my article "Cursus in Old English: Rhetorical Ornament or Linguistic Phenomenon?", scheduled for early publication in *Speculum*.

glosses. It seems to me very probable that Old English writers used such glosses as the bases for many of their translations; indeed, I believe that practical common sense would dictate this course whenever a gloss was available. In some translations, the traces of an underlying gloss (Latinate syntax, awkward phrases, unnecessary synonyms, dialect relics, etc.) may have been more thoroughly obliterated by revision than in others. Miss Whitelock doubts that my "postulated gloss fully explains Mercian vocabulary and Mercian sympathies[1] in a work by Alfred." It is true that Alfred would harldy use Mercian words like *leoran* and *nemne* in place of the words normal to his own dialect – if he were wholly on his own. If, on the other hand, he was revising an old gloss, he might easily overlook Mercianisms, especially if he were working hastily or if his Mercian advisers or his Mercian wife, Ealhswið, had already familiarized him with some of the commoner Mercian words.

On one point, I am afraid that Miss Whitelock and I are in total disagreement. I cannot accept her summary dismissal of the testimony of reputable witnesses concerning the authorship of the Bede. Noting that Ælfric's homily on Gregory the Great was composed almost a century after Alfred's death, she remarks: "One could find parallels for a wrong attribution at this distance" (p. 59). She dispatches William of Malmesbury with: "This shows that the belief in Alfred's authorship was not confined to Ælfric, but it does not prove the attribution correct" (*ibid.*). With regard to the inscription in Cambridge University Library MS. Kk. 3. 18, she notes that N. R. Ker[2] believes the handwriting to be of the sixteenth century, then affirms that the inscription "merely represents the opinion of an antiquary, probably based on William of Malmesbury" (p. 60). Primary sources for the history of the Middle Ages cannot safely be treated in this manner.

Ælfric of Eynsham was born only about a half-century after King Alfred's death. He studied at Winchester, where Alfred had spent most of his life and produced his literary works. Ælfric's master was Aþelwold,

---

[1] I was about to point out (1) that certain family and political connections might account for Mercian sympathies on Alfred's part, and (2) that some of the Mercian sympathies could have been those of the glossator which Alfred merely allowed to stand – when I noticed that Miss Whitelock (pp. 63–64) argues that the OE Bede shows no real Mercian sympathies at all.

[2] *Catalogue of Manuscripts Containing Anglo-Saxon* (Oxford, 1957), p. 37.

born less than a decade after the death of Alfred. Æþelwold must have been acquainted with men who had known Alfred personally, and Ælfric must have known men whose fathers had known Alfred. Who would be more likely than Ælfric to know whether the king had authored the Old English Bede? Ælfric's accuracy and his extreme caution are well known, as well as his reputation for integrity. Who would be less likely than he to report an idle rumor or a fancy of his own as fact? Malmesbury is about forty miles from Winchester, and William was the librarian of the monastery there. If evidence linking Alfred to the Old English Bede was available anywhere in the twelfth century, there are few places more likely to have had it than Malmesbury, few persons more likely to have had access to it than William. His other attributions to Alfred are commonly accepted without question. As for the comment on the inscription, that is a simple *non sequitur*. If the inscription as we have it was written in the sixteenth century, it could have been composed by the one who placed it at the beginning and end of the manuscript, but it could equally as well have been copied from one of the now lost or damaged manuscripts of the Old English Bede. The substitution of the spelling *Alured* for *Ælfred* (see fn. 3, p. 172) suggesst that the inscription existed elsewhere, but of course the alteration can be explained in other ways.

For the sake of completeness, I should perhaps mention Miss Whitelock's argument from Laȝamon's ignorance (p. 59). The poet certainly did not possess the sort of learning that William and Ælfric had. When historians accept his "Seint Beda" as evidence that the Venerable Bede was canonized, or his attribution of the Latin Bede as evidence that it was written by St. Albin and St. Austin, it will be time enough for serious consideration of his attribution of the Old English Bede.[1]

I am as certain of Alfred's authorship and as sure that he lightened his labors by the use of an older Mercian interlinear gloss as I was in 1947. On one rather important point, however, I have changed my mind. In 1947, I accepted the widely-held view that the Old English Bede, if it was Alfred's, must have been one of his earliest works, made before his style had matured. It now seems to me more probable that it was his last work, written at a time when renewed invasions of England and the task of carrying out his ambitious domestic programs left the king little leisure for

---

[1] I hope that my emphatic rejection of a small part of Miss Whitelock's article will not be construed as an attack upon the validity of the article as a whole.

polishing his work. This chronology would place the Bede after the departure of Werfrið, Plegmund, and John the Old Saxon, which left Alfred with fewer assistants to share the burden. It would explain why Asser, who had also left Winchester by that time, failed to mention the Old English Bede among Alfred's works. Finally, the later date would account for the fact (noted by Miss Whitelock, p. 76) that several passages of the translation are extremely well written, by no means the work of a novice. Such passages suggest that the author, when deeply interested, could rise rather high, even though on the next leaf his work might lapse into something resembling a half-revised interlinear gloss. Some of the differences between the style of the best parts of the Bede and that of the earlier translations (also noted by Miss Whitelock) [1] could be attributed (1) to changes in Alfred's tastes as he grew older, and (2) to the adoption of poetic turns of phrase and poetic compounds from his Mercian source.

The University of Michigan
Ann Arbor, Michigan

SHERMAN M. KUHN

[1] Pp. 76 and 89 (notes 160–166).

CURSUS IN OLD ENGLISH: RHETORICAL ORNAMENT OR LINGUISTIC PHENOMENON?

I. HISTORICAL PREAMBLE

DURING the first quarter of this century, there was a brief flurry of interest in cursus (the late Latin rhetorical device) as used, or apparently used, by vernacular writers of the Old English period. The chief results of this interest were embodied in three articles by P. Fijn van Draat and one by G. H. Gerould. In his "Voluptas aurium,"[1] Van Draat rejected the view that cursus had been introduced into English prose, as a result of Classical influence, during the sixteenth century. He held that the device had been used in English prose from Old English down to modern times (p. 419):

> In Old English, then, it is the same as in Modern English: you can take up no prose but you find cursus-forms in it: they may be more numerous in one author than in another, but they are never absent.

His second article, "The Cursus in Old English Poetry,"[2] demonstrated that, if cursus is common in Old English prose, it is about equally common in the poetry. In 731 verses of the *Juliana*, for example, he found 245 instances of *cursus planus*, 82 of *cursus tardus*, and 35 of *cursus velox*.[3] Other poems in which he found a comparable abundance include *Beowulf* and *Widsið*, in neither of which can the cursus-forms be attributed to the influence of a Latin original.[4] He held that the cursus in Old English poetry was derived, by a sort of rhythmic amplification, from the basic rhythms of the poetry itself and that it was native rather than borrowed.

> These rhythmic formulas, *occurring as they do both in alliterative poetry and in prose*, especially the younger rhythmical prose, go to prove that there is no essential difference between the construction of O.E. poetry and that of rhythmical prose.[5]

The third article, "The Authorship of the Old English Bede: A Study in Rhythm,"[6] is an examination of the tautologies (the use of two words in the Old English to translate one word of the Latin) in the Old English Bede and in King Alfred's translation of Gregory's *Pastoral Care*, with some consideration of the

---

[1] *Englische Studien*, XLVIII (1914-15), 394-428.

[2] *Anglia*, XXXVIII (1914), 377-404.

[3] Hereafter, I shall not italicize these terms.

[4] In my opinion, Van Draat took some unjustified liberties with the rhythms, e.g., in giving a major stress to the unemphatic *to* of *to his winedrihtne* (*Beowulf* 360b) and no stress to *stod* in *oð ðæt idel stod* (*ibid.*, 145b). A closer adherence to what many of us believe to have been the real rhythm of Old English poetry would have reduced the amount of cursus, although not enough to invalidate his argument.

[5] (1914), p. 403. Italics are mine. The referent of *formulas* is not entirely clear, but Van Draat must have been referring to the cursus-forms; otherwise his statement as a whole is untenable.

[6] *Anglia*, XXXIX (1915-16), 319-346.

Reprinted by permission from *Speculum*, 47 (1972), 188-206, published by the Medieval Academy of America.

same feature in Werfrið's translation of Gregory's *Dialogues*. Van Draat noted that, in many instances, a tautological phrase could be analyzed as some variety of cursus-form. In the work of Alfred, the production of cursus through tautology is comparatively rare, according to Van Draat; whereas, in the Bede and in the *Dialogues*, it is much more frequent and more aesthetically pleasing. He granted that a considerable number of the tautologies in the Bede were better explained as due to the translator's efforts to render the Latin more precisely, or even to his "garrulous longwindedness." But for the most part, he favored a different explanation (p. 322).

> For though not rarely the tautological phrases may be accounted for in the way indicated above, yet, in the majority of instances they are due to the translator's conscious endeavor to render by means of planus, tardus, or velox, the cursus-form which he found in his Latin text.

Turning to Alfred's work, he noted a sharp contrast between its style and that of the Old English Bede (pp. 332–333).

> For in spite of the fact that Gregory's Latin text is hardly less rhythmical than Bede's, the conscious endeavor to create planus, tardus and velox which is characteristic of the Bede, is as good as absent in Alfred's Pastoral Care . . . Nor is the difference only quantitative. When reading Bede, a man with an ear attuned to cursus-forms cannot fail to be delighted with the numbers winging its pages. But let him turn from this work to the Pastoral . . . gone is the charm. The prose moves with difficulty, jerkily . . . There is a planus, a tardus, a velox even, occasionally, but they are felt to be there almost in spite of the author. There are double-phrases, but two out of three yield groups, which from a rhythmical point of view are simply detestable.

Van Draat concluded that the translator of the Bede could not possibly have been King Alfred.

Gerould's article, "Abbot Ælfric's Rhythmic Prose,"[7] as its author candidly admitted, was motivated by a desire to remove Ælfric from the ranks of the poetasters and establish him as the inventor of a new and highly artistic form of prose.[8] It does, indeed, seem unfair to regard the metrical works of this great master of Old English style as merely a feeble imitation of the older alliterative poems (*Beowulf*, the Caedmonian Poems, and the like). Instead, Gerould argued that the abbot was imitating the sophisticated prose of the late Latin writers, with its cursus, its rime, and its balanced clauses. Ælfric, so goes the argument, adopted the balance and cursus of his sources but substituted alliteration for their rimes. Gerould seems to have taken it for granted that cursus was foreign rather than native, a feature of prose rather than of poetry.

After 1925, interest in the Old English cursus declined. Gerould's view of Ælfric's *Lives of Saints* was widely accepted, but few saw fit to examine the evidence and arguments on which it was based.[9] Scholars were so happy to find a

---

[7] *Modern Philology*, XXII (1924–25), 353–366.

[8] *Ibid.*, pp. 353–355.

[9] A notable exception was Dorothy Bethurum's article, "The Form of Ælfric's Lives of Saints," *Studies in Philology*, XXIX (1932), 515–533. Although Miss Bethurum agreed with Gerould in regarding the *Lives* as prose, she demonstrated that Ælfric seldom imitated the style of his immediate sources, also that his style was essentially English rather than foreign.

means of rescuing Ælfric's literary reputation that they scarcely noticed how much of Gerould's argument had been vitiated by Van Draat's first two articles, in which he had shown that cursus in Old English was neither a foreign importation nor a feature confined to prose. As for the Old English Bede, few scholars were then prepared to reject the testimony of men like Ælfric and William of Malmesbury to the Alfredian authorship of the Bede. Van Draat's handling of his evidence also left much to be desired, his aesthetic pronouncements were repellent to those who do not regard either tautology or cursus as the crowning glory of prose style, and his whole argument seemed to be contradicted by the findings of his earlier articles. Literary scholars went on attributing the Bede translation to Alfred; while a few philologists, without reference to rhythms, argued for a Mercian origin because of the many Mercian words, spellings, and grammatical forms in the text. So marked was the decline of the cursus that, in the 1940's, I felt safe in ignoring Van Draat's views in an article of my own on the tautologies of the Old English Bede.[10] Until recently, I have had no cause to regret that decision.

The 1960's saw a revival of interest in the Old English cursus. Dorothy Whitelock apparently accepts without question Van Draat's explanation of the tautologies — which would imply acceptance of the views on cursus set forth in his third article.[11] Minnie Cate Morrell, although she mentions Bethurum's article, accepts in large part Gerould's view that Ælfric's *Lives* are in rhythmic prose similar to that written by those mediaeval authors who cultivated cursus.[12] J. C. Pope rejects much of Gerould's argument, especially with regard to cursus.

> In the second place, imitation of anything as peculiarly Latin as the *cursus* is rare in Ælfric and likely to be purely accidental unless it occurs at a point where he is echoing several features of his immediate source.[13]

He accepts the view that the *Lives* are in prose but, like Bethurum, believes that the form used by Ælfric was native.

> What is valuable in Gerould's essay is simply, I think, the notion that Ælfric, in developing a semi-metrical form, may well have felt that he was acting in harmony with the spirit of the Latin prose-writers. The form itself is unique, but essentially native.[14]

Frances Randall Lipp regards Ælfric's *Lives* as a prose work.[15] Although granting that the style was influenced by "Latin rhetorical tradition," she rejects the view that "the distinctive characteristics of his mature style" were drawn from the Latin (p. 690). She includes a lengthy discussion of cursus in Ælfric's Latin works, in the writings of other Mediaeval Latin authors, in Ælfric's vernacular

---

[10] "Synonyms in the Old English Bede," *JEGP*, XLVI (1947), 168–176.

[11] "The Old English Bede," *Proceedings of the British Academy 1962*, XLVIII (1963), 80; "The Prose of Alfred's Reign" in E. G. Stanley (ed.), *Continuations and Beginnings* (London, 1966), p. 78.

[12] *A Manual of Old English Biblical Materials* (Knoxville, 1965), pp. 15–18.

[13] *Homilies of Ælfric: A Supplementary Collection*, I (EETS, No. 259; 1967), 105. Pope does not say whether he has in mind Van Draat's conception of cursus or that of some writers on Latin cursus, whose rules would exclude much of the cursus which Van Draat found in Old English.

[14] *Ibid.*, pp. 108–109.

[15] "Ælfric's Old English Prose Style," *SP*, LXVI (1969), 689–718.

works, and in *Beowulf* (pp. 707–717).[16] One of her principal conclusions is that the rhythm of the *Lives* is modeled after that of Old English poetry.

With this revived interest in mind, I feel that my own ideas and findings in the far out field of cursus may be of more value to scholars than they would have been twenty years ago.

II. WHAT IS CURSUS?

The rhetorical device known as cursus was used by post-Classical Roman writers and by Mediaeval Latin writers for several centuries, it is believed, although the rules for it were not written down until near the end of the Middle Ages. Cursus consists of ordering the elements within clauses, and sometimes within smaller rhetorical units, in such a way that units will end in one of three rhythmic patterns: cursus planus, e.g., retributiónĕm mĕrétŭr, prudéntĕr ĕt cáutĕ, qúi mĕ prĕmébănt; cursus tardus, e.g., felicitátĭs pĕrcípiĕnt, dirigéntŭr ĭn éxŭŭs, úndă pĕrfúsŭs sŭm; and cursus velox, e.g., exhíbĭŭm rèpŭĭábō, subsídĭŭm mĭhĭ détĭs, respóndĕăt prò mĕ vóbĭs. These are the basic types approved by the Roman Curia and recognized by all writers on the subject of cursus.[17] Since I wish to concentrate first upon Van Draat's analyses, I shall postpone consideration of the cursus trispondaicus[18] and some other rhythmic patterns until section VI. In the cursus-forms, the primary and secondary stresses (/and\) are generally those of speech; and quantity is disregarded. Some writers permit an extra unstressed syllable, usually in the first part of the cursus-form; e.g., planus, dónă sĕntĭámŭs; tardus, virtútĭs ŏpĕrátĭŏ; velox, incéndĭŏ prăvòrŭm vídĭt or flétĭbŭs sŭpplĭcántĭŭm.[19] The possibility that much of the supposed cursus in Latin prose is not actually rhetorical, but the inevitable consequence of Latin word structure and accentuation, should always be borne in mind. The presence of rhetorical cursus in a text is difficult to confirm unless one compares it with texts by writers who were not striving for cursus or unless one compares the clause endings of the text itself with the other, "non-rhythmic,"[20] portions of its clauses.[21] Because my main concern at this point is with the application of cursus theory to Old English, I shall not pursue the Latin cursus further.[22]

[16] Mrs. Lipp includes so many things which are not strictly cursus that I should prefer a term like "phrase-end rhythm."

[17] My examples are taken from various modern writers on cursus. In some of them, the treatment of monosyllabic and dissyllabic words would not be approved by *some* of the authorities. In others, the lack of regard for correct placement of the caesura will probably call forth objections.

[18] Called "dispondaique ou trispondaique," by Mathieu G. Nicolau in *L'Origine du "Cursus"* *Rhythmique*, Collection d'Études Latines, v (Paris, 1930), 2. This pattern did not figure in Van Draat's studies.

[19] This last velox, ending in two unstressed syllables, has not figured significantly in discussions of OE cursus.

[20] This is the expression used by writers on cursus. I do not subscribe to the view that there is no prose rhythm other than cursus.

[21] This important principle has been very well stated by Nicolau, p. 34, and by A. W. de Groot, *Revue des Études Latines*, IV (1926), 43 (*Prose métrique des Anciens*, p. 21).

[22] Those who wish to investigate further may consult De Groot and Nicolau; A. C. Clark, "The Cursus in Mediaeval and Vulgar Latin," *Oxford Philological Society 1910*, pp. 5–19; Karl Polheim,

Van Draat's conception of cursus in Old English is similar to that outlined above, but there are some important differences. As with the Latin, quantity is disregarded, and the main word accent is of greatest importance. Secondary stress, as on a strong affix or the second element of a compound, may be elevated to major stress or reduced to non-stress, depending upon the surrounding pattern of stressed and unstressed syllables. In this respect, Van Draat's practice seems to me more flexible than that of the Latinists. He is especially apt to vary in the treatment of monosyllables, with which Old English is better supplied than Latin. He also permits strings of three and four monosyllables to substitute for polysyllables in a manner which I believe the writers on Latin cursus would not tolerate. He presents four types of cursus-forms, with two varieties of each. The fourth type Van Draat believed to be of English origin and without parallel in the Latin rhetoric.[23] The examples which follow have been culled from various parts of his three articles to illustrate his practices. Because many were taken from the tautological phrases of the Old English prose works with which Van Draat was dealing in his third article, there is an abundance of &'s. He substituted & for the Tironian nota (shaped like an Arabic 7) of the Old English manuscripts — a practice which, to avoid confusion, I shall follow. Needless to say, an & is not an essential part of any cursus-form.

1. Planus (/xx/x): *lóng is þis ónbid, þéaw wæs & régol, éorl under lýfte, éalle*[24] *ofercómon, þónne æt níhstan, mýnster gedón wæs, wýlme onstýred, wíseste wíste, licettúnge & léase,* hundséofontig *míla.* (/xxx/x): *ǽnlic is þæt íglond,* mid *héte & miþ níþe,* hu *néarwe & hu ǽnge, fóron æfter búrgum, Héorogar & Hróðgar, récene & hráþe, aléfde & forgéfe, héofonrices dúru, míldheortnesse séaldon.*

2. Tardus (/xx/xx): *hád & gegýrelan, hréoh under héofonum, féodun þurh fírencræft, Gódes word bódade, snýtro & wísdomes, méorda & édleana, stílnes & swígung wæs, tíntregum wǽced wæs, magíster*[25] *& éaldormonn.* (/xxx/xx): *sórh is me to sécganne,*[26] *wæs se féorða stiell in býrgenne, þone méte & þa swǽsendo, sǽgdon & gemýngedon, þurhgóten & gefúlwad wæs, Babylónium to fúltume.*

3. Velox (/xx\x/x): *sé þe wið Brécan*[27] *wúnne, þæt sár & seo ádl*[28] *ón wæs, swá he his wèorc*[29] *wéorpað, swá þone màgan cénde, ða he him óf dyde ìsern-býrnan, ídel stod hùsa sélest, géonge men týdde wǽron, fóre him ènglas stóndaþ, wǽron & fórþ geléorde, wýrcnisse scàn & béorhte, begángum his èaldordómes, hwéorfende mè gehéhton, ágenes fìrenlústes.* (/xxx\x/x): *þone grénan wong ofgìefan scéoldan, þæs hálgan lifes wòrd & láre, gebúnden & getògen tó me, swǽslice & hìwcuplíce,*

Die Lateinische Reimprosa, Berlin, 1925; Eduard Norden, *Die Antike Kunstprosa* (Leipzig, 1898; repr. Darmstadt, 1958), esp. pp. 923–960; and many works cited in the articles by Gerould and Lipp.

[23] First noted in modern English by Clark, *op. cit.,* p. 11.

[24] The final *e* is elided, according to Van Draat.

[25] He assumes that the Latin accentuation was retained.

[26] Usually emended to *secgan.*

[27] Apparently, Van Draat regarded \, not as a secondary stress, but as equal to /; see his treatment of cursus in OE poetry. To assume only a secondary stress in *Brecan* would fly in the face of everything that we know about OE accent.

[28] The *l* is syllabic.

[29] A pause after this word substitutes for x, according to Van Draat.

*néownesse & ùncupnésse, bíscopa gemòt & séonoð, atémige & òferwìnne, mìdde-
weardum hìera ríce.*

4. English: (/xx/): he *slóh hi & þærsc, stýring & líf*, fornóm *& forléas, héofende
téon*, forðfóre *is néah, asódene béon.* (/xxx/): *béne & gehát, afýlde & fornóm, alýsde
& unbánd.*

As we examine these cursus-forms, we may note a number of Van Draat's
practices which he apparently took so completely for granted that he did not
bother to explain them. We observe the varying treatment of the prefixes *ofer-*
(stressed in *oferwinne*, unstressed in *ofercomon*) and *un-* (stressed in *uncupnesse*,
unstressed in *unband*).[10] If *forþ geleorde* is regarded as a verb with two prefixes,
it presents another example of a stressed prefix. Among the suffixes, *-ung-* may
be stressed as in *licettunge* or unstressed as in *swigung*; *-lic-* may be stressed as in
hiwcuplice or unstressed as in *swæslice*; *-nes-* may be stressed as in *uncupnesse* or
unstressed as in *mildheortnesse*; *-dom-*[11] is stressed in *ealdordomes* but unstressed
in *wisdomes*. The second elements of compounds may contain stress, as in *isern-
byrnan* and *firenlustes*, or no stress, as in *firencræft*, *ealdormonn*, *hiwcuplice*,
heofonrices, and *mildheortnesse*. In short, the amount of stress given to a living
suffix or to the second element of a compound is governed by the pattern of
stresses in the surrounding syllables rather than by the stress patterns of the
words taken in isolation. The same principle holds true, but to a lesser degree,
in the treatment of prefixes.

The monosyllables *me*, *to*, and *word* occur both with and without stress in the
examples. Usually unemphatic words like *se* (pron.) and *swa* (conj.) may be
stressed if stressing them results in cursus-forms.[12] Relatively important words
like *men*, *stod*, *wong*, *stiell* may be as unstressed as *seo*, *mid*, *he*, *his*, or *æt*. Dissyllables may be stressed on the first syllable (*þonne*, *fore*, *wæron*, *hiera*, *foron*) or on
the second (*gedon*, *gemot*, *unband*), and the stress in these is determined by the
normal stress of the word without regard to sentence patterns.[13] However, words
normally stressed on the first syllable may be totally unstressed if the exigencies
of cursus so require: *æfter*, *dyde*, *þone*, *under*, and *lifes* (cf. stressed *lif* above).
Van Draat did not treat in this manner dissyllables stressed on the second syllable
— at least not in these examples. A trisyllable is stressed on the first or the second
syllable (*recene*, *forgefe*),[14] the stress being the normal stress of the word. A tetrasyllable may be stressed on the first syllable, on the second, on the third, or on the
first and third: *heofonrices*, *gemyngedon*, *ofercomon*, *uncupnesse*. In these, the

---

[10] The *on-* of *onbid* was usually stressed in OE poetry; hence, Van Draat's stress on this word does
not really contrast with his unstressed *on-* in *onstyred*, etc.

[11] Perhaps *-dom-* should be regarded as the second element of a compound in OE, although it was
certainly reduced to a suffix in Middle English.

[12] In *þæt sar & seo adl on wæs*, the *on* may be regarded as either an adverb or a transposed preposition, in either case being entitled to more stress than a simple preposition. The examples of stressed
forþ and *of* could be regarded as monosyllables or as prefixes.

[13] Except in the case of *unband*, in which the normal poetic stress was on the prefix and the prose
stress is hard to determine.

[14] Possibly also on the third syllable (cf. the tetrasyllable *ofercomon*) or on the first and third (cf.
tetrasyllable *oferwinne*).

normal main stress of the word is retained; the presence or absence of a second stress and its position if present are determined by the needs of the cursus pattern. Longer words are too rare for any generalization at this time.

My purpose in calling attention to these variations is not that of discrediting Van Draat by demonstrating that he is inconsistent. It is one of the facts of language that the same word or syllable may receive greater or lesser stress in different contexts. Those of us who scan Old English poetry (or modern poetry, for that matter) have long recognized and accepted this fact. I wish rather to clarify Van Draat's methods of analysis, which coincide only in part with those of the writers on Latin cursus. In so doing, I hope that I shall be of some assistance to anyone who wishes to pursue the Old English prose rhythms on his own — as I shall be doing presently.

One is impressed by the multitude of ways in which a cursus-form can be put together. In the paragraphs below, the three types of dissyllable found in the Van Draat examples are represented by 'x, x', and xx; the two kinds of trisyllable by 'xx and x'x; the four kinds of tetrasyllable by 'xxx, x'xx, xx'x, and 'x'x; the four cursus-forms by their initials, P, T, V, and E.

If a clause ends in a monosyllable, there will be cursus if the monosyllable is preceded by three other monosyllables (E): by three monosyllables, 'x, and a monosyllable (V); by 'x and a monosyllable (E); by 'x and x' (P); by 'x, a monosyllable, and 'x (T); by 'xx (E); by 'xx and 'x (T); by x'x and a monosyllable (E); by x'x, a monosyllable, and x'x (T); by x'x, a monosyllable, x'x, and a monosyllable (V); or by x'xx (E).

If the clause ends in 'x, there will be cursus if it is preceded by four monosyllables and a pause (V); three monosyllables (P); three monosyllables and 'x (V); a monosyllable and xx (P); a monosyllable, xx, and 'x (V); 'x and a monosyllable (P); 'x and two monosyllables (P); 'x, a monosyllable, and 'x (V); 'x, a monosyllable, and x'x (V); 'x, xx (P); 'x, xx, and two monosyllables (V); 'xx (P); 'xx and a monosyllable (P); 'xx and two monosyllables (V); 'xx, x', and a monosyllable (V); 'xxx (P); 'xxx and 'x (V); x'xx (P); or 'x'x and a monosyllable (P). If the clause ends in x', there will be cursus if it is preceded by 'x and a monosyllable (E); x' and a monosyllable (E); or x'x and a monosyllable (E).

If the clause ends in 'xx, there will be cursus if it is preceded by four monosyllables (T); a monosyllable and xx (T); 'x and a monosyllable (T); 'x and two monosyllables (T); or x'x and a monosyllable (T). If the clause ends in x'x, there will be cursus if it is preceded by 'x (P); 'x and two monosyllables (V); 'xx and a monosyllable (V); or x'x and a monosyllable (P).

If the clause ends in x'xx, there will be cursus if it is preceded by two monosyllables (T) or by 'x and a monosyllable (T). If the clause ends in xx'x, there will be cursus if it is preceded by a monosyllable (P). If the clause ends in 'x'x, there will be cursus if it is preceded by a monosyllable and xx (V); 'xx (V); 'xx and a monosyllable (V); x'x and a monosyllable (V); or x'xx and a monosyllable (V).

This has been a dull recital of unadorned facts, and I apologize if I have tried the patience of any literary critic accustomed to more lively fare. Every rhythmic pattern in the last four paragraphs can be verified in the Van Draat examples previously listed. I would now try the patience of critics and scholars somewhat further by asking them to go back to those examples and verify my statements. There is no other way to comprehend fully the looseness of Van Draat's system.

The fifty cursus-producing combinations recited above include only those which can be found in the limited body of examples taken from Van Draat's articles. Many more are theoretically possible; e.g., x′xx here shows cursus-forms only when preceded by two monosyllables or by ′x and a monosyllable. At least six other combinations preceding could also produce tardus: three monosyllables, x′ and a monosyllable, ′xx, x′x, x′xx, and xx′x. Only two among the forms of words occurring in the examples could not produce cursus if they preceded x′xx; i.e., x′[35] and ′xxx. Thus, of ten patterns likely to occur in Old English prose, eight result in cursus. Taking this single example is a great oversimplification; to calculate the actual probabilities for the natural and involuntary production of cursus would require the best computers, plus detailed information concerning word frequencies in Old English which we do not have. It should be obvious, however, that the cursus-forms are neither accidental nor, necessarily, due to conscious striving after rhetorical effect. Given the language and the system, their presence in large numbers is inevitable.

III. CURSUS IN A BOUNDARY DESCRIPTION

In his article "Voluptas aurium" (p. 401), Van Draat skirted the edges of the idea stated above, apparently without seeing it: he called attention to cursus-forms in modern English conversational, nonrhetorical utterances; e.g., "Gíve me an ápple" (P). One does not have to look far for comparable examples by the dozen: Páss the aspáragas, sócial secúrity, Mádison Ávenue (T); potátoes and grávy, cárdigan swéater, léft-handed bátter (P); I thínk it's the cárburétor, loóking for húckleberries, congréssional invéstigátion (V); etc. These forty centuries we have been talking cúrsus and néver knéw it.[36]

Very little informal conversation was recorded in Old English times, but there may be passages in Old English that can be presumed to be completely free from rhetorical flourishes. Many otherwise Latin charters granting land contain short paragraphs in the vernacular giving the boundaries of the land; that is, the Latin describes the tract in very general terms, and if greater exactness is required, the Old English passage traces the boundaries in detail. A paragraph of this sort is as utilitarian as a telephone directory.[37] It is unlikely, moreover, that a landowner would risk losing a few acres of his property here and there by permitting the landmarks to be changed for the sake of rhetorical ornament.

The following paragraph is taken from a grant made by King Edward the Elder to Friðestan, Bishop of Winchester, A. D. 909.[38] I have left misspellings

---

[*] Cf. Mrs. Lipp's rhythm *a* in section VI.

[36] With acknowledgments to Molière — or apologies if you prefer.

[37] Cursus-forms also appear in the directories if one cares to look for them.

[38] Walter de Gray Birch (ed.), *Cartularium Saxonicum*, II (London, 1887), ~~284–285~~; British Museum, *Facsimiles of Ancient Charters*, IV (1878), pl. 10. The document itself, Harley Charter 43. C. 1,

uncorrected, partly because they are all transparent and partly because they may suggest that the writer was not overly concerned with the effect created by his work as literature. I have silently expanded the Tironian nota to *and*, both by itself and as a part of other words, and have also expanded ·the abbreviation for *þanon* (i.e., *þ̄*, which often = *þæt* in other OE texts). I have normalized word division in a few cases but not in any instance where the change could affect the rhythm significantly. The manuscript punctuation has been retained because, with two exceptions, all of the important syntactic units are followed in the manuscript by points. There can be no argument as to where the cursus, if any, should appear. Each type of cursus is marked with the appropriate initial, lack of cursus with (O).

Ǽrest on *ícenan æt brómbrigce* (T) up andlang *wéges to hlídgeate*. (T) þanon andlang *sládes to béanstede*. (T) þanon be hagan to *seárnægles fórda*. (P) þanon up be *swæðelínge to sùgebróce*. (V) ðæt forð be *méarce to cúles félda*. (V) forð be gehrihtum *gemǽre to stódleage*. (T) swa to ticnes felda. (O) *þánon to meárcdene*. (T) swa to tæppeleage. (O) *swá forð to scípleage*. (T) *þánon to bràdan érsce*. (V) swa to þære ealdan cwealmstowe. (O) *þánon forð be dèopan délle*. (V) þanon be craweleainga *meárce to bàcegéate*. (V) forð be *méarce to ðæm èaldan fálde*. (V) swa norð and east to hearpaðe. (O) a be *hearpáðe to hèafod stóccum*. (V) swa be hideburninga *gemǽre on ícenan*. (T) *þánon up be stréame*. (P) þanon swa wið easton wordige (O) þonan be rihtre mearce to ðæm gemærðornan. (O) þanon to ðære readan rode. (O) swa forð be *éaldormonnes méarce*. (P) a be mearce. (O) þanon *hít cimð on ícenan*. (T) up be *stréame to àlres fórda*. (V) *þónan on tìccebúrnan*. (V) *úp andlang búrnan*. (P) to hearpaðe swa to tyrngeate wiðinnan ða *ǽfisc to scéapwican*. (T) þanon be riht *gemǽre to èllenfórda*. (V) swa to bradan dene. (O) *þánon to mèolluc- cúmbe*. (V) swa to meolænbeorge. (O) andlang weges to *wealthǽminga méarce*. (P) be rihton *gemǽre to hìge léage*. (V) *þánon to clènefélda*. (V) swa on are dene forð be *hágan on scèatteléage*. (V) þanon forð on icenan be norðan stanforde. (O) swa mid streame ðæt hit *cýmð eft on brómbricge*. (T)

This simple, unpolished boundary paragraph, analyzed in accordance with Van Draat's own practices, has yielded five examples of cursus planus, ten of tardus, fourteen of velox. Out of forty units, twenty-nine, or 72.5 percent, end in cursus-forms. I believe that, if I have erred, it has been on the side of caution. I could not bring myself to stress the *to* in *to ðære readan rode*, although Van Draat stressed a simple preposition in its normal position at least once. By assuming that the analogical *i* in *wordige* was not pronounced, and that *hear-* represents *here-* rather than *her-*, I could have added two more examples of velox. I have eschewed all pauses and elisions within units. I have made no use of rhythmic patterns not used by Van Draat; e.g., the cursus trispondaicus, Clark's variant of the velox which ends in *'xx*,[39] and Mrs. Lipp's *a* and *b*. Unless I have misunderstood these rather badly, they would have yielded eight additional cursus-forms or related rhythms: *swá norð and eàst to héarpaðe* (V); *swá to meolænbéorge* (Tr.); *éaldan cwéalmstowe, éaston wórdige, nórðan stánforde* (a); *tícnes félda, reádan róde, brádan déne* (b). In other words, my analysis does not exaggerate the amount of cursus in the paragraph.

---

is a copy made somewhat later than the date of the transaction, but probably not enough later to affect the rhythm materially.

[39] *Op. cit.*, p. 19.

IV. CURSUS IN THE OLD ENGLISH BEDE

As we have seen, Van Draat proved, to his own satisfaction and to that of a number of other scholars, that King Alfred could not have made the Old English translation of Bede's *Ecclesiastical History*. The proof hinges upon cursus — not all of the cursus at the ends of clauses, but only those cursus-forms produced by double translation of Latin words; e.g., *legerit: hy rædeþ & leornaþ* (P). He found 304 such tautologies in the Bede, 260 of which contained some kind of cursus; 156 tautologies in Alfred's translation of the *Pastoral Care*, only 60 of which had cursus.[40] As it relates to the Bede, Van Draat's argument is in effect a twofold one: (1) the tautologies were introduced for the purpose of making cursus-forms; (2) the author of the translation was imitating the cursus-forms which he found in the original Latin. We shall examine the first branch of the argument now.

Of the 304 tautological translations in the Bede, 44 do not produce cursus-forms (as Van Draat observes); i.e., the crusus theory alone leaves about 14.5 percent of the tautologies to be accounted for by other explanations. The 260 examples of cursus include, according to Van Draat, 25 in which the cursus produced by double translation is redundant, unnecessary, since the clause would end in cursus even if the tautology were absent (p. 325). In 9 other instances, the tautological cursus is in the body of a clause and followed immediately, or very closely, by another cursus-form (pp. 331–332). Here, then, are 34 tautologies to be subtracted from the 260, since the translator could have had cursus at these points without resorting to double translation.[41] The cursus-forms which might be evidence of the translator's purpose are thus reduced to 226, or about 74.3 percent of 304, very close to the percentage found in the boundary paragraph above. Here one might let the matter rest.

But Van Draat's evidence must be further reduced. Roughly, about two-thirds of the 226 should have been classified as redundant and added to the 25 which he recognized as unnecessary. Few scholars today are sufficiently interested in Old English prose rhythm to wade through a complete catalogue of the redundant cursus-forms; hence, I offer some representative examples, all taken from Van Draat's lists of "double-forms used . . . for no other purpose than that of rhythm" (pp. 325–330).

1. mæssepreostas betwih wibedum wæron *slægene & cwylmde* (P)*
   wibedum wæron cwylmde (V)[42]
2. in þa tid wæs micles mægenes *tald & gelefed* (P)*
   mægenes tald (E)
   mægenes gelefed (P)*

---

[40] (1915–16), p. 332.

[41] Perhaps seven other instances of tautological cursus within a clause should also be thrown out, but Van Draat felt that in each case one would make a rhetorical pause when reading the translation aloud (p. 331).

[42] It would be a mistake to suppose that the second member of the tautological pair is necessarily the one added. A translator with the ingenuity assumed by Van Draat could easily place the added synonym first.

3. hræðe him læcedom gebæron & brohton (P)*
        læcedom gebæron (P)*
        læcedom brohton (P)*
4. mid smolte mode aberan & aræfnan (P)*
        mode aberan (P)*
        mode aræfnan (P)*
5. maran cirican & hyrran stænenne *timbran & wyrcan* (P)
        stænenne timbran (P)
        stænenne wyrcan (P)
6. þæt heo him þone heofonlican weg *forsette & fortynde* (P)
        heofonlican weg forsette (V)*
        heofonlican weg fortynde (V)*
7. oð hluttorne dæg in gebedum *astode & awunade* (T)*
        gebedum astode (P)
        gebedum awunade (T)*
8. þa het se cyning sona neoman þone *mete & þa swæsendo* (T)*
        neoman þone mete (P)
        neoman þa swæsendo (T)*
9. þa georn þær sona upp genihtsumlic *yrþ & wæstm* (V)
        genihtsumlic yrþ (E)
        genihtsumlic wæstm[a] (P)*
10. mid gelomlicra wundra *wyrcnisse scan & beorhte* (V)
        wyrcnisse scan (E)
        wyrcnisse beorhte (P)

Reducing 226 by two-thirds leaves somewhere between 70 and 80 of the 304 tautologies (about 25 percent) still usable as evidence that the translator of the Bede was trying to achieve cursus by this means. Comparison with the boundary paragraph suggests that he could have accomplished as much without even trying.

The second branch of the argument, that the translator was imitating the cursus-forms of his Latin original, also falls apart under close scrutiny. Of Van Draat's 260 cursus-producing tautologies, some are of the sort which he called English, a type which could not have been modeled after the original because no such cursus-form is recognized in the Latin (p. 331). Others appear in the Old English at points where there is no cursus in the original (p. 330). About 100 of the Old English cursus-forms do not match the forms in the Latin clauses being translated (pp. 325–327). Such examples are hardly evidence of direct imitation. It is possible, as Van Draat argued, that in these instances the translator was imitating the Latin cursus in general rather than the specific cursus-forms before him. It is equally possible, however, in view of the abundant cursus of the boundary paragraph, that he was not imitating anything, that his cursus came naturally.

Van Draat listed only 86 of his "about 100" non-matching examples: 9 planus for Latin tardus, plus page-line references[a] of 22 others (p. 328); 8 planus for velox, plus references for 5 others (p. 328); 10 tardus for planus, with references

---

[a] The *m* is syllabic.

[a] Van Draat used Thomas Miller (ed.), *The Old English Version of Bede's Ecclesiastical History of the English People*, Part I, EETS, OS, No. 95, 96 (1890–91).

for 21 others (p. 329); 2 tardus for velox (p. 329); 7 velox for planus (pp. 329–330); and 2 velox for tardus (p. 330). He listed 68 of his "about 70 instances" in which the Old English cursus matches the Latin: 27 planus for Latin planus, plus page-line references for 27 others (pp. 325–326); 12 tardus for tardus (p. 327); and 2 velox for velox (p. 327).

It is in the 68 matching examples that one might find some basis for an argument that the translator was imitating his original. My ten examples of redundant cursus above were drawn from both the matching and the non-matching examples in Van Draat's article; and those cursus-forms which match the forms of the Latin being translated are marked with an asterisk. It will be seen that the cursus-forms already present in the translation match the Latin somewhat oftener than do the tautological cursus-forms; i.e., in 1, the tautology matches while the other does not; in 6 and 9, the tautology does not match but the other does; in 2, 3, 4, 7, and 8, both provide matches; and in 5 and 10, neither matches. I have not checked to see whether proportions like these hold true for all of Van Draat's examples, but I know that there are many more instances in which the translator could have echoed the Latin cursus without resorting to tautology.

If we examine Van Draat's 154 best examples (68 matching, 86 non-matching) as a group, we shall see that

92 Latin planus are rendered in OE by 54 P, 31 T, 7 V;
45 Latin tardus   by 12 T, 31 P, 2 V;
17 Latin velox   by 2 V, 13 P, 2 T.

It seems that any Latin cursus-form is much more likely to be matched up with an Old English planus than with either of the other two types. This suggests the operation of chance rather than of conscious art. It is well-known that, in Latin, planus is by far the easiest cursus to obtain, with tardus second, and velox third. As far as Old English is concerned, the cursus-forms of the boundary paragraph indicate that planus was not invariably the commonest. The synonymous pairs in the Bede, however, contain a large proportion of inflected nouns and verbs with a single unstressed syllable after the stressed root: ′x or x′x. Placing an unstressed & between two of these automatically results in planus.

The numbers of the three types in the Old English are 98 P, 45 T, and 11 V; therefore, if we assume that the translator paid no attention at all to the Latin cursus-forms and that his own use of the three types was governed by pure chance, we can see that *any* Latin cursus-form would have about 9 chances in 14 of being matched with an Old English planus, about 4 in 14 of being matched with tardus, and a little better than 1 in 14 of being rendered by a velox. By a very crude arithmetical calculation, we should expect between 54 and 63 of the 92 Latin planus forms to be matched with Old English planus, between 12 and 16 of the Latin tardus forms to be matched with Old English tardus, and one or two of the Latin velox forms to be rendered by Old English velox. A glance at the actual numbers will suffice to indicate that we have here a distinct possibility that the matching is random and governed by chance.

With the aid of formulas provided me by skilled mathematicians, I was able to refine my own primitive calculations considerably.[45] These are the results. The chances are about 19 to 1 (95 percent) that the number of Latin planus (92) matched with Old English planus at random will lie between 52.67 and 64.42. The actual number is 54. The chances are also about 19 to 1 that the number of Latin tardus (45) matched with Old English tardus at random will lie between 7.999 and 18.299. The actual number is 12. The chances are the same that the number of Latin velox (17) matched with Old English velox will fall between zero and 3.11. The actual number is 2. Further refinement of these results is possible, of course, by means of the highly sophisticated techniques available in a good statistical laboratory, but my goal is not to pursue the mathematical probabilities to their ultimate refinement, but merely to demonstrate that Van Draat's findings can be explained by the workings of pure chance.

It would be difficult, under these circumstances, to argue that the translator made any conscious effort whatever to imitate the cursus-forms of his original. The second branch of Van Draat's argument is, therefore, as invalid as the first.

V. CURSUS IN THE PREFACE TO THE *PASTORAL CARE*

Since Alfred's alleged incapacity for cursus has been made a sort of touchstone with which to determine his authorship or non-authorship of literary works, an examination of his best known and best authenticated piece of original Old English prose should be revealing. The text below is the first part (about one-third) of King Alfred's preface to the *Pastoral Care*, as it appears in MS. Hatton 20.[46] My division of the text into rhetorical units is as objective as I can make it. I assume a rhetorical pause wherever a new grammatical clause begins, the only exceptions being before ðæt in line 19, swa in 23, and hwelce in 26.[47] I have treated two long and important phrases as rhetorical units: ægðer ge . . . woruldcundra (line 4) and & eac . . . hadas (10–11). I have retained the manuscript punctuation, which supports many of my rhetorical divisions, only substituting periods and commas for the points, inverted semicolons, etc., of the original. The marks after sibbe (7), siodo (8), wige (10), liornunga (12), and utanbordes (13) seem to me much less likely to be preceded by cursus than the others.[48] I have no doubt that anyone who reads the passage will disagree with some of my decisions, but probably no one will reverse enough of them to change my conclusions significantly.

[45] I wish to acknowledge the very kind assistance of James G. Wendel and Charles F. Brumfiel of the University of Michigan Department of Mathematics. I did not ask them to check my accuracy in carrying out their instructions, however, and any blunders in the calculations are my own.

[46] N. R. Ker (ed.), *The Pastoral Care*, Early English Manuscripts in Facsimile, VI (Copenhagen, 1956). I have also made use of my own notes on the MS taken in 1958.

[47] The line numbers in the margin are my own and are for convenience of reference in this article. Again & has been substituted for the Tironian nota. I ignore alterations in the text which, in my opinion, could not be contemporary.

[48] They serve to emphasize sets of phrases within the clauses. If one looks for cursus in these phrases, the result will be about as follows: ægðer ge hiora sibbe (V), ge hiora siodo (P), ge hiora onweald (P), ægðer ge mid wige (P), ge mid wisdome (O), ægðer ge ymb lare (P), ge ymb liornunga (O), & hu man utanbordes (V).

✠ ĐEOS BOC SCEAL TO WIOGORA CEASTRE.[49]

Ælfred kyning hateð gretan Wærferð biscep his wordum
luflice & freondlice, (T) & ðe cyðan hate ðæt me com swiðe
oft on gemynd, (E) hwelce wiotan iu *wæron giond Angelcynn*, (T)
ægðer ge godcundra *hada ge woruldcundra*,[50] (V) & hu gesælig-
5 lica tida ða *wæron giond Angelcynn*, (T) & hu ða kyningas ðe
ðone onwald hæfdon ðæs *folces on ðam dagum*,[51] (P) Gode & his
ærendwrecum hyrsumedon,[52] (O) & hie ægðer ge hiora sibbe, ge
hiora siodo, ge hiora onweald innan*borðes gehioldon*, (P)
& eac ut hiora *eðel gerymdon*,[53] (P) & hu him ða speow, (O)
10 ægðer ge mid *wige, ge mid wisdome*, (T) & eac ða *godcundan
hadas*, (P) hu giorne hie wæron ægðer ge ymb lare ge ymb
liornunga, ge ymb *ealle ða ðiowotdomas*, (V) ðe hie *Gode
don*[54] *scoldon*, (P) & hu man utanbordes, wisdom & lare *hieder
on lond sohte*, (P) & hu we hy[52] nu sceoldon *ute begietan*, (P)
15 gif we hie habban sceoldon. (O) Swa[55] clæne hio wæs oð*feallenu
on Angelcynne*, (V) ðæt swiðe feawa *wæron behionan Humbre* (V)
ðe hiora ðeninga cuðen under*stondan on Englisc*, (P) oððe furðum an ærendgewrit of Lædene on *Englisc areccean*, (P) & ic
wene ðæt[56] noht monige begiondan Humbre næren. (O) Swa[55] *feawa*
20 *hiora wæron*, (P) ðæt ic furðum anne anlepne ne mæg geðencean
besuðan Temese, (O) ða ða ic to rice feng. (O) Gode Ælmihtegum
sie ðonc (O) ðæt[56] we nu ænigne *onstal*[57] habbað *lareowa*, (T)
& forðon ic ðe bebiode, (P) ðæt ðu do swa[55] ic ge*liefe ðæt ðu
wille*, (P) ðæt ðu ðe ðissa woruldðinga to ðæm geæmetige (O)[58]
25 swæ ðu oftost mæge, (O)[59] ðæt ðu ðone *wisdom ðe ðe God sealde* (T)
ðær ðær ðu *hiene befæstan mæge* (V) befæste. (O) Geðenc hwelce
witu us ða becomon for ðisse worulde, (O)[60] ða ða we hit no-
hwæðer ne *selfe ne lufodon*, (T) ne eac oðrum *monnum ne lefdon*.
(P) Ðone naman *ænne we lufodon* (T) ðæt[56] we Cristne wæren, (O)[61]
30 & swiðe *feawa ða ðeawas*. (P)

There is nothing rough or unpolished and nothing pedestrian about this prose.
The clauses and phrases are worked into an intricate pattern of balance and

[49] My analysis does not include the superscription, which ends in cursus planus.

[50] The first *d* of this word has been added above the line by a contemporary, perhaps the original
scribe. The cursus is not affected.

[51] *On ðam dagum* has been added above the line by what seems to me a contemporary scribe (11th-
century according to Ker, p. 24). If the insertion is rejected as non-Alfredian, the clause still ends
in planus: *hæfdon ðæs folces*.

[52] The *y* on erasure. Rhythm not affected.

[53] The *ge* is crowded but may be a contemporary insertion. If *ge-* is rejected, the clause probably
ends in velox: *ut hiora eðel rymdon*.

[54] *don* is above the line, I think by a contemporary scribe (11th-cent., Ker); the reading is supported
by the Cottonian MS.

[55] From *swæ* by erasure.

[56] From *ðætte* by erasure.

[57] *On stal* can be read as a phrase, but it is more probably the word *onstal*, which (in poetry at
least) has stress on the first syllable.

[58] ? *to ðam geæmetige* (V).

[59] ? *oftost mæge* (Mrs. Lipp's *b*).

[60] ? *for ðisse worulde* (T).

[61] ? *ðætte we Cristne wæren* (V).

parallelism.[62] To take the first large unit alone (the first sentence, if you like), we see eight parallel clauses: (a) *hwelce wiotan* . . . (lines 3–4), (b) *& hu gesæliglica* . . . (4–5), (c) *& hu ða kyningas* . . . (5–7), (d) *& hie ægðer* . . . (7–9), (e) *& hu him ða speow* . . . (9–10), (f) *& eac ða godcundan* . . . (10–13), (g) *& hu man* . . . (13–14), (h) *& hu we* . . . (14–15). Yet, apparently because the Anglo-Saxons found perfect symmetry too monotonous for their taste, the parallelism seems to be deliberately broken in several ways. Three clauses (a, d, and f) begin differently from the others. Each clause varies in some detail or details from the others in its internal structure, some being simple, others containing sub-clauses, and others having varying sets of balanced phrases within them. Within the series of eight are three sub-series (clauses a and b, c to f, g and h), each sub-series linked together by similarities of thought and structure. Within clauses, *godcundra* is balanced against *woruldcundra* (a); *hiora sibbe* against *hiora siodo*, *hiora onweald*, and *hiora eðel* (d); *gehioldon* against *gerymdon* (d); *mid wige* against *mid wisdome* (e); *ymb lare* against *ymb liornunga* and *ymb ealle ða ðiowotdomas* (f); and *wisdom* against *lare* (g). Between clauses, *iu wæron giond Angelcynn* (a) is paralleled by *ða wæron giond Angelcynn* (b); *hyrsumedon* (c) by *gehioldon* and *gerymdon* (d); the first series of *ge*-phrases (d) by the second and third (e, f); and *ðe hie Gode don scoldon* (f) by *gif we hie habban sceoldon* (h). This is a highly sophisticated prose, which makes the balanced antitheses of the Church Fathers look rather simple in comparison. It is loaded with rhetorical devices, the prose of a literary king exhibiting his virtuosity. As he gets into the meat of his preface, his earnestness increases and his rhetoric becomes less ornate.

If Alfred indeed lacked an ear for cursus, we might expect that trait to appear most conspicuously in a work like the preface, in which he wrote with conscious artistry, not willingly permitting any syllable to slip in "in spite of the author." Yet, in the forty units of the passage above, we find 14 examples of planus, 8 of tardus, 5 of velox, and 1 of the type called English, for a total of 28 units (70 percent) ending in some kind of cursus.[63] This is not a translation text, but there are two roughly synonymous pairs joined by *&*, each making a cursus-form, one at the end of a clause and the other in the interior: *luftice & freondlice* (T), *wisdom & lare* (P). Perhaps *ge ymb lare ge ymb liornunga* (T) should be added to these, since correlative *ge*'s join constructions comparable to those joined by *&*.

I do not for a moment believe that Alfred consciously worked to produce these cursus-forms, any more than I believe that the authors of the boundary paragraph and the Old English Bede consciously sought after such rhythms. Alfred was much too busy, I am sure, with his intricate tapestry of phrases and clauses to think about planus and tardus. His cursus-forms were inevitable.

If, however, there is any doubt about this point, I shall offer the logical refuta-

---

[62] This is not the sort of parallelism which is *typical* of the OE poetry. In the latter, the parallel elements are similar in thought but not necessarily similar in form. Here, the elements are similar in form, usually different in thought.

[63] There may be more cursus than this. I have read the passage so many times over a long period of years that, even when the principles implicit in Van Draat's practices would permit a cursus-form, I may not recognize it if it fails to conform to my own notions of how the preface should be read.

tion, not unknown to rhetoric, known as the *reductio ad absurdum*; to wit, King Alfred, with his bad ear for cursus, could not have written his preface to the *Pastoral Care*; hence, the latter is a forgery from beginning to end.[54]

VI. THE RHYTHMS OF ÆLFRIC'S *LIVES OF SAINTS*

Writers on cursus in the *Lives of Saints* and Ælfric's other metrical works have already been mentioned in section I of this article. How much cursus one sees in Ælfric's "rhythmical prose" depends to a great extent on whether one is a strict or a loose[55] constructionist where cursus is concerned. Gerould was generally a strict constructionist, confining his statements to the three types of cursus-form expressly recognized and approved by the best authorities of the eleventh to thirteenth centuries, taking no liberties with those forms except for an occasional irregular placement of the caesura, and looking only at the rhythmical patterns of clause-endings. As one might expect, he found relatively few cursus-forms. His corpus was small, of course: his discussion of cursus in Ælfric (pp. 360–365) includes not more than twenty-five clauses in short passages which he had chosen because they seemed to illustrate Ælfric's adoption of Latin prose features. Gerould listed 7 examples of cursus planus (*wundurlíce afýrhte, wénde þa óngean, béah to martíne, gástlican lífe*, etc.); 1 of tardus (*cristes gebýsnungum*); and 3 of velox (*mánega mỳnecéne, hǽþenum hère-tógan, swimman on ánum flóde*). Two of these are objectionable, in that they distort the natural rhythm of Old English: *wénde þa óngean* (rightly *ongéan*) and *béah to martíne* (rightly *mártíne* or *mártìne*).[56] Regardless of Latin word structure, I take it that the grave accent in Old English cursus velox may be at least as strong as either of the acutes;[57] consequently, I shall not cavil at *mỳnecéne* or *hèretógan*, but shall take advantage of this rule when I begin to play the game myself.

To Gerould, the chief importance of Ælfric's cursus lay in the supposed fact that it was modeled after the cursus of the Latin prose writers and, therefore, indicated that Ælfric's intention was to write prose rather than poetry.

Dorothy Bethurum noted five examples of planus and one of tardus in a passage from the *Lives* (pp. 524–525, 527), without indicating precisely which lines contained planus and which one tardus. I am sure that I can identify the forms on my own, however, and I judge that her conception of cursus was very similar to that of Gerould. Although she referred to Ælfric's *Lives* as "prose," Miss Bethurum called attention (p. 530) to Van Draat's earlier articles, which tended to prove that cursus in Old English was neither derived from Latin nor confined to prose.

As noted in section I, Pope regards most of Ælfric's cursus-forms as "purely accidental." I agree with this verdict, with one modification, i.e., the substitution

---

[54] I believe, of course, that Alfred was author of the OE Bede — see the article referred to in fn. 10 and, in the near future I hope, an article in a volume honoring Tauno Mustanoja.

[55] For the former, e.g. Nicolau; for the latter, e.g. Van Draat.

[56] In the first 600 lines of *St. Martin*, for example, Ælfric alliterates the forms of this name on *m* 34 times, on *t* never. The OE accent is evidently on the first syllable.

[57] Cf. Mrs. Lipp's *ʒeleafan to langum fyrste* (below) and Van Draat's practices. The grave may also, of course, be much weaker than the acutes.

of "rhetorically" for "purely." From a linguistic standpoint, these cursus-forms are no more accidental than those in the boundary description; they are an inescapable part of the language.

Mrs. Lipp's study (pp. 712–717) is much too broad to be called a study of cursus, even with loose construction, but it is an excellent study of Ælfric's rhythms. She began by analyzing about 200 clause-endings in his Latin writings to discover what types of rhythm he preferred. She then analyzed 537 half-lines of Ælfric's vernacular *Life of St. Oswald* and found that many of the half-lines end in the rhythms which Ælfric preferred at the ends of his Latin clauses.[68] Lastly, she analyzed 537 half-lines of *Beowulf* in order to compare poetic with prose usages. The rhythms which she found most frequently in the Latin are: cursus planus (33 instances), tardus (33), velox (25), the controversial trispondaicus (36), and three additional rhythms which she labels *a* (16), *b* (22), and *c* (17). These seven patterns accounted for about 91 percent of the clause-endings. About 73 percent of the half-lines from *St. Oswald* ended in one or another of these seven patterns, although the distribution of the types differed from that found in the Latin, and the caesura was correctly placed in only 58 percent (of the 537). Of the half-lines from *Beowulf*, about 61 percent ended in one or another of the seven rhythms, and in nearly 50 percent (of the 537) the caesura was correctly placed. Here are the rhythmic types with examples of each:[69]

1. Planus (/x, x/x):[70] *línguam verténdo, fréondum and mágum.* (/xx, /x): *geléaffulla cýning.*[71]

2. Tardus (/x, x/xx): *práge gepólode, gehéolde on wórulde.* (/xx, /xx): *gúðsearo géatolic.*[72] (? Error): *éodon to pam geféohte.*

3. Velox (/xx, \x/x): *témpore relevátus, síðode on his fótum, Hábbað we to pæm mǽran.* (/x, x\x/x): *geléafan to langum fýrste, baptismáte ablurerétur.*

4. Trispondaicus (/x, \x/x): *propríis impraegnátam, léoda to geléafan, ǽnne ofer ýðe.* (/x\, x/x): *síngalum gebédum,*[73] *Héorogar ond Hróðgar.*[74]

5. *a* (/x, /xx): *gehwánon cúmene.*[75]

---

[68] In treating such short units, Mrs. Lipp departs from all of the best cursus theory. In fact, comparison of *clausulae* with the interior parts of clauses is one of the methods for determining whether rhetorical cursus exists in a text — see Nicolau, p. 34. Since Mrs. Lipp finds as much cursus within clauses as at clause-ends, some authorities would say that she has demonstrated a lack of cursus in the *Lives*.

[69] Angus McIntosh had found similar rhythms in Wulfstan's *Sermo Lupi ad Anglos* — see "Wulfstan's Prose," *Proceedings of the British Academy 1949*, xxxv, 135. McIntosh's pattern *1* corresponds to planus, *2* to trispondaicus, *3* to *b*, *4* to tardus, *6* to *c*, and *7* to *a*. No pattern on this page corresponds to velox, but on p. 134 there are seven examples of two patterns which look like two variants of velox. The same rhythmic patterns turn up in his brief study of Ælfric's *St. Oswald*, p. 137.

[70] Comma within the parentheses indicates the caesura of the rhythmic pattern; this was unnecessary in sections II–V, which were based on Van Draat's system.

[71] Cf. Polheim's "Kursus *u*," pp. 82–83.

[72] Cf. Polheim's "Kursus *s*," p. 82.

[73] If, as I believe, a trispondaicus can hardly be pronounced without at least a secondary accent on the third syllable, *singalum* is not in keeping with the natural rhythm of OE.

[74] Van Draat, planus.

[75] Cf. Polheim's "Kursusform *o*," p. 80; Clark, tardus.

6. *b* (/x, /x): *féasceaft fúnden.*[76]

7. *c* (/xx, x/xx): *libentíssime suscípitur,*[77] *dúguðe ond géoguðe.* (/x, xx/xx): *recíténtur in ecclésia, háleð under héofenum.*[78]

Mrs. Lipp concludes (p. 717), after the comparisons described above, that the model for Ælfric's rhythms in the *Lives* was provided by Old English poetry rather than by the Latin cursus — a conclusion with which I am in complete agreement. She further suggests that the later vernacular poetry would show a closer relationship to the *Lives* than does *Beowulf*, "since his [Ælfric's] ear would have been attuned to late Old English poetry, which shows a higher percentage of unstressed syllables than *Beowulf*." I am sure that she is correct, and I should have been better satisfied had she chosen for comparison a relatively late poem like *Judith*. The latter would have been especially appropriate, inasmuch as we have evidence that Ælfric was familiar with a vernacular poem on the subject of the ancient prototype of Al Fateh, and there seems to be no reason to doubt that it was the poem of which a fragment is preserved in MS. Cotton Vitellius A. 15.[79]

I should prefer that Mrs. Lipp perform the suggested analysis, but for the present I offer my own findings in lines 2–51 (the first 100 complete half-lines) of *Judith*, listing all examples so that it will be seen where I have followed the rules of the game and where I may inadvertently have violated them. The results of my examination are as follows:

1. Planus: *trúmne geléafan, árest gesóhte, béncum gelóme, féorran gehýran, góda gehwýlces, níða geblónden, béagum gehláste, lǽdan ongúnnon, búnan ond órcas, ríca ne wénde, dréncte mid wíne, réste on sýmbel; gúmena báldor, ýldestan ðégnas, drýhtguman síne, dúguðe éalle, gúmena áldor, -wígena brégo, wígena báldor, hǽleða béarna.* (20)[80]

2. Tardus: *tíðe gefrémede, déaðe geslégene, hríngum gehródene, fǽder on róderum, stýrmde ond gýlede, módig ond médugal, ýmbe þæs fólctogan; góldwine gúmena, gírwan up swǽsendo.* (9)

3. Velox: *égesful éorla drýhten,*[81] *néalǽhte niht seo þýstre; hýldo þæs héhstan déman, wlánce to wíngedrínce, éalle his wéagesíðas.* (5)

4. Trispondaicus: *mánode genéahhe.*[82] (1)

5. *a: féorðan dógore, ídes álfscinu, ófstum fétigan, hráðe frémedon, fúndon férhðgleawe.* (5)[83]

6. *b: gínnan grúnde, géarwe fúnde, mǽran þéodne, mǽste þéarfe, héhstan brógan. frýmða wáldend, wýrcean géorne, wúndrum þrýmlic, ófstum míclum, rícan þéodne,*

---

[76] Cf. Polheim's "Kursusform *r*," pp. 81–82.

[77] Cf. Polheim's "Form *w*," p. 83; Clark, Van Draat, tardus.

[78] Van Draat, tardus.

[79] C. W. M. Grein (ed.), *Ælfrik de Vetere et Novo Testamento*, etc., in Grein and R. Wülker, *Bibliothek der angelsächsischen Prosa*, I (Cassel & Göttingen, 1872), 11.

[80] With questionable caesura: *gleaw on geðonce, ða to ðam symle.*

[81] Cf. Polheim's *oótúlerit iustas réi*, p. 74.

[82] See fn. 73.

[83] With questionable caesura: *þær was eallgylden, hu se stiðmode, Swa se inwidda, to his bedreste, to ðam gysterna, þær hie Iudithðe, ond ða fromlice.* There are other faults besides the caesura in some of these.

fólces ráswan, Iúdith hýne, síttan éodon, bóllan stéape, fǽge þégon, sínces brýtta,
swíman lágon, fíra béarnum, béarhtme stópon, ríca hýne, nihtes ínne, fléohnet fǽger,
hýne nǽnig. (23)[84]

7. *c: hlýnede ond dýnede.* (1)

If my decisions as to what to include and what to reject have been in accordance
with the principles used by Mrs. Lipp in analyzing Ælfric, this *Judith* passage
shows 64 percent of Ælfric's Latin rhythms, as compared with 58 percent in
St. Oswald.[85] The percentages of the seven types are: planus 20, tardus 9, velox
5, trispondaicus 1, *a* 5, *b* 23, and *c* 1. In two of these, planus and *a*, the percentages for the *Judith* passage are identical with those for the 537 half-lines of
St. Oswald. In two others, tardus and velox, the *Judith* passage is closer to Ælfric's
Latin usage than is *St. Oswald*. In the remaining three, the half-lines from *St.
Oswald* are closer to the Latin usage than is the *Judith*. These rhythms, it is clear,
belong as much to poetry as to Ælfric's so-called "rhythmic prose."[86]

VII. SOME CONCLUSIONS

The so-called cursus in Old English literature is nothing more than a part of
the natural rhythm of the language. It is not a rhetorical ornament either of
prose or of poetry, for it appears in unpolished, non-rhetorical Old English
boundary descriptions, as well as in modern everyday speech. If methods similar
to those employed in this article were used to test the things which pass for cursus
in Mediaeval Latin, Middle English, and other languages, I suspect that much of
the supposed cursus would turn out to be simple linguistic phenomena having
little or no connection with the true cursus.

Two literary controversies are affected by this conclusion and by the investigations which led to it: the controversy over the Alfredian authorship of the Old
English Bede and the argument as to whether Ælfric's alliterative writings are
prose or poetry. Although Alfred's authorship may be disputed on other grounds,
the argument based on cursus is no longer tenable; for (1) the supposed cursus
in the Old English Bede is not cursus, (2) the tautologies in the Bede translation
were not introduced for the purpose of creating cursus, either real or apparent,
and (3) Alfred's own preface to the *Pastoral Care* contains abundant evidence
that his clause-end rhythms were not unlike those found in the Bede tautologies.
The second controversy also remains unsettled. Obviously, the argument that
Ælfric was writing prose because he used cursus, or other rhythms favored by
Latin prose-writers, can no longer be entertained. But what of other alleged prose
features of Ælfric's work? And what of the poetic features in which he is allegedly
deficient? It remains to be seen whether arguments based upon these things can
stand the test of close examination any better than the argument from rhythm.

UNIVERSITY OF MICHIGAN

[84] With questionable caesura: *hloh ond hlydde, bed ahongen.* Lacking caesura: *gytesalum, bealofulla,*
and three occurrences of *Holofernus.*

[85] See her comparative table, p. 717. She excludes, as I do, examples in which caesura is lacking or
misplaced.

[86] I am now putting the finishing touches on an article which rejects the view that Ælfric wrote
metrical prose, and which places him in the later alliterative tradition in the company of such
poets as Laʒamon.

Was Ælfric a Poet?[1]

There was a time, roughly about fifty years ago, when one could have compiled an impressive list of contemporary or recently departed scholars who treated Ælfric's alliterative homilies and translations as poetry. The list would have included such well-known names as Richard Wülker,[2] Jakob Schipper,[3] W. W. Skeat,[4] and Eduard Sievers.[5] There were also notable dissenters at that time, such as Bernhard ten Brink,[6] Adolf Ebert,[7] and Alois Brandl,[8] who held Ælfric's alliterative works to be some kind of prose. Both parties recognized that Ælfric's alliterative style differed in several respects from that of *Beowulf* and other poems composed in an earlier stage of the poetic tradition: Ælfric's alliteration was looser, did not obey some of the traditional rules; his rhythm differed, mainly because his lines contained many more unstressed syllables than the earlier style allowed; his diction was short on kennings, epithets, poetic compounds, and other traditional ornaments. The one party felt that these faults showed merely that Ælfric was writing a different kind of poetry, while the other party judged that any verse so faulty must be classified as prose.

Scholarly opinion began to swing to the side of the prose faction about the time that Gordon Hall Gerould published his article, "Abbot Ælfric's Rhythmic Prose," in 1924.[9] After calling attention to some of the alleged faults of Ælfric's alliterative style,

---

[1] This article formed the basis of a paper read before the Old English section of the Fifth Biennial Conference on Medieval Studies, Kalamazoo, May 20, 1970.

[2] *Anglia*, 2 (1879), 141.

[3] *Englische Metrik*, Part I—*Altenglische Metrik* (Bonn, 1881), pp. 60-66; *Grundriss der englischen Metrik* (Vienna and Leipzig, 1895), pp. 39-43.

[4] *Ælfric's Lives of Saints*, EETS, OS, 76, 82, 94, and 114 (1881-1900; rpt. Oxford U. Press, 1966), 2 vols.; esp. II, l-liii.

[5] "Metrische Studien IV" *Abhandlungen der phil.-hist. Klasse der sächsischen Akademie der Wissenschaften*, 35 (Leipzig, 1919), 211-19.

[6] *Geschichte der englischen Literatur*, I (Berlin, 1877), 136.

[7] *Allgemeine Geschichte der Literatur des Mittelalters*, III (Leipzig, 1887), 513.

[8] *Geschichte der altenglischen Literatur* (Strassburg, 1908), pp. 163-64.

[9] *MP*, 22 (1924-25), 353-66.

Reprinted by permission from *Philological Quarterly*, 52 (1973), 643-62, published by The University of Iowa.

Gerould argued that the abbot, so far from writing poor poetry, was writing a new kind of English prose in imitation of the ornate Latin prose which he found in his sources. This Latin style was characterized by rime, parallelism, antithesis, and rhythmical clause-ends (i.e. *cursus*). According to Gerould, Ælfric adopted all of these features except rime, for which he substituted alliteration. Gerould made no real effort to demonstrate Ælfric's use of antithesis and parallelism, although he quoted numerous examples in the Latin writers. Nearly half his article was devoted to Ælfric's supposed imitation of the *cursus* in his sources (pp. 359-65).

Very little of Gerould's argument has survived. Dorothy Bethurum demonstrated that Ælfric's alliterative style was of English rather than foreign origin and that he seldom showed any tendency to imitate the characteristic features of his Latin sources.[10] On two of Gerould's specific points she was able to show, by comparing Ælfric's *Life of St. Agnes* with its source in Ambrose, (1) that Ælfric's alliteration differed in both form and function from Ambrose's rimes, (2) that Ælfric's occasional cursus-forms were unrelated to those used by Ambrose (pp. 526-27). P. Fijn van Draat had already proved that *cursus* was about as common in the Old English poetry as in the prose;[11] hence, any *cursus* found in Ælfric's works is irrelevant to the problem of determining whether he wrote prose or poetry. Two of the most recent writers on Ælfric's style, J. C. Pope[12] and Frances Randall Lipp,[13] while accepting the view that Ælfric was writing prose, reject nearly all of Gerould's arguments.

It is generally recognized, moreover, that Ælfric's alliterative lines obey the most essential rules of Old English alliterative verse. The short rhythmic-syntactic unit generally consists of four syllables with major stress, plus a varying number of syllables with lesser stress or none. With some exceptions, each of these units is further divisible into two parts, each containing two of the major stresses. The pairs of sub-units are normally linked by alliteration,

---

10 "The Form of Ælfric's *Lives of Saints*," *SP*, 29 (1932), 515-33. Miss Bethurum, however, regarded Ælfric's alliterative works as prose.

11 "The Cursus in Old English Poetry," *Anglia*, 38 (1914), 377-404. In an article entitled "Cursus in Old English: Rhetorical Ornament or Linguistic Phenomenon," *Speculum*, 47 (1972), 188-206, I believe that I have shown that all of the so-called *cursus* thus far found in OE literary works is, not the rhetorical device, but merely a natural concomitant of the structure of OE.

12 *Homilies of Ælfric. A Supplementary Collection*, EETS, Nos. 259 and 260 (Oxford U. Press, 1967-68), 2 vols.; see esp. I, 105-36.

13 "Ælfric's Old English Prose Style," *SP*, 66 (1969), 689-718.

which usually falls on the syllables with major stress. This alliteration, unlike that of the Latin prose writers, is not an occasional
added ornament; it is structural, i.e., a regular part of the fabric
of discourse, without which the latter would fall apart. Most of
the units are readily scannable by the Sievers system.[14] Obviously, these units and sub-units bear a close resemblance to the lines
and half-lines of the older poetry. There are troublesome lines
(just as in the older poetry), but the typical line is much like
line 2 of the *Life of St. Oswald:*

> wæs sum *Eðele cyning*   *Oswald gehaten.*

Nor are the divisions between lines the invention of modern scholars. Several of the earliest and best manuscripts of the *Lives* and
other alliterative pieces by Ælfric frequently mark the line divisions, and not infrequently the half-line divisions, with points or
other marks of punctuation; for example, Cotton Julius E. 6,
which Skeat used as the base manuscript for most of his edition of
the *Lives* (see I, pp. vi-vii) ; Cotton Vitellius C. 5, which provides
one of the facsimiles at the front of volume I of Pope's collection;
Trinity College, Cambridge, B xv. 34[15] and Corpus Christi College, Cambridge, MS. 178, facsimiles from which appear at the
front of Pope's volume II. Whether the manuscript punctuation
is authorial or scribal, it indicates that the metrical divisions were
somehow heard or felt by eleventh-century Anglo-Saxons.[16] As
Miss Bethurum has admitted, "if the test of verse is a purely metrical one, then there is little doubt that the *Lives of Saints* is poetry"
(p. 515).

Nevertheless, the view that Ælfric was writing prose prevailed,
not so much, I believe, because of the reasoning and evidence supporting it, as because of the emotional power of Gerould's plea on
behalf of Ælfric and his literary reputation.

A man so learned in the things that mattered to a monk, so curious and critical of mind as he showed himself to be throughout his writings, and so eager
to spread enlightenment as well as true religion among the people of England,
would scarcely have blundered into a style that was neither verse nor prose,
when he composed his maturest set of legends. At least, he ought not to be
accused of having done so until his manner has been more carefully studied
than has been done hitherto. (pp. 354-55)

---

[14] Or, I believe, by Andreas Heusler's system or by J. C. Pope's or by
Robert P. Creed's.

[15] See the editor's note, "Nearly constant half-line pointing by the original
scribe."

[16] The punctuation of verses in these MSS is less consistent than that of the
Parker copy of the *Battle of Brunanburh*, more consistent than that in the
Beowulf MS.

The argument that a scholarly man with a critical mind and a desire to spread enlightenment and true religion must necessarily be a skilled poet is intellectually empty but emotionally satisfying. Pope also speaks to the emotions when, after describing Ælfric's "rhythmical prose" as "a loosely metrical form" (I, 105), he suggests that "It is better regarded as a mildly ornamental, rhythmically ordered prose than as a debased, pedestrian poetry." If Ælfric's poetry is, in fact, debased and pedestrian, can one really improve it by calling it prose—a mere change in nomenclature?[17] Mrs. Lipp (p. 695) frankly recognizes the subjective nature of the present-day answer to the question of whether Ælfric wrote prose or poetry. "The answer," she says, "hinges ultimately on one's own private ideas of the borderline between the two or on one's conclusions on the complex problem of what medieval writers themselves felt to be the difference." She feels that the abbot felt himself to be a prose writer. "Modern readers," she adds, "recognizing Ælfric's undeniable skill as a stylist, but finding that he makes a poor poet, are . . . more comfortable with the prose label."[18]

The question involves more than a simple matter of nomenclature. Emotional involvement of the sort illustrated above tends to induce a certain mental set, which leads a scholar to accept with a minimum of scrutiny any evidence or argument supporting the one side of the controversy while inhibiting any investigation which might lead to results favoring the other side. The purpose of this present article is to reexamine those features of Ælfric's alliterative works which have been regarded as either confined to prose or out of place in poetry. Before I have finished, I hope that we shall have better notions of what the later alliterative poetry was like and a truer understanding of Ælfric's place in the alliterative tradition.

The prose features most frequently pointed out in Ælfric are these: (1) rime, (2) balance and antithesis, (3) wordplay, and

---

[17] Angus McIntosh solves the nomenclatural problem in another way: "The *Life of St. Oswald* may be verse, it is hardly poetry"—"Wulfstan's Prose," *Proceedings of the British Academy 1949*, 35, 111. Can we devise standards which, when applied to several writers (not just one), will separate the true poets from the mere versifiers?

[18] Peter Clemoes accepts without question the view that the metrical homilies are prose, but suggests that their rhythm and alliteration are derived from OE poetry of the sort found in the *Paris Psalter*—"Ælfric" in E. G. Stanley, ed., *Continuations and Beginnings* (London, 1966), pp. 203-06.

(4) *cursus.*[19] I do not wish to be misleading at this point. No one, as far as I know, has classified these four as absolutely non-poetic or as exclusively prose features. Much is made, however, of their occurrence in the Latin prose works which could have influenced Ælfric's style; and special emphasis is invariably given to any instance found in the *Lives of Saints* or other Ælfrician alliterative pieces. I shall discuss the first three, omitting *cursus* for reasons previously suggested.

Writers on Ælfric's style easily find rimes in the Latin works which he could have imitated, as well as in Ælfric's own Latin prose, e.g., *infirmitas—humilitas—divinitas, infantia—potentia, sugebat—pascebat, omnibus—fidelibus,* and *insistere—predicare* in passages quoted by Mrs. Lipp (pp. 702-03). These are merely inflectional rimes, of course, but the Latin endings are full enough to provide rimes which catch the eye and ear; and the rimes usually fall at the ends of parallel syntactic units, so that rime and parallelism reinforce each other. The instances which are found in Ælfric's Old English are much less impressive. In a passage from one of his letters, Mrs. Lipp (p. 693) singles out four successive half-lines ending in *-e* as a conspicuous example of riming: *godcundnesse—wunigende—mægenþrymme—gecynde.* Three of the words are datives at the ends of parallel expressions, but the rimes are phonetically and graphically so feeble that I wonder whether an Anglo-Saxon would recognize the *-e's* as rhetorical ornament. They look more like inevitable results of the Old English morphological system, no more significant than the endings *-um, -on, -on, -um* of the first four lines of *Beowulf.*[20] On the other hand, the rime *tihting—rihting* (p. 703) must be deliberate, and the two syntactic units involved have parallel structure. This, as I see it, is the one clear example of rime which Mrs. Lipp has drawn from Ælfric's vernacular writings. In one of the *Catholic Homilies,* Pope (p. 115) notes one example of a rough sort of assonance (*scinende—stymende*) in a line which possesses parallel structure and one example of rime (*brohte—rohte*) in a line which lacks parallelism and is, therefore, not of a typically prose type. I am not finding fault with Mrs. Lipp or with Pope for finding so little

---

[19] See, for example, Gerould, p. 358, Pope, I, pp. 109-10, and Lipp, pp. 692-94.

[20] A better example of inflectional rime might be the four lines ending *fæstenum, adrifan, wederum, biddan* in the *Exhortation to Christian Living* (see pp. 660-61). Despite the obvious parallelism in the lines, I would regard this instance as accidental.

rime, any more than with Gerould who found even less. The fact is that Ælfric, in the vernacular, made little use of any kind of rime that can be positively identified as stylistic.

Rime is not, moreover, a distinctive feature of prose in Old English. Occasional rimes occur in most Old English poems of any length. Although many of them could be accidental, there is at least one in *Beowulf* which was surely deliberate: *fylle gefægon, fægere geþægon* (1014). In *Judith*, the very abundance of the rimes seems to preclude the possibility of accidental riming, e.g., lines 2, 20, 29, 36, 60, 63, 115. In line 115, the syntactic units are parallel: *wyrmum bewunden, witum gebunden*; and in lines 59-60, the rime reinforces antithesis: *Ne wolde þæt wuldres dema geðafian, þrymmes hyrde, ac he him þæs ðinges gestyrde.* The clearest evidence that rime was accepted as a form of poetic ornament is found in well-known passages like *Elene* 1236-50, in which Cynewulf used six sure rimes (*fus—hus, þreodude—reodode, nearwe—gearwe, asæled—gewæled, onband—onwand, onleac—breac*), four irregular rimes (*riht—geþeaht, miht—þeaht, onwreah—fah, amæt—begeat*), four assonances (*wæf—læs, gebunden—beþrungen, onlag—had, ontynde—gerymde*), and possibly one mere inflectional rime (*geoce—unscynde*).[21] In lines 1237, 1238, 1243, 1244, and 1249, the rimes or assonances link syntactic units with parallel structure. There are other rimed poetic passages, shorter than this one but almost as obvious: *Elene* 114-15, *Phoenix* 15-17 and 53-55, *Guðlac* 829-30, *Gnomic Verses* (Exeter) 120-21, etc. A Latin proverb with English translation, which appears at the end of Ælfric's own grammar and glossary in MS. Cotton Faustina A. 10,[22] shows that at least one Anglo-Saxon versifier of Ælfric's century was able to render rimed Latin in rimed Old English:

Ardor frigescit,	nitor squalescit,
amor abolescit,	lux obtenebrescit.
Hat acolað,	hwit asolað,
leof alaðaþ,	leoht aðystrað.

Mrs. Lipp observes the "careful architectural structuring" of Ælfric's sentences (p. 694).[23] This is, indeed, a notable feature

---

[21] The irregular rimes become much more regular when transposed back into the Mercian dialect of Cynewulf's period.

[22] E. V. K. Dobbie, ed., *The Anglo-Saxon Minor Poems*, The Anglo-Saxon Poetic Records, VI (Columbia U. Press, 1942), p. 109.

[23] This, as well as rime and wordplay, she places among the features which appear only occasionally in Ælfric or are typical in a general way of his style, rather than with those features which appear rather constantly, i.e., division into lines and half-lines, use of structural alliteration.

of Ælfric's style in all of his works, metrical and non-metrical, although it seems to me no more remarkable than the precision with which the *Beowulf*-poet knits together his complicated sets of phrases and clauses. In general, careful structure seems to me at least as characteristic of the best Anglo-Saxon poets as it is of the best prose writers. It is the use of balance and antithesis, especially balanced structure combined with antithesis, rather than sentence structure in general, which Mrs. Lipp emphasizes in her treatment of the vernacular specimens from Ælfric; and it is the same balance combined with antithesis which Gerould, Bethurum, and Pope have emphasized when discussing Ælfric's debt to Latin prose.

One notices, however, that Ælfric's rhetoric in the vernacular is very subdued in comparison with that of the writers whom he might have imitated. First, let us look at the latter part of a passage from Sulpicius Severus quoted by Gerould (p. 358).

> Illos confusis plausibus populorum honoret insania.
> Martino diuinis plauditur psalmis,
> Martinus hymnis caelestibus honoratur.
> Illi post triumpos suos in tartara saeua trudentur.
> Martinus Abrahae sinu laetus excipitur,
> Martinus pauper et modicus caelum diues ingreditur.

Compare this with the lines from Ælfric's *Life of St. Edmund* which Mrs. Lipp quotes as an example of Ælfrician balance and antithesis (p. 694).

> þæt he nolde abugan   to bysmorfullum leahtrum,
> ne on naþre healfe   he ne ahylde his þeawas,
> ac wæs symble gemyndig   þære soþan lare.

Surely Ælfric could have made his antithesis more Sulpician had he been truly interested in antithesis for its own sake. He contrasts the ideas clearly, but simply and without fanfare. His lines have balance, but it is the balance of ideas alone rather than of idea plus grammatical structure. Another example is quoted by Pope from another of Ælfric's alliterative works: *lufian ealle menn, and nænne hatian* (p. 133). This one shows formal as well as semantic balance, but how tame is the antithesis! I suspect that the abbot could have composed lines like these without ever having heard of the Latin rhetoricians. There are long stretches in his *Lives* and other alliterative works which do not afford an example

of antithesis emphasized by balance even as strong as these two.[24]
The poetry of the Anglo-Saxons affords instances of antithesis
with balance at least as striking as any of Ælfric's; for example,
the well-known passage from *Beowulf* (183-88), arranged here to
emphasize the balanced structure:[25]

Wa bið þæm ðe sceal þurh sliðne nið sawle bescufan
  in fyres fæþm,   frofre ne wenan, wihte gewendan.
Wel bið þæm þe mot   æfter deaðdæge   Drihten secean
  ond in Fæder fæþmum   freoðo wilnian.

Another example appears in *Riddle 40*, 74, 76:[26]

hefigre ic eom micle   þonne se hara stan . . .
leohtre ic eom micle   þonne þes lytle wyrm . . .

I shall offer only a few further examples from the poetry: from
Beowulf, the *Seafarer*, *Elene*, *Guðlac I*, the *Fates of Men* (or *For-
tunes of Men* or *Be Manna Wyrdum*), *Gnomic Verses* (Exeter),
the *Wanderer*, and the *Dream of the Rood*. These are a fairly representative selection, some with grammatical balance, some with
balance of ideas only, some with the antithesis expressed by *ne*
. . . *ac* or the like, some with the contrasted expressions merely
juxtaposed.

Ne weox he him to willan   ac to wælfealle
ond to deaðcwalum   Deniga leodum.   (*Beo.* 1711-12)
Dol biþ se þe him his dryhten ne ondrædeþ;
cymeð him se deað unþinged.
Eadig bið se þe eaþmod leofaþ;
cymeð him seo ar of heofonum.   (*Sea.* 106-07)
Is his rice brad
ofer middangeard.   Min is geswiðred,
ræd under roderum.   (*Ele.* 916-18)
No hy hine to deaðe   deman moston,
synna hyrdas,   ac seo sawul bad
in lichoman   leofran tide.   (*Guð.* 549-51)
Sumum eadwelan.   sumum earfeða dæl,
sumum geogoþe glæd,   sumum guþe blæd.   (*Fat.* 67-68)
Metod sceal in wuldre,   mon sceal on eorþan.
Laþ se þe londes monað,   leof se þe mare beodeð.   (*Gno.* 7, 59)
Waraðhine wræclast,   nalæs wunden gold,
ferðloca freorig,   nales foldan blæd.   (*Wan.* 32-33)

---

[24] I should mention *swelte ic, lybbe ic* in the *Life of St. Edmund* 83b. The
passage from Ælfric's translation of St. Basil's *Hexameron* quoted by Clemoes,
pp. 176 and 203, shows skillful use of parallel structure and sounds more like
the Latin rhetoricians than either of the examples above; however. Clemoes
correctly labels the contrastive structures "paradoxes" rather than antitheses.

[25] This has been attributed to Latin influence. I do not care to argue the
point at this time, since the presence of the lines in an OE poem is all that
is relevant here.

[26] The example is a free paraphrase of two lines in Aldhelm's *De Creatura*.
The OE has more precise grammatical balance than the original.

Hwilum hit wæs mid wætan bestemed . . .
hwilum mid since gegyrwed. (*Dre.* 22-23)

I submit that among the Anglo-Saxons balance and antithesis could not have been regarded as exclusively, or even predominantly, prose features. Ælfric could as easily have had his inspiration from the older vernacular poetry as from Latin prose.

Wordplay of the flamboyant kind which delighted many of the Church Fathers is also hard to find in Ælfric's alliterative works. There is nothing comparable to Augustine's *miserius, misero, miserante* in a single clause, or to his pun on *error* "wandering" and *error* "sin," both in one chapter of the *Confessions* (*Lib.* II, *cap.* 13). Pope quotes a passage in which the related words *gesceop* and *gesceafta* are juxtaposed and another in which *Ælmihtig* seems to be punningly etymologized as *mæg eal* (p. 110). Elsewhere (pp. 131-32), he quotes a number of examples of repetition, wordplay, and punning, of which the following are typical:

Heo spræc *ongean* God and *ongean* Moysen.
Matheus se *godspellere* us sæde on ðysum *godspelle.*
For þan ðe we *rædaþ* ðas *rædinge* foroft.
Good (good) is þæs lichoman wæcce, þe for *Gode* (God) bið gefremod.

Mrs. Lipp (p. 692) quotes a four-line passage in which *þridda* and *þrynnysse* occur in one line, *froforgast* and *frefrað* in another, and *gife* and *forgyfð* in the second and fourth lines respectively. Some of these examples could be unintentional; others look like deliberate wordplay. In any case, the wordplay is restrained, and the instances are widely scattered in Ælfric's works. A more striking example appears in the passage quoted by Clemoes (see above):

And se wæs *hafenleas* for us,   se þe *hæfð* ealle þing,
þæt he us *gewelgode*   on his eceum *welum.*

Once more, we are dealing with a feature which is not confined to prose in Old English, as a few examples from the poets will show.

þæt he þonne wile *demam,*   se ah *domes* geweald. (*Dre.* 107)

þurh agne *gecynd* eft *acende.* (*Phoenix* 256)

sceop and scyrede   ond *gesceapo* ferede. (*Fat.* 95)

Til mon *tiles*   ond tomes meares.
þing sceal gehegan   *frod* wiþ *frodne.* (*Gno.* 141, 18-19)

spowende sped   spreca ond dæda. (*Guð.* 254)

Halig is se *halga,*   heahengla god. (*Ele.* 750)

grimme wið god gesomnod;   him þæs *grim* lean becom.
hehsta heofones wealdend wearp hine of þan *hean* stole. (*Genesis* 46, 300)

sceþþendum sceaþan   þonne þinum scyppende.   (*Christ* 1395)

Most of these examples of wordplay are tame in comparison with the sort that one finds in Ælfric's Latin sources, but they are comparable to the specimens to be seen in Ælfric's alliterative works. Here are a few probable puns from Old English poetry:

scyldum (sinfully) sceððan,   ac *gescylded* (shielded) a.   (*Pho.* 180)

god (good) bið genge,   ond wiþ *god* (God) lenge.
wif sceal wiþ *wer* (man)   *wære* (faith) healdan.   (*Gno.* 120, 100)

þurh morðres *man* (crime) *mannum* (from men).
geara (of years) gongum.   Ge þæt *geare* (readily) cunnon.
                                        (*Ele.* 626, 648)

men (men) on mode   þonne man (evil) hwæt.   (*Christ* 1600)[27]

In short, none of the stylistic features which have been used to link Ælfric's alliterative works with the Latin prose tradition can be regarded as a valid criterion for differentiating Old English prose from Old English poetry. The stylistic differences, apart from meter, between the prose and the poetry are in need of further study. As soon as someone brings forward better criteria than we now have, I shall be glad to reconsider the views expressed here.

Much has been made of the features of alliterative poetry in which Ælfric's metrical works are deficient. The list is impressive and, so long as we insist upon *Beowulf* as the norm, incontrovertible. (1) Ælfric's alliteration is irregular. (2) He uses too many unstressed words (articles, prepositions, copulas, etc.), which rob his lines of the compactness of the traditional Old English poetry. (3) He occasionally overloads a half-line, so that it seems to have more than two stresses or beats. (4) He lacks certain features of diction and style (kennings, epithets, poetic variation, poetic compounds) which are characteristic of the traditional poetry. (5) He lacks the emotional fire of some of the traditional poets. Coming straight from *Beowulf*, we cannot but be impressed

---

[27] Since this article was written, I have seen Roberta Frank's "Some Uses of Paronomasia in Old English Scriptural Verse," *Speculum*, 47 (1972), 207-26, to which I refer the reader for many additional examples. I wish to call special attention to the abundant examples of *God—gōd, man—mān, māga—mǣgð*, and *ēðel—æðeling* (pp. 214, 220-21); to the etymological wordplays on *wyrd—weorðan, dōm—gedēman, nama—nemnan, mihtig—Ælmihtig*, and *wig—wiga* (pp. 214, 219, 222, 225); and to the clear puns on *bēot* (it beat)—*bēot* (danger) in *Daniel* 264, on *æþele—ēðel* in *Aldhelm* 3-4, on *wlite—wlītan* in *Gen.* 1825, and on *trēo—trēow* in *Gno.* 159.

by these differences. We see Ælfric as either a very inept poet or no poet at all.

We may have been too narrow in our comparisons. There are many alliterative works which differ from the traditional Old English poetry in some respects, but which are nevertheless regarded as poems, some of them even as great poems.[28] There are also works in the traditional style which fall far short of the standards of *Beowulf* and yet are generally conceded to be poems. For purposes of close comparison, I have chosen lines 51-150 of Ælfric's *Life of St. Edmund*;[29] lines 51-150 of Laʒamon's *Brut*, about two centuries later than Ælfric and a representative of the later tradition;[30] and all 82 lines of *An Exhortation to Christian Living*, roughly contemporary with Ælfric and written in the traditional style.[31] I do not disregard the work of scholars who have studied these poems as wholes nor the work of J. P. Oakden, who has taken the entire alliterative tradition in Middle English as his province.[32] My little study cannot compete with their analyses in completeness, but it has the advantage of permitting manageable portions of three works to be studied by the same person with one set of methods and criteria for all.

The alliteration of Edm. is thinly spread in comparison with that of *Beowulf*, which has two alliterating syllables in the *a*-half of about half its lines. In Edm. only 15 of the 100 *a*-halves are like *þæt ic on feohte feolle* (66a). In Brt. also there are just 15 such *a*-halves, and in Exh. 14 (i.e. about 17 percent).[33] If closeness to the Old English classical tradition is to be our only criterion, all three

---

[28] For example, J. P. Oakden says of Laʒamon's *Brut*: "here is great poetry born of a vivid imagination and written for its own sake" in *Alliterative Poetry in Middle English*, II: *A Survey of the Traditions* (Manchester, 1935), p. 20.

[29] Skeat, *Lives*, II, 318-24. (Abbreviated Edm.)

[30] Caligula version in G. L. Brook and R. F. Leslie, eds., *Laʒamon: Brut*, EETS, No. 250 (Oxford U. Press, 1963), I, 4-8. (Brt.) (I have also analyzed lines 51-150 of the Prologue to *Piers Plowman B*, which a number of critics regard as one of the great alliterative poems. Evidence from *PPl. B* might, however, be challenged as irrelevant to this discussion because of its lateness.)

[31] Dobbie, *Minor Poems*, pp. 67-69. (Exh.) I agree with McIntosh (*op. cit.*, pp. 110-111) that, whatever we may decide to call Ælfric's metrical works, they do not belong in the same category as the "debased" poetry in late Old English; e.g., the poem on the death of Prince Alfred in the *Chronicle*. Exh. has its faults but is still recognizably traditional.

[32] *Alliterative Poetry in Middle English*, I. *The Dialectal and Metrical Survey* (Manchester, 1930).

[33] The *PPl. B* passage might be condemned for excessive alliteration, for it shows double alliteration in 79 of the *a*-halves, plus triple alliteration in some others. It has 2 examples of cross alliteration, none of the embraced.

must be judged inferior, perhaps non-poems. Edm. has 4 examples
of cross alliteration (e.g., *bedde wurdon . . . bearnum . . . wifum*,
76); Brt. only 2; and Exh. 5 (about 6 percent of the lines). In
Edm. there are 8 instances of embraced alliteration (e.g., *gewende
. . . ærend- . . . ardlice aweg*, 94); in Brt. 5; and in Exh. 1 (about
1.2 percent). Judged by their richness in these two types of ornament, the three passages are to be ranked: Edm., Exh., Brt.

The faults in Ælfric's alliteration are of seven types: (1) three
alliterations in the *a*-half of the line, (2) two alliterations in the
b-half, (3) alliteration on the second beat only of the *b*-half, (4)
alliteration falling on an unstressed syllable, (5) the half-line alliterating only within itself, (6) non-traditional alliteration of
consonant clusters, and (7) lack of any alliteration in a line. Although Ælfric is sometimes guilty of the first fault, no instance
occurs in the 100-line passage, nor is there any example in Brt. or
Exh.[34] The second fault appears 3 times in Edm., e.g., *þæt heafod
mid him* (139b); 5 times in Brt.; twice in Exh. (about 2.5 percent). Alliteration on the second beat only of the *b*-half is limited
to 3 occurrences in Edm., e.g., *ofslagen þurh eow gif hit swa god
fore-sceawað* (89).[35] There are 16 examples in Brt., none in Exh.[36]

It is often hard to be certain whether a line in one of the later
alliterative poems has alliteration on a weak syllable or whether it
lacks alliteration altogether. In several instances, I must admit
that I am guessing; but my guesswork in all three passages is based
upon the same kinds of objective hints and the same kinds of subjective impressions. Edm. 60b is a clear example, in which *cwæþ*
obviously carries the alliteration, while the beats are obviously on
ræd and *þuh-*.[37] A less certain example is 110b: *and hine eft
swuncgon*, with alliteration, if any, on *hine*. In 142a, *eodon* alliterates, but its alliteration is not necessary to the poetic structure
of the line. There are 6 other lines like these: 57, 68, 84, 90, 103,
and 150.[38] There are 12 lines of this sort in Brt.: 56, 66, 68, 82,
104, 108, 112, 115, 118, 135, 137, and 147. In Exh. there are only

---

[34] The *PPl. B. passage* has 7 *a*-halves like *And leue þe lede þi londe* (126a).
[35] I am assuming that *swa* has purely accidental alliteration. For the alliteration of *sc* with *s*, see below.
[36] There are 2 in the *PPl. B* passage, and 8 examples of double alliteration
in the *b*-half.
[37] This could be considered a three-stress half-line, but cf. *Beowulf* 199b.
[38] In 71, 83, 115, 116, and 139, normally unstressed words alliterate, but
they probably have stress in these lines because of the word order; e.g., in 71,
butan is the first word in an A-type having only one strong syllable.

3 lines with alliteration on unstressed syllables: 25, 33, and 46.[39]

Ælfric occasionally has a half-line containing alliteration within itself but not linked by alliteration to the other half of the line. No instance of this fault occurs in the passage. In Brt. there are 4 half-lines like *þer þa sea wasceð þat sond* (63b), 106b, 126b, and 128b; in Exh., only line 12, a single half-line with vocalic alliteration, and 11b, if we assume false analysis of *adwæscan*.[40] The sixth fault, non-traditional alliteration of consonant clusters, appears 3 times in Edm. (*sc* alliterating with *s*, 89, 117, 138); twice in Brt. (*sc* with *s*, 52, 129); not at all in Exh.[41] In my opinion, 2 lines of Edm. lack alliteration, 140 and 143. The repetition of *wæs*, stressed in both halves of 140, can be regarded as a substitute for alliteration, but it is not alliteration. The alliteration of *ge*-with unstressed *geond* in 143 is sheer accident, and I cannot accept the supposed "lisping" alliteration (*secende—þyfelas*). There are 5 non-alliterating lines in Brt.: 113, 117, 122, 136, and 140. Line 123 is incomplete. Two lines have assonance, 113 and 140, but neither rime nor assonance can substitute for alliteration in the traditional Old English poetry. Exh. has 4 lines without alliteration (4.9 percent): 2, 9, 56, and 66; while 39 and 67 are incomplete.[42]

A tabulation of the seven deadly faults will show how Ælfric compares with two accepted alliterative poets.

	1	2	3	4	5	6	7	Total % of violations.[43]
Edm.	0	3	3	9	0	3	2	20
Brt.	0	5	16	12	4	2	5	44
Exh.	0	2.5	0	3.6	2.5	0	4.9	13.5

We have two choices here: we may say that Laȝamon was a worse poetaster than Ælfric, perhaps call his work some kind of prose, or we may allow him to be a poet who followed rules of alliteration which were more relaxed than Ælfric's already relaxed rules. I prefer the latter course, not because it saves Laȝamon's literary

---

[39] It is hard to be certain in some cases, but there would seem to be 17 in the *PPl.* B passage.

[40] There are 7 in the *PPl.* B passage.

[41] In the *PPl.* B passage, 5 examples of *s* (or *c*) alliterating with *sh*, *sp*, or *st*.

[42] There is only 1 such line in the *PPl.* B passage, i.e. 103, which has *vertues* in each half, and 1 example of *f* alliterating with *v*.

[43] The totals are not intended to be taken too seriously, for the violations are not all of comparable magnitude; e.g., one line absolutely lacking in alliteration should probably weigh more heavily than several with non-traditional alliteration. (The 100-line passage from *PPl.* B shows similar results; i.e., *1*, 7; *2*, 8; *3*, 2; *4*, 17; *5*, 7; *6*, 6; *7*, 1; total % of violations, 47.)

reputation, but because it may force us to stop talking vaguely about the breakdown of the alliterative tradition and begin trying to understand what the new rules were.

Proceeding to the second stricture upon Ælfric's meter, his excessive use of unstressed syllables, we may observe that the 100 lines of Edm. contain 1343 syllables—in the spelling. In arriving at that number, I did not take into account any possible elisions or syncopations. There were, of course, fewer pronounced syllables than the spellings would indicate, but in specific cases i felt much too uncertain to assert my opinion. Of the 200 half-lines, 1 has four syllables, 27 have five, 63 have six, 60 have seven, 37 have eight, 10 have nine, and 2 have ten. The median is 7, the average 6.7, and the range 4—10. There are 1446 spelling syllables in Brt. Again, I am sure that there were elisions and syncopations not reflected by the spelling, but I counted as though they did not exist. On the basis of an uneasy compromise between Wace's probable pronunciations and Laȝamon's alliterations, rimes, and apparent rhythms, I have treated the difficult foreign names as follows: dissyllabic, *Lingoe, Troie, Tyure*; trisyllabic, *Creusa, Eneas* (? accented on the first syllable, 68, 103), *Lauine, Priames;* and tetrasyllabic, *Asscanius* (? alliterating on *c,* 104, 121), *Italiȝe, Lauinion.* Of the 199 complete half-lines, 3 have four syllables, 18 have five, 44 have six, 62 have seven, 33 have eight, 19 have nine, 14 have ten, 3 have eleven, 2 have twelve, and 1 has fourteen. The median is 7, the average 7.26, the range 4—14.[44] The 161 complete half-lines of Exh. contain 855 syllables. Two half-lines have only three syllables (defective as Old English alliterative verse), 37 have four, 63 have five, 36 have six, 17 have seven, 3 have eight, and 3 have nine. The median is 5, the average about 5.3, the range 3—9.

In compactness, the three passages would be ranked thus: Exh., Edm., Brt.

In the matter of overloaded half-lines, Ælfric is an occasional offender, as is each of the other authors. I find 5 half-lines of this sort in Edm., 23 in Brt.,[45] and 1 in Exh.[46] Nearly all of these

---

[44] The syllable count for the *PPl. B* passage is higher than that for Ælfric, lower than that for Laȝamon.

[45] I.e., 55a, 55b, 60a, 63a, 65a, 86a, 88a, 95a, 96a, 97b, 99a, 100a, 106a, 106b, 107b, 110a, 111a, 126b, 127a, 128a, 128b, 142a, 150a. Although overloaded, all of these are scannable with the possible exception of 97b.

[46] In the *PPl. B* passage, the following half-lines are overloaded: 51b, 62a, 67a, 72a, 81a, 83a, 109a, 122b, 125a, 126a, 152a.

half-lines can be scanned by the Sievers system;[47] but, in a number of cases, only if some of the rules are relaxed. Because of changes in English syntax, the poets probably learned to tolerate more and longer anacruses, longer theses in all types of half-lines, more than two syllables in the second thesis of a B-type, two or more extra syllables in the first foot of a D-type or an E-type, perhaps even a two-syllable final thesis in an A-type or a C-type. As the ancient poetic compounds became less intelligible, the poets used them less frequently but, at the same time, learned to treat some set phrases and frequent combinations as though they were compounds.[48] It is probable, also, that the poets became less careful about excluding important words from theses and anacruses. If the rules are modified to allow for such natural changes as these, one can scan all of the 12 half-lines below, but all of them can also be read as three- or four-stress half-lines. Structural alliterations and rimes or assonances are indicated by italics. In scanning Brt., I have assumed the usual lengthenings and shortenings of early Middle English vowels, excepting only lengthening in the open syllable. These examples will show how Ælfric compares with the other two poets.

80b: and se *ǽ*lmihtiga *g*ód wát—❘ xx) $\acute{}$ xxx $\acute{}$ / $\acute{}$ (E).
91a: ne abíhð nǽfre *eá*dmund—❘ xxx) $\acute{}$ x / $\acute{}$ x (A).
99b: *é*alle *ǽ*pan scéoldon—❘ $\acute{}$ x / $\acute{}$ x $\acute{}$ x (D).
109a: to anum éorðfǽstum *tr*éowe—❘ xxx) $\acute{}$ xx / $\acute{}$ x (A).
142a: Hi *e*odon þá sécende *é*alle—❘ xxxx) $\acute{}$ xx / $\acute{}$ x (A).

Brt.

55b: þar Róme nóu ón stóndeð—❘ xxxx $\acute{}$ / $\acute{}$ x (C).
100a: æfter þa *f*éourðe ʒére he was déad—❘ xxx $\acute{}$ / xxxxx $\acute{}$ (B).
106b: ah heo néfden noht áne *m*óder—❘ xx) $\acute{}$ xxxx / $\acute{}$ x (A).
110a: Asscánius héold þis *dr*ihliche lónd—❘ x) $\acute{}$ xxxx / $\acute{}$ xx $\acute{}$ (D).
128a: þis child hefde his *é*ames nóme—❘ x) $\acute{}$ xxx / $\acute{}$ x $\acute{}$ x (D).
142a: þat þeo wimon was mid ane súne—❘ xx $\acute{}$ / xxxxx $\acute{}$ x (B).

Exh.

74b: þu scealt glǽdlice *sw*íðe *sw*incan—❘ xxxxx) $\acute{}$ x / $\acute{}$ x (A).

My suggested scansions are a crude, tentative performance, which could be vastly improved upon by anyone who would analyze

---

[47] The system which I use is actually a simplification of the original, rather cumbersome, Sievers system; the nearest thing to it in print is the section on meter in J. R. Hulbert, *Bright's Anglo-Saxon Reader* (New York, 1935), pp. 229-40. I am less at home with other systems, but I believe that the half-lines in question are also scannable by the systems of J. C. Pope, Robert Creed, A. J. Bliss, and Andreas Heusler.

[48] This idea is only partly my own. For much of the theoretical basis and many practical applications of the idea, see James A. Eby's dissertation, *The Alliterative Meter of Piers Plowman A* (U. of Michigan, 1971).

the *Lives of Saints* or the *Brut* with the thoroughness which they deserve. My main purpose was to demonstrate that Ælfric fares at least as well under the Sievers system as does the later representative of the alliterative tradition. A secondary purpose was to suggest that, when the later poetry does not conform in every detail to older standards, we need not give it up as hopelessly amorphous and undisciplined; it might be more profitable to look for the new forms and disciplines which I am convinced are there. I have passed over some uncertainties, therefore, indicating only one scansion for several half-lines which admit of two or more possibilities (at least in the present state of *my* knowledge) and leaving the reasons for my decisions unstated. A few points should be made, however, with regard to probable changes in the alliterative style which are illustrated by the examples. By Ælfric's time, *ælmihtiga god* almost certainly had the stress pattern of a compound, at least part of the time.[49] Similarly *feourðe ʒere, drihliche lond,* and perhaps *eames nome,* may have been treated as compounds. *Anum* in Edm. 109b is no longer a numeral (stressed) but has become an article (unstressed). The same is true of *ane* in Brt. 142a, but *ane* in Brt. 106b seems to be a stressed "one." By the rules of the earlier Old English poetry, *on* in Brt. 55b has an obvious major stress, but Laʒamon may have preferred to treat *onstondeð* as a prefixed form, in which case *on-* would be unstressed.

The fourth non-poetic feature of Ælfric's alliterative works is thought to be their lack of the traditional poetic diction. There are no kennings in the 100-line passage from *St. Edmund,* nor do we find any in Exh. or Brt. None of the passages contains any epithet of the traditional type; *Asscanius þe kene* (Brt. 121) is of a different kind, more closely related to the Homeric epithets.[50] The Old English poetic variation is rare in all three passages. Edm. has two examples of what Claes Schaar calls "close variation,"[51] the type most characteristic of the traditional poetry: *hingware . . . hæþenum here-togan* (91b, 92a) and *hingwar, se arlease flot-man* (119). In the first example, the variation carries over from the *b*-half to the next *a*-half—a traditional feature. A

---

[49] Cf. *Guðlac* 242a: *An is ælmihtig god.*

[50] For a comparison of the two types, see Ann Chalmers Watts, *The Lyre and the Harp* (Yale U. Press, 1969), pp. 100-17; esp. pp. 101-02.

[51] *Critical Studies in the Cynewulf Group* (Lund, 1949), pp. 184 ff.

fair example of Schaar's "loose variation" (but one which, minus meter and alliteration, would not be inappropriate in a vigorous prose narrative) appears in lines 142-43: *Hi eodon þa secende ealle, endemes to þam wuda, secende gehwær geond þyfelas and bremelas.* There are four possible examples of loose variation in Brt., although the first three could have been conceived outside the alliterative tradition and may not have been intended as poetic variation at all: *wið Eneam he nom an feiht . . . hond wið honde fuhten þa heʒe men* (88-89), *His moder . . . Eneas . . . forleas inne þane fehte; his feon heo him binomen* (107-09), *þa luuede he a maid . . . mid darnscipe he heo luuede* (130b, 131b), *þat boa sculde fallen fader & his moder, þorh him heo sculden deiʒen & þene deað þolien* (143-44). Exh. contains four close variations which are technically superior to any presented above: *wuldres god, ece ælmihtigne* (28b, 29a), *heofena drihten . . . milde mundbora* (50a, 51a), *læne stapelas, eard and eþel* (59a, 60b), and *lifes . . . eardes on eþle* (62b, 63a).[52]

One clearly identifiable poetic compound appears in Edm., *flothere* (130), which occurs, as far as I can discover, only here and in *Beowulf* 2915. One compound, *eorð-fæstum* (109), I have found only here and in Ælfric's metrical *De Auguriis* 130; perhaps this was a poetic word to Ælfric's contemporaries. The remaining compounds occur elsewhere in prose texts or in both poetry and prose. Of the compounds of Old English origin in Brt., only one belongs to the poetic vocabulary of both Old and Middle English, *drihtfolcke* (57).[53] One quasi-compound, really a suffixed form, was used in both prose and poetry in Old English but is not found outside the *Brut* in Middle English, *drihlice* (OE *dryhtlic*) 75. This may have become a poetic word by Laʒamon's time. Of the compounds unattested in Old English, one is confined to poetry in Middle English, *dweomerlakes* (137). Four others are peculiar to the *Brut* and are classified as poetic by Oakden: *kiʒe-lond* (93), *luf-þing* (86), *wen-siðes* (53), and *wiðer-craftes* (138). We are on shaky ground here, of course: if the critics should decide that the *Brut*, because of its irregular alliteration, etc., is "alliterative prose," all words peculiar to Laʒamon would instantly become

---

[52] *Heremites on an hepe . . . Grete lobyes and longe* (*PPl. B* prol. 53a, 55a) is at least akin to poetic variation.
[53] My remarks on Brt. owe a great deal to Oakden's *Allit. Poetry in ME*, Part II, pp. 134-65.

prose words. I have a subjective impression that the *Brut* contains many compounds which look and sound like the poetic compounds of the Old English traditional verse, and that in this respect Laӡamon is closer to the tradition than Ælfric. Exh. contains three compounds which seem to have been confined to poetry in Old English: *eard-wic* (78), *eþel-rices* (75), and *hilde-rinc* (57). All other compounds in the piece occur in prose, and the following compounds and quasi-compounds are confined to prose except for the occurrences in Exh.: *ælmes-sylen* (14), *cyric-socnum* (48), *dyrne-geligere* (44), *forhæfdnessum* (47), *hwilwendan* (5), and *oferfylle* (77).[54]

For quick comparison, the tabulation below summarizes the traditional features of poetic diction in the three passages. Numbers in parentheses indicate the dubious examples.

	Edm.	Brt.	Exh.
Kennings	0	0	0
Epithets	0	0 (1)	0
Variations	2 (1)	1 (3)	4
Compounds	1 (1)	2 (5)	3

The fifth and last of the criticisms which, to my knowledge, have been leveled at Ælfric the poet is that he lacks poetic fire, the capacity to stir our feelings strongly or deeply. This charge may not be unfounded. Speaking subjectively and emotionally, I may say that the *Lives of Saints* has never stirred me as *Beowulf* has and does. I find some of the legends very interesting as Ælfric tells them—but not exciting. Nevertheless, I hold that Ælfric possesses enough of the divine spark to justify our regarding him as a poet. One cannot refute a subjective criticism with evidence, but one may undermine it, perhaps, with an illustration. Let the reader decide for himself whether the first passage below is more inspired than the second.

```
Warna þe georne        wið þære wambe fylle,
forþan heo þa unþeawas        ealle gesomnað
þe þære saule        swiðost deriað;
þæt is, druncennes        and dyrnegeligere,
ungemet wilnung        ætes and slæpes;
þa man mæg        mid fæstenum
and forhæfdnessum        heonon adrifan,
```

---

54 *Kyngriche* (cf. OE *cynerice* and late OE *kynyngriche*) in *PPl. B* is not a poetic word in OE or early ME, but it almost never occurs outside of poetry after about the middle of the 14th century.

and mid cyricsocnum cealdum wederum[55]
eadmodlice   ealluncga biddan
heofena Drihten   þæt he þe hæl gife,
milde mundbora,   swa him gemet þince.
Exhortation 41-51.

þa geseah Hingwar,   se arlease flot-man,
þæt se æþela cyning   nolde Criste wið-sacan,
ac mid anrædum geleafan   hine æfre clypode,
het hine þa beheafdian,   and þa hæðenan swa dydon.
Betwux þam þe he clypode   to Criste þa git,
þa tugon þa hæþenan   þone halgan to slæge,
and mid anum swencge   slogon him of þæt heafod;
and his sawl siþode   gesælig to Criste.
St. Edmund 119-126.

If we decide to call Ælfric's alliterative compositions poetry, what are the consequences beyond a change in nomenclature? First, we are under no real compulsion to think of Ælfric as a poetaster. His works are different from the traditional alliterative poetry but not necessarily inferior. Technically, we have seen that his work is at least equal to later writings which everyone recognizes as poetry. In the matter of poetic inspiration, I suspect that many will judge him superior to some poets (like the author of the *Exhortation*) whose techniques are closer than his to the older tradition. Second, we shall still see Ælfric as an innovator, as the originator of a new poetry[56] rather than a new prose in English. He composed, not for the warrior aristocracy and the learned elite, who could best appreciate *Beowulf* and the poems of Cynewulf, but for the cross section of Anglo-Saxon society which might be expected at church on an average Sunday. The finest of the poems in the older tradition, however edifying they might be at times, were intended primarily to give pleasure; Ælfric's were intended primarily to instruct, only secondarily to entertain. The language of the older poems was very archaic by the eleventh century, although poetry could still be composed in it. Ælfric's language was much closer to the common speech of his day. With his own audience, his own purposes, and his own English in mind, Ælfric invented, or popularized, a new kind of poetry. Third, although it has been said that his rhythmic prose had no imitators, we shall see that, as a poetic innovator, he had many and distin-

---

[55] I interpret this line "and by church attendances in cold weather."

[56] The germ of it may, perhaps, be found in metrical lines which occur sporadically in the homiletic prose of the 9th and 10th centuries; see Otto Funke, "Studien zur alliterierenden und rhythmisierenden Prosa in der älteren altenglischen Homiletik," *Anglia*, 80 (1962), 9-36.

guished followers. Transpose his style into the language of the twelfth century, adapt it to a secular audience and the subject matter of historical romance, allow some French influence in the metrics, and flavor it with Laȝamon's personality; it is the poetry of the *Brut*. All of the later alliterative tradition, although it is a complicated thing with many sources, owes something to Ælfric.

FURTHER THOUGHTS ON *BRAND HEALFDENES*

Sherman M. Kuhn, University of Michigan

Beowulf contains two passages which, to be fully appreciated, must be seen together:

> Forgeaf þa Beowulfe   brand[1] Healfdenes,
> segen glydenne   sigores to leane—
> hroden hiltecumbor,[2]   helm ond byrnan.
> Mære maðþumsweord   manige gesawon
> beforan beorn beran.   (ll. 1020–24)

(*He* gave then to Beowulf the blade of Healfdene, a golden standard as a reward of victory—a decorated staff-banner, a helmet, and a coat of mail. Many looked upon the famous treasure-sword borne before the warrior.)

> Het ða in beran   eafor—heafodsegn,[3]
> heaðosteapne helm,   hare byrnan,
> guðsweord geatolic;—   gyd æfter wræc:
> "Me ðis hildesceorp   Hroðgar sealde,
> snotra fengel," [etc.]   (ll. 2152–56)

(*He* then ordered the boar brought in—the head-banner, the battle-steep helmet, the gray coat of mail, the splendid battle-sword;—afterward *he* uttered a speech: "To me Hroðgar, the wise prince, gave this war-garment," etc.)

My afterthoughts on these passages are concerned with five matters:[4] (1) *bearn* as a substitute for *brand*, (2) unexpressed subjects, (3) repetition with variation and change of emphasis, (4) syntactic structure and punctuation, and (5) the meaning of *brand*.

In my 1943 article (pp. 83–84), I objected to the emendation of MS *brand* to *bearn* as unnecessary (i.e., *brand* makes sense in the context) and implausible (i.e., it violates the principle of *lectio difficilior*). I have since tried in various ways to reconstruct a situation in which a scribe might reasonably mistake *bearn* for *brand*. If we suppose, for example, that some scribe in copying *Beowulf* came upon a metathesized form

---

[1] Sometimes unnecessarily emended to *bearn*.
[2] Unnecessarily emended to *hildecumbor*.
[3] Incorrectly printed *eaforheafodsegn* by some editors.
[4] For my previous thoughts on this subject, see "The Sword of Healfdene," *JEGP*, 42 (1943), 82–95. I shall repeat as little as possible of what I said in that article, hoping the readers will go back to it for a better understanding of the present article.

Reprinted by permission from *Journal of English and Germanic Philology*, 76 (1977), 231-37.

of *bearn,* such as *bran* or *bron,* we might conceive of his mistaking it for a form of *brand* or *brond* lacking the final *-d.* This conjecture is so improbable that I mention it only because it seems to illustrate the futility of such speculations. Old English metathesis of *ra* to *ar,* as in *arn, orn* from earlier **ran,* is well-attested; but the reverse of this, *ar* to *ra,* is too rare to allow of our positing a *bran* or *bron* form of *bearn.* Equally rare is the loss of final *-d* in *brand, brond.*[5] The supposed error, *brand* for *bearn,* will probably never be explained as a simple scribal error.

If we are truly dealing with an error, it can only be of the sort which Eduard Prokosch described as either "a 'slip of the tongue' on the part of a speaker" (if one assumes that *Beowulf* was dictated) or "a mental aberration on the part of a copyist."[6] Although he accepted the emendation, Prokosch has warned us that "this is the most elastic class [of errors], permitting the greatest latitude of emendation." To this, I would add that, as soon as we begin to assume irrational blunders, almost anything goes. No editor should fall back on such explanations except in desperate cases—and probably not even in these. Prokosch suggested that "the speaker's (or writer's?) thought may have strayed ahead to the sword (l. 1023), which was the most precious of the four gifts." But if this is so, why should the absent-minded speaker or the aberrant scribe have chosen so unusual a synonym as *brand?* Why not *sweord, mece, bil*—something commoner that would come to mind without extensive cogitation? There is too much method in this madness.

Hertha Marquardt's objection to *bearn* seems to me of questionable validity. She observed that, while *bearn*-formulas (e.g., *bearn Ecgþeowes*) are used of Beowulf and other young warriors, the poet uses different formulas (e.g., *sunu Healfdenes*) for older men and for kings, especially for *Hroðgar* and *Hygelac.* She concluded, from this and some supporting evidence, that *bearn* always implies "young" or "young man" (*jung oder Jüngling*) and that the poet could not have used an expression like *bearn Healfdenes* for the aged king Hroðgar.[7] Two instances, both noted by Marquardt, contradict this argument: *Ongenðioes bearn* (l. 2387), applied to King Onela, who must have been well on in years at the time of the second war of the Geats and Swedes, and *bearn*

[5]Hitherto, I have been unable to find any examples.
[6]"Two Types of Scribal Errors in the *Beowulf* MS," *Studies in English Philology: A Miscellany in Honor of Frederick Klaeber,* ed. Kemp Malone and M. B. Ruud (Minneapolis: Univ. of Minnesota Press, 1929), p. 203.
[7]Hertha Marquardt, "Fürsten- und Kriegerkenning im *Beowulf,*" *Anglia,* 60 (1939), 390–95, esp. pp. 391–93.

Ecgðeowes (l. 2425), used of Beowulf after he had been king for fifty years. Marquardt explained away the first on the ground that the emphasis in the passage is on Beowulf and that Onela is unimportant, a *Nebenperson,* to whose rank and age the poet was indifferent. I cannot read the passage in this way. It is Onela who attacks the Geats, kills Heardred, and then leaves the kingdom to Beowulf. Onela acts and controls the action of others. We cannot even be sure that Beowulf was present; it is more likely that he had retired to his estate when Heardred was old enough to rule the kingdom. The second instance is brushed aside as the mechanical repetition of a familiar formula. But if the poet could forget himself in line 2425, why not in line 1020?

The supposed limitations on the use of *bearn* do not apply outside of *Beowulf.* Byrhtnoð, the *har hilderinc* (*Maldon* 169), whose hoary head was of a "swanlike whiteness" to one early historian,[8] is called *Byrhtelmes bearn* (l. 92). St. Joseph is called *Iacobes bearn* (*Christ* 164)[9] in a lyric obviously based on medieval traditions according to which Mary was a temple virgin (l. 186) and Joseph was an old man when he took her to wife.[10] Ælfwine, that is, Alboin of the Langobards, is *bearn Eadwines* (*Widsith* 74). Alboin's age at the time referred to in the poem is uncertain, but he was unquestionably a king. Although I cannot accept Marquardt's argument, I agree that *bearn* for *brand* is an undesirable emendation.

Three unexpressed subjects have been supplied in my modern rendering of the two *Beowulf* passages—out of respect for modern fashions in syntax. *Forgeaf* (l. 1020), *Het* (l. 2152), and *wræc* (l. 2154) lack expressed subjects because Hroðgar, Beowulf, and Beowulf can be picked up from the contexts. In my article mentioned above, I pointed out that *brand Healfdenes,* which makes a better object than subject, is not needed as subject of *Forgeaf.* I cited eminent authorities (p. 84), especially Alois Pogatscher,[11] and presented supplementary evidence of my own (pp. 85–92). Since 1943, one editor has expressed

---

[8]*Non reminiscens cigneam canitiem sui capitis;* see *Vita Oswaldi Archiepiscopi Eboracensis,* in James Raine, *The Historians of the Church of York and its Archbishops,* 1 (Rolls Series, 71; London, 1879), 456.

[9]Cf. Matthew 1:16.

[10]The traditions stem from early New Testament apocrypha, especially the *Gospel of the Birth of Mary* and the *Protevangelion.* Ælfric, without mentioning Joseph's age, drew upon the same traditions: Benjamin Thorpe, *The Homilies of the Anglo-Saxon Church,* (London: The Ælfric Society, 1844–46), 1, 196.

[11]Alois Pogatscher, "Unausdrücktes Subject im Altenglischen," *Anglia,* 23 (1901), 261–301. Although Pogatscher was dealing with Old English in general, prose and poetry, his examples include many from *Beowulf.* His article clarifies the syntax of *Beowulf* at several points, yet it is not listed in bibliographies of scholarship on *Beowulf,* and some editors seem unaware of its existence.

something which might be construed as skepticism on this point,[12] but without attempting to discredit the authorities or the evidence.

The repetition in the two passages is not verbal, nor is it one-for-one. The concept "sword" occurs three times, differently worded and with different emphasis each time: *brand Healfdenes* (origin), *Mære maðþumsweord* (fame and value), *guðsweord geatolic* (beauty and function). The idea of the banner or standard appears four times with similar variations in wording and emphasis: *segen gyldenne* (amplified by the phrase *sigores to leane*), *hroden hiltecumbor, eafor,*[13] and *heafodsegn*. The helmet occurs as *helm* and, varied and augmented, in *heaðosteapne helm*. The coat of mail appears three times: *byrnan, hare byrnan,* and *hildesceorp*. As far as space and number of repetitions are concerned, the banner or standard seems most emphatic; but the sword and the coat of mail are the items singled out for special praise (after the actual enumerations are complete) in lines 1023–24 and lines 2155–56, respectively. The *Beowulf*-poet apparently preferred not to say the same thing twice in the same way.

He also varied the order in which the gifts are listed: sword, standard, helmet, coat of mail; standard, helmet, coat of mail, sword. J. Hoops's statement that the four gifts are enumerated in identical order in the two passages[14] has already been rebutted.[15] Since 1943, it has occurred to me that a parallel example of the *Beowulf*-poet's practice would strengthen my argument. The last of the four passages on the subject of Hygelac's raid upon Friesland (ll. 2912–21) enumerates the foes of the Geats in greatest detail: *Froncum, Frysum, Hugas, Hetware, Merewioingas,* in that order, that is, "Franks, Frisians, Hugas (perhaps another name for the Franks), the Hetware, and the Merovingian." In lines 1202–14, the poet gives only the first two, in reverse order: *Frysum, Francna,* the other three being de-emphasized. In lines 2501–2508, he mentions only the *Huga cempan* (cf. *Hugas*) and the *Frescyninge* (cf. *Frysum*), and not in the order in which the Frisians and the Hugas appear in the first passage cited. In lines 2354–66, only the Hetware are mentioned, although Frisians are implied in *Freslondum*. The Frisians are mentioned or implied in all four passages; Franks, Hugas, and Hetware, in two each; the Merovingian, in only

---

[12]*Schon dies ließe sich wohl bestreiten!*—Else von Schaubert, *Beowulf*, ii (Paderborn: Ferdinand Schöningh, 1961), 71.

[13]I.e., *eofor* "boar." The function of this variation is that of further describing the appearance of the *segen*. It suggests that the latter was not a "banner" as now generally understood, i.e., a flag. It must have been a boar image attached to a staff, something comparable to the eagles of the Roman legions.

[14]J. Hoops, *Kommentar zum Beowulf* (Heidelberg: Carl Winter, 1932), p. 236.

[15]See my 1943 article, p. 94 and n. 37.

one. The analogy between the two sets of passages is not perfect, but I believe that it is close enough to clinch the argument.

E. V. K. Dobbie objected to my interpretation of *brand Healfdenes* on the ground that "bringing a sword into the picture at this point would make *maðþumsweord,* l. 1023, a rather awkward repetition."[16] This misconception is due, not to anything the poet said, but solely to the tortured syntax and illogical punctuation imposed upon lines 1020–24 by some modern scholars. Sentences of the modern literary type are frequently hard to identify in Old English texts, but the one which ends with *byrnan* is exceptionally easy. The enumeration of gifts is complete with *byrnan,* which should be followed by a full stop. With *Mære maðþumsweord,* a new sentence is launched, one which is concerned, not with all of the gifts, but only with the sword; just as *Me ðis hildesceorp,* and so forth in the second passage concerns only the coat of mail. Once scholars had agreed to emend *brand* to *bearn,* however, there was no longer a sword in the first enumeration. Eduard Sievers suggested placing a colon or semicolon after *maðþumsweord.*[17] Such punctuation would move the sword back into the list of gifts, thus eliminating one problem—while creating two others: *helm ond byrnan, mære maðþumsweord* does not make typical Beowulfian syntax, and *beran* (l. 1024) is left without an object. Verbs with unexpressed objects are permissible in Old English, but it seems very unlikely that a skilled poet would use *beran* as an objectless verb, while at the same time placing *maðþumsweord* where it could easily be taken for the object. Sievers' recommendation was accepted by some editors,[18] although most rejected it. Dobbie rejected the punctuation after *maðþumsweord* but used only a comma after *byrnan,* thus creating an ambiguous construction in which the sword can be both the fourth item of the list and also the object of *beran.* This is not normal Beowulfian syntax. When the lines are correctly punctuated, the awkwardness decried by Dobbie vanishes.

When I wrote the article which was published in 1943, I had not yet seen Hertha Marquardt's "Fürsten- und Kriegerkenning." Upon seeing it, I was impressed with the plausibility of her argument for *brand Healfdenes* as a figure for Hroðgar; I felt that it was really a toss-up whether one accepted her interpretation or mine. I have since

---

[16]E. V. K. Dobbie, *Beowulf and Judith,* Anglo-Saxon Poetic Records, IV (London, for the Columbia University Press, 1954), pp. 167–68.

[17]Eduard Sievers, "Zum *Beowulf,*" *Beiträge zur Geschichte der deutschen Sprache und Literatur,* 9 (1884), 139.

[18]E.g., Ferdinand Holthausen, *Beowulf nebst dem Finnsburg Bruckstück* (Heidelberg: Carl Winter, 1905–1906); W. J. Sedgefield, *Beowulf* (Manchester: The University Press, 1910).

changed my mind. Dobbie's objection to Marquardt's use of *helm* "protector" (e.g., in *helm Scyldinga*, l. 371) as a parallel to *brand Healfdenes*—"since the development of *helm* from 'protection' to 'one who affords protection' is remote from the semantic development which she assumes for *brand*" (p. 167)—seems to be well-taken although it could have been stated in more exact terms. There is a further objection to the analogy. The *Beowulf*-poet uses *helm* in the sense of "protector" only with plural genitives (ll. 182, 371, 456, 1321, 1623, 2381, 2462, 2705), in all instances except one with designations of peoples or tribes. He never uses it with a singular genitive or a personal name (as if he were to say *helm Healfdenes*). Similarly, outside *Beowulf*, the Old English poets use *helm* "protector" rather frequently but only three times with singular genitive (*Daniel* 16, *Christ* 463, 566) and never with the name of an individual person. Negative arguments based on the absence of evidence should not be pushed too far; the *Beowulf*-poet frequently modified established formulaic patterns to suit his own purposes. Nevertheless, in the absence of a single example like *helm Healfdenes*, it seems to me that positing a *brand Healfdenes* designating Hroðgar is unwarranted.[19]

The most recent objection to my interpretation of *brand Healfdenes* as "the sword (or blade) of Healfdene" is, I believe, that of Neil Isaacs.[20] After remarking that my reading "makes perfectly good syntactical and contextual sense," he adds "but there seems little reason to suppose that the poet took his weapon-plus-genitive-of-proper-name formula, which in every extant usage is a figure for a person not mentioned—a hero, chief, or leader—and suddenly used it in the literal sense of the weapon of the expressed person" (p. 126).[21] Unless

---

[19]It is surely an error to label OE *brand* "sword" a borrowing from Old Norse (p. 393). Jan de Vries is also mistaken, in his *Altnordisches etymologisches Wörterbuch* (Leiden: E. J. Brill, 1962), when he attributes OE *brand* in the sense of "sword" or "swordblade" to Old Norse and states that it occurs once in Old English. *Brand* in one or the other of these senses occurs at least four times in Old English: twice in *Beowulf*, once in Ælfric (see Thorpe, *Homilies*, II, 510), and once in the will of Æðelstan Æðeling, a document written in the neighborhood of Winchester about the year 1050 (see Dorothy Whitelock, *Anglo-Saxon Wills* [Cambridge: The University Press, 1930; rpt. New York: AMS Press, 1973], p. 58). In Middle English, the occurrences are much more frequent and are well scattered geographically, most of them outside the area of the former Dane-law; see, for example, the *Middle English Dictionary* and the *New English Dictionary*. The Norse uses of *brandr* "sword" are not extraordinarily numerous, and they appear in Old Icelandic texts of later date than the OE examples; in fact, the OIc. evidence is roughly contemporary with that in Middle English.

[20]Neil Isaacs, "Six *Beowulf* Cruces." *JEGP*, 62 (1963), 119-28.

[21]The *Beowulf*-poet used figurative compounds in the unusual literal senses; see A. G. Brodeur, *The Art of Beowulf* (Berkeley: Univ. of California Press, 1969), p. 37. What the poet could do with a figurative compound, he could undoubtedly do with a figurative phrase.

I have misunderstood this argument, it is refuted by *sweord Biowulfes* (l. 2681). An instance outside *Beowulf* is *Holofernes sweord (Judith* 336–37). The word *lāf* as applied to weapons or armor is not quite the same as a weapon-name, but it may be close enough to have been included in formulaic systems with *sweord* and *brand.* If so, *Hrædlan laf* (l. 454), *Hreðles lafe* (l. 2191), *Eanmundes laf* (l. 2611), and *Ælfheres laf (Waldere* 18) may also be relevant here.

In short, the sword of Healfdene is still as much a part of *Beowulf* as it was a thousand years ago.

[212]

OLD ENGLISH *AGLǢCA* –
MIDDLE IRISH *OCLACH*[1]

1. The word *āglǣca*, variously spelled, occurs unmistakably 34 times in Old English: *Beowulf* 19, *Christ and Satan* 5, *Andreas* 3, *Juliana* 3, *Elene* 1, *Guðlac A* 1, *Phoenix* 1, and *Whale* 1. There are two other probable instances: *Riddle 3*, line 7, and *Riddle 93* 23.[2] In the first of these, *Nah ic hwyrftweges of þam aglaca*, the intended reading was probably *aglacan* (a nasal stroke having been obliterated or perhaps omitted by a scribe), a variation on *min frea* back in line 1. The line should, therefore, be interpreted: 'I have no escape from that ____ (i.e. my Lord).' The suggested emendation is simpler and more plausible palaeographically than the usual emendation to *aglace* 'misery, torment,' and the result is certainly in keeping with the Old English poetic style. In the second instance, *ac ic aglæca ealle þolige*, I agree with Mackie that *aglæca* is in apposition with *ic* and should be construed as the one who 'suffers all' rather than as a genitive plural governed by *ealle*. The addition of these two instances brings the total to 36.

The root *āglǣc-, āglāc-* appears in three compounds: *āclǣc-cræft-um* (*Andreas* 1362), *āglāc-hād-e* (*Riddle 53* 5), and *āglǣc-wīf* (*Beowulf* 1259); and three times as a separate noun: *āglāc* (*Daniel* 237, *Riddle 81* 6)[3] and *ǣglǣc-e* (*Elene* 1187). A derived adjective, *ēglēche*, occurs five times in Middle English: *South English Legendary* (Laud MS) 3, *Proverbs of Alfred* 1, and Robert of Gloucester (B-version) 1.

All instances of these words occur in poetry, none in prose. The Old English examples appear in poems believed to be of Anglian origin, although the surviving copies were made by late West Saxon scribes. In several poems, the dialect relics preserved in the copies point to the Mercian dialect rather than to Northumbrian or to general Anglian, e.g. *Beowulf, Elene, Juliana*. This is especially relevant to the aim of the present article, for the etymology which I propose hinges upon an intermediate Mercian stage in the transmission. The Middle English poems containing *ēglēche* are all either Southwestern or Southwest

Reprinted by permission from *Linguistic Method: Essays in Honor of Herbert Penzl*, ed. Irmengard Rauch and Gerald F. Carr (The Hague: Mouton, 1979), pp. 213-30.

Midland, and their dialects appear to be mixtures derived from Mercian and West Saxon.

The forms show much variation. The first element is most often *āg-*, with presumably a voiced velar spirant /g/: 26 times in *Beowulf, Daniel, Christ and Satan, Juliana, Guðlac A, Phoenix, Whale*, and the riddles. The by-form *æg-* (12 times in *Beowulf, Christ and Satan, Andreas*, and *Elene*) had a raised and fronted vowel due to *i*-umlaut and might be expected to contain a palatalized and assibilated /ġ/, phonetically [j]. The Middle English evidence supports the vowel but not the assibilated consonant, for the latter would have become /i/ in Middle English (spelled *i*, *y*, etc.), and we should find something like **eileche* instead of *egleche*. It is possible that the velar g of the *æg-* forms is due to analogy with the *āg-*forms; but it is more probable that in *æglǣca* the assibilation of *g* was prevented when, through loss of an intervening *i*, the *g* came to be followed immediately by a consonant.[4] The rare variant *āh-* (*Beowulf* 646, 989) can be explained as analogical; cf. the *āh- æg-* in *āhwā-æghwā, āhwǣr-æghwǣr, āhwæðer-æghwæðer, āhwonan-æghwanan*.[5] It is not easy to find a phonetic explanation of the first *c* in *æclǣca* (*Elene* 901) and *āclǣccræft* in the *Andreas*. I am reminded of the Middle Irish *óclach*, in which the first element was spelled *óc-* but pronounced [ōg-]. One might speculate that the two *c*-spellings are survivals from a period when Anglo-Saxons were unsure of the spelling of a borrowed word.[6]

The second element is normally *-lǣc-* (31 times in *Beowulf, Christ and Satan, Andreas ,Juliana, Elena, Guðlac A, Phoenix, Whale*, and the riddles), also *-lǣce-* (*Beowulf* 2520, 2534, 2557, 2592, 2905), *-lēc-* (*Christ and Satan* 712), *-lēc-* (*ibid.* 73), and *-lēch-* (5 Middle English examples). The *c*, as indicated by the Middle English spellings and the five instances of the plural *āglǣcean* in *Beowulf*, was the affricate /ċ/, [tʃ]. There are four instances of the by-form *-lāc-* (*Daniel* 237, *Riddle* 3 7, 53 5, 81 6). These may have contained the phoneme /c/, phonetically [k].

The meanings assigned to *āglǣca* by modern scholars are contextually derived and frequently ad hoc.[7] When the word was used of Grendel or the dragon, Friedrich Klaeber 1950 glossed it 'wretch, monster, demon, fiend,' but 'warrior, hero' when it was used of someone, like Sigemund or Beowulf, who was obviously not covered by 'wretch', etc. C. L. Wrenn 1953 glossed in a similar manner: 'terrible being; monster, fiend; terrifying warrior or hero (of Sigemund) ... terrible beings (of Beowulf and the dragon)'. Else von Schaubert 1961 has 'trefflicher Kämpfer, Held' for Sigemund (line 893) and Beowulf (2592), 'Unhold,

Dämon, Ungeheuer' for all other instances. It would be tedious and unprofitable to catalogue here all of the glosses and renderings used by editors and modernizers of Old English poems; unless the *āglæca* in a particular passage is obviously of high moral character, he will be a 'wretch, a monster, a miserable creature, an evil creature,' or (if in any way supernatural) 'a demon.' R. K. Gordon 1926 was more imaginative than most in his modernizations. He used 'hero' for Sigemund and 'fighters' for Beowulf and the dragon (pp. 22, 58); 'warriors' for the Mermedonians in *Andreas* 1131 and 'magician' for St. Andrew in 1359 (pp. 221, 226); and 'creature' for the beast in *Whale* 52 (p. 283). In *Elene* 1187, he rendered *æglæce* 'warriors,' a good rendering if the word in that instance were truly *āglæca* (p. 257). The dictionaries give us a double definition without indicating that it is double: Bosworth-Toller, (BT) 'A miserable being, wretch, miscreant, monster, fierce combatant'; Clark Hall, (CH) 'wretch, monster, demon, fierce enemy'; F. Holthausen (AEW) 1963 'Elender, Untier, böser Geist, Feind'. The *Oxford Dictionary* tried to provide a single definition which would cover all varieties of *āglæca*, 'cruel person, fierce warrior.'[8] This interpretation of the word is not far removed from my own notion of its meaning. C. M. Lotspeich 1941 was also on the right track, I believe; at least, he saw that the different kinds of *āglæca* were more alike than different: 'one who goes in search of his enemy, an attacker, stalker, pursuer,' not essentially different from 'adventuring hero' – i.e. the pursuer could be evil or good, 'detested or admired.'

Other words of the *āglæca* group are generally defined in terms of the 'wretch, monster' concept. *Aglæccræft* is 'evil art' (BT, CH), but 'magic art' (Gordon 1926:226); *āglāchād* is 'Misery-hood, a state of misery' (BT), 'state of misery' (CH), 'torment' (Mackie 1934:145), but 'downfall' (Gordon 1926:337); *āglæcwīf* is 'A wretch of a woman, vile crone' (BT), 'female monster' (CH), 'wretch, or monster, of a woman' (Klaeber 1950), 'monster of a woman' (Wrenn 1953), 'dämonenhaftes Weib, Unholdin' (von Schaubert 1961), 'she-monster' (Gordon 1926:30); *āglāc, æglæc* is 'misery, grief, trouble, vexation, sorrow, torment' (BT), 'trouble, distress, oppression, misery ,grief' (CH), 'Elend, Unglück, Bedrückung, Kummer' (AEW), 'misery' and 'torment' (Mackie 1934:91, 219), 'torment' and 'tribulation' (Gordon 1926:134, 321), 'terror' (Cook 1919). Middle English *ēglēche*, on the other hand, is defined '? Valiant' (Oxford) and 'Brave, fearless' *(Middle English Dictionary)*, both definitions stemming from the heroic concept.

2. Although the meanings assigned are usually dictated by the referent of the word (and the presumed attitude of the author) in a specific context, no one has tried, it seems, to look at all of the contexts and all of the referents simultaneously (but see note 28). This, I shall attempt to do now. Six instances of *āglǣca* alone are used of Grendel in contexts of attack or combat: *Beowulf* 159, 425, 433, 739, 989, 1000. In all of these, Grendel may be miserable, monstrous, devilish, but he is also, or has been, a formidable fighter. Four instances have as referent the dragon, also in contexts of battle or attack; and the dragon is also a dangerous fighter, as well as a monstrous and devilish creature: *Beowulf* 2520, 2534, 2557, 2905. Two are used of sea creatures: *Beowulf* 556 and *Whale* 52. In the first of these, the creature is vicious and no doubt monstrous, but he is important as a fighter who attacks Beowulf and continues fighting until slain. In the second, the sea beast is monstrous in size, wicked, and symbolic of the Devil; he is, however, a dangerous attacker as well, although his attacks are more insidious than violent. Twice *āglǣca* is used of a devil in the guise of an angel, who assaults Juliana verbally and spiritually, until the saint turns the combat into a physical one: *Juliana* 268, 319. This devil is angelic rather than monstrous in appearance, yet he is a devil and inwardly miserable no doubt. Just as importantly, I think, he is a fighter, an adversary who is vanquished in rough-and-tumble combat. The word is once used of Sigemund, one of the foremost of Germanic heroes, a victorious fighter, who has just finished killing a dragon: *Beowulf* 893. He is neither monster nor devil, and although he has endured misery in the past, his present state is one of fame and affluence. In the plural, the word is used of two fighters in the midst of combat, one of them a hero and the other a monster: *Boewulf* 2592. The plural is again used of the Mermedonians who attack St. Andrew: *Andreas* 1131. These warriors lead a miserable life, and their actions are wicked, but they are represented neither as monsters nor as demons. In *Andreas* 1359, it is Andrew himself who is the *āglǣca*. The word is used of him by one of the enemies who have come to attack him, and it may be that his foes regard Andrew as a monster of some kind. But they clearly recognize in him a heroic warrior, for they have been using a whole army to subdue one man.

There are five disputed instances of *āglǣca*: *Beowulf* 646, 1269, 1512, *Riddle* 3 7, and *Riddle* 93 23. In the first, *wiste þǣm ahlǣcan to þǣm heahsele hilde geþinged* ('he knew battle to be appointed at the high hall for the ____'), the referent can be either Beowulf or Grendel. If the poet and his audience felt the word to have two meanings, 'monster' and 'hero', the ambiguity would be troublesome; but, if by *āglæca* they understood a 'fighter', the ambiguity would be of little consequence, for battle was destined for both Beowulf and Grendel and both were fierce fighters. The second ambiguous example, *þær him aglæca ætgræpe wearð* ('there the ____ came to grips with him'), is in a passage recounting the fight between Beowulf and Grendel, either of whom could be the referent. The third has been treated as ambiguous but is not really so when one considers the syntax: *sædeor monig hildetuxum heresyrcan bræc, ehton aglæcan* ('many a sea beast with battle tusks tore at the mail shirt, pursued the ____'). The word must be singular, genitive or accusative, referring to a warrior, i.e. Beowulf.[9] From the standpoint of form alone, *āglæcan* could also be nominative plural and refer to the sea beasts. The verb *ēhtan*, however, nearly always takes an object; in fact, I have been unable to find a single clear instance in Old English poetry in which *ēhtan* is used intransitively. The syntax is not an absolutely deciding factor, for the *Beowulf*-poet was capable of combining words in unusual ways. Nevertheless, in the absence of any conflicting evidence, we have little choice but to bow to the syntax. In the remaining disputed instances, the word is often taken to be *āglāc, -læc* rather than *āglæca*. A consideration of contexts and possible referents will probably strengthen the view that the word is *āglæca* in both cases. In both, the context is one of defeat, vanquishment after a struggle. In both, the speaker is not a person but a thing, which has been overcome. The Lord *(min frea)*, as a victorious *āglæca*, has conquered and imprisoned a natural force of some kind, and the latter cannot escape from him, *Riddle 3*. The *āglæca* of *Riddle 93* is a stag's horn, which has been wounded by iron and steel *(mec isern innanweardne brun bennade ... mec heard bite stiðecg style);* which would have taken revenge on the warrior, its enemy, but was unable *(ic ... ne wrecan meahte on wigan feore wonnsceaft mine);* and which has now been forced into an ignoble life as an inkhorn.

In thirteen instances, *āglæca* is modified by *atol* 'terrible, horrible' or *earm* 'miserable, wretched.' In these, the unfavorable sense of the phrase evidently inheres in the adjective, not the noun. The term *atol āglæca* is applied to Grendel in contexts of attack or combat (*Beowulf* 592, 732, 816); to a devil in a context of attack (*Andreas* 1312); to a devil, or the Devil, in a context of verbal assault (*Elene* 901); and to the Devil or a devil as a vanquished antagonist (*Christ and Satan* 160). The phrase *earm āglæca* refers to Satan or the devils in defeat after warfare (*Christ and Satan* 73, 446, 578, 712); to a vanguished devil (*Juliana* 430); to demons in a context of spiritual and verbal assault (*Guðlac A* 575);

and to either devils or simply enemies in a context of either spiritual or physical attack (*Phoenix* 442).

The context in each of these thirty-six uses of *āglǣca* is one of combat or attack. The struggle is usually physical but may also be spiritual. The fight may be in progress, or it may be an anticipated conflict, or it may be a past struggle, from which the *āglǣca* has emerged either victorious or defeated. The referent may be a monster, a miscreant, a hero, a saint, a devil, God, a soldier, an inanimate object, or a force of nature. The only factor common to all members of this seemingly ill-assorted group is that they are, or have been, or will be, fighting. In a case like this, in which specific definition based wholly on context leads to incongruous results, it is sometimes best to look for some general definition which will fit all of the contexts without doing violence to any of them. I suggest, therefore, that we define *āglǣca* as 'a fighter, valiant warrior, dangerous opponent, one who struggles fiercely'.[10]

The three compounds should also be redefined in the light of what has been said above. Andrew's resistance to the Mermedonians was accomplished with an *āglǣc-crǣft* which may or may not have been wicked or miserable or magical to his enemy (*Andreas* 1362), but which was certainly regarded as 'fighting-strength' or 'skill in fighting.' The tree which was cut down and carved into a battering ram may have endured torment, but 'torment' is not exactly the meaning of *āglāchād* in *Riddle 53* 5. For *aglachade deope gedolged*, one should read something like 'by violence (or violent attack) deeply wounded.' Grendel's mother was an *āglǣcwīf* 'a female warrior' (*Beowulf* 1259). There is no more reason to introduce the idea of monstrosity or of misery here than there is in line 1519, where she is called *merewīf*, defined simply as 'water-woman, woman of the mere' (Wrenn).

The noun *āglāc, -lǣc* is probably a back-formation from *āglǣca* itself, the essential idea being that of conflict or attack. Suffering and misery may also be implied, but these are not essential. In *Elene* 1187, the word is used in a context of anticipated warfare; the referent is something to be resisted, but the attitude toward it is confident rather than timorous or miserable. One might read *þis bið beorna gehwam* WIÐ ÆGL ÆCE *unoferswiðed wǣpen æt wige* thus: 'This shall be for each one of men AGAINST ATTACK an invincible weapon in battle'. In *Daniel* 237, the *āglāc* which the boys experienced in the fiery furnace may have been a torment (although the narrative indicates that their sufferings were negligible), but essentially it was an 'attack' designed to overcome them and to assure the triumph of idolatry. In *Riddle 81* 6, it is the onslaught of wind, rain, and hail upon the weathercock which forms the context and suggests the referent. One should read *Aglac dreoge* as 'I endure the attack'.

In the Middle English adjective, also derived from *āglæca*, we see the basic idea sometimes generalized, sometimes weakened. Such developments are not surprising, for the Middle English texts are at least two centuries later than any of the Old English poems mentioned above. In the B-version of the Gloucester Chronicle, *þe lefdi was egleche*, i.e. 'the lady was warlike' (Wright 1887:847). The lady referred to was unquestionably brave and warlike – her name was Matilda, and she made war on King Stephen. In the *Proverbs of Alfred* (Arngart 1955: 70-71), the knights characterized as *ēglēche* were not fighting at the moment, but presumably they had already shown themselves 'fierce' or 'warlike' in battle. In the legend of Mary Magdalene (Horstmann 1887: 462-480), what must have been the original sense of the word is less clear. The first instance, *Sleiʒe men and egleche* (line 1), is part of a complimentary address to the listeners, not all of whom, I suspect, were warlike. The second, *Marie was egleche; Crist hire hauede aboute isent to sarmoni and to preche* (157), has to do with spiritual and ideological conflict, and we have no reason to doubt that Mary was courageous. The third, *egleche wordes and bolde* (281) is extremely weak, for the words referred to are neither hostile nor daring.

3. Various etymologies have been proposed for words of the *āglæca* group. In Bosworth-Toller 1882, there is an entry *ag* 'wickedness, nequitia'; and from this, plus *lāc* '*ludus, donum,*' the word *aglāc* is derived. In the Supplement (1908), *ag* is deleted; and for *āglāc, -læca*, one is referred to ME *egleche* and to OHG *aigi-laihi* 'phalanx.' Holthausen (1906-7:316) cited Greek *aixµή* 'spear' and suggested that *āglæca* originally meant 'warrior.' In his *Altenglisches etymologisches Wörterbuch* (1934), he discarded both the dubious etymology and the admirable definition. He ignored the BTS *aigi-laihi*, derived *āglæca* from *āglāc*, and labeled the latter as of unknown origin. The *Middle English Dictionary's* etymology for *ēglēche* ('Cp. OE *æ-glæcea* warrior, hero, monster; *-glæcea* may be from the same root as OE *glæm* radiance, splendor') seemed like a plausible conjecture in 1952 – no worse than most of the others. It does not, however, take account of all of the Old English evidence; and placing the morpheme boundary after *æ-* and interpreting the latter as the Old English privative prefix can lead to serious phonological difficulties.

Viewed in isolation, the OHG *aigi-laihi* looks like a possible cognate of some prehistoric form of *āglæca*, perhaps **aigilaikijō*. The latter would antedate the Old English monophthongization of Germanic /ai/ and would be dated in the third or fourth century at the latest. One might suppose that the Old High German word survived until the eighth or ninth century and was then lost. Semantically, of course, the meaning 'phalanx' is rather remote from the meanings of the OE *āglæca* group; and the first element of *aigi-laihi* is difficult to account for in terms of Old High German. The word appears as a gloss to *Falanx* in three Latin-German glossaries which must have been derived from a common ancestor. The forms are as follows: *eikileihhi* (St. Gallen, Stiftsbibliothek, MS. 911; eighth century), *aigilaihi* (Paris, Bibliothèque Nationale, Lat. 7640; eighth or ninth century), and *eingilihi* (Karlsruhe, Landesbibliothek, Aug. 111; tenth century).[11] It is not easy to reconstruct the original shape of the gloss, but the suggestion that it represented *eingileihhi* [12] seems to me most plausible, both semantically (i.e. as a gloss for *phalanx*) and phonologically.

I have already mentioned Lotspeich's article of 1941. He derived the second element of *āglæca* from OE *lāc* 'battle', *lācan* 'to jump', etc. I believe that this explanation is, in a certain sense, correct, as I shall try to make clear presently. For the first element, he offered as cognates Greek *δίχομαι* 'to go away, be ruined,' etc., and a Lithuanian *eigà* [13] 'a going, a march.' The original meaning of *ag-* was 'pursuing,' he argued, and an *āglæca* was 'one who goes in search of his enemy,' etc. This derivation would be more acceptable if *eigà* were attested and if the meanings of *δίχομαι* were different. The common meanings of the latter were all of a passive [14] sort: 'to be gone, have gone, be departed, be dead, be ruined, be vanished,' etc. The meaning 'to go, rush,' etc., which seems essential to Lotspeich's etymology, was very rare and appears to have been used only of things, not of persons. Subject to correction by those who are more expert than I in Greek etymology and semasiology, I would suggest that the more active sense of the verb was probably a secondary development within Greek itself and, therefore, not likely to have been shared with Germanic. The 1963 edition of Holthausen's *AEW* makes no mention of Lotspeich's view, although Von Schaubert accepted it.

4. The Middle Irish *óclach* or *ócláech*, phonetically [oːglɑx] or [oːglɑɪx], could mean 'young man,' thought by many to be the original sense of the word.[15] It could also mean 'attendant, servant, vassal,' apparently a rather late sense in Middle Irish which became common in early modern Irish. The most frequent meaning, especially in the sagas and other heroic literature, was 'young warrior,' often simply 'warrior.' These three senses are supported by etymology and bolstered by translation usages. Even more importantly, they are distinguished from one another by a number of clear defining contexts; that is, contexts in which the young man is clearly neither a warrior nor a servant, or the servant is neither warlike nor young, or the warrior cannot be either young or a servant.[16] The sense 'warrior,' without regard to age, is neatly illustrated in the *Táin Bó Cúailnge*,[17] in which the youthful Cuchulainn is referred to as an *óclach* (*Co naccai in nÓCLAIG oca fothrocod isinn abaind*, 745), as is also the middle-aged King Conchobor (*Ní fil ind Ére ÓCLAIG bus amru*, 372). On a number of occasions, the word is used of divine, or semi-divine, timeless heroes like Lug (TBC 1802, LU 6304) and Midir (*Tochmarc Étaíne*, LU 10793). The semantic resemblance between this word, as used in Middle Irish heroic literature, and *āglēca*, as used in Old English poetry, is obvious enough to require no further demonstration.

There is also a formal resemblance between the patterns of *ócláech* and *āglēc-*, which could be purely accidental but which certainly invites speculation: long vowel from earlier diphthong in both; /g/, stop in Middle Irish, spirant in Old English but still phonemically the same as the stop; /l/, phonetically and phonemically the same in both; an earlier /ai/-diphthong, still preserved in Middle Irish, monophthongized and umlauted in Old English; an original /k/, lenited in Middle Irish, palatalized and assibilated in Old English. I accepted the invitation to speculate many years ago. It would be unprofitable to recount my various futile attempts to derive the Middle Irish word from the Old English, or to equate the two somehow as cognates. My efforts came to nothing, without leaving even the residue of an interesting discarded hypothesis. But I believe that a rather convincing case can be made for a prehistoric borrowing by English from Irish.

I have been unable to find *óclach, -láech* in texts of the Old Irish period, but it is used in the *Book of the Dun Cow*, which contains a mixture of Old Irish and Middle Irish forms, and is treated as at least possibly Old Irish by Thurneysen 1946. I suspect that its absence from the glosses on Biblical commentaries, which make up most of the Old Irish corpus, is an accident. There is little occasion to use the concept 'warrior, hero' in such glosses; and *óclach* also has a rival, *míl*, a less colorful word which means simply 'soldier' without the heroic connotations. A derivative, *óclachas* 'age of manhood' (? 'age at which a youth took arms'), occurs in the Milan glosses. One would infer from this that the simplex *óclach* must have existed in Old Irish, and very probably in prehistoric times.

The first element is *óc*, phonetically [o:g], 'young,' also 'young man' and 'warrior.' A dissyllabic *óac* [o:ɑg] appears in Old Irish, beside *óc*, and there are traces of an even more archaic *óec*, presumably [o:eg] (Pokorny 1927:128). It is not surprising that the adjective should have been pressed into service as a noun, nor that 'warrior' (in a warlike society) should have developed as an extension of the 'young man' sense. The extension of meaning would certainly have been facilitated by association with *óclach, -láech*, which already had, or was developing, this sense, and with *láech*, which certainly meant 'warrior' from very early times. The sense 'warrior' for *óc* is attested in earliest Middle Irish and in Old Irish; for example, *It é óic innso condricset* [read: *condricfet*] *frit indiu*, 'These are the *warriors* who will fight with you today' (TBC 720, LU 5199);[18] and *oaic féne* 'warriors of the Féni' (verses in the ninth-century *Codex Sancti Pauli* (see Stokes 1903:2.293). An earlier example appears in the Milan glosses on the Psalms (*c* 800): *fobith romatar indarmthi á oic*, in which *á oic* 'its young men,' or more probably 'its warriors,' refers to the armed men of Idumæa (Stokes 1903:1.267). Etymologically, *óc, óac, óec* is derived from a prehistoric **jouenk-*; cf. Cornish *iouenc*, Welsh *ieuanc*, Gaulish *Jovinc-illos*, Latin *juvencus*, OE *geong, gung*, etc. The loss of initial [j], the shift of [ou] to [o:], the loss of [n] before [k], nasalizing the latter to [g], and the shift of [e] to [ɑ] are all normal phonetic changes in prehistoric Irish. The last phonetic change to affect the word was the contraction of [o:e] or [o:ɑ] to [o:], which was most likely to occur when the dissyllabic form was combined with one or more following syllables.

The second element of the Middle Irish word is variable. Sometimes it was apparently felt to be *-lach*, as in *echlach* fem. 'messenger, courier, attendant' or *midlach* fem. and mas. 'coward, weakling,' or perhaps as in *teglach* neut. 'a household,' although this last seems to me a bit unlikely. When *óclach* was associated with *-lach*, it was apt to be declined as a feminine noun, e.g. sg. gen. *óclaigi*. At other times, the second element was felt to be *láech* [lɑɪx] 'warrior,' and then *ócláech* was declined as a masculine, e.g. sg. gen. *ócláich*. Both types appear in the MSS equally early, but the masculine type becomes much more frequent in later Middle Irish, a fact which has no doubt influenced those who see -*láech* as a secondary development and -*lach* as the primitive form.[19] One should bear in mind that *midlach* and *echlach* are strictly Middle Irish words and that the etymology of the suffix (or whatever it was) -*lach* is still unsettled. As a separate word, *láech* meant 'a ṇayman' (cf. Latin *lāicus*) or, more frequently, 'a warrior'. I do not find the word itself in texts of the Old Irish period, but it occurs in the earliest Middle Irish manuscripts (LU and the *Book of Leinster*) and is treated by Thurneysen in the same manner as *óclach*. The collective noun *láechrad* 'warriors,' occurring in mid-ninth-century verses in the St. Gall Priscian (*Thesaurus*, II, 290), would be an impossible form unless *láech* were already well established in the language. The lenited *c* and a Welsh cognate *lleyg* also suggest that the word had been in Irish from early times. *Láech* is either a very early borrowing from Latin (Pedersen 1909: 1.203), or a native Celtic word, cognate with Greek λᾱϊκός and Hittite *laḫḫa* 'military expedition,' having an original Celtic form *law-iko* (Watkins 1963:241). Either derivation would make it a fairly ancient word.

Equating the second element of *óclach* with the noun *láech* is such a natural thing to do that one would suppose that the association was made in very early times. But one might go even further. It seems possible, indeed rather probable, that the compound itself was not built upon *óc* alone but arose out of a phrase *óc láech* (in prehistoric form, of course) and originally meant 'young-warrior.' This suggestion is so obvious that I am sure it must have occurred to others before me; yet I have been unable to find it in print. If this is the correct explanation, then it is the -*lach*-forms which represent a secondary development, due to analogy or to some factor at present unknown to us. In any case, an ancestral form of the MIr. *óclach* variant *ócláech* surely existed in prehistoric Irish. Its first element would be something like [oː-eg] or [oː-ɑg]; the second something like [lɑɪk-] [20] before Irish lenition, probably [lɑɪx-] afterward.

5. The resemblance of this word to OE *āglǣc-* would, of course, be greatest before the assibilation of Old English palatal /ċ/ was complete, while the sound was still closer to [k] than to [tʃ], and before the Irish lenition had transformed Irish intervocalic [k] into [x]. The exact dates of these sound changes are not easy to pin down, although we can see that both

antedated the earliest written records in both languages; i.e. they occurred before the eighth century. There is reason to believe that assibilation took place in the seventh century, perhaps in the second half (Kuhn
1970:23; Penzl 1947:42; Moulton 1954:24). The date of lenition has long
been controversial. I shall not attempt to catalogue all of the views
that have been expressed, contenting myself rather with giving the opin-
ions of three great Celticists, whose views are representative in their
diversity. According to Holger Pedersen (1909:1.436) lenition took place
in all of the Celtic languages some time before A.D. 300. Kenneth
Jackson (1953:10,143) rejects this early dating and would place the lenitions (Irish, British, Cornish, Breton) in the second half of the fifth
century. Thurneysen (1946:59, 74) refuted no one but merely stated that
the Irish lenition occurred before the loss of vowels in final syllables, and
that the latter preceded the earliest OIr. texts. I prefer Thurneysen's
cautious dating, partly because it is irrefutable, and partly because of
objections to the other two which cannot be presented briefly and which
would create an intolerable digression if stated here in full.[21] Before
leaving this difficult subject, I should like to call attention to the earliest
glosses in the Würzburg MS of the Pauline Epistles (*Thesaurus*, I, p. xxiv,
prima manus), which may be as early as *c* 700, certainly not much earlier.
As Stokes and Strachan (1901-03:xxiv) point out (following Thurneysen),
the scribe was archaic in his spellings. He indicated lenition part of the
time, but almost as frequently failed to indicate it: *cetarcoti* for *cethar-
choti*, *comtinol* for *comthinól*, *ercomlassat* for *erchomlassat*, *forcanit* for
forcanith, etc.[22] Such uncertainty in spelling practices frequently, although
not invariably, marks a period during or shortly after the completion of
a sound change, a time when the orthography has not quite caught up
with the language.

I admit that I am prejudiced in favor of the seventh century, for this
was the period most favorable to Anglo-Saxon borrowing from Irish.
This is the century of Irish missionaries in Northumbria and Mercia:
Aidan, Finan, and Colman, bishops of Lindisfarne; Diuma and Ceollach,
earliest bishops among the Mercians; and many others. It was a period
when many young Angles studied under Irish masters in Ireland or at
Iona or Melrose or Lindisfarne: Ecgberht and Æðelhun (Bede III, 27);
Bishop Cuðberht, later bishop of Lindisfarne; Chad and Trumhere,
later bishops in Mercia; Oswald, later king of Northumbria, etc. It
was also the century of Cædmon, with whom the history of English
poetry begins.

Anglo-Saxons of the seventh century would find it difficult to assimilate a word which was pronounced [o:eglɑɪk-] or [o:ɑglɑɪk-] or [o:glɑɪk-][23] without some modification, for their language lacked the sequences [o:e], [o:ɑ], and [ɑɪ].[24] If there was borrowing, it must have been by means of morpheme substitution; that is, by the substitution of somewhat similar native elements for those foreign elements which most Anglo-Saxons would find meaningless and difficult to pronounce. Morpheme substitution is a sort of unenlightened loan-translation. When it appears in modern English *crayfish, sparrowgrass,* or *woodchuck,* we call it 'folk etymology'. Interesting examples are not hard to find in Old English: *mere-grot* 'sea particle' or 'sea groats' for Latin *margarīta; milt-estre* 'spleen,' plus feminine suffix, for L. *meretrix; bi-scop* for *episcopus; Eofor-wīc* for *Eboracum;* and *lēah-tric* or *lēctric* [25] for *lactūca.* There are other explanations for *Wyrt-georn* from British Latin *Vortigernus,* (Luick 1921:105, 186; Jackson 1953:273, 280, 282, 453, 655), but 'eager for herbs' is too pat to be a phonological accident. Moreover, it bears a close resemblance to native names like *Friðugeorn* 'eager for peace' and *Here-georn* 'eager for war' in the Durham *Liber Vitae* (Sweet 1885: l. 225, 267, 345).

A native substitute for the second element could easily be found in a group of words containing the closely related roots *-lāc-* [-lɑ:k-] and *-læc-* [-læ:tʃ-] (Lotspeich 1941); for example, *lācan* 'to move quickly, play, fight,' etc.; *læcan* 'to move quickly, spring, leap'; *gelāc* 'motion, commotion, play' (*sweorda gelāc* 'play of swords, combat with swords'); *gelæca* 'competitor'; *ellenlæca* 'champion'. The seventh-century pronunciations of the two roots would be nearly identical with those of the historical period. As for phonetic differences between the substitute morphemes and the Irish original, they would be considerable but certainly not too great to permit of substitution. Meanings which an Anglo-Saxon might attach to the reshaped second element would be in keeping with the sense of the Irish word.

It would be more difficult to find a general Old English substitute for the first element of **oeg-laik-.* The only really plausible substitute would seem to be the element *ōg-* or *ōeg-* in the Mercian equivalents of West Saxon words like *æghwilc* 'every, each' and *æghwær* 'everywhere'.[26] For example, the eighth-century *Epinal Glossary* has *oeghuuelci* and *oghuuaer;* the *Corpus Glossary* of the same century has *oeghwelce* and *oeghuer;* and the early ninth-century gloss of the *Vespasian Psalter* has *oghwelc* and *oeghwelc* (Sweet 1885:35-106; Lindsay 1921; Kuhn 1965). These Mercian forms were due either to a substitution of /ō/ for the /ā/, which was the reflex of Gmc. /ai/ in **aig-, *aigi-,* or to generalization of

a different original ablaut base. There is no clear evidence of this development in any dialect except Mercian. About the middle of the seventh
century, $\bar{o}g$- and $\overline{oe}g$- were probably pronounced [o:g] and [ö:g], the
g representing a voiced velar spirant in each case, and the oe representing
a vowel similar to an umlauted German $\bar{o}$. The phonetic differences
between these and the prehistoric Irish [o:eg], etc., are far from negligible
but hardly so great as to stand in the way of morpheme substitution.[27]
The sense of an element lifted out of words meaning 'every,' 'everywhere,' etc., would perhaps be felt as that of a general intensive when
combined with something else to form a noun.

To conclude, I would posit a seventh-century Mercian noun, *$\bar{o}gl\acute{æ}ca$
(a masculine -jan-stem), with variants *$ægl\acute{æ}ca$, *$\bar{o}gl\bar{a}ca$, and *$ægl\bar{a}ca$,
as a reshaping of the prehistoric form of the Irish $\acute{o}clach$, $\acute{o}cl\acute{a}ech$. The
Mercian word meant 'fighter, warrior' and was perhaps analyzed (by
those who thought about such matters) as 'an all-fighter, one who
fights anybody anywhere, a great fighter'. Compounds and derivatives
would arise naturally. The Irish etymon would be forgotten as time went
on and words like *$\bar{o}gl\bar{a}c$ or *$ægl\acute{æ}c$, *$\bar{o}gl\bar{a}ch\bar{a}d$ or *$ægl\bar{a}ch\bar{a}d$, became
an accepted part of the poetic vocabulary. Much later, when the poetic
texts were turned into West Saxon, the scribes carefully respelled words
like $oghwelc$, oeg⹂ and $oghwer$, oeg- as $æghwilc$, -$hwylc$ and $æghwær$ (or
$ahwær$), and the like. This is one Mercian feature which has left no clear
trace in those West Saxon poems believed to have been copied from
Mercian originals. While they were altering other og-, oeg- spellings, the
West Saxon scribes would undoubtedly respell the first elements of
words in the *$\bar{o}gl\acute{æ}ca$ group.[28]

University of Michigan

NOTES

[1] Portions of this article formed the basis of a paper read before the Old English
Section of the Seventh Conference on Medieval Studies, Kalamazoo, May 1, 1972.
[2] I use the numbering in G. P. Krapp and E. V. K. Dobbie (1936). This riddle is
no. 92 in W. S. Mackie
[3] Mackie's no. 80.
[4] The palatal g would then revert to velar, just as palatal c reverted under similar
circumstances; see my article (1970).
[5] I call attention to the ease with which a late West Saxon might associate the $æg$-
of $ægl\acute{æ}ca$ with the $æg$- of $æghw\bar{a}$, etc. The relevance of this observation will appear
later.

[6] See below, note 23.

[7] There has, of course, been very little other than context on which to base definitions. Latin originals, where they exist, offer nothing helpful. Etymology has hitherto been of little or no use, although the etymology which I propose may, if accepted, remedy this defect.

[8] See *Egleche*.

[9] This interpretation was adopted by Dobbie (1953); see his note to this line.

[10] If there were one clear instance of *āglæca* referring to an unwarlike monster, a peaceful demon, or the like, this definition would fall apart.

[11] See Elias von Steinmeyer and Eduard Sievers (eds.), *Die althochdeutschen Glossen* (Berlin, 1879-98), I, 142-143; IV, 401, 459, 595.

[12] See Elisabeth Karg-Gasterstädt and Theodor Frings (1952). I know that I should let well enough alone at this point, but I think that a discarded conjecture of my own, with my reasons for rejecting it, could be useful. It seemed to me possible that the Karlsruhe form might be a mere rationalization, a scribe's attempt to make sense of something incomprehensible; and that the form underlying St. Gallen and Paris could have been a garbled and misunderstood *āglæca*, as copied by a High German scribe ignorant of Old English. The library at St. Gallen has five MSS containing Old High German glosses or glossaries, together with a few glosses in Old English; Karlsruhe has three MSS of this sort (probably from Reichenau); see N. R. Ker (1957:477-78, 480-81). A major obstacle to acceptance of this view is the fact that *āglæca* does not occur in any of the surviving Old English glosses, although *phalanx (falanx)* does and is glossed by other words.

[13] Inferred from the words for 'a coming in' and 'a going out'; see Émile Boisacq (1950:694).

[14] In a semantic, not a grammatical, sense.

[15] This view is inferred from the etymology (and the assumption that *-lach*, not *-láech*, was the original second element). Without going beyond the hard evidence, all we can say is that the senses 'warrior' and 'young man' appear simultaneously in the written records.

[16] I shall not be able to catalogue and classify all examples here as I have done with *āglæca*, nor does it seem necessary to do so. In the first place, the Irish word is many times more frequent than the Old English word; to catalogue even the instances which are immediately available would require an inordinate amount of space. Secondly, the senses of *óclach, -láech* are relatively clear and not in dispute. Thirdly, the tools for research in Middle Irrish are less fully developed than those for Old English – another way of saying that Irish heroic literature lacks a Grein's *Sprachschatz*. My data and examples are drawn from the Royal Irish Academy's *Dictionary of the Irish Language* (DIL) and *Contributions to a Dictionary of the Irish Language* (CDIL); Alexander MacBain, *An Etymological Dictionary of the Gaelic Language* (Revised by Calum MacPharlain; Stirling, 1911); Rudolph Thurneysen, *A Grammar of Old Irish* (Transl. and rev. by D. A. Binchy and Osbern Bergin; Dublin, 1946); occasionally from other sources indicated in the notes; and partly from my own reading in the Old and Middle Irish texts.

[17] The edition of John Strachan and J. G. O'Keeffe (1912), quoted by line (TBC). This ed. is based on the version in the *Yellow Book of Lecan*, but the same word is used in both passages in the earliest version of TBC; see R. I. Best and O. Bergin (1929:1. 5223, 4861), LU.

[18] Mugain spoke figuratively (no doubt jocularly), but the fact that the 'warriors' were actually naked women does not affect the meaning of *óic* itself.

[19] CDIL, art. *óclach*, says: 'Prob. orig. fem., a formation from *óc* analogous to *echlach, midlach;* later analysed as *óc + laech* and freq. written *óclaech (-láech)* in

Mid. Ir. down to the classical period.' This is speculative, of course, and is not presented as fact by the arranger.

[20] Since the [x] from [k] was made possible by a following vowel, we must assume the presence of a vocalic ending. I omit the endings and their possible variant forms for this word and for *aglǽca* in order to reduce the number of prehistoric forms to be reconstructed.

[21] It is hard to dismiss Jackson's work in this manner. His book is a gold mine of information and generally a model of scholarship. Even his position with regard to the date of lenition, with which I strongly disagree, is brilliantly argued and supported with immense erudition.

[22] Even in MIr. texts, spelling is not consistent. On any leaf of the *Book of the Dun Cow*, one will find at least an example or two of *t* or *c* where the lenited consonant should be spelled with *th* or *ch*. The glosses referred to above differ from the usual Old and Middle Irish in having a vastly larger proportion of unindicated lenitions.

[23] If an Anglo-Saxon saw the word in writing, the first element would be something like *oec-*, *oac-*, or *oc-*; the second element, *-laic-*, *-laec-*, or something of the sort.

[24] I exclude cases in which a sequence straddles a morpheme boundary, e.g. *dōan*, variant of *dōn* infinitive.

[25] Holthausen (*AEW* 1963) suggests that *-tric* is connected with OE *trog* 'trough.'

[26] Instead of the *ōg-*, *ōēg-*forms, Northumbrian has *ēg-* (rarely *ǣg-*), usually regarded as containing an umlauted reflex of Gmc. *ai*. It seems to me possible that Nhb. *ēg-* could have developed from *ōēg-*, but positive evidence is lacking.

[27] If one assumes that an epenthetic *i* was first induced after after every vowel undergoing *i*-umlaut, the phonetic differences are decreased; one could suppose that the umlauted [oː] first became [oːi], then [oːɛ], and then [öː]. I would prefer, for reasons too lengthy for discussion here, not to become entangled in the epenthetic theory and its troublesome ramifications.

[28] Some time after this article was written, I 'discovered' Doreen M. E. Gillam 1961. Gillam examines 34 examples in context, somewhat as I have done. On the basis of connotations (i.e. the presumed connotations the word would have had for Anglo-Saxons), she divides the occurrences into three groups: I. monsters – 19, II. devils – 13, III. human beings – 4. (*Whale* 52 is counted in both I and II; *Beowulf* 2592, in both I and III.) The first group is treated as primary, the second as derivative, and the third as a sort of bold innovation derived from the other two. The analysis is most interesting, but I suspect that it is more useful as a stimulus to the modern reader than as an explanation of what actually happened to the word in Old English. As regards the latter objective, I would raise the following questions: Is it safe to assume that 'monster' was the original meaning without some kind of linguistic or historical support? Why should one assume that the religious poetry, in which the sense 'devil' developed, is all later than *Beowulf* and the *Whale*, when most scholars are convinced that the Caedmonian poems are roughly contemporary with *Beowulf*? Is it not a bit unreasonable to treat occurrences in *Beowulf* and *Andreas* as though they were late innovations, when the former poem is one of the earliest in Old English and the latter is probably contemporaneous with the Cynewulfian poems at the latest? Is it safe to assume that the Anglo-Saxons, with their presumably wider knowledge of *aglǽcan*, would form the same association as we do, with our very limited knowledge?

REFERENCES

ARNGART, OLOF. 1955. Proverbs of Alfred. Vol. 2. Lund: C. W. K. Gleerup.
BEST, ROBERT I., and OSBORN BERGIN. 1929. Lebor na huidre; Book of the Dun Cow. Dublin: Hodges, Figgis, and Company.

BOISACQ, ÉMILE. 1950. Dictionnaire étymologique de la langue grecque. Heidelberg: Carl Winter.

BOSWORTH, JOSEPH, and T. NORTHCOTE TOLLER. 1882. An Anglo-Saxon dictionary ... Oxford: Oxford University Press.

CLARK HALL, JOHN R. 1960. A concise Anglo-Saxon dictionary. 4th ed. Cambridge, England: University Press.

COOK, A. S. 1919. The Old English Elene, Phoenix, and Physiologus. New Haven: Yale University Press.

DOBBIE, ELLIOTT V. K. 1953. Beowulf and Judith. (ASPR, 4.) New York: Columbia University Press.

FRINGS, THEODOR, and ELISABETH KARG-GASTERSTÄDT. 1952. Althochdeutsches Wörterbuch. Berlin: Akademie-Verlag.

GILLAM, DOREEN M. E. 1961. The use of the term 'æglæca' in Beowulf at lines 893 and 2592. Studia Germanica Gandensia 3.145-69.

GORDON, ROBERT K. 1926. Anglo-Saxon poetry. London: J. M. Dent and Sons.

GREIN, CHRISTIAN. 1912. Sprachschatz der angelsächsischen Dichter. (Bibliothek der angelsächsischen Poesie.) Heidelberg: Carl Winter.

HOLTHAUSEN, FERDINAND. 1907. Etymologien. Indogermanische Forschungen 20.316.

—. 1934, 1963. Altenglisches etymologisches Wörterbuch. Heidelberg: Carl Winter.

HORSTMANN, CARL. 1887. The early South-English legendary. (EETS, OS, 87.) London: N. Trübner.

JACKSON, KENNETH. 1953. Language and history in early Britain. Edinburg: University Press.

KER, NEIL R. 1957. Catalogue of manuscripts containing Anglo-Saxon. Oxford: The Clarendon Press.

KLAEBER, FRIEDRICH. 1950. Beowulf and the fight at Finnsburg. 3rd ed. Boston: D.C. Heath.

KRAPP, GEORGE P., and ELLIOTT V. K. DOBBIE. 1936. The Exeter Book. (ASPR, 3.) New York: Columbia University Press.

KUHN, SHERMAN M. 1965. The Vespasian Psalter. Ann Arbor: University of Michigan Press.

—. 1970. On the consonantal phonemes of Old English. Philological Essays: studies in Old and Middle English language and literature in honor of Herbert Dean Meritt, ed. by James L. Rosier, 16-49. The Hague: Mouton.

KURATH, HANS, and SHERMAN M. KUHN. 1952-. Middle English dictionary. Ann Arbor: University of Michigan Press.

LINDSAY, WALLACE M. 1921. The Corpus glossary. Cambridge, England: University Press.

LOTSPEICH, CLAUDE M. 1941. Old English etymologies. Journal of English and Germanic Philology 40.1-4.

LUICK, KARL. 1921. Historische Grammatik der englischen Sprache. Vol. 1, part 1. Leipzig: Tauchnitz.

MACBAIN, ALEXANDER. 1911. An etymological dictionary of the Gaelic language. Stirling: E. MacKay.

MACKIE, WILLIAM S. 1934. The Exeter Book, part 2. (EETS.) London: N. Trübner.

MARSTRANDER, CARL J. S. 1913-70. Contributions to a dictionary of the Irish language. Dublin: Royal Irish Academy.

—. 1913-70. Dictionary of the Irish language. Dublin: Royal Irish Academy.

MOULTON, WILLIAM G. 1954. The stops and spirants of early Germanic. Language 30.1-42.

MURRAY, JAMES A. H., et al. 1884-1933. A new English dictionary on historical principles. Oxford: The Clarendon Press.

PEDERSEN, HOLGER. 1909. Vergleichende Grammatik der keltischen Sprachen. Vol. 1. Göttingen: Vandenhoeck and Ruprecht.

PENZL, HERBERT. 1947. The phonemic split of Germanic *k* in Old English. Language 23.34-42.
POKORNY, JULIUS. 1927. Archaisch irisch *óëc* 'jung.' Zeitschrift für celtische Philologie 17.128.
SCHAUBERT, ELSE VON. 1961. Beowulf. Paderborn: F. Schöningh.
STEINMEYER, ELIAS VON, and EDUARD SIEVERS. 1879-1922. Die althochdeutschen Glossen. Vols. 1 and 4. Be lin: Weidmann.
STOKES, WHITLEY and JOHN STRACHAN. 1901-03. Thesaurus palaeohibernicus. 2 vols. Cambridge, England: University Press.
STRACHAN, JOHN, and JAMES G. O'KEEFFE. 1912. Táin Bó Cúailnge. Dublin: Royal Irish Academy.
SWEET, HENRY. 1885. The oldest English texts. (EETS, OS, 83.) London: N. Trübner.
THURNEYSEN, RUDOLPH. 1946. A grammar of Old Irish. (Trans. and rev. by D. A. Binchy and Osbern Bergin.) Dublin: Dublin Institute for Advanced Studies.
WATKINS, CALVERT. 1963. Indo-European metrics and archaic Irish verse. Celtica 6.241.
WRENN, CHARLES L. 1953. Beowulf with the Finnesburg fragment. London: G. Harrap.
WRIGHT, WILLIAM A. 1887. The metrical chronicle of Robert of Gloucester. (Rolls Series, 86.) London: Eyre and Spottiswoode.

CORRIGENDA

Page 5 (5), fn. 13. *for* ætrendian, *read* ærendian
Page 11 (11), line 36: *for* hefæn-, *read* hefaen
Page 17 (17), fn. 59: *for* Wylde, *read* Wyld
  fn. 63. *for* woegas, *read* weogas
Page 23 (85), line 18. *for* 2889, *read* 2899
Page 24 (86), line 4: *for* underscored, *read* italicized
Page 36 (633), fn. 13: *delete* comma
Page 37 (634), line 34; *for* unnæhtigo, *read* unmæhtigo
Page 40 (637), fn. 30: *for* 17, 149, *read* 17, 14
Page 44 (641), fn. 41: *for* χοινή, *read* κοινή
Page 46 (643), line 27: *delete* comma
Page 47 (644), line 5: *for* onsaecest, *read* onsæcest; *for* onsækeþ,
  onsaekeþ
Page 55 (652), line 6: *add* semicolon *after* 23
Page 57 (654), line 11: *for* sesægan, *read* gesægun
  line 13: *for* 28, 5, *read* 28, 15
Page 63 (660), line 28: *for* gelfeað, *read* gelefað
Page 64 (661), line 12: *for* forbecun, *read* forebecun
  line 27: *for* āē, *read* ǣ
Page 65 (662), line 8: *substitute* colon *for* semicolon *at end of line*
  line 22: *for first* gæþ, *read* gaeþ
  line 23: *for* gæ, *read* gae
  line 24: *for* gaeþ, *read* gaeð
Page 66 (663), line 17, *for* w, *read* æ
  line 29: *for* 16, 25, *read* 16, 28; *for* 28, 2 , *read* 25, 2
Page 67 (664), line 17: *for* sacredes, *read* sacerdes
Page 70 (667), line 37: *add* (2) *before* unrounding
Page 72 (669), fn. 111: *delete* apostrophe *and add* comma *after* Mercia
Page 74 (169), line 15: *replace final* comma *with a* period
  line 16: *omit* and . . . unstable y
Page 82 (491), fn. 2: *for* New, *read* (New
Page 88 (525), line 11: *for* pppl., *read* p.ppl.
Page 91 (528), fn. 28: *for* set, *read* sets
Page 96 (533): Table II *should follow the first paragraph of* #3
Page 99 (536): Table IV *should follow the first paragraph of* #5

[231]

CORRIGENDA

Page 100 (537), Table V *should follow the first paragraph of* #6
Page 109 (250), line 38: *for* oðbær, *read* oþbær
Page 114 (255), fn. 32: *for* 81a, *read* 81b
Page 120 (261), line 15: *for* totaling . . . But, *read* certainly do not impede
the action of the poem materially, but
    line 18: *for* is One, *read* One is
Page 127 (19)   line 11: *The l-liquids should be moved to the right so as to fall between the* Labial *and* Dental *columns; the r-liquids should be moved to the right so as to fall between the* Dental *and* Palato-velar-glottal *columns*
    line 15: *for* Voceless, *read* Voiceless
    line 16: *for* g, *read* ğ
    line 17: *for* Usualy, *read* Usually
Page 129 (21)   line 2: *for* rougly, *read* roughly
Page 165 (179) line 19: *for* suggesst, *read* suggests
Page 192 (649) line 20: *for* triumpos, *read* triumphos
Page 193 (650), line 38: *for* nales, *read* nalæs
Page 206 (231), line 4: *for* glydenne, *read* gyldenne
Page 207 (232), line 6: *add superscript 5 after* rare
    line 7: *omit superscript 5*
Page 208 (233), fn. 10: *omit second* comma *in third line*
Page 213 (213), title: *for* AGLAĒCA, *read* ĀGLAĒCA
Page 216 (216), line 28: *for* Boewulf, *read* Beowulf
Page 227 (227), fn. 16: *for* Irrish, *read* Irish
Page 228 (228), fn. 27; *delete second* after *in first line*
Page 230 (230), line 12: *for* oldest, *read* Oldest

TABULA GRATULATORIA

Richard Abbot, Enosburg Falls, Vermont
G. W. Abernethy, *The Middle English Dictionary*
A. J. Aitken, *Dictionary of the Older Scottish Tongue*
John Algeo, University of Georgia
John G. Allee, George Washington University
Ashley Crandell Amos, University of Toronto - Centre for Medieval Studies
Earl R. Anderson, Cleveland State University
Richard W. Bailey, University of Michigan
Roy Barkley, *The Middle English Dictionary*
Larry D. Benson, Harvard University
Robert E. Bjork, Arizona State University
F. H. Brengelman, California State University, Fresno
Daniel Brink, Arizona State University
Ronald E. Buckalew, Pennsylvania State University
R. W. Burchfield, *The Oxford English Dictionaries*
Sharon Butler, University of Toronto - Centre for Medieval Studies
Daniel G. Calder, University of California at Los Angeles
Frederic G. Cassidy, University of Wisconsin
William A. Chaney, Lawrence University
Francelia Mason Clark, University of Michigan
John Riddle Cleaveland, Vincentown, N. J.
James E. Cross, University of Liverpool
Joseph P. Crowley, Auburn University at Montgomery
Michael Cummings, York University

Rosemary Laughlin, Urbana, Illinois
Patricia V. Lehman, *The Middle English Dictionary*
Winfred P. and Ruth P. M. Lehmann, University of Texas
Robert Thomas Lenaghan, University of Michigan
Patrizia Lendinara, Università di Palermo
Roy F. Leslie, University of Victoria
Robert E. Lewis, *The Middle English Dictionary*
G. M. Logsdon, University of Tennessee
Peter J. Lucas, University College, Dublin
Robert A. Lucas, California Polytechnic State University
Charles D. Ludlum, San Jose State University
Angelika Lutz, Universität München
Robert L. Kyes, University of Michigan
R. M. Lumiansky, New York, New York
Michio Masui, Hiroshima University
Lister M. Matheson, *The Middle English Dictionary*
Vincent P. McCarren, *The Middle English Dictionary*
Raven I. McDavid, Jr., University of Chicago, Emeritus
Virginia G. McDavid, Chicago State University
Angus McIntosh, University of Edinburgh
Meradith T. McMunn, Rhode Island College
Paul Mertens, Liège, Belgium
Marilyn Miller, *The Middle English Dictionary*
Tauno F. Mustanoja, Helsinki, Finland
Ann Eljenholm Nichols, Winona State University
Michiko Ogura, Tsuru University
Akio Oizumi, Doshisha University
Marijane Osborn, University of California, Davis
Gillian R. Overing, Wake Forest University
Robert A. Palmatier, Western Michigan University
Joseph P. Pickett, *The Middle English Dictionary*
John C. Pope, New Haven, Connecticuit
Randolph Quirk, University of London
Irmengard Rauch, University of California, Berkeley
Allen Walker Read, Columbia University
John Reidy, *The Middle English Dictionary*
Paul G. Remley, Cornell University
Robert C. Rice, Christendom College
Jane Roberts, King's College, London

Fred C. Robinson, Yale University
Jay L. Robinson, University of Michigan
Thomas M. Rodgers, Jr., Atlanta, Georgia
H. L. Rogers, University of Sydney
James Rosier, University of Pennsylvania
Bertil Sandahl, Uppsala University
Karl Inge Sandred, Uppsala University
Donald B. Sands, University of Michigan
Seminar für Englische Philologie der Georg-August-Universität
Ann Shannon, *The Middle English Dictionary*
Cyril L. Smetana, York University
E. G. Stanley, Oxford University
Robert P. Stockwell, University of California at Los Angeles
Bertil Sundby, University of Bergen
Paul E. Szarmach, State University of New York at Binghamton
Paul Beekman Taylor, University of Geneva
Erik Tengstrand, Uppsala University
John Tinkler, University of Tennessee, Chattanooga
Thomas E. Toon, University of Michigan
Sylvia L. Thrupp, Ann Arbor, Michigan
Joseph B. Trahern, Jr., University of Tennessee
Lazaros A. Varnas, University of North Carolina at Charlotte
Richard L. Venezky, University of Delaware
John Frederick Vickrey, Lehigh University
Linda Ehrsam Voigts, University of Missouri, Kansas City
Cory L. Wade, University of Santa Clara
Anthony Warner, University of York
Horst Weinstock, Technical University of Aachen
Mary Jane Williams, *The Middle English Dictionary*
H. Rex Wilson, London, Ontario
Joyce M. Wolford, *The Middle English Dictionary*
R. F. Yeager, Warren Wilson College